BECAUSE GOD
...I CAN

Register This New Book

Benefits of Registering*

- ✓ FREE **replacements** of lost or damaged books
- ✓ FREE **audiobook** – *Pilgrim's Progress*, audiobook edition
- ✓ FREE information about new titles and other **freebies**

www.anekopress.com/new-book-registration

*See our website for requirements and limitations.

BECAUSE GOD ... I CAN

12 Themes on Following Jesus

Daily Devotional

STEPHEN A. GAMMON

aneko
PRESS

www.walkingwithgodforlife.com
Because God . . . I Can
© 2021 by Stephen A. Gammon
All rights reserved. Published 2021.

Please do not reproduce, store in a retrieval system, or transmit in any form or by any means – electronic, mechanical, photocopying, recording, or otherwise, without written permission from the publisher.

Scripture quotations are from the ESV® Bible (The Holy Bible, English Standard Version®), copyright © 2001 by Crossway, a publishing ministry of Good News Publishers. Used by permission. All rights reserved.

Cover Design: Jonathan Lewis
Editors: Sheila Wilkinson and Ruth Clark

Aneko Press
www.anekopress.com
Aneko Press, Life Sentence Publishing, and our logos are trademarks of
Life Sentence Publishing, Inc.
203 E. Birch Street
P.O. Box 652
Abbotsford, WI 54405

RELIGION / Christian Living / Devotional
Paperback ISBN: 978-1-62245-714-4
eBook ISBN: 978-1-62245-715-1
10 9 8 7 6 5 4 3 2 1
Available where books are sold

TABLE OF CONTENTS

Foreword xvii
Introduction xxi

January – I Can *Believe* Today . . .
Because God Saves 2
Because God's Son Has Risen 3
Because God Knows Me 4
Because God Does Miracles 5
Because God Loves His Children 6
Because God Has Made Me His Child 7
Because God Provides Daily Bread 8
Because God Protects 9
Because God Forgives 10
Because God Keeps Me From Falling 11
Because God Will Never Fail Me 12
Because God Gives Faith 13
Because God Is Good 14
Because God Is Truth 15
Because God Cannot Lie 16
Because God Woke Me Up Today 17
Because God Has Revealed The Ending 18
Because God Is Very Near 19
Because God Is Omniscient 20
Because God Is Omnipotent 21
Because God Is Omnipresent 22
Because God's Promises Are Assured 23
Because God Is Speaking Today 24
Because God Is Leading 25
Because God Is Merciful Today 26
Because God Is Eternal 27
Because God Is Glorious 28
Because God Enables Today 29

    Because God Has Compassion 30
    Because God Delivers 31
    Because God Enters Through Locked Doors 32

February – I Can *Trust* Today . . .
    Because God Has Been Faithful 34
    Because God Has Fed Us 35
    Because God Promises A Good Future 36
    Because God Answers Whenever I Call In Trouble 37
    Because God Sees Me 38
    Because God Is With Me In Every Battle 39
    Because God Even Cares For The Birds 40
    Because God Has Given Me A Mission 41
    Because God Keeps His Word 42
    Because God Invites Me To Trust Him Fully 43
    Because God Bids Me To Come In The Storm 44
    Because God Is A Refuge For Me 45
    Because God Is Able 46
    Because God Loves Me So 47
    Because God Is With Me 48
    Because God Is Inviting Me To Come Near 49
    Because God Works Wonders 50
    Because God Does Not Change 51
    Because God Gives Perfect Peace 52
    Because God Is Good To Me 53
    Because God Avails Us Of His Power Today 54
    Because God Gives Living Water Today 55
    Because God Has Numbered Our Days 56
    Because God Forgives 57
    Because God Is Here And There Today 58
    Because God Redeems Me 59
    Because God Brings Good Out Of Trials 60
    Because God Is The Antidote For Fear 61
    Because God Gave Us This Day 62

March – I Can *Receive* Today . . .
    Because God Saves 64
    Because God Loves 65
    Because God Gives 66
    Because God Forgives 67
    Because God Knows 68
    Because God Leads 69

    Because God Strengthens The Weak 70
    Because God Prepares Us Well 71
    Because God Anoints 72
    Because God Restores 73
    Because God Heals 74
    Because God Comforts 75
    Because God Holds Me Close 76
    Because God Sees 77
    Because God Speaks 78
    Because God Provides 79
    Because God Sustains 80
    Because God Transforms 81
    Because God Relates 82
    Because God Hears 83
    Because God Seeks 84
    Because God Reconciles 85
    Because God Conquers 86
    Because God Cares 87
    Because God Accompanies Us 88
    Because God Welcomes Me 89
    Because God Keeps Me 90
    Because God Foreordains 91
    Because God Teaches 92
    Because God Prunes 93
    Because God Sacrificed 94

April – I Can *Pray* Today . . .
    Because God Invites Our Prayer 96
    Because God Hears When I Pray 97
    Because God Teaches How To Pray 98
    Because God Commands Me To Pray 99
    Because God Rewards Us As We Pray 100
    Because God Loves It When His Children Pray 101
    Because God Surprises Us As We Pray 102
    Because God Draws Us Close When We Pray 103
    Because God Strengthens Us As We Pray 104
    Because God Gives Hope When We Pray 105
    Because God Blesses When We Pray 106
    Because God Is Glorified When We Pray 107
    Because God Gives Peace When We Pray 108
    Because God Sanctifies When We Pray 109
    Because God Demonstrates How To Pray 110

Because God Rewards Persistence As We Pray 111
  Because God Lets Us Joinin His Work As We Pray 112
  Because God Gives Victory Over Evil As We Pray 113
  Because God Makes Prayer Available 114
  Because God Teaches Humility As We Pray 115
  Because God Binds Us With Others As We Pray 116
  Because God Lets Us Hear And Heed As We Pray 117
  Because God's Sacrifice Allows Us To Pray 118
  Because God Changes Us As We Pray 119
  Because God Reveals Himself As We Pray 120
  Because Prayer Can Be Our Way Of Life 121
  Because God Invites Us To Pray Boldly 122
  Because God Offers Escape From Temptation As We Pray 123
  Because God Invites Us To Pray Anytime 124
  Because God Lets Us Pray Anywhere 125

May – I Can *Praise* Today . . .
  Because God Is Praiseworthy 127
  Because God Is My Savior 128
  Because God Opens Access Through Praise 129
  Because God Dwells In Our Praise 130
  Because God Has Ordained Praise 131
  Because God Chases Away Despair Through Our Praise 132
  Because Praise Is A Weapon Against The Devil 133
  Because God Is Worthy Of My Praise 134
  Because God's Son Is Soon Returning 135
  Because God Is Alpha And Omega 136
  Because God Is *I Am* 137
  Because God Heals The Brokenhearted 138
  Because God Sets Captives Free 139
  Because God Rescues Us From Enemies 140
  Because God Sets Me High Upon A Rock 141
  Because God Comforts Us In Our Troubles 142
  Because God Desires Praise From All Who Live 143
  Because God Is Praised By Vast Multitudes 144
  Because God Hides Me Beneath His Wings 145
  Because God Delivers From Evil 146
  Because God Is My Blessed Redeemer 147
  Because God Sought And Found Me 148
  Because God Defends Me 149
  Because God Is My Provider 150
  Because God Leads His Dear Children Along 151

   Because God Is Merciful 152
   Because God Makes All Things New 153
   Because God Grants The Desires Of Our Heart 154
   Because God Is Deserving 155
   Because God Has Spoken 156
   Because I Know God Loves Me 157

June – I Can *Love* Today . . .
   Because God Is Love 159
   Because God Commands Loving Him And People 160
   Because God Has Loved Me Sacrificially 161
   Because God Shows Me How To Love 162
   Because God Is The Source Of Love 163
   Because God Will Never Stop Loving Me 164
   Because God Lives In Me And Loves Through Me 165
   Because God's Love Is Given, Not Earned 166
   Because God Always Abounds In Love For Us 167
   Because God Delights In Those He Loves 168
   Because God Has Made Me His Child 169
   Because God's Love Is The Perfect Model 170
   Because God's Love Expels Fear 171
   Because God's Love Has Very Deep Roots 172
   Because God's Love Keeps Me Safe 173
   Because God's Love Is Vast 174
   Because God Adopted Me In Love 175
   Because God Gave His Own Son For Me 176
   Because God Loves Us Even When We Rebel 177
   Because God's Love Lets Me Grow 178
   Because God Bought Me With Jesus' Blood 179
   Because God The Holy Spirit Helps Me Love 180
   Because God Cares For People In Anguish 181
   Because God's Mercies Are New Today 182
   Because God Demonstrates His Love Through Me 183
   Because God Allows Us To Remain In His Love 184
   Because God Protects His Own 185
   Because God First Loved Me 186
   Because God Put Love In My Wardrobe 187
   Because God Has Loved Me Extravagantly 188

July – I Can *Listen* Today . . .
   Because God Wants Me To Know Him 190
   Because God Is Speaking 191

Because God Is Here Now 192
Because God's Word Is For My Good 193
Because God Is Speaking In A Whisper 194
Because God Calls Me 195
Because God Redirects 196
Because God Speaks In Our Exile 197
Because God Opens His Word To Us 198
Because God Welcomes Me To Sit With Him 199
Because God Invites Children To Come 200
Because God Speaks Through His Word 201
Because God Speaks Through Gifted Teachers 202
Because God Teaches Through Difficulties 203
Because God Empowers By The Holy Spirit 204
Because God Speaks Through His Creation 205
Because God Speaks In Dreams And Visions 206
Because God Speaks In Surprising Ways 207
Because God Speaks Words Of Love 208
Because God Speaks Through My Circumstances 209
Because God Speaks Through Wise Counsel 210
Because God Speaks Through Peace 211
Because God Speaks In Our Thoughts 212
Because God Speaks Uniquely To Me 213
Because God Wants Me To Hear, Then Do 214
Because God Calls Me To A Listening Way Of Life 215
Because God Speaks That I Might Obey 216
Because God Heals That I Might Hear 217
Because God Is My Good Shepherd 218
Because God's Word Is Guaranteed 219
Because God Speaks To His Friends 220

August – I Can *Rest* Today . . .
Because God Rested 222
Because God Restores Me As I Rest 223
Because God Commands Me To Rest 224
Because God Gives Me A Longing For His Rest 225
Because God Gives Rest To His Beloved 226
Because God Makes Me Safe Enough To Rest 227
Because God Created Me With A Need For Rest 228
Because God Knows My Frame 229
Because God's Presence Brings Rest 230
Because God Gives Rest In Peace 231
Because God Is Granting A Sabbath Rest 232

Because God Gives Peace In Times Of Trouble 233
Because God Displaces Anxiety With Peace.. 234
Because God Makes Us Restless Without Him 235
Because God Keeps The Watch.. 236
Because God's Salvation Includes Peace And Rest...................................... 237
Because God Is My Shelter In Time Of Storm... 238
Because God Gives Me Rest As I Trust In Him.. 239
Because God Replenishes Weary Souls 240
Because God Offers Rest In Worship... 241
Because God Provides Needed Rest Stops 242
Because God Is Holding Me As His Child 243
Because God Is With Me In The Lions' Den 244
Because God Goes With Us Into The Storm 245
Because God Fights My Battles.. 246
Because God Bestows Rest In Quietness 247
Because God Calls Me To Come Away With Him...................................... 248
Because God Relieves Me Of My Worries... 249
Because God Gives Rest To Those Who Return.. 250
Because God Sustains Me In Every Way 251
Because God Always Keeps His Promises.. 252

September – I Can *Testify* Today . . .
Because God Tells Me To Testify 254
Because God Has Given Me A Story To Tell 255
Because God's Love Compels Me 256
Because God Gave Jesus As The Only Way.. 257
Because God Washes Me Clean 258
Because God Uses Unlikely People 259
Because God Doesn't Want Anyone To Perish 260
Because God's Son Will Return When All Nations Have Heard................ 261
Because God Opens Eyes To See 262
Because God Causes Me To Grow... 263
Because God Edifies Others When I Testify 264
Because God Uses My Trials 265
Because God Gives Me What I Need 266
Because God Changes Me 267
Because God Has Made Me A Witness 268
Because God Has Divine Appointments For Me 269
Because God's Light Shines In Me.. 270
Because God Alone Vaccinates.. 271
Because God's Truth Is Wholly True.. 272
Because God Changes Lives Through Testimony 273

Because God Is Present In The Valley Of Death 274
Because God Prepares Me 275
Because God Says Don't Be Ashamed.. 276
Because God Lets Me Speak Of His Love.. 277
Because God Brings Faith From Hearing.. 278
Because God Is Glorified In My Testimony 279
Because God Touched Me 280
Because God Reveals His Majesty To Me.. 281
Because God Sacrificed For Me 282
Because God Has Given Me Eternal Life.. 283

October – I Can *Serve* Today . . .
Because God Is The Master Servant... 285
Because God Enables Me To Live As His Servant... 286
Because God Elevates Servant Leadership 287
Because God Sees All I Do As Service To Him 288
Because God Is Greater Than His Servants.. 289
Because God Gives Me Opportunity 290
Because God Gave His Life For Me.. 291
Because God Washes My Feet... 292
Because God Came As A Suffering Servant... 293
Because God's Gospel Is Adorned In Service 294
Because God Makes Leaders Who Serve 295
Because God Gifts Us To Serve... 296
Because God Is My Supreme Example 297
Because God Sends Me Where He Goes... 298
Because God Made Me His Servant... 299
Because God Blesses Us To Serve The Least Of These................................. 300
Because God Frees Us To Serve 301
Because God Gives Fervor For Service.. 302
Because God Loves Through Me 303
Because God Raised Jesus 304
Because God Notices People 305
Because God Helps Me Serve Only Him 306
Because God Flips My Definition Of ***Great***..***307***
Because God Fills Me With Himself 308
Because God Helps Me Say No, So I Can Say Yes 309
Because God Uses Servant Leaders As Examples 310
Because God Heals To Serve 311
Because God Rewards Faithful Service 312
Because God Judges Unfaithful Service 313
Because God Has Done Great Things.. 314

Because God Invites Me To Choose 315

November – I Can *Give* Today . . .
Because God Gives Good Gifts 317
Because God Gives Out Of Love 318
Because God Loves And Gives To The Unlovely 319
Because God Gives Priceless Treasures 320
Because God Blesses In Proportion To What We Sow 321
Because God Gives Me What I Need 322
Because God Expects Me To Give 323
Because God Freely Gives His Best 324
Because God Has Delivered Me 325
Because God Gave Himself 326
Because God Gives Me Time 327
Because God Shows The Blessedness Of Giving 328
Because God Gives Peace 329
Because God Gives Life 330
Because God Designed Me To Give 331
Because God Gives Joyfully 332
Because God Became Poor For Me 333
Because God Through Christ Has Saved Me 334
Because God Gives Great Grace Through Giving 335
Because God Encourages Through Giving 336
Because God Sees Every Giver's Heart 337
Because God Gives What He Has 338
Because God Uses What We Can Give 339
Because God Loves Joyful Giving 340
Because God Rewards The Giving Of Our Best 341
Because God Holds Me Responsible 342
Because God Has A Giving Nature 343
Because God Is Glorified In Grateful Giving 344
Because God Is So Generous To Me 345
Because God Gave Himself For Me 346

December – I Can *Hope* Today . . .
Because God Offers Hope In Him 348
Because God Promises Hope 349
Because God Is My Very Present Help 350
Because God Invites Me To The Mountaintop 351
Because God Sees And Acts 352
Because God Brings Hope To Hopelessness 353
Because God Makes A Straight Path For Me 354

Because God Shines A Great Light 355
Because God Changes *Shall* To *Is* 356
Because God Enters My Warfare 357
Because God Called Mary Who Said Yes 358
Because God Made A Way For Me To Hope 359
Because God Says The Days Are Coming 360
Because God Is Present In The Hardest Times 361
Because God Enables Patient Endurance 362
Because God Speaks Hope To Catastrophe 363
Because God Promises Eternal Life 364
Because God Raised Jesus From Death 365
Because God Comes To Unnoticed People 366
Because God's Son Lay In A Feeding Trough 367
Because God Is Planning A Surprise Party 368
Because God Invites Expectancy 369
Because God Remembers His Covenant 370
Because God Dispels Gloom 371
Because God Incarnate Was Born 372
Because God Fills My Longing With Joy 373
Because God Promises Another Christmas 374
Because God Makes Me Be Resolute 375
Because God Is Patient With Me 376
Because God Satisfies Fully 377
Because God Makes All Things New 378

About The Author 379

FOREWORD

Although Dr. Stephen Gammon can accurately say he has known me my entire life, I cannot say the same about him, since he was already two and a half years old when we first met. I was blessed to be born into the same family; Stephen was the second of six children, and I was the fourth of the bunch. Yes, our often-exhausted mother gave birth to six children in six years and lived to tell about it. So we grew up in the same loving, happy, noisy, and encouraging but disciplined home. Our dad was a busy and devoted small-town Baptist pastor, and our mom a well-organized, mostly stay-at-home teacher. Our home-cooked meals were eaten together around a large family table. Following our early-morning breakfast, the routine was to take turns reading a Bible passage, then a daily devotional, followed by family prayer and a praise song or two to the Lord.

Illustrating the centrality of daily prayer in our household, I remember our mom laughing as she recounted the time when I was only eighteen months old and it was my "turn" to pray. I was already talking quite fluently, so I was expected to participate. But when I was urged to start praying, I adamantly refused by saying, "This little girl ain't gonna pray!!" According to Mom, that earned me a swift and sad timeout in my bedroom, but then I was cheerfully compliant the next time around. Daily family devotions were assuredly not an option in our home, and our willing participation was a given.

Family devotions were not the only spiritual discipline we witnessed in our parents. They also prayed together as a couple every night for everyone in our family; they named each person individually as they prayed for God's protection and blessings in their lives. They continued to do so for their entire sixty-five years of marriage, adding our spouses and later our children and grandchildren to their ever-burgeoning list. To this day, I remember the security and love I felt as a child when I overhead them praying for me by name. What a priceless gift we experienced by having faith-filled, praying parents during our formative years.

As Stephen and I entered adulthood and went our separate ways, I was quite astounded that my very ordinary, often obnoxious and misbehaving elder brother went into full-time ministry and became a powerful man of God, one whom I will always admire. At times I have secretly envied his numerous supernatural encounters with God and his intimate and comfortable friendship with Jesus that he appears to come by so naturally. How blessed were the countless sailors and marines who listened to his wise counsel as a U.S. Navy Chaplain, and received his heartfelt prayers and encouragement. And thousands of people have since been touched and have had their lives changed by his kind pastoral care, his powerful biblical preaching, and the two inspirational *Walking with God* books he has authored. My own adult life took a much different road than his, as I chose to enter the medical field and served thirty years' active duty in the U.S. Public Health Service. Following retirement, I spent many months living and volunteering in Israel, serving in numerous houses of prayer, and completing graduate degrees while studying in Jerusalem.

But what my brother Stephen and I will always have in common, besides our upbringing, is that we are both incurably in love with Jesus. Our lives revolve around Him. We wake up thinking about Him and go to bed grateful that He is always there; we even pray He will visit us in our dreams. We cannot imagine life without Him and have each desperately clung to our Lord through numerous life events such as parenting challenges, traumatic losses, illnesses, and other crises. But now it is time for a true confession. I have not been nearly as disciplined as Stephen throughout my life in my personal time with God. Currently, I do have my favorite meeting place – a private, wooden gazebo overlooking a small lake where my husband and I live in Georgia. This is my "happy place," where I open the Word of God, turn my gaze to Jesus, and anticipate what He will say to me. There is nothing better than sitting at His feet, reading His Word, hearing His voice, and basking in His presence. Other times I experience His glory while sitting at my keyboard, singing and worshipping Him alone. Tears often flow in the "secret place" as I am once again awed by

His boundless love, mercy, and goodness to me. But as much as I want and intend to, I have not consistently and daily spent time alone with Jesus as Stephen faithfully does. Admittedly, I let my erratic schedule, busyness, and cares of this life interfere too often, and I will bet many or most of those reading this can readily identify with my shortcomings. It also has been too long since I have read the whole Bible in a year, how about you?

But this is what makes this new devotional book so exciting and timely for me (and you). It is high time for a change and a recharge. I intend to delve into *Because God* daily and to discipline myself once again to put first things first – *Because God* is worth it all. Without a doubt, the 365 days I spend with this Holy Spirit-inspired devotional book, my Bible, and most importantly with Jesus will radically transform my life and effect an abiding practice of seeking Him daily. I am truly still a work in progress (always will be) and so are you. The Lord is lovingly and patiently wooing and drawing all of us closer still. And He has wonderfully promised to complete the work He has started in us. Jesus is waiting, and oh, how much we need Him. So let's dive in!

Cheryl L. Tyler

With love and praise I dedicate this book to God
With forever gratitude to my parents
Glendon and Marjorie Gammon
From whom I learned how to love,
How to live in loving family and personal relationships,
And most of all, how to enjoy closeness with the One
Who made, and knows, and loves me and all of us.

INTRODUCTION

A Good Habit

I have done few things in my life more consistently and habitually than daily devotions. For this I am incredibly grateful. My parents started it, as our family of eight followed up breakfast each morning with family devotions, except on Sundays because we were preparing for church. During this time every day we turned our individual and collective focus to God, hearing and reflecting on His Word, reading and considering devotional thoughts centered on His Word, spending time in prayer, and singing together songs of worship. It wasn't long before I was also doing this on my own.

A Great Invitation

Perhaps because of this childhood discipline, I found it easier to continue this personal practice through life. Having daily quiet times with Jesus, knowing He is with me now just as He promised to be, and hearing Him speak through the Holy Spirit to my heart each day as we have shared life together has been my lifelong privilege and pleasure. Many days, and in many ways, this daily practice has enriched and changed my life. Many mornings I have awakened with anticipation, because I knew my God was inviting me to come near to Him again.

I knew that in a few short minutes my Lord and I would enjoy quiet time together. I anticipated hearing Him speak to me, and I looked forward to sharing my heart with Him. I have wanted and needed God to be with me and to lead me each day, and He has done so to the extent I have listened, believed, and allowed Him to change and lead me. Every day God invites His children to come near for quiet time with Him. And when we do, we become conscious throughout the day that He is there.

A Growing Relationship

Personal relationships grow by people spending time together. It is the same in our personal relationship with God. If we want to know God more, knowing His heart and His truth, we will choose to come near and spend time with Him often and as a way of life. To know God a little is better than not at all, but to know Him intimately and increasingly, up close and personal, is far better. There is no greater honor.

We marvel that God desires a personal and growing relationship with us and that He is willing and available to all who come near to Him. But He does not force this on us. God loves us, but as is the nature of love, He wants us to want to love Him. We must therefore willingly come near and make it our personal priority to seek Him first. This includes taking time daily to enter His presence for quiet time and being still.

A Grand Gift

God has spoken to us through His Word, and by it He is still speaking. After more than sixty years of daily devotions with Jesus, I can speak personally of wonderful tools God has used to help and bless me in drawing near to Him each day. The ones that have blessed me most are Scripture focused, drawing truths from the Bible that are from God and about God; they speak to me about living with and for Him today.

Concerning God's Word, I hope to encourage a discipline I have long practiced, which has enriched me greatly: I read the entire Bible again and again. Each time we prayerfully read and hear God's Word, He opens our eyes and ears to things we have not yet seen or heard. We can easily accomplish this by following an annual schedule that includes an Old Testament and a New Testament reading for each day. These can easily be read in just a few minutes each day.

By following such a schedule, over the course of a year we will have read the entire Bible. Why is this important? Because God's Word says, *All Scripture is breathed out by God and profitable for teaching, for reproof, for correction, and for training in righteousness, that the man of God may be complete, equipped for every good work* (2 Timothy 3:16-17). These verses do not say *some* Scripture is inspired of God, they say *all* Scripture.

If we believe this, isn't it reasonable to want to read it all, asking and trusting God to give us ears to hear what the Holy Spirit is saying? Of course, some portions of Scripture will speak to us more than others. But it is all God's Word, and there are spiritual truths revealed throughout it. Most years I have followed this practice, and I have been blessed in doing so. I hope you prayerfully consider this discipline in your own daily quiet time with God. To encourage this, following each daily devotion in this book, I have included the assigned readings for that day to read the Bible through in a calendar year. The schedule included here is not copyrighted but was graciously provided to me by Day of Discovery ministry. This same schedule is included with their popular daily devotional, *Our Daily Bread*.

A Gracious Privilege

Perhaps you have noticed that over time we tend to pick up characteristics from those we hang around. For this reason it is wise for us to look for opportunities to be with people we wish to be like. All the more is this true regarding our personal relationship with God. If we desire to follow Jesus and become like Him, we will surely and gladly take time to be with Him. If we say that we love God and want to be like Him but neglect to seek quiet time at His feet to pray, read, listen, and enjoy His presence, then our words and actions do not agree.

The disciples of Jesus loved following Him, each one utterly astounded that they had been given this privilege. When Mary sat at Jesus' feet, she was so glad for the privilege to be with the Lord and sit with Him. When Mary's sister Martha wanted her to get up and assist with the busywork of the day, Jesus said of Mary and by extension of you and me, that she *"has chosen the good portion, which will not be taken away from her"* (Luke 10:42). Sitting at Jesus' feet and enjoying quiet time with Him each day is a gracious privilege He offers to us. We need only do what Mary did and do this as a way of life. This means sitting in His presence today and every day.

A Glorious Transformation

The more that we enter God's presence to listen, learn, and love, the more we are transformed by Him and become more like Him. In His presence, as we hear His voice and respond to Him in faith, He anoints and equips us to be more like Him. So we are blessed to love, emulate, obey, honor, serve, and please Him. As we enter into His holy presence every day for quiet time with Jesus, and as He reveals Himself to us through His Word, God the Holy Spirit equips us to live each day according to His Word. The principle we can apply in His presence each day is this: *Because God . . . I Can.* Because God what? Because He speaks, acts, reveals, empowers, and loves today, I can . . . I can what? As the apostle Paul declared, *I can do all things through him who strengthens me* (Philippians 4:13).

What things can Christians do today because of God? This devotional focuses on twelve life practices that we are called and blessed to live every day as we walk with God. In each month a different life practice is emphasized that we can live, **Because God.** Each day of that month a particular truth about God is highlighted related to that theme, which leads us to consider how we can walk with God by living out that life practice that day.

Each month and day, as we make it our practice to have quiet time with Jesus, we see again that *Because God . . . I Can.* The twelve life-practice themes focused on in this yearlong devotional are foundational in following Jesus Christ, as we walk with Him through all of life and into eternity. Following God includes all of these: Believing, Trusting, Receiving, Praying, Praising, Loving, Listening, Resting, Testifying, Serving, Giving, and Hoping. This devotional focuses on one of these twelve themes each month, as day after day we grow in love for and obedience to God by living these life practices before Him. Our schedule is as follows:

January:	Because God . . . I Can *Believe* Today
February:	Because God . . . I Can *Trust* Today
March:	Because God . . . I Can *Receive* Today
April:	Because God . . . I Can *Pray* Today
May:	Because God . . . I Can *Praise* Today
June:	Because God . . . I Can *Love* Today
July:	Because God . . . I Can *Listen* Today
August:	Because God . . . I Can *Rest* Today
September:	Because God . . . I Can *Testify* Today
October:	Because God . . . I Can *Serve* Today
November:	Because God . . . I Can *Give* Today
December:	Because God . . . I Can *Hope* Today

As 2020 was approaching its end, as is my practice, I asked my Lord how He would have me proceed in my daily devotions in 2021. I heard His assignment clearly. In addition to again reading prayerfully through the whole Bible this year as I encourage you to prayerfully consider doing too, I was given a new assignment from my Lord. This year I was to write a daily devotional that focused on twelve particular themes that are all part of following Him. It has been my honor and joy to listen, learn, write, share, and pray.

I appreciate and thank my sister Cheryl L. Tyler who graciously wrote the Foreword for this devotional. She and I were blessed to be raised together, learning these same treasured and lifelong lessons on following Jesus, and enjoying daily devotions in fellowship with Him.

Now I pray for you. I am praying that the Lord of all blesses you greatly as you make it your practice to enter His presence for a special quiet time with Him each day. Come prayerfully, expecting to meet and hear Him. Come without pretense, just as you are. Come loving God, believing and receiving His deep and tender love for you. Come ready to be changed in His presence. The door is open wide for you. Every day God awaits your coming, and He covers you with His love. I know in faith that you will never be the same again.

Daily Devotions
For a Special Time with God Today

12 Themes on Following Jesus

JANUARY

Because God . . .
I Can *Believe* Today

January 1

I CAN *Believe* TODAY . . .
BECAUSE GOD SAVES

Say to those who have an anxious heart, "Be strong; fear not! Behold, your God will come . . . He will come and save you." Then the eyes of the blind shall be opened, and the ears of the deaf unstopped; And the ransomed of the Lord shall return and come to Zion with singing; everlasting joy shall be upon their heads; they shall obtain gladness and joy, and sorrow and sighing shall flee away. (Isaiah 35:4-5, 10)

As we look forward to this new year and what follows, with hope we can hear God's Word that everlasting joy is coming, for God comes to save. He declared this through His prophet Isaiah, and seven centuries later, the promised Messiah was born. His name was *Jesus,* meaning "God saves." God has come to save. And when we have been saved through believing the good news, we want this for others.

Harriet Tubman's story illustrates this. She was a slave who had suffered harshly, then ran north and discovered freedom. She became so grateful for this that she determined to risk her life so others could escape their slavery too. Harriet could neither read nor write, and she was frail, but she was undeterred. Altogether, she made nineteen trips south, freeing over three hundred former slaves, including several of her own family.

Could we who believe in the Lord Jesus Christ, having been saved from the slavery of our own sin through faith in Him, be content to simply rest in our own salvation? Or like Harriet Tubman, can we who know that this salvation is available to all, proactively show others the way? Looking ahead to whatever the future may hold, let us be supremely glad that God saves today, and that the Way is Jesus.

For Prayerful Reflection: In what ways have you been saved from slavery, and what has this meant to you? What will it mean for you today to believe that Jesus saves all who will believe and follow Him?

Bible in a Year: *Genesis 1-3; Matthew 1*

January 2

I CAN *Believe* TODAY . . .
BECAUSE GOD'S SON HAS RISEN

"We have seen the Lord." (John 20:25)

"Jesus of Nazareth, a man attested to you by God with mighty works and wonders and signs that God did through him in your midst, as you yourselves know—this Jesus, delivered up according to the definite plan and foreknowledge of God, you crucified and killed by the hands of lawless men. God raised him up, loosing the pangs of death, because it was not possible for him to be held by it." (Acts 2:22-24)

The resurrection of Jesus Christ is a firm pillar of Christian faith. We have not, as some presume, laid aside reason to blindly believe, as children do when believing in Santa or the Tooth Fairy. Rather, we have sought God's truth; we have heard and examined evidence, and by God's great grace we have become convinced that it is true. Today it is true that God has raised Jesus from the grave.

There is much evidence. The testimony of His disciples affirms that it is true. Everything for which they had worked, longed, hoped, and prayed died when Jesus died on that cross. If He had not risen from the grave, they would have sadly returned to their former lives. In fact, after His death they gathered in fear and grief in secret behind closed doors, lest His suffering and horrible death should become their fate too.

But something happened to radically change all of them. Despite the dangers, they repressed their fears and became filled with great joy; they all boldly announced to everyone who would listen that Jesus Christ is Lord, and He is risen. The only plausible explanation for such change and for their lifelong passion and devotion is that Jesus was risen. He remains alive today.

For Prayerful Reflection: How and when did you come to believe in the resurrection of Jesus Christ? How does believing that He is risen affect the way you live today?

Bible in a Year: *Genesis 4-6; Matthew 2*

January 3

I CAN *Believe* TODAY...
BECAUSE GOD KNOWS ME

O Lord, you have searched me and known me! You know when I sit down and when I rise up; you discern my thoughts from afar. You search out my path and my lying down and are acquainted with all my ways. Even before a word is on my tongue, behold, O Lord, you know it altogether. You hem me in, behind and before, and lay your hand upon me. Such knowledge is too wonderful for me; it is high; I cannot attain it. (Psalm 139:1-6)

Now the word of the Lord came to me, saying, "Before I formed you in the womb, I knew you, and before you were born I consecrated you." (Jeremiah 1:4-5)

Much like the psalmist, it blows my mind to consider that God knows everything about me. He knows my nature and yours, and everything we have ever thought, said, or done. God knows our every desire, including the things that shame us. Nevertheless, God wanted us even before we were conceived and formed in our mother's womb. God knows each of us completely, and He has always been, is now, and will forever be with us in every moment of every day – even today.

Haven't you experienced being misunderstood by others? Haven't you been dishonest in a personal relationship, perhaps due in part to shame or fear of rejection if they should know who you really are? But being in a personal relationship with God through Jesus Christ isn't like that. Nothing about us is hidden from God, yet He still loves us. Today we can believe this good news.

For Prayerful Reflection: What are some implications of believing God knows you completely and still loves you? How is such belief impacting you today?

Bible in a Year: *Genesis 7-9; Matthew 3*

January 4

I CAN *Believe* TODAY . . .
BECAUSE GOD DOES MIRACLES

The official said to [Jesus], "Sir, come down before my child dies." Jesus said to him, "Go; your son will live." The man believed . . . and went on his way. As he was going down, his servants met him and told him that his son was recovering. So he asked them the hour when he began to get better, and they said to him, "Yesterday at the seventh hour the fever left him." The father knew that was the hour when Jesus had said to him, "Your son will live." And he himself believed, and all his household.
(John 4:49-53)

This father's son lay dying, so he came to Jesus. Desperately needing a miracle, he begged Jesus to heal his boy. Seeing the man's faith, Jesus spoke the word, and from a distance the boy was healed. When this father arrived home the following day, he learned that the fever had left the boy at the very moment Jesus proclaimed his healing. Then the Bible says *he himself believed, and all his household.*

Miracles alone do not evoke faith, for like the soldiers who guarded Jesus' tomb and were there when He arose, many can witness God's power, yet rationalize it away. But when people seek truth and hear about or see God's miracles of grace, they are blessed with faith to believe. This has been true of me, for I have often been reminded of the miraculous power of God.

My grandfather and my mother told a story that especially touched me. They told of how God healed my mother from polio as she lay in a hospital, paralyzed and dying, while from a distance, her parents and others prayed for God's miraculous touch. I am blessed to be alive today, as many others are also, because God still works miracles today.

For Prayerful Reflection: Do you believe in the gospel accounts of Jesus' miracles? Do you believe He still does miracles today? How does such belief impact you?

Bible in a Year: *Genesis 10-12; Matthew 4*

January 5

I CAN *Believe* TODAY . . .
BECAUSE GOD LOVES HIS CHILDREN

[Jesus] put [a child] in the midst of them and said, "Truly, I say to you, unless you turn and become like children, you will never enter the kingdom of heaven. Whoever humbles himself like this child is the greatest in the kingdom of heaven." (Matthew 18:2-4)

Jesus said, "Let the little children come to me and do not hinder them, for to such belongs the kingdom of heaven." (Matthew 19:14)

Jesus loved and welcomed children, and urged us to come to Him like children do. Today I am remembering God's precious children in Myanmar. I was there in 2017. A decade earlier, after horrendous flooding, many little ones were left homeless. Led of the Lord Jesus, the church established a children's home where boys and girls would be raised in Christ's love. Because of widespread persecution against Christians there, the group home "parents" and all the children were often evicted, with little notice, from the large houses they were renting.

That Sunday morning as I worshipped with them, the children fervently prayed with evident intensity and faith, so I leaned toward the interpreter and inquired what they were praying for. After listening for a moment, he said they were asking God for a permanent home, so they wouldn't have to move again and again. The church there had few material resources, but these children, whom God so loved, believed God would accomplish this. When I heard this, the Holy Spirit told me to join in their prayer of faith, for God was going to answer their request. Now, by His love and grace, it is so. These dearly loved children are now living in a beautiful and permanent home that has been provided by God. My faith was stretched by the faith of the children. Because God loves His children, we can believe today.

For Prayerful Reflection: What does it mean to have childlike faith? How does God's love for children, and His affirmation of childlike faith, apply in your life today?

Bible in a Year: *Genesis 13-15; Matthew 5:1-26*

January 6

I CAN *Believe* TODAY . . .
BECAUSE GOD HAS MADE ME HIS CHILD

To all who did receive [Jesus], who believed in his name, he gave the right to become children of God, who were born, not of blood nor of the will of the flesh nor of the will of man, but of God. (John 1:12-13)

But you have received the Spirit of adoption as sons [and daughters], by whom we cry, "Abba! Father!" (Romans 8:15)

Some of us were blessed to be raised in a Christian home, where Jesus was known and loved. Others were raised in homes where He was not yet personally known or loved. Regardless of our upbringing, to be in God's forever-family as His child, we must personally believe in Jesus and out of faith choose to love and follow Him. God has many children, but no grandchildren. No one whose parents believed in Jesus automatically becomes God's child too. We must each believe that Jesus Christ is Savior and Lord, and that He loves us, and so we will want to love and follow Him. When this happens within us, God adopts us.

My children never asked me, "Are you still my dad today?" They knew and they loved me, for I knew and loved them. We are not God's children today because we have attained a standard of perfection, for no one has and no one can. Because of Jesus' perfect love and sacrifice for us, and through our faith in Him, God loves us today as His own children, and He will forever. And we are now blessed with many dear brothers and sisters. How blessed we are to believe this.

For Prayerful Reflection: What does it mean to be God's child, and when did you first know you were His? How does believing that you are God's own child affect you today?

Bible in a Year: *Genesis 16-17; Matthew 5:27-48*

January 7

I CAN *Believe* TODAY. . .
BECAUSE GOD PROVIDES DAILY BREAD

Then the Lord said to Moses, "Behold, I am about to rain bread from heaven for you, and the people shall go out and gather a day's portion every day, that I may test them." (Exodus 16:4)

Pray then like this: . . . "Give us this day our daily bread." (Matthew 6:9, 11)

The people of Israel were hungry and upset, as they had no idea where their next meal would come from. Perhaps if they had paused, pondered, and prayed, they would have realized how wonderful God had been thus far. He had miraculously led them out of bondage in Egypt and now was leading them toward the land of promise. But instead, they worried about their daily needs.

But God did watch over and care for them; He provided all they needed each day. God wanted His people then, and He wants His people now, to believe that He loves us and that today He will provide what we need. For the people of Israel, when they awoke each morning, they were vividly and visually reminded of God's personal care and provision, for fresh manna awaited them. God had once again provided their daily bread.

Our Lord calls us to share similar dependence on Him for our daily needs. He has taught us to pray, *"Give us this day our daily bread."* Because He has always been faithful to His promises by providing our daily bread, and because we have had all that we have needed, we can know that today He will do the same.

For Prayerful Reflection: How has God provided all you have needed through the years, when you needed it? How does it bless you today to believe God will provide all that you need?

Bible in a Year: *Genesis 18-19; Matthew 6:1-18*

January 8

I CAN *Believe* TODAY . . .
BECAUSE GOD PROTECTS

God is our refuge and strength, a very present help in trouble. Therefore we will not fear though the earth gives way, though the mountains be moved into the heart of the sea, though its waters roar and foam, though the mountains tremble at its swelling. (Psalm 46:1-3)

In this often-chaotic world, there is much trouble and fear. Sometimes this world seems like it is out of control. Rather than discount or deny this, the psalmist affirms it is so. In the face of this reality, when life for us is hard, we who believe in the Lord are reminded that we're never in this alone, for God is *a very present help in trouble.* And whenever we turn to Him in faith, we are blessed to find an oasis in the desert, a safe harbor in the storm, a haven of tranquility in the midst of chaos.

I assure you it is so, for I have experienced this truth over and over again. In times when I've faced the winds of uncertainty and weakness from cancer, a pandemic, or other struggles, God is my strength. When my heart has been flooded with grief from profound loss or from the pain of a broken relationship, He is my refuge. When the ground around my heart has been shaken because of prolonged absence from people I dearly love, God has been my fortress. He has been, is today, and will always be for me and you a *very present help in trouble.* Today we can believe God is with us, protecting us, no matter what the storms are.

For Prayerful Reflection: When and how has God been a refuge, strength, and fortress for you in times of trouble? How does this assurance bless you as you face today's challenges?

Bible in a Year: *Genesis 20-22; Matthew 6:19-34*

January 9

I CAN *Believe* TODAY . . .
BECAUSE GOD FORGIVES

[Jesus said,] "Therefore I tell you, her sins, which are many, are forgiven—for she loved much. But he who is forgiven little, loves little." And he said to her, "Your sins are forgiven." And he said to the woman, "Your faith has saved you; go in peace." (Luke 7:47-48, 50)

How sweet to be forgiven and to realize the wonder of it. In the scene that is described in Luke 7, a woman has entered the home of a Pharisee who is hosting a dinner party for Jesus. She is described as a sinner, for this was her public reputation. She knew it, others knew it, and Jesus knew she was a sinner. But though her sins were great, the wonderful grace of Jesus was greater.

She knelt at Jesus' feet, knowing her sinful condition and humbly owning it. And Jesus gave her what she needed more than anything else. He gave her what He offers us today – His forgiveness. When we believe this today, like the woman that day, we are set free from the burden of our sin.

As the woman described in this text, I too have received His forgiveness, and I have witnessed His grace of forgiveness to others. I will always remember the young man I visited in a Mexican prison who had been convicted of a horrible crime. The weight of his sin was heavy upon him. But God spoke to him through His Word and brought conviction of sin and His offer of grace. I was blessed to confirm to him the excellent news of God's love and forgiveness that day. And he believed.

All of us are sinners, invited by Jesus to come to Him in faith today. How wonderful to believe this and to receive His forgiveness.

For Prayerful Reflection: When and how have you realized your sin, and that Christ offers you forgiveness? How are you blessed today in believing and receiving His forgiveness?

Bible in a Year: *Genesis 23-24; Matthew 7*

January 10

I CAN *Believe* TODAY . . .
BECAUSE GOD KEEPS ME FROM FALLING

"Watch yourselves lest your hearts be weighed down with dissipation and drunkenness and cares of this life, and that day come upon you suddenly like a trap. For it will come upon all who dwell on the face of the whole earth. But stay awake at all times, praying that you may have strength to escape all these things . . . and to stand before the Son of Man." (Luke 21:34-36)

Now to him who is able to keep you from stumbling and to present you blameless before the presence of his glory with great joy, to the only God, our Savior, through Jesus Christ our Lord, be glory, majesty, dominion, and authority, before all time and now and forever. Amen. (Jude vv. 24-25)

God wants us to stand with Him against corruption and the temptations that can make us fall. Because we have all physically fallen at one time or another and have been hurt, we wisely take precautions to keep ourselves from falling. Perhaps we hold on to someone when we feel unstable. Spiritually, Jesus holds us tightly, and we hold on to Him. He reminds us that in this world there are slippery places where we could easily stumble and fall. For example, this happens when we place our own desires over His, the pleasures of sin over the joy of obedience, or the anguish of worry over the peace of trusting Him.

Jude's benediction reminds us that in Jesus Christ we do not walk alone. He has held us up and picked us up when we have stumbled. In faith we know that He keeps us from falling, and He will surely present us *blameless before the presence of his glory with great joy.* We can believe this today.

For Prayerful Reflection: How and when has God held you up from spiritually falling? How are you blessed today by believing that Christ will surely present you blameless before God's heavenly throne?

Bible in a Year: *Genesis 25-26; Matthew 8:1-17*

January 11

I CAN *Believe* TODAY . . .
BECAUSE GOD WILL NEVER FAIL ME

"And now I am about to go the way of all the earth, and you know in your hearts and souls, all of you, that not one word has failed of all the good things that the Lord your God promised concerning you. All have come to pass for you; not one of them has failed." (Joshua 23:14)

I have walked with the Lord many years now, gladly ministering in His name wherever He has called me. Today I joyfully remember forty years ago when in the first church I was called to serve, I was set apart and ordained for pastoral ministry. Looking back now, I can testify with praise and joy that God has never failed me. He has been faithful in every situation – always present, meeting every need, keeping every promise, walking beside me every step, guiding me all along the way. And so, I know God will not fail me today. And looking ahead now with confidence, I can believe that in all my remaining days and forever, God will never fail me.

As Joshua approached the end of his own earthly sojourn, his testimony was similar. He had experienced God's deliverance from bondage in Egypt. He had received daily manna from heaven. In the dry desert, his thirst was quenched by water from a rock. He had heard and received God's revelation, and now God's people were at last in the promised land. Remembering all this, Joshua reminded God's people that God had never failed them. Surely, we can believe today and know that God will never fail us.

For Prayerful Reflection: What is your own testimony of how God did not fail you? Today, and looking to the future, what is the effect for you of believing that God is never going to fail?

Bible in a Year: *Genesis 27-28; Matthew 8:18-34*

January 12

I CAN *Believe* TODAY . . .
BECAUSE GOD GIVES FAITH

I am reminded of your sincere faith, a faith that dwelt first in your grandmother Lois and your mother Eunice and now, I am sure, dwells in you as well. Do your best to present yourself to God as one approved, a worker who has no need to be ashamed, rightly handling the word of truth. (2 Timothy 1:5; 2:15)

I think I've always believed in the Lord Jesus. Like Timothy, I was raised in a family where He was loved. In my own heart, even as a little boy, Jesus Christ was as real to me as the other members of my family. I knew and loved Him, and I knew He loved me. As I grew, my understanding grew, as did my faith. But I have always been aware that the reason I believe is not because I was smart enough to figure it out. Rather, it is because in God's grace, He gave me sincere faith.

At whatever point in our lives we come to believe in the Lord, we must not passively rest upon it. As Paul urged young Pastor Timothy, we are all responsible to utilize, live, and grow in our faith by learning, understanding, and living in God's Word. The King James Version translation of 2 Timothy 2:15, which I remember memorizing as a boy, says we are to *study to shew thyself approved unto God, a workman that needeth not to be ashamed, rightly dividing the word of truth.* Believing in God today means wanting to grow in love for the Lord and in faith and understanding.

For Prayerful Reflection: How and when, by God's grace, did you first believe in Him? Today, how are you demonstrating a sincere desire to grow in your love, faith, and understanding?

Bible in a Year: *Genesis 29-30; Matthew 9:1-17*

January 13

I CAN *Believe* TODAY . . .
BECAUSE GOD IS GOOD

Know that the Lord, he is God! It is he who made us, and we are his; we are his people, and the sheep of his pasture. For the Lord is good; his steadfast love endures forever, and his faithfulness to all generations. (Psalm 100:3, 5)

"No one is good except God alone." (Mark 10:18)

God is light, and in him is no darkness at all. (1 John 1:5)

God is the One who made us; He is the Creator of all that is and the One who gave to each of us the gift of life. So we are His. And goodness is His character. The Hebrew word *tōv* means "pleasant, agreeable, delightful, good." Contrary to an all-too-popular perception, God is not an irritated despot looking for reasons to smash us or crush our happiness. God is good. His truth and guidance flow from His love.

Jesus said, *"No one is good except God alone."* Regrettably and admittedly, we have all experienced and demonstrated that we are not wholly good. No matter what our stated intentions, we can all sin, disappoint, and break promises. But not God. The apostle John rightly declared it: *God is light, and in him is no darkness at all.* Of course, for God is good.

We can therefore believe today that God can be wholly counted on to act in accordance with His nature, which is always what is right, true, and good. God is the gold standard of goodness. We can count on God to be good today. And so, we can believe.

For Prayerful Reflection: What does it mean that God is good, and how have you experienced His goodness? What are implications for you today of believing that God is good?

Bible in a Year: *Genesis 31-32; Matthew 9:18-38*

January 14

I CAN *Believe* TODAY . . .
BECAUSE GOD IS TRUTH

And the Word became flesh and dwelt among us, and we have seen his glory, glory as of the only Son from the Father, full of grace and truth. (John 1:14)

"You will know the truth, and the truth will set you free." (John 8:32)

"I am the way, and the truth, and the life. No one comes to the Father except through me." (John 14:6)

Because we live in a sin-filled world, and we have all sinned and been sinned against, our perspective may be corrupted by falsehoods. We can devise our own truth and believe falsehoods that are unholy, destructive, and degrading.

But when we meet Jesus and believe in Him, we begin to learn that in His character, word, and deed, He is the complete embodiment of truth. When we grasp God's truth that Jesus is *the way, and the truth, and the life,* and the only way to God the Father, our outlook changes for the good.

The ugly duckling of Hans Christian Andersen's tale illustrates that what we believe to be true determines our life-perspective and behavior. Hatched with other ducks, this duckling was considered ugly, was told so, and believed it. Degrading self-perception contributes to depression, feelings of worthlessness, and rejection. But in the spring, perspective changed when this ugly duckling for the first time met beautiful swans and discovered that, in fact, it was a beautiful and graceful swan.

God has made you and me to be like Him. Believing in Jesus, who is ultimate truth, means we can increasingly become like Him, the beautiful sons and daughters He created us to be.

For Prayerful Reflection: How has the truth of Christ altered your perspective of this world and of yourself? What are some implications for you today for believing that God is truth?

Bible in a Year: *Genesis 33-35; Matthew 10:1-20*

January 15

I CAN *Believe* TODAY . . .
BECAUSE GOD CANNOT LIE

"God is not man, that he should lie, or a son of man, that he should change his mind. Has he said, and will he not do it? Or has he spoken, and will he not fulfill it?" (Numbers 23:19)

In hope of eternal life, which God, who never lies, promised before the ages began. (Titus 1:2)

God has promised to always be with us and to hear and answer our prayers. God has promised that He loves us and will never stop. And He promised that He is preparing a place for us with Him in heaven, and we will be with Him forever. God has made many wonderful promises to us. But do we struggle to believe?

Because people may be dishonest and untruthful, and because we have all experienced this, we can at times struggle to believe what we have been told. This struggle can carry over to our belief in God. But we must remember that God can never lie, for truth is His everlasting character. The Lord Jesus said of Himself, *"I am . . . the truth"* (John 14:6). He not only spoke truth, He also was and is truth.

The only way your child or grandchild would know that tomorrow they will receive a new bicycle, or puppy, or a visit to the zoo from you is for you to promise it to them. They then believe that you will do what you have said, because you have done so before. It is humanly possible that you might not do as you have said, for something unforeseen could happen to preclude it, or you could change your mind, or you could even lie. But not God. God has never failed to keep a promise, nor can He ever.

For Prayerful Reflection: What struggles have you had with believing God? Why? What are some implications for believing today that God can never lie to you?

Bible in a Year: *Genesis 36-38; Matthew 10:21-42*

January 16

I CAN *Believe* TODAY . . .
BECAUSE GOD WOKE ME UP TODAY

I lay down and slept; I woke again, for the Lord sustained me. (Psalm 3:5)

And rising very early in the morning, while it was still dark, [Jesus] departed and went out to a desolate place, and there he prayed. (Mark 1:35)

"Awake, O sleeper, and arise from the dead, and Christ will shine on you." (Ephesians 5:14)

When I was a little child, before going to bed each night, I prayed something like this: "Now I lay me down to sleep, I pray the Lord my soul to keep. If I should die before I wake, I pray the Lord my soul to take. Please guide me safely through the night and wake me with the morning light." After this I would lift my various petitions before the Lord. I can recall the childlike confidence I had that God had heard me and would surely answer my prayer and that He would watch over me through the night. I knew that whether I died or awoke, I would be in God's presence. I carry that confidence today.

In many hotels we can request and receive a wake-up call the next morning if we so desire. Today God has awakened us with a new day to live in His presence. This day is filled with possibilities.

Being by nature a morning person, I like rising early. With morning coffee in hand and before the demands of the day begin, I first treasure a quiet time of fellowship with the Lord. Mark tells us that Jesus did something similar, often starting His days in quiet fellowship with His Father. God woke us up again today, so we can live this day with Him.

For Prayerful Reflection: To what extent have you realized that God wakes you every day? What are some implications of believing that you will live all of today with Him?

Bible in a Year: *Genesis 39-40; Matthew 11*

January 17

I CAN *Believe* TODAY . . .
BECAUSE GOD HAS REVEALED THE ENDING

Then I saw a new heaven and a new earth, . . . And I heard a loud voice from the throne saying, "Behold, the dwelling place of God is with man. He will dwell with them, and they will be his people, and God himself will be with them as their God. He will wipe away every tear from their eyes, and death shall be no more, neither shall there be mourning, nor crying, nor pain anymore, for the former things have passed away." And he who was seated on the throne said, "Behold, I am making all things new." (Revelation 21:1, 3-5)

Some days our battles can be exhausting and hard. Stress is higher when it feels like we are losing. But if we know with complete surety that victory is ahead, how improved our perspective can be!

As a football fan and New England native, I have long been a fan of the Patriots. When watching their football games, I feel stressed when the team is getting battered or beaten. If you are a sports fan, you understand this. When my team scores, I cheer, and when the game has been won, I share in the celebration. I have video recordings of every Super Bowl game won by the Patriots. Watching those recorded games is not stressful for me now, because even when my team is behind, I know that victory lies ahead. And so, the trial is tempered with faith, and the stress with joy.

Christians, we are blessed with a great hope, for God has shown us the triumphant end that is soon coming. His victory is assured. And so, no matter what today may look like now, we can rejoice and believe.

For Prayerful Reflection: When facing life's battles, do you tend to remain in the stress, or hold on in faith, anticipating with joy the victory that will come? How is believing God helping you today?

Bible in a Year: *Genesis 41-42; Matthew 12:1-23*

January 18

I CAN *Believe* TODAY . . .
BECAUSE GOD IS VERY NEAR

The Lord is near to all who call on him, to all who call on him in truth. (Psalm 145:18)

I bless the Lord who gives me counsel; in the night also my heart instructs me. I have set the Lord always before me; because he is at my right hand, I shall not be shaken. (Psalm 16:7-8)

The Lord is at hand; do not be anxious about anything, but in everything by prayer and supplication with thanksgiving let your requests be made known to God. And the peace of God, which surpasses all understanding, will guard your hearts and your minds in Christ Jesus. (Philippians 4:5-7)

Some think God is very far away. But in fact, He is very near. This truth is revealed in both the Old and New Testaments. Psalm 145 was the last of King David's recorded psalms. In it he testified of this truth which he had learned and lived: *The Lord is near to all who call on him, to all who call on him in truth.* Also, in Psalm 16, recalling times in the night when his heart was troubled, yet believing in the nearness of God, the psalmist testified, *Because he is at my right hand, I shall not be shaken.* I can relate to this.

Writing from prison to Christians in Philippi, the apostle Paul shared a wonderful truth he had learned firsthand – that the Lord is near. Believing this today means we need *not be anxious about anything.* Rather, as we come to our Lord who is near, praying in faith and gratitude, His peace becomes ours.

For Prayerful Reflection: To what extent have you believed the Lord is always near, and how has this affected you? How is believing that God is near helping you today?

Bible in a Year: *Genesis 43-45; Matthew 12:24-50*

January 19

I CAN *Believe* TODAY . . .
BECAUSE GOD IS OMNISCIENT

Great is our Lord, and abundant in power; his understanding is beyond measure. (Psalm 147:5)

Have you not known? Have you not heard? The Lord is the everlasting God, the Creator of the ends of the earth. He does not faint or grow weary; his understanding is unsearchable. (Isaiah 40:28)

"Even the hairs of your head are all numbered." (Matthew 10:30)

God is omniscient, which is to say He is all-knowing. Because our own wisdom and knowledge are limited and can thus be misguided, we may face hard consequences. Perhaps you've heard of the vacuum cleaner salesman who years ago knocked on the door of a remote farmhouse. When the farmer's wife opened the door, he entered and dumped a bag of dirt on the floor. The salesman said, "If this amazing vacuum cleaner doesn't pick up every bit of this dirt, I will eat what's left."

The farmer's wife gave him a spoon and said, "We don't have electricity." The man's lack of knowledge created the mess. Can you relate?

But God knows everything past, present, and future, including everything there is to know about you and me. God is all-knowing! So when we are confused, uncertain about what is true or right, or what we should do, or the way we should go – we can turn in faith to our omniscient God. This privilege lifts the weight of our responsibility to somehow figure it all out and fix everything. God blesses and guides those who do not lean on their own understanding but rather believe in Him and lean on Him today.

For Prayerful Reflection: When have you ever trusted your own knowledge and been left with a mess to clean up? Today, what effect does or could believing in the omniscience of God have in your life?

Bible in a Year: *Genesis 46-48; Matthew 13:1-30*

January 20

I CAN *Believe* TODAY . . .
BECAUSE GOD IS OMNIPOTENT

"Ah, Lord God! It is you who have made the heavens and the earth by your great power and by your outstretched arm! Nothing is too hard for you." The word of the Lord came to Jeremiah: "Behold, I am the Lord, the God of all flesh. Is anything too hard for me?" (Jeremiah 32:17, 26-27)

God is omnipotent, which is to say He is all-powerful. He is more powerful than all the forces of nature that He has created and all the forces of evil that must tremble before Him. The omnipotence of God means He is more powerful than every struggle and circumstance in this world, even our own.

When the world was in utter chaos and it seemed like all was lost, the prophet Jeremiah looked to God and prayed, *"Ah, Lord God! It is you who have made the heavens and the earth by your great power and by your outstretched arm! Nothing is too hard for you."* He then painfully confessed that the people of God had ceased believing this, so they were now living the consequences of unbelief. Omnipotent God then spoke to Jeremiah and to us today and asked, *"Is anything too hard for me?"* What is your answer today?

Believing God is omnipotent includes believing He is able in my life and circumstances today. As A. W. Tozer put it, "Anything God has ever done, He can do now. Anything God has ever done anywhere, He can do here. Anything God has ever done for anyone, He can do for you."[1] Amen.

For Prayerful Reflection: What powerful things has God done for you that you have lately forgotten? What affect could belief in the omnipotence of God have in your life today?

Bible in a Year: *Genesis 49-50; Matthew 13:31-58*

---

[1] Cited from *Leadership Weekly* (October 9, 2002).

January 21

I CAN *Believe* TODAY . . .
BECAUSE GOD IS OMNIPRESENT

Where shall I go from your Spirit? Or where shall I flee from your presence? If I ascend to heaven, you are there! If I make my bed in Sheol, you are there! If I take the wings of the morning and dwell in the uttermost parts of the sea, even there your hand shall lead me, and your right hand shall hold me. (Psalm 139:7-10)

Could you imagine sending an emergency 9-1-1 call to God in prayer asking for help, but there is no signal? You are unable to get through, for you are out of range. Or imagine going somewhere, as Jonah once thought possible, where God is not present. Thankfully, such imaginations are foolish and futile, for the omnipresence of God assures us such things cannot be.

The psalmist spoke of God's omnipresence, which is to say that God is everywhere. This can be hard for us to grasp. We could more easily perceive God's omnipotence in part, for we all have some measure of strength. Or we might more easily understand God's omniscience, for we all have some measure of knowledge. But omnipresence? We have no frame of reference for this because we are all limited to just one location at a time. But God is omnipresent, and this truth is remarkable, and a great blessing to those who believe.

The omnipresence of God means God is with us today and will be with us always, no matter where we are or where we go. This truth has carried me through life. I've been in places I could not have imagined in every state across the USA, on six continents, and on many islands. I've been with God on mountains and in valleys, in the air, on the seas, and under the seas. In foreign places, stressful places, and dangerous places, I have never doubted that the omnipresent God is with me. He is with us all today and will be forever.

For Prayerful Reflection: When have you learned and how have you appreciated the omnipresence of God? How does believing this truth bless you today?

Bible in a Year: *Exodus 1-3; Matthew 14:1-21*

January 22

I CAN *Believe* TODAY . . .
BECAUSE GOD'S PROMISES ARE ASSURED

Now faith is the assurance of things hoped for, the conviction of things not seen. (Hebrews 11:1)

Notice this verse is in the present tense. Yes, it speaks to the past, but it is not primarily addressing history. And though it applies to tomorrow, it is not primarily addressing the future. This speaks to today. *Faith **is** the assurance of things hoped for, the conviction of things not seen* (emphasis added).

True faith is defined here as *assurance* and *conviction*. It is not merely wishful thinking or vague hope. Faith is confidence today that what God has promised will assuredly happen. Even if we do not see the fulfillment yet, with assurance and conviction we can believe, for we know God will keep His promises.

A sweet Christmas memory for me happened when I was just eight years old. I had longed for a new bicycle, and my parents said that if I would be patient and wait, in time it would come. So when Christmas morning came, I hoped this would be the day. But at the family Christmas tree, I saw other blessings and gifts but not the bicycle I was most longing for.

On the tree, however, there was a small box with my name on it. Opening it, I found a folded picture of a red-chrome bicycle with a personal note saying I must patiently wait just a little bit longer. I was happy with that promise, for I believed it. I didn't yet have the promised bike, but I knew with certainty that soon I would. Later that day, the promised bike was mine. And of course, I was a very happy boy.

We who trust in Christ can know today with certainty that all God's promises to us are entirely assured.

For Prayerful Reflection: What promises has God made to you for which you have been patiently waiting? Today, how are you blessed by knowing that God's promises to you are assured?

Bible in a Year: *Exodus 4-6; Matthew 14:22-36*

January 23

I CAN *Believe* TODAY . . .
BECAUSE GOD IS SPEAKING TODAY

And [Samuel] said to the people of Israel, "Thus says the Lord, the God of Israel, 'I brought up Israel out of Egypt, and I delivered you from the hand of the Egyptians and from the hand of all the kingdoms that were oppressing you.' But today you have rejected your God." (1 Samuel 10:18-19)

They said to each other, "Did not our hearts burn within us while he talked to us on the road, while he opened to us the Scriptures?" (Luke 24:32)

In the 1970s the stock brokerage firm E. F. Hutton launched a great advertising slogan. Their first commercial took place in a crowded restaurant in which businessmen are at a table. One says, "My broker is E. F. Hutton. And E. F. Hutton says, . . ." at which everyone in the restaurant suddenly stops what they're doing and leans forward, straining to hear. Then the slogan is heard: "When E. F. Hutton talks, people listen."

Shouldn't people who believe in God respond like this, always eager to hear as He speaks? But as in Samuel's day, sometimes we don't listen, do we? In unbelief, rather than listening carefully to what God is saying, we can choose to reject Him by not listening to His voice. But let us notice the beautiful testimony revealed in Luke 24. These two men who had walked along with Jesus on His resurrection day were forever changed from being with Him and hearing His voice.

I want to be like them today, don't you? We are blessed to be with God now, listening carefully and hearing His voice. Because God is speaking, we can believe today. We can in fact hear His word and take it into our own hearts by faith, thus being changed. God speaks. Are we listening today?

For Prayerful Reflection: When have you been astounded with the realization that God is speaking to you now, and that you are so blessed to hear? How does this privilege affect you today?

Bible in a Year: *Exodus 7-8; Matthew 15:1-20*

January 24

I CAN *Believe* TODAY . . .
BECAUSE GOD IS LEADING

Then the cloud covered the tent of meeting, and the glory of the Lord filled the tabernacle. Throughout all their journeys, whenever the cloud was taken up from over the tabernacle, the people of Israel would set out. But if the cloud was not taken up, then they did not set out till the day that it was taken up. For the cloud of the Lord was on the tabernacle by day, and fire was in it by night, in the sight of all the house of Israel throughout all their journeys. (Exodus 40:34, 36-38)

And [Jesus] said to them, "Follow me." (Matthew 4:19)

Throughout human history, God has desired and called a people who will follow Him. Exodus tells a portion of this story. God led Israel's descendants out of centuries-long bondage in Egypt and then along their wilderness journey until, at last, they were ready to enter the land of promise. How beautiful is the picture painted in the last chapter of Exodus, for God was among them, leading them – visibly evidenced by the pillar of cloud by day and fire by night. Their great but underappreciated blessing was simply to go as God would lead them. But did they do it? Do we?

Jesus came among us and called people to follow him. Then and now, some who are called to follow Jesus choose to walk away. Others leave all to follow Him. If we follow, we do not ask, "Where are we going, Lord?" as though we might then choose whether or not we will go. Following is the holy privilege of being with our Lord, wherever He may lead. To believe in Jesus is to be a Christ-follower, which is to go when and where He leads, regardless of our particular preference. To believe God is leading means I can follow Him today.

For Prayerful Reflection: When have you ever resisted following Jesus or waiting for His lead? When have you experienced the peace and joy of following His lead? How does this speak to you today?

Bible in a Year: *Exodus 9-11; Matthew 15:21-39*

January 25

I CAN *Believe* TODAY . . .
BECAUSE GOD IS MERCIFUL TODAY

[Bartimaeus] began to cry out and say, "Jesus, Son of David, have mercy on me!" And Jesus stopped and said, "Call him." And they called the blind man, saying to him, "Take heart. Get up; he is calling you." And throwing off his cloak, he sprang up and came to Jesus. And Jesus said to him, "What do you want me to do for you?" And the blind man said to him, "Rabbi, let me recover my sight." And Jesus said to him, "Go your way; your faith has made you well." And immediately he recovered his sight and followed him on the way. (Mark 10:47, 49-52)

And [one of the criminals beside Jesus] said, "Jesus, remember me when you come into your kingdom." And he said to him, "Truly, I say to you, today you will be with me in paradise." (Luke 23:42-43)

God extends mercy to all who come to Him believing, having recognized their need, calling out to Him, and asking in faith. Bartimaeus was a poor, blind beggar who needed God's touch. So when Jesus passed by that day, Bartimaeus loudly and repeatedly cried, *"Jesus, Son of David, have mercy on me!"* Jesus heard his cry and extended mercy to him. Today, yes even today, our Lord hears and extends to us His mercy – to all who come to Him believing.

As Jesus was dying on the cross for my sins and yours, a sinful criminal beside him looked toward Jesus in faith. Believing, he asked the Savior for mercy. Lovingly, Jesus granted him sweet salvation and everlasting life. Like this remarkable recipient of our Lord's grace and mercy, we are blessed today to believe that He extends such mercy to us.

For Prayerful Reflection: When have you called to the Lord for mercy and known that you received it? What will it mean for you to come to Jesus today, believing like Bartimaeus and the dying thief?

Bible in a Year: *Exodus 12-13; Matthew 16*

January 26

I CAN *Believe* TODAY . . .
BECAUSE GOD IS ETERNAL

In the beginning, God. (Genesis 1:1)

Before the mountains were brought forth, or ever you had formed the earth and the world, from everlasting to everlasting you are God. (Psalm 90:2)

"And now, Father, glorify me in your own presence with the glory that I had with you before the world existed." (John 17:5)

Jesus Christ is the same yesterday and today and forever. (Hebrews 13:8)

"I am the Alpha and the Omega," says the Lord God, "who is and who was and who is to come, the Almighty." (Revelation 1:8)

God is eternal. This truth is not within our comprehension, for we have all had a beginning, and our mortal bodies are going to have an end. But there has never been a time when God has not been, nor will there ever be a time when He will not be. Transcending the boundaries of linear time, God exists eternally and concurrently in past, present, and future.

In Dr. David Jeremiah's audio message *How Big is Your God?* he offers an illustration of God's eternal perspective compared to our own experience. He said if we were to attend the Rose Bowl Parade, we would see each float, marching band, animal, or performer as it passes us. Perhaps we could see a little of what has already passed and a little of what is about to come, but primarily we would only see what is right before us. Eternal God, however, sees the entire parade all at once – what has already passed, what is now passing, and what is yet coming.

Believing that God is eternal means we can leave our past with Him, we can walk with Him today in our present, and we can trust Him without worry for our future, for we know He is already there.

For Prayerful Reflection: Though understandably God's eternal nature is difficult to grasp, what has it meant to you in your walk with Him? How does belief that God is eternal help you today?

Bible in a Year: *Exodus 14-15; Matthew 17*

January 27

I CAN *Believe* TODAY . . .
BECAUSE GOD IS GLORIOUS

Arise, shine, for your light has come, and the glory of the Lord has risen upon you. For behold, darkness shall cover the earth, and thick darkness the peoples; but the Lord will arise upon you, and his glory will be seen upon you. (Isaiah 60:1-2)

"I am the light of the world. Whoever follows me will not walk in darkness, but will have the light of life." (John 8:12)

The city has no need of sun or moon to shine on it, for the glory of God gives it light, and its lamp is the Lamb. (Revelation 21:23)

God's glory magnificently shines, even today, here and now. Into the darkness of this world, God promised that His light would come. Then He announced that His light *has* come. The Lord Jesus is *the light of the world.* So in heaven, no sun or moon will shine, *for the glory of God gives it light, and its lamp is the Lamb.*

In *God in the Dock,* C. S. Lewis described a day in his garden toolshed when he noticed a sunbeam was shining across the shed. He had likely seen this before, but that day it captivated him. He traced the beam of light to a crack at the top of the closed shed door and peered through the crack. It struck him that though within the shed it appeared that the light was coming from the crack itself, in truth, the ultimate source was a blazing star ninety million miles away! Believing in God today allows us to look beyond our many visible blessings to see and exalt the glorious God, who is the source of it all.

For Prayerful Reflection: How have you noticed God's glory shining around you? In what ways is the light of God's glory blessing you or those around you today?

Bible in a Year: *Exodus 16-18; Matthew 18:1-20*

January 28

I CAN *Believe* TODAY . . .
BECAUSE GOD ENABLES TODAY

"Not by might, nor by power, but by my Spirit, says the Lord of hosts." (Zechariah 4:6)

I can do all things through [Christ] who strengthens me. (Philippians 4:13)

Every person who walks with God can know by faith that God will enable them for everything He calls them to do. In our personal estimation of what is needed for challenges awaiting us, we could easily presume that we cannot do something because our strength is weak and our resources are few.

The Bible, however, shows many examples of weak people being called by God for seemingly impossible challenges. But God enabled them. When the shepherd Moses was called by God to lead Israel out of bondage in Egypt, he repeatedly told the Lord there was no way he could do this. But God enabled him. And against all odds and in the low estimation of everyone, the shepherd boy David went out boldly in the name and power of God, and the giant warrior Goliath fell. Overwhelmed by grief and fear, the Lord's apostles, who previously hid themselves, joyfully, boldly, without fear, and in the power of the Holy Spirit publicly proclaimed the wonderful news of Jesus, and His victory for us over sin and death.

I have lived this lesson, for I have often been called to things beyond my own ability or strength. But knowing and believing that God enables means we too are enabled by God for whatever He calls us to do, as He enabled Moses, David, the apostles, and many more. Like Paul, we can believe today and confidently say, *I can do all things through [Christ] who strengthens me.*

For Prayerful Reflection: What situations have you faced for which you felt unable, but God enabled you? What could you face today or in coming days for which you will believe for God's enabling grace?

Bible in a Year: *Exodus 19-20; Matthew 18:21-35*

January 29

I CAN *Believe* TODAY . . .
BECAUSE GOD HAS COMPASSION

> *When Jesus heard this, he withdrew from there in a boat to a desolate place by himself. But when the crowds heard it, they followed him on foot from the towns. When he went ashore he saw a great crowd, and he had compassion on them and healed their sick.* (Matthew 14:13-14)

Jesus had compassion on them, and He has compassion on us. The day described in this passage was very hard for Jesus, for He was informed that morning that John the Baptist had been killed by Herod. This grievous news was painful, and Jesus wanted to get away, undoubtedly to grieve and pray. Scripture says *he withdrew from there in a boat to a desolate place by himself.* But when He arrived, a crowd was waiting, for they had seen his boat on the lake and walked or ran around the lake to join Him there. Rather than being annoyed at this or frustrated by the demands they placed upon Him, the Bible says *he had compassion on them.*

I love that. Don't you? We can believe today that God always cares for His children, even for us. He loves you and me and has compassion on us. Let that sink in. Believe that wherever you are today and whatever needs you may have or burdens you may carry, the Lord has compassion on you today.

In this account we see Jesus healing the sick and feeding the hungry. Today He is meeting each of us right where we are. He sees our needs, and with compassion He cares for us. We can believe it.

For Prayerful Reflection: How have you experienced God's compassion? What needs do you carry that the Lord sees and will surely meet? How are you helped today by believing God has great compassion for you and for everyone you meet today?

Bible in a Year: *Exodus 21-22; Matthew 19*

January 30

I CAN *Believe* TODAY . . .
BECAUSE GOD DELIVERS

Then the Lord said [to Moses], "I have surely seen the affliction of my people who are in Egypt and have heard their cry because of their taskmasters. I know their sufferings, and I have come down to deliver them out of the hand of the Egyptians and to bring them up out of that land to a good and broad land, a land flowing with milk and honey." (Exodus 3:7-8)

An incredible reality of life is that our God comes to deliver us. That day on Mount Sinai began as an ordinary day with Moses tending his father-in-law's flock. Then heaven came down. As Moses came near to examine a bush that was burning without being consumed, God called Moses by name and called Himself *I am*. Though Moses heard and saw this, at first he resisted the leap of faith required to believe it fully.

In the above verses, God told Moses of four actions He has done and is doing to save us:

1. God sees: *"I have surely seen the affliction of my people."*

2. God hears: *"I have . . . heard their cry."*

3. God knows: *"I know their sufferings."*

4. God comes: *"I have come down to deliver them."*

This was and is astounding news, for *I am* reveals Himself as personal, loving, and proactive on our behalf. God sees our afflictions, hears our cries, knows our sufferings, and in great love comes to deliver us. God has done this through the incarnation of Jesus Christ. And because He has come to deliver us, we can believe Him today.

For Prayerful Reflection: How has the personal nature and actions of *I am* affected your outlook? How does believing that God sees, hears, knows, and comes to deliver you affect you today?

Bible in a Year: *Exodus 23-24; Matthew 20:1-16*

January 31

I CAN *Believe* TODAY . . .
BECAUSE GOD ENTERS THROUGH LOCKED DOORS

Eight days later, his disciples were inside again, and Thomas was with them. Although the doors were locked, Jesus came and stood among them and said, "Peace be with you." Then he said to Thomas, "Put your finger here, and see my hands; and put out your hand, and place it in my side. Do not disbelieve, but believe." Thomas answered him, "My Lord and my God!" Jesus said to him, "Have you believed because you have seen me? Blessed are those who have not seen and yet have believed." (John 20:26-29)

We can all relate to Thomas, when after Jesus' resurrection he refused to believe his friends and fellow disciples who had excitedly told him Jesus was alive. Thomas had erected a door in his heart and closed it tight. His door was a firm refusal to believe unless he could see the risen Lord with his own eyes and touch Him with his own hands.

We too can erect barriers to our believing – refusals to accept God's truth unless or until certain conditions of our making are met. But the story of Thomas is a story of sweet grace that God extended to him and now to us, for as Jesus came through the locked door to reach Thomas, He does the same for you and me.

God is not blocked by locked doors. And when by grace Jesus presents Himself to us, it is not a matter of whether we are able to believe. Rather, as with Thomas, the Lord's presence summons our belief. We can believe today, and we are blessed for it, even though we have not yet physically seen Him. Because God enters through locked doors, today we can believe.

For Prayerful Reflection: What locked doors have you erected that keep you from believing all that is true? Today, will you ask God to enter through any locked doors in your heart, thus to fully believe?

Bible in a Year: *Exodus 25-26; Matthew 20:17-34*

12 Themes on Following Jesus

FEBRUARY

Because God . . .
I Can *Trust* Today

February 1

I CAN *Trust* TODAY . . .
BECAUSE GOD HAS BEEN FAITHFUL

After the death of Moses the servant of the Lord, the Lord said to Joshua the son of Nun, Moses' assistant, "Moses my servant is dead. Now therefore arise, go over this Jordan, you and all this people, into the land that I am giving to them, to the people of Israel. . . . Just as I was with Moses, so I will be with you. I will not leave you or forsake you." (Joshua 1:1-2, 5)

Sometimes the challenges before us can seem overwhelming, and we might wonder how we will make it through them. We can face personal challenges in our schooling, relationships, work, health, or other areas of life. Sometimes our responsibilities can weigh heavy upon us.

I expect that Joshua felt this way after Moses died. Moses had been his longtime friend and mentor, the one whom God had so powerfully used to lead Israel out of bondage in Egypt, through the wilderness for forty years, and then to the very edge of the promised land. But Moses was gone, and Joshua was called to lead this nation across the river and into the land of promise.

Was Joshua feeling overwhelmed? Wouldn't you be overwhelmed with such an enormous responsibility? But God knew exactly what Joshua needed, and He knows what you and I need too. Joshua needed to trust the Lord, and so do we. God said, *"Just as I was with Moses, so I will be with you. I will not leave you or forsake you."* In other words, "Just as I have been faithful before, so I will be faithful to you now, and I will make a way for you." God wants us to trust Him like this today.

For Prayerful Reflection: What challenges have you faced before or are you facing now with which you have at times felt overwhelmed? How does the Lord's promise affect your trust today?

Bible in a Year: *Exodus 27-28; Matthew 21:1-22*

February 2

I CAN *Trust* TODAY...
BECAUSE GOD HAS FED US

"And you shall remember the whole way that the Lord your God has led you these forty years in the wilderness, that he might humble you, testing you to know what was in your heart, whether you would keep his commandments or not. And he humbled you and let you hunger and fed you with manna, which you did not know, nor did your fathers know, that he might make you know that man does not live by bread alone, but man lives by every word that comes from the mouth of the Lord."
(Deuteronomy 8:2-3)

We can be prone to take for granted the blessings we have enjoyed from the Lord and forget how God has blessed us thus far. In the eighth chapter of Deuteronomy, the Lord makes this point clear, as the people of Israel had received many blessings. God had miraculously delivered them from slavery in Egypt, and as they wandered for forty years in the wilderness, God had given them all that they needed.

Day after day and year after year, in that wilderness God had rained down manna from heaven to feed them. Initially they celebrated God's provision with gratitude, but over time they took it for granted and even complained. They had not earned, nor have we earned, God's grace or provision. Yet He provided daily manna to teach them and to teach us that He is loving and able, and we can trust Him every day for our every need – physical and spiritual. Yes, we can fully trust Him today.

For Prayerful Reflection: What areas of God's provision have you taken for granted? In what areas of life today will you trust God for what you need and thank Him for all He has provided?

Bible in a Year: *Exodus 29-30; Matthew 21:23-46*

February 3

I CAN *Trust* TODAY . . .
BECAUSE GOD PROMISES A GOOD FUTURE

These are the words of the letter that Jeremiah the prophet sent from Jerusalem to the surviving elders of the exiles, and to the priests, the prophets, and all the people, whom Nebuchadnezzar had taken into exile from Jerusalem to Babylon. "For thus says the Lord: When seventy years are completed for Babylon, I will visit you, and I will fulfill to you my promise and bring you back to this place. For I know the plans I have for you, declares the Lord, plans for welfare and not for evil, to give you a future and a hope." (Jeremiah 29:1, 10-11)

Their outward circumstances were tough, and the people were in despair, for the world as they once knew it was no more. Jerusalem had fallen; many had died, and they were exiled far away in Babylon. Their circumstances were a direct consequence of the sins of their nation, including their own individual sins. As they feared to envision their future, God sent them this message of love, hope, and promise through His prophet Jeremiah, letting them know they could still trust Him.

God reminded His people then, and reminds us today, that though life can be hard for a while, He is still faithful, and His plan is still good. When we experience loss, disappointment, and sorrow, our pain can be great, for life as we knew it is no more. But God remains faithful, and to all who will trust Him, He gives His message of hope and the promise of a future filled with blessing. Yes, we can trust Him today.

For Prayerful Reflection: When have hard circumstances brought you to despair? What, if anything, could keep you from fully trusting God today for His promise to you of a hope and a good future?

Bible in a Year: *Exodus 31-33; Matthew 22:1-22*

February 4

I CAN *Trust* TODAY . . .
BECAUSE GOD ANSWERS WHENEVER I CALL IN TROUBLE

Is anyone among you suffering? Let him pray. (James 5:13)

"Because he holds fast to me in love, I will deliver him; I will protect him, because he knows my name. When he calls to me, I will answer him; I will be with him in trouble; I will rescue him and honor him." (Psalm 91:14-15)

The Bible often speaks of people who were in dire trouble, calling out to God in faith. And when they did so, and today when we do so, God hears and answers. The Scriptures quoted above are words of God to us. He invites, reminds, and promises that when we are in trouble, we can call Him, and He will answer.

I have often seen the reality of this promise. One precious time occurred in the Intensive Care Unit at the National Naval Medical Center in Bethesda, Maryland. It was wartime, and I was then a Navy Reserve Chaplain. I had been activated for a month to support the Hospital Pastoral Care Department, which had been stressed by a sustained influx of wounded warriors.

Making my rounds one day and praying for divine appointments, I came through the Intensive Care Unit. A medical flight had just arrived with wounded service members. A wounded Marine noticed the cross on my collar and called out, "Chaplain, please pray with me!" When I approached him, I saw that his legs were gone, and he was about to be wheeled into surgery. Though this man was suffering and afraid, I knew that he knew Jesus, and in faith he was calling upon the Lord. As we prayed that day, our Lord powerfully met us. Whatever we may be facing today, we too can trust Him, knowing that He always answers His children who cry to Him in trouble.

For Prayerful Reflection: When have you faced trouble and called upon the Lord, knowing that He heard and answered? How does this invitation and promise impact your trust today?

Bible in a Year: *Exodus 34-35; Matthew 22:23-46*

February 5

I CAN *Trust* TODAY . . .
BECAUSE GOD SEES ME

The angel of the Lord found [Hagar] by a spring of water in the wilderness, the spring on the way to Shur. And he said, "Hagar, servant of Sarai, where have you come from and where are you going?" She said, "I am fleeing from my mistress Sarai." The angel of the Lord said to her, "Return to your mistress and submit to her." The angel of the Lord also said to her, "I will surely multiply your offspring so that they cannot be numbered for multitude." So she called the name of the Lord who spoke to her, "You are a God of seeing," for she said, "Truly here I have seen him who looks after me." (Genesis 16:7-10, 13)

Hagar had been having a rough time, as Sarai had treated her horribly. Hagar despaired; she concluded she could not take it anymore, so she ran away. She was angry, afraid, alone, and without direction or hope. Have you known some of what Hagar was experiencing? Have you felt frustration, anger, fear, or loneliness in times of personal pain? I have.

God is doing today what He did for Hagar that day. He met her and spoke precious promises to her that she needed to hear and believe. She believed God that day, and her life was changed. She was reminded that God is real and personal and, yes, that God saw her. Hagar's reply to God was, "*You are El-Roi,*" which means "the God who sees me." She could henceforth remember and know that God saw her then. We can know this too, and how blessed we are to know it today.

No matter what discouragements we might be facing today or in coming days, we can know and trust that God is here, God cares, and He sees us now. This conviction allows us to face today with hope.

For Prayerful Reflection: What does it mean to you, and how has it helped you to know that God sees you? How does this assurance make a difference in your life today?

Bible in a Year: *Exodus 36-38; Matthew 23:1-22*

February 6

I CAN *Trust* TODAY . . .
BECAUSE GOD IS WITH ME IN EVERY BATTLE

"It is the Lord who goes before you. He will be with you; he will not leave you or forsake you. Do not fear or be dismayed." (Deuteronomy 31:8)

"You will not need to fight in this battle. Stand firm, hold your position, and see the salvation of the Lord on your behalf . . . Do not be afraid and do not be dismayed. Tomorrow go out against them, and the Lord will be with you." (2 Chronicles 20:17)

These are God's words of assurance to us when we are facing conflict and overwhelming odds. He promises to be with us in life's battles. Such assurance brings confidence and help.

I love the amazing true story in Booton Herndon's book *Redemption at Hacksaw Ridge* and the subsequent movie *Hacksaw Ridge*. Desmond Doss was a World War II conscientious objector who refused to bear arms to kill or injure others, yet he volunteered to serve as an Army medic, treating wounds and saving lives.

With the 77th Infantry in the Battle of Okinawa, as thousands fought and died, Desmond Doss braved bullets, grenades, and snipers to rescue many wounded soldiers. Though he had been wrongly accused by other soldiers of cowardice, with extraordinary faith and remarkable courage, he rescued many. After each rescue, though utterly exhausted and facing continued grave danger, he prayed, "Lord, please let me find one more." God answered Desmond's prayers. He was credited with saving seventy-five wounded men. For such heroism he was awarded the Medal of Honor.

Today, in every battle we are facing, we too can know and trust that our God is with us.

For Prayerful Reflection: When have you been in trouble and called upon God, knowing He was with you? How can His promise to be with you in life's battles help you today?

Bible in a Year: *Exodus 39-40; Matthew 23:23-39*

February 7

I CAN *Trust* TODAY . . .
BECAUSE GOD EVEN CARES FOR THE BIRDS

"Look at the birds of the air: they neither sow nor reap nor gather into barns, and yet your heavenly Father feeds them. Are you not of more value than they?" (Matthew 6:26)

On the deck outside the sliding glass door in our living room, Helen and I have placed a bird feeder. We enjoy watching birds arrive each day to enjoy an all-they-can-eat buffet of bird seed. And with the aid of our illustrated manual of Minnesota bird species, we can identify various species that come each day.

Knowing our propensity to worry and wanting us to know that we can fully trust Him, Jesus encourages us to *look at the birds of the air* to learn what they teach us about God's care and provision. As we do this, we can clearly see that God, the Father of creation, feeds His birds every day. And since He cares for birds and provides what they need, surely we can trust Him to care and provide for us today.

Our part is to trust that God does care for us and always will. God has provided, is providing, and will always provide what we need. We can trust Him by doing what the birds in our backyard do – return every day in faith, enjoy His care and provision, and receive His love and blessings for the new day.

For Prayerful Reflection: For what have you been worrying more than trusting? How does God's lesson about His care for birds speak to you about trusting Him?

Bible in a Year: *Leviticus 1-3; Matthew 24:1-28*

February 8

I CAN *Trust* TODAY . . .
BECAUSE GOD HAS GIVEN ME A MISSION

[Jesus] called the twelve together and gave them power and authority over all demons and to cure diseases, and he sent them out to proclaim the kingdom of God and to heal. And he said to them, "Take nothing for your journey, no staff, nor bag, nor bread, nor money; and do not have two tunics." And they departed and went through the villages, preaching the gospel and healing everywhere. (Luke 9:1-3, 6)

Jesus teaches that anytime He calls us to do something in His name, He always makes a way for us to do it. So we can trust Him fully. We are never called to do His work in self-reliance, depending only on our own abilities or resources. Our Lord calls us to depend on Him and trust Him fully for anointing and provision. This theme was taught by Jesus when He sent the twelve out to minister in His name. They could not possibly do this in their own strength or wisdom, so our Lord gave them His own power and authority to accomplish His mission, as He gives to us today.

Why did the Lord say, *"Take nothing for your journey"*? He wanted His apostles to know experientially that they needed to trust Him for their daily bread and for all that they needed. Likewise, we must trust Him. We do not need to fret about His care or provision. We can trust God for everything and give Him our praise for His love and gracious provision, even through those whom He may stir to welcome and bless us. Whenever God assigns us a mission, we can fully trust Him to provide – even today.

For Prayerful Reflection: When has God assigned you a mission that you resisted out of worry about your ability or His provision? How could you step out for the Lord today and trust His provision?

Bible in a Year: *Leviticus 4-5; Matthew 24:29-51*

February 9

I CAN *Trust* TODAY . . .
BECAUSE GOD KEEPS HIS WORD

"God is not man, that he should lie, or a son of man, that he should change his mind. Has he said, and will he not do it? Or has he spoken, and will he not fulfill it?" (Numbers 23:19)

The saying is trustworthy, for: If we have died with him, we will also live with him; if we endure, we will also reign with him; if we deny him, he also will deny us; if we are faithless, he remains faithful—for he cannot deny himself. (2 Timothy 2:11-13)

Haven't we all experienced the sting of broken promises? I read about a sixty-seven-year-old carpenter who died in 1994 in Marion, Illinois. In his last will and testament, he had bequeathed $2.4 billion to the town of Cave-In-Rock, $2.4 billion to the city of East St. Louis, $1.5 billion for projects in southeastern Illinois, and $6 trillion to the Federal Reserve to apply to the national debt. The problem was, when the man died, the only thing he actually owned was an eleven-year-old car. No one can give what they do not have. But our God is able, and we can trust Him to keep every promise He has made.

As we have been recipients of broken promises in this broken world, we might easily apply our wounded skepticism to God. But He wants us to know that unlike those who have sinned against us and have broken their promises, God has never, can never, and will never break a single promise He has made. No matter what our circumstances are today, God's promises are trustworthy and true, and we can trust Him.

For Prayerful Reflection: What promises were made to you but later broken, thus wounding you? What promises of God have you struggled to trust? Why? How are you blessed today by knowing that God will keep His Word?

Bible in a Year: *Leviticus 6-7; Matthew 25:1-30*

February 10

I CAN *Trust* TODAY . . .
BECAUSE GOD INVITES ME TO TRUST HIM FULLY

Trust in the Lord with all your heart, and do not lean on your own understanding. In all your ways acknowledge him, and he will make straight your paths. (Proverbs 3:5-6)

Here God invites us to trust Him fully and promises that when we do, He will direct our path. He will steer us toward His will, which will always be for our good and His glory. This invitation with a promise is extended by God to us today. It is given within the context of the major theme in this book of wisdom that *the fear of the Lord is the beginning of knowledge* (Proverbs 1:7). So trusting God fully means leaning on Him today, even if life has become hard, and we do not understand what is happening. We can draw near in faith and trust in God's infinite wisdom, not in our own limited understanding.

I have often experienced the truth of this invitation and promise. Haven't you also defaulted to self-reliance or feeble attempts to determine for yourself the best way to go when you are experiencing pain or confusion and are unsure of the way forward? But mercifully, God calls us back to Himself, invites us again to trust Him fully, and promises that He knows the way and will lead us. We cannot always see what is ahead, for our wisdom is limited and our vision is myopic. But God sees, and we can trust Him fully to lead us today.

For Prayerful Reflection: When have you realized that this invitation and promise is extended to you? In what areas of your life do you need to trust Him today, and what effect will His promise have?

Bible in a Year: *Leviticus 8-10; Matthew 25:31-46*

February 11

I CAN *Trust* TODAY . . .
BECAUSE GOD BIDS ME TO COME IN THE STORM

In the fourth watch of the night [Jesus] came to them, walking on the sea. But when the disciples saw him . . . they cried out in fear. But immediately Jesus spoke to them, saying "Take heart; it is I. Do not be afraid." And Peter answered him, "Lord, if it is you, command me to come to you on the water." He said, "Come." So Peter got out of the boat and walked on the water and came to Jesus. But when he saw the wind, he was afraid, and beginning to sink he cried out, "Lord, save me." Jesus immediately reached out his hand and took hold of him, saying to him, "O you of little faith, why did you doubt?" And when they got into the boat, the wind ceased. (Matthew 14:25-32)

What a story. We have been there, haven't we? In one of life's many storms, we find ourselves in trouble. But our Lord sees us and comes to us, perhaps in ways we could not imagine. That night Jesus came out to His disciples in a storm in the middle of the lake, walking on water. Addressing their fear, our Lord said to them, *"It is I."* Then Jesus bade Peter to come to Him.

In the storms of our lives, He bids us come too. On that stormy night, trusting in Jesus, Peter got out of that boat and walked toward Jesus on the water. If Peter's faith and focus had remained steady, he would have made it the whole way. But his faith wavered, as ours can also, and he began to sink. We can relate, can't we? Sometimes when storms are raging, our faith wavers too. But Jesus, who loves us so, extends hands of grace and strength to us as He did to Peter, teaching us again that we can always trust Him fully, no matter the strength of the storm.

For Prayerful Reflection: When have you ever been in a storm and heard the Lord calling you to come? In what storm do you want to trust Him fully today?

Bible in a Year: *Leviticus 11-12; Matthew 26:1-25*

February 12

I CAN *Trust* TODAY . . .
BECAUSE GOD IS A REFUGE FOR ME

In you, O Lord, do I take refuge; let me never be put to shame! Be to me a rock of refuge, to which I may continually come; you have given the command to save me, for you are my rock and my fortress. For you, O Lord, are my hope, my trust, O Lord, from my youth. Upon you I have leaned from before my birth; you are he who took me from my mother's womb. My praise is continually of you. Do not cast me off in the time of old age; forsake me not when my strength is spent. (Psalm 71:1, 3, 5-6, 9)

This psalm was penned by someone who, like me, has been blessed to know the Lord since childhood. This psalmist, who was older, is looking back and remembering how faithful God has been, but in the current season, there is trouble again, and his strength is spent. He needed the Lord that day.

I have been there, haven't you? Perhaps it was profound grief or a hard diagnosis. Or perhaps it was loneliness, fear, disappointment, conflict, financial strain, a fractured relationship, or some other pain. If we are not facing such struggles today, we can rejoice. But we can also know with certainty that we will face struggles again.

Because the Lord has been our fortress and refuge in times of trouble, and since He has always been faithful, even when life for us has been hard, we can surely trust Him today. We can know with the certainty of faith that God walks with us now, and He will see us through whatever today brings.

For Prayerful Reflection: What times of struggle can you recount when you ran to God in faith and found Him faithful? Can you trust God fully today, even in the struggles?

Bible in a Year: *Leviticus 13; Matthew 26:26-50*

February 13

I CAN *Trust* TODAY . . .
BECAUSE GOD IS ABLE

The Lord said to Abraham, ". . . Is anything too hard for the Lord? At the appointed time I will return to you, about this time next year, and Sarah shall have a son." (Genesis 18:13-14)

The angel answered [Mary], "The Holy Spirit will come upon you, and the power of the Most High will overshadow you; therefore the child to be born will be called holy—the Son of God. For nothing will be impossible with God." And Mary said, "Behold, I am the servant of the Lord; let it be to me according to your word." (Luke 1:35, 37-38)

God is infinite in power and love. He is the One who by His own word created the vast universe, including this earth, and who by His own will formed each of us in our mother's womb and by grace chose to breathe into us the breath of life. God is the One who has loved us with an everlasting love, despite our sinful condition, and who freely gave His incarnate Son to suffer and die in our place as the perfect sacrificial Lamb for our forgiveness and salvation. God is able today.

In light of who God is and all He has done for us, how could we doubt Him? Yet some days we do, don't we? Sometimes when facing trials, we can make little or no sense of this world. Yet we hear God calling us again to believe His Word and to trust Him fully, as Abraham and Mary did. Because God is able today, and because nothing is impossible with Him, we can trust Him fully.

For Prayerful Reflection: When and how has God shown you that He is able, for nothing is impossible with Him? In what areas of life do you need to trust Him today?

Bible in a Year: *Leviticus 14; Matthew 26:51-75*

February 14

I CAN *Trust* TODAY . . .
BECAUSE GOD LOVES ME SO

In all these things we are more than conquerors through him who loved us. For I am sure that neither death nor life, nor angels nor rulers, nor things present nor things to come, nor powers, nor height nor depth, nor anything else in all creation, will be able to separate us from the love of God in Christ Jesus our Lord. (Romans 8:37-39)

[Jesus said,] "As the Father has loved me, so have I loved you. Abide in my love." (John 15:9)

Happy Valentine's Day. Do you know that God loves you very much? Ponder this question for a moment, as you consider God's very deep love for you. He really loves you, for He has often said so. He has also proved His love in countless ways, most powerfully by willingly suffering and dying to wash away your sins and save you, so that you can be forgiven and live forever in His loving presence. On His way to doing this for you and for me, He declared that love was His reason. Jesus said, *"Greater love has no one than this, that someone lay down his life for his friends"* (John 15:13).

Today God loves us deeply, and He will never stop. If this truth has made its way into the core of our hearts by faith, then we know He is inviting us today to *abide in [his] love*. Considering the struggles of today or the hurts or discouragements that could come our way, let us hear and trust His personal love for us. Let us hear His kind invitation to each of us to pause in His presence right now and soak in His love, being prayerfully determined to trust Him wholly.

For Prayerful Reflection: When and how did you come to realize that God loves you very much? Today, how will your realization of God's great love for you affect your trust in Him?

Bible in a Year: *Leviticus 15-16; Matthew 27:1-26*

February 15

I CAN *Trust* TODAY . . .
BECAUSE GOD IS WITH ME

[Moses said,] "Be strong and courageous. Do not fear or be in dread of them, for it is the Lord your God who goes with you. He will not leave you or forsake you." (Deuteronomy 31:6)

[Jesus said,] "Behold, I am with you always, to the end of the age." (Matthew 28:20)

How blessed we are to have this amazing promise. And because God is faithful in all His promises, we can know with complete certainty that we will not be alone today or ever. God is with us in this season and in every season and situation. We can be wholly sure of this, and we can trust Him.

I can never forget the morning of that day when I was to enter the hospital for a stem-cell transplant as treatment for multiple myeloma. Helen and I would be physically apart for some time, because COVID-19 protocols precluded her hospital visits. That morning we held each other's hand, shared heart to heart, and prayed together.

The stem cells had already been harvested and frozen. Now I was to receive megadoses of chemotherapy, which would strip away what remained of my immune system while also destroying cancer cells. Then the stem cells would be transplanted back into my body, making their way to my bone marrow. After this, we would patiently wait for my immune system to be slowly reborn.

Because Helen and I had to be apart from each other while I lived in a sterile bubble, we worried about each other. I was concerned for Helen because she was alone in Nashville, removed from our family and friends. And she tearfully expressed her worries about me, that I would be all alone and even that I could die alone. As we prayed together that morning, God reminded us both of His wonderful promise to be with us always. God is with each of us today, and He will be every day.

For Prayerful Reflection: In what circumstances has God reminded you that He is with you now, so you are not alone? What will you face today in which it will help to remember this and trust Him?

Bible in a Year: *Leviticus 17-18; Matthew 27:27-50*

February 16

I CAN *Trust* TODAY . . .
BECAUSE GOD IS INVITING ME TO COME NEAR

[Jesus said,] "Come to me, all who labor and are heavy laden, and I will give you rest. Take my yoke upon you, and learn from me, for I am gentle and lowly in heart, and you will find rest for your souls. For my yoke is easy, and my burden is light." (Matthew 11:28-30)

These days we might not often see two animals yoked together, pulling a heavy load or plow. In Jesus' day this was a common sight. Two oxen, for example, shared a yoke. The first could be older, made stronger from years of labor. The second might be inexperienced and weaker. But in sharing the yoke, the load was lighter, because the younger, weaker one had to simply walk step-by-step beside the strong one, thus becoming stronger day after day.

Jesus invites us to be yoked with Him today and walk alongside Him every step that we take. As we do this, we see that His yoke is very good, for He is with us and bears the heavy weight of the burdens. How blessed we are to be yoked with Jesus today, for He is strong, loving, and good. We can trust Him fully, for He knows the way for us to go, and He has all the strength needed to pull the load and see us through.

For Prayerful Reflection: In what hard situations have you learned or are you learning to trust the Lord, leaning on Him to pull a heavy load? What does it mean for you today to face each challenge walking step-by-step alongside Jesus?

Bible in a Year: *Leviticus 19-20; Matthew 27:51-66*

February 17

I CAN *Trust* TODAY . . .
BECAUSE GOD WORKS WONDERS

And leaping up, he stood and began to walk, and entered the temple with them, walking and leaping and praising God. And all the people saw him walking and praising God, and recognized him as the one who sat at the Beautiful Gate of the temple, asking for alms. And they were filled with wonder and amazement at what had happened to him. (Acts 3:8-10)

What a beautiful account! The Scriptures give many accounts of people experiencing God's miraculous touch. Sarah's barren womb was opened when she was ninety years old, causing her to "laugh," which was the meaning of *Isaac,* her baby's name. Elijah was miraculously fed by God through the widow of Zarephath and her child in a time of dire famine. Daniel was protected from the mouths of hungry lions. Jairus' daughter and Lazarus were raised from the dead by Jesus. And the man described in Acts 3, who had never before walked, was walking, leaping, and praising God! All these people were never again the same, for God works wonders.

What happens when we face a situation that seems impossible to us, and God reminds us of His miracle-working power? Our faith is stretched when we remember that today God is able. I have been blessed to witness God's wonder-working power at various times through the years. And so, in trying circumstances when God reminds me of His wonder-working power and love, my faith has been stretched to believe and see again His miraculous authority. God is able today.

For Prayerful Reflection: What miraculous accounts in Scripture have especially blessed you? What miracles have you encountered that God has used to stretch your faith? What difficult situations are you facing today in which you are trusting God and remembering He is able?

Bible in a Year: *Leviticus 21-22; Matthew 28*

February 18

I CAN *Trust* TODAY . . .
BECAUSE GOD DOES NOT CHANGE

"For I the Lord do not change." (Malachi 3:6)

Jesus Christ is the same yesterday and today and forever. (Hebrews 13:8)

Every good gift and every perfect gift is from above, coming down from the Father of lights, with whom there is no variation or shadow due to change. (James 1:17)

As the days go by, which become months, then years, then decades, and then generations, we change. We all do, and we must. No pause button will allow us to remain *as* we are or *where* we are. This is especially evident in little children, who are growing and changing so quickly. I have been reminded of this lately while watching family videos that I recorded in years gone by. I have reminisced over video clips of various places and stages of Helen's and my life together, including times with our beloved and now-departed parents, and our children at various stages of their childhood.

While watching and remembering, I have laughed, cried, and rejoiced in how God has blessed us through the years. In each season and every generation, God has been present, blessing His people. We can never go back to what once was, for we must continue moving forward toward the destiny God has in store for those who love Him, when time will be for us no more.

As changes keep coming, let's not be pining for days gone by, nor fretting for days that will come. May we know in faith today that as God has always been faithful, He cannot and will not change.

For Prayerful Reflection: How have you been reminded that God is forever the same? Looking ahead to the future, how does God's unchanging nature affect your trust in Him today?

Bible in a Year: *Leviticus 23-24; Mark 1:1-22*

February 19

I CAN *Trust* TODAY . . .
BECAUSE GOD GIVES PERFECT PEACE

"You keep him in perfect peace whose mind is stayed on you, because he trusts in you. Trust in the Lord forever, for the Lord God is an everlasting rock." (Isaiah 26:3-4)

Is it really possible to experience calm and be at peace while a storm is raging around us? Yes. It is very possible – by trusting God who is with us in the storm.

During a severe thunderstorm one summer night, a mother was tucking her little boy into bed. As she was about to turn off the light, the boy asked with a trembling voice, "Mommy, will you stay with me all night?"

The mother gave her son a reassuring hug and said tenderly, "I can't dear. I have to sleep in Daddy's room."

After a long silence, and with a shaky voice, the little boy said, "The big sissy!"

We might chuckle, but we understand that little boy's sentiment, don't we? It can be hard to remain unafraid and calm when a storm rages without or within. But we are not alone in the storms of life. God has promised to always be with us, even when life is hard and storm winds blow – even today.

What is our part in experiencing God's peace in times of storm? It is to focus on Him in faith, knowing He is with us. And because we know this, we can trust Him fully today and receive His peace.

For Prayerful Reflection: In what storms of life have you been fearful and lacked God's perfect peace? What will it mean for you to keep your mind stayed on the Lord today, trust in Him, release fears, and receive His peace?

Bible in a Year: *Leviticus 25; Mark 1:23-45*

February 20

I CAN *Trust* TODAY . . .
BECAUSE GOD IS GOOD TO ME

Though an army encamp against me, my heart shall not fear; though war arise against me, yet I will be confident. I believe that I shall look upon the goodness of the Lord in the land of the living! Wait for the Lord; be strong, and let your heart take courage; wait for the Lord! (Psalm 27:3, 13-14)

We can all share stories of how God has been good to us. We can think of times in our lives when something beautiful happened that we neither earned nor deserved, and yet we received it. Perhaps it was a wedding day, or the birth of a child or grandchild. Or perhaps it was a magnificent sunrise or sunset or another glorious scene in God's creation. Or beneath a clear nighttime sky, did you behold the glory of our magnificent God? Or was there a time when things were going so well for you that you became overwhelmed by His blessings and love? Along the way in our walk with God, it is good to gratefully pause and consider again the goodness of God.

Those who make it a practice of seeing and acknowledging God's goodness are fortified to continue seeing His goodness, to trust Him even on the hard days. Psalm 27 expresses such confidence through many circumstances in life, even if an army should encamp against us. I have lived this lesson along my own journey of walking with God, even while facing cancer. Remembering His goodness from before cancer, I experienced it again. Because God has been and is so good, He can be fully trusted today.

For Prayerful Reflection: How have you experienced God's goodness, even when life was hard? What would it mean for you to fully trust the goodness of God today?

Bible in a Year: *Leviticus 26-27; Mark 2*

February 21

I CAN *Trust* TODAY ...
BECAUSE GOD AVAILS US OF HIS POWER TODAY

May the Lord answer you in the day of trouble! May the name of the God of Jacob protect you! Some trust in chariots and some in horses, but we trust in the name of the Lord our God. (Psalm 20:1, 7)

Psalm 20 was penned by David who knew very well the power of God to help in the day of battle. He could recall what he learned as a youth. Though others trembled in fear and relied on armies and warriors to win battles, David learned to trust not in his own strength, nor in armies, chariots, and horses, but to *trust in the name of the Lord*. This is what young David did when in the name of the Lord, he faced Goliath. We've all faced giants in life, and we will again. The question for us is, In whose strength do we fight?

I like the story of the old woodsman who had always cut down trees with an ax and a handsaw. But when a hardware shopkeeper told him of a chainsaw that would let him cut many more trees per day, the aging woodsman decided to try it. Later that day the woodsman returned to the hardware store – tired, sweaty, and upset. "You said this thing would cut more trees, but I worked all day and only felled one."

"That cannot be," said the shopkeeper. "Let me see what the problem is." He inspected the chainsaw closely, then pulled the choke and the starter rope.

The startled woodsman yelled, "What's that noise?"

Are we still attempting to complete the hard tasks in our own strength? Today, may our God mercifully help us become more familiar with trusting and applying His amazing and wonderful power.

For Prayerful Reflection: What battles have you been fighting in your own strength? What will it mean for you to approach every situation today, trusting and depending on God's presence and power?

Bible in a Year: *Numbers 1-3; Mark 3*

February 22

I CAN *Trust* TODAY . . .
BECAUSE GOD GIVES LIVING WATER TODAY

Jesus said to her, ". . . whoever drinks of the water that I will give him will never be thirsty again. The water that I will give him will become in him a spring of water welling up to eternal life." (John 4:13-14)

O God, you are my God; earnestly I seek you; my soul thirsts for you; my flesh faints for you, as in a dry and weary land where there is no water. (Psalm 63:1)

Water is essential for life, and we have all known physical thirst. This is true spiritually too, for God created us in His own image and gave us all an inner thirst for relationship with Him.

Jesus offered *living water* to the woman He met that day at the well at Sychar in Samaria. Like her, our lives can sometimes be a mess. She had often failed, and she was deeply scarred. She carried shame, loneliness, and pain, and her future seemed to hold little promise. But all of that changed when she met Jesus. With tender love and grace, our Lord offered her what He offers us – *a spring of water welling up to eternal life.* Today we can come and drink as often as we wish; we can drink deeply of God's grace in faith and personal relationship with the Lord Jesus Christ.

Let us come to the Lord today with the same longing expressed by David in Psalm 63:1, thirsting for Him, *as in a dry and weary land where there is no water.* Because God offers living water, we can come to Him right now, drink deeply, and trust fully.

For Prayerful Reflection: Reflecting on what it means to be intensely thirsty, when have you known the sort of spiritual thirst alluded to by David? What will it mean for you today to trust enough to drink deeply of the living water offered by Jesus?

Bible in a Year: *Numbers 4-6; Mark 4:1-20*

February 23

I CAN *Trust* TODAY . . .
BECAUSE GOD HAS NUMBERED OUR DAYS

Your eyes saw my unformed substance; in your book were written, every one of them, the days that were formed for me, when as yet there was none of them. (Psalm 139:16)

The years of our life are seventy, or even by reason of strength eighty; yet their span is but toil and trouble; they are soon gone, and we fly away. So teach us to number our days that we may get a heart of wisdom. (Psalm 90:10, 12)

Even before we were born, eternal and almighty God knew us and loved us; He had a wonderful plan for our lives. And God has numbered our days. Over the years of my life, in the precious days when I was ill and facing my own mortality, God gave me His peace and hope through these precious truths.

The fact is, in our mortal bodies all of us have a finite number of days. If we picture in our minds an hourglass in which grains of sand are steadily falling, and if each grain represents a single day of our mortal life, we can clearly see that it won't be long before all the grains of sand have fallen, and the days of this mortal life are gone. Though this realization causes some to despair, for God's children it brings rejoicing, for we know we are in His hands for time and eternity. We know God has a good purpose for us, and His plans for us include eternal life. So we can trust Him fully today.

For Prayerful Reflection: What has been your experience when reflecting on your mortality? How and why can your thoughts, attitudes, and trust be positively affected today by knowing that God who loves you numbers your days?

Bible in a Year: *Numbers 7-8; Mark 4:21-41*

February 24

I CAN *Trust* TODAY...
BECAUSE GOD FORGIVES

When Jesus saw their faith, he said to the paralytic, "Son, your sins are forgiven." Now some of the scribes were sitting there, questioning in their hearts, "Why does this man speak like that?... Who can forgive sins but God alone?" And immediately Jesus... said to them, "Why do you question these things in your hearts? Which is easier, to say to the paralytic, 'Your sins are forgiven,' or to say, 'Rise, take up your bed and walk'? But that you may know that the Son of Man has authority on earth to forgive sins"—he said to the paralytic—"I say to you, rise, pick up your bed, and go home." And he rose and immediately picked up his bed and went out before them all, so that they were all amazed and glorified God. (Mark 2:5-12)

Two miracles happened that day: forgiveness and physical healing. Jesus addressed the greatest need first, the man's forgiveness. Then Jesus healed his body. People were amazed, and they glorified God. Which of these miracles impressed them more? And what impressed the one whom Jesus forgave and healed?

My mom taught me about this. Like the man described in this passage, she too received from the Lord forgiveness and healing from paralysis. From her hospital bed where she lay paralyzed and dying from polio, her parents and others fervently prayed for her from a distance and asked God for a miracle. And by His mercy, God heard and answered.

She told me that because of her paralysis, she could not speak that day, but she could still hear. She heard a doctor say she would never rise from her bed. That was when she heard Jesus tell her to rise. So she did, utterly astounding everyone present. She later married and had six children, of whom I am the second. My mom knew what the man in today's gospel account knew: He is a miracle-working, prayer-answering God, and His miracles include forgiveness. I know this too, and I pray you do also.

For Prayerful Reflection: How does knowing that God is able and that He forgives affect your trusting Him? Today, how are you treasuring God's forgiveness?

Bible in a Year: *Numbers 9-11; Mark 5:1-20*

February 25

I CAN *Trust* TODAY . . .
BECAUSE GOD IS HERE AND THERE TODAY

The official said to him, "Sir, come down before my child dies." Jesus said to him, "Go; your son will live." The man believed the word that Jesus spoke to him and went on his way. As he was going down, his servants met him and told him that his son was recovering. So he asked them the hour when he began to get better, and they said to him, "Yesterday at the seventh hour the fever left him." The father knew that was the hour when Jesus had said to him, "Your son will live." And he himself believed, and all his household. (John 4:49-53)

God is here and there today, for He is everywhere. Like us, the incarnate Lord Jesus was fully human, so He could be in just one location at a time. But being divine, He had authority everywhere. So the man described in John 4 came to Jesus and pleaded for his dying son. And from a distance, Jesus healed that boy.

One day in San Diego, California, where I was serving as a Navy Chaplain, a very distraught sailor came to me. His family was far away in Cameroon, Africa, where his wife was in a hospital close to death from a burst appendix. I asked him if he believed in Jesus and that He is with us and also with his wife, and if he believed Jesus heals. He answered yes to every question. We then prayed together in Jesus' name and asked God to enter that far-off hospital room in Cameroon and heal his wife.

After we prayed, I urged him to call his sister in my presence, as he had said she was with his wife in her hospital room. When she answered, we heard her screaming with delight, for just at that moment his wife had awakened from unconsciousness and was getting up out of bed. Hallelujah! Our God is everywhere today. He is here where you are, and He is there where the people are who are on your heart. God is able, and we can surely trust Him.

For Prayerful Reflection: How have you been blessed by believing that God is able and everywhere? How does knowing that God is with you throughout this day affect your trust today?

Bible in a Year: *Numbers 12-14; Mark 5:21-43*

February 26

I CAN *Trust* TODAY . . .
BECAUSE GOD REDEEMS ME

"Fear not, for I have redeemed you; I have called you by name, you are mine. When you pass through the waters, I will be with you; and through the rivers, they shall not overwhelm you; when you walk through fire you shall not be burned, and the flame shall not consume you. For I am the Lord your God, the Holy One of Israel, your Savior." (Isaiah 43:1-3)

"Blessed be the Lord God of Israel, for he has visited and redeemed his people." (Luke 1:68)

The biblical concept of redemption is about being ransomed, delivered, and rescued. This is what Jesus Christ has done for us. Motivated by profound love, He gave His life, dying for us on a cross to save us and all who will trust in Him from the eternal consequence of our sin, which is death and the wrath of God. By grace and through faith in the Lord Jesus who bore the judgment we deserve, we are made righteous and thus redeemed from God's wrath.

We might be nervous about the future and unsure of what it holds. We might be facing some hard times. But God says to us and to all whom He has redeemed at great cost, that no matter what our future holds, He is going to see us through, for He has redeemed us. If we should face deep waters or flames of fire, by faith in Jesus we can know that the One who redeemed us will be with us today and to the end. Corrie ten Boom endured great trials through the Holocaust but still trusted in God through it all. She learned and exhorted others to "never be afraid to trust an unknown future to a known God." Amen.

For Prayerful Reflection: Reflecting prayerfully on this truth that God redeemed you at great cost, what is God saying about His love for you? How does God's act of redeeming you impact your trusting Him today?

Bible in a Year: *Numbers 15-16; Mark 6:1-29*

February 27

I CAN *Trust* TODAY . . .
BECAUSE GOD BRINGS GOOD OUT OF TRIALS

Joseph said to [his brothers], ". . . As for you, you meant evil against me, but God meant it for good, to bring it about that many people should be kept alive, as they are today. So do not fear; I will provide for you and your little ones." Thus he comforted them and spoke kindly to them. (Genesis 50:19-21)

And we know that for those who love God all things work together for good, for those who are called according to his purpose. (Romans 8:28)

We have all experienced the harsh reality that horrible things happen in this broken world. The Word of God makes this clear and calls God's children to trust Him, even in and beyond our trials. For out of the trials God brings good to us and glory to His name.

Joseph was abused by his own brothers, sold as a slave, and taken far away to Egypt. He was then falsely accused and imprisoned for many years. But God never abandoned Joseph, and in His time, Joseph was highly elevated in Egypt. At the end, Joseph looked back and said to his brothers, *"You meant evil against me, but God meant it for good."*

Paul expressed a similar confession in Romans 8 that those who love God and *are called according to his purpose,* can know that *all things work together for good.* The *good* that is mentioned here doesn't refer to earthly satisfaction. It refers to our conformity to Christ and closer fellowship with Him, thus bearing fruit for His kingdom.

I have experienced this. As I look back now upon various times of struggle, I see His glory and my good.

For Prayerful Reflection: When have you seen God bring glory to Himself and good to you or others through your trials? How does this perspective affect your trusting God today?

Bible in a Year: *Numbers 17-19; Mark 6:30-56*

February 28

I CAN *Trust* TODAY . . .
BECAUSE GOD IS THE ANTIDOTE FOR FEAR

Fear not, for I am with you; be not dismayed, for I am your God; I will strengthen you, I will help you, I will uphold you with my righteous right hand. For I, the Lord your God, hold your right hand; it is I who say to you, "Fear not, I am the one who helps you." (Isaiah 41:10, 13)

Who of us has not struggled with fear? We might fear being alone, new situations and challenges, potential failures and future uncertainties, declining health and approaching death, or the suffering of someone we love. All of us face fear. The question is, When we are afraid, what do we do? In his book *Fearless,* Max Lucado said this: "The presence of fear does not mean you have no faith. Fear visits everyone. But make your fear a visitor and not a resident."[2] I like that.

How do we make fear "a visitor and not a resident"? By bringing all our fears to God and holding on to Him in faith. When we do this, we realize He is here now, walking with us through it all, step-by-step and day by day. God is so big and so mighty that our fears become smaller and smaller. In faith, we hear the Lord saying, *"Fear not, I am the one who helps you."* Yes, today I can trust Him.

For Prayerful Reflection: What have you been most afraid of? Why? What will the impact be of your bringing every fear to the Lord today and holding on to Him in faith throughout the day?

Bible in a Year: *Numbers 20-22; Mark 7:1-13*

---

[2] Max Lucado, *Fearless* (Nashville, TN: Thomas Nelson, 2009).

February 29

I CAN *Trust* TODAY . . .
BECAUSE GOD GAVE US THIS DAY

This is the day the Lord has made; let us rejoice and be glad in it.
(Psalm 118:24)

So teach us to number our days that we may get a heart of wisdom.
(Psalm 90:12)

When I was a boy, a friend told me one day that a man in our town was celebrating his eighteenth birthday. I didn't understand this, for he looked old to me. In fact, he had lived seventy-two years. That was when I learned about leap year.

Today is leap day, which shows up once every four years. It was created when the Gregorian calendar was introduced in the 1700s. The earth's orbit around the sun does not take precisely 365 days. About six more hours are needed, so a "leap day" was added every four years.

Trusting God means knowing that today and every day *is the day the Lord has made.* Our God gave us today to live with and for Him. Suppose a benevolent billionaire said that on the stroke of midnight he would deposit a gift of $86,400 in your bank account, and in the following twenty-four hours you would have to spend it all, or it would vanish. Not likely, you say. Well, how about 86,400 seconds? This is the exact number of seconds in this leap day and every day, and when midnight strikes, it will all be gone.

Every day is a gift from God, and we are blessed to live it with Him and for Him. God calls us to live today well, for we will only see it once.

For Prayerful Reflection: What does it mean to trust that each day is a gift from God to us, to be lived well with Him and for Him? What does this perspective mean for you today?

Bible in a Year: *If a leap year, no scheduled reading.*

12 Themes on Following Jesus

MARCH

Because God . . .
I Can *Receive* Today

March 1

I CAN *Receive* TODAY . . .
BECAUSE GOD SAVES

He came to his own, and his own people did not receive him. But to all who did receive him, who believed in his name, he gave the right to become children of God. (John 1:11-12)

Zacchaeus stood and said to the Lord, "Behold, Lord, the half of my goods I give to the poor. And if I have defrauded anyone of anything, I restore it fourfold." And Jesus said to him, "Today salvation has come to this house, since he also is a son of Abraham. For the Son of Man came to seek and to save the lost." (Luke 19:8-10)

There is great joy in being saved – snatched from fire or flood, danger or destruction, suffering, or death itself. Those who are saved have been liberated from whatever threatened or enchained them. A reasonable response among those who have been set free is gratitude.

But the nature of any offered gift, even the gift of salvation, is that it has to be freely received. We could choose to ignore or reject an offered gift, or we might receive it freely and gratefully. These options are true of God's gift of salvation. It is inestimable in value and freely offered by God. Yet we can refuse it. To receive God's gift of salvation, we must first believe and then receive His great gift through faith in the Lord Jesus Christ.

Receiving God's salvation means believing who Jesus is and trusting in what He has accomplished for us through His sacrificial death and resurrection for our salvation. Through faith we are thus spiritually born again and are thus determined to hereafter love and live for the Lord Jesus who has saved us.

Zacchaeus was saved that day when he met and received Jesus. The Lord declared to him and declares to us and to all who have received Him, *"Today salvation has come to this house."*

For Prayerful Reflection: When and how were you first aware of God's offer of the free gift of salvation? What has been your response to His gift? What does it mean for you to fully receive this gift today?

Bible in a Year: *Numbers 23-25; Mark 7:14-37*

March 2

I CAN *Receive* TODAY . . .
BECAUSE GOD LOVES

"God so loved the world, that he gave his only Son, that whoever believes in him should not perish but have eternal life." (John 3:16)

God is love. (1 John 4:8)

I am sure that neither death nor life, nor angels nor rulers, . . . nor anything else in all creation, will be able to separate us from the love of God in Christ Jesus our Lord. (Romans 8:38-39)

To receive something is to accept what has been offered. God offers us His love. But as is true in all personal relationships, we must choose to receive what has been offered. We must receive His love and return it. Though we might at times feel unloved or unworthy of being loved, the blood of the Lord Jesus Christ makes us worthy. When we do receive God's love, He changes us from the inside out.

If we should ever doubt God's love for us, we must look again at the cross of Jesus. There, with truly extraordinary love, God sacrificed His sinless and beloved Son who suffered and died for us. He did this so that all who believe in Him will not perish. Having been forgiven, we will live with Him now and forever. To receive Jesus is to receive God's love extended to us – today, tomorrow, and forever.

When we receive God's great love for us, it flows through us as water flows through water pipes. As water pipes are designed to carry water from one place to another, we are designed to carry God's love. When the pipe is hooked to water, and the water is turned on, it flows through the pipe and then out. When we are connected to God's love and receive it every day, His love flows through us to others.

For Prayerful Reflection: How and to what extent have you been believing and receiving God's love for you? What does it mean for you to receive His love and let it flow through you to others today?

Bible in a Year: *Numbers 26-27; Mark 8:1-21*

March 3

I CAN *Receive* TODAY . . .
BECAUSE GOD GIVES

For the wages of sin is death, but the free gift of God is eternal life in Christ Jesus our Lord. (Romans 6:23)

"If you then, who are evil, know how to give good gifts to your children, how much more will your Father who is in heaven give good things to those who ask him!" (Matthew 7:11)

"Peace I leave with you; my peace I give to you. . . . Let not your hearts be troubled, neither let them be afraid." (John 14:27)

A few years ago on *America's Funniest Home Videos,* a boy is seen on Christmas morning. Running to a large present beside the tree, he tears the gift open. With wrapping paper flying everywhere, he suddenly breaks into a dance, jumping around the room, repeatedly yelling, "It's just what I wanted. I love it!" After a little while, he looks at it again. Then he asks, "What is it?"

What gifts has God given us, and have we truly received them? We are reminded again today that our heavenly Father loves to give good gifts to His children, because of His great love. As such gifts come from God, should we not treasure and gladly receive every one? To do this is to adore God who so lovingly gives to us and to gratefully receive what He has given.

This means looking appreciatively at each gift from God and treasuring it because of the giver. God's priceless gifts to us are many, especially forgiveness, everlasting life, the presence and power of the Holy Spirit, His Holy Word, and His peace. He also gives precious family and friends, the blessing of His church, a measure of good health, and much more. Because God continues giving good gifts to us, we can receive them today.

For Prayerful Reflection: What gifts has God given to you that you have especially treasured? Why? What will it mean for you to receive God's gifts today?

Bible in a Year: *Numbers 28-30; Mark 8:22-38*

March 4

I CAN *Receive* TODAY . . .
BECAUSE GOD FORGIVES

Have mercy on me, O God, according to your steadfast love; according to your abundant mercy blot out my transgressions. Wash me thoroughly from my iniquity, and cleanse me from my sin! (Psalm 51:1-2)

And [Jesus] said to her, "Your sins are forgiven." Then those who were at table with him began to say among themselves, "Who is this, who even forgives sins?" And he said to the woman, "Your faith has saved you; go in peace." (Luke 7:48-50)

Forgiveness is a most wonderful gift. God's gift of forgiveness wipes away the insurmountable debt we owe and could never repay. It sets us free from carrying this crushing burden any longer. What glorious release! God forgives, and we can receive His forgiveness.

King David had sinned egregiously when he committed adultery with Bathsheba and ordered the death of her husband Uriah. He then lied, as we too can be prone to do, presuming he could hide his sin from God. But when confronted and convicted of his sin, with a repentant heart, there was only One to whom David could turn, or to whom any of us can turn. He turned to God who alone forgives and removes the sin from our record.

The woman whose story is told in Luke 7 carried a very heavy load of sin. But when convicted of it, she was sorrowful and repentant and knew whom to turn to. She came to Jesus, and with much love and tender mercy, He forgave her. That day she received His forgiveness. Our God forgives. And we, like David and the dear woman who knelt before Jesus, are offered God's forgiveness today. And when we receive it, we are released from the heavy weight of our sin. And as Jesus has taught us and now enables us, we will forgive even as we have been forgiven.

For Prayerful Reflection: When have you needed and received God's forgiveness? What would it mean for you to fully receive God's forgiveness today?

Bible in a Year: *Numbers 31-33; Mark 9:1-29*

March 5

I CAN *Receive* TODAY . . .
BECAUSE GOD KNOWS

"Remember the former things of old; for I am God, and there is no other; I am God, and there is none like me, declaring the end from the beginning and from ancient times things not yet done, saying, 'My counsel shall stand, and I will accomplish my purpose.'" (Isaiah 46:9-10)

God is greater than our heart, and he knows everything. (1 John 3:20)

There is nothing God does not know. God knows everything in every place. From eternity past God determines and declares the beginning and the end; He accomplishes His good purpose. We who believe in Him are blessed to receive this assurance that He will accomplish His good plan for us and in us. Because God knows, and we love Him, we can live His good will for us today.

In David Jeremiah's book *Prayer, the Great Adventure*,[3] he quoted the great Puritan thinker and writer Richard Baxter, who understood the blessing of trusting and following the Lord who knows. Whenever Baxter was asked to sign one of his books, he wrote, "Lord, what Thou wilt, where Thou wilt, and when Thou wilt." In the Puritan way of speaking, he was saying, "Lord, whatever you want, wherever you want it, and whenever you want it, that is what I want."

Such a response comes from those who know that He is God; He is worthy of my all, and He knows the way for me. So today I can gladly receive Him and accept His good will for me, whatever it may be.

For Prayerful Reflection: How did you come to realize that God knows all, including what is His good will for you? How does knowing that His will for you is good affect your willingness to receive it today?

Bible in a Year: *Numbers 34-36; Mark 9:30-50*

---

[3] David Jeremiah, *Prayer, the Great Adventure* (Colorado Springs, CO: Multnomah, 1997), 106.

March 6

I CAN *Receive* TODAY . . . **BECAUSE GOD LEADS**

I will instruct you and teach you in the way you should go; I will counsel you with my eye upon you. Be not like a horse or a mule, without understanding, which must be curbed with bit and bridle, or it will not stay near you. (Psalm 32:8-9)

Starting out as a young pastor and dearly loving the Lord, I longed to serve and follow Him effectively. But I was nervous about two things. First, I worried that I might somehow resist His leading and go my own way, not His. Second, I was nervous that I might fail to lead my congregation as my Lord would lead them. The weight of my responsibility was heavy on me, for I understood that the church and I were the Lord's.

I still recall how God brought my attention to these verses in Psalm 32. This was music to my soul, for God was assuring me that I would never be alone; His eye was always upon me, and He would always lead me. Wherever we are today, or whatever we are called to do, God is going to instruct us and teach us the way we should go and counsel us along the way.

God warns against resisting His voice and His leading, lest we pull hard to go the way we want to go as a stubborn horse or mule, for then we are foolishly fighting against God. God leads you, me, and His church. Our responsibility is first to desire and then to gladly receive His leading to go however and wherever He leads us today.

For Prayerful Reflection: When have you resisted God's leading like a stubborn horse or mule? When have you said yes to Him? What will it mean for you to receive and gladly follow His leading today?

Bible in a Year: *Deuteronomy 1-2; Mark 10:1-31*

March 7

I CAN *Receive* TODAY . . .
BECAUSE GOD STRENGTHENS THE WEAK

Have you not known? Have you not heard? The Lord is the everlasting God, the Creator of the ends of the earth. He does not faint or grow weary; his understanding is unsearchable. He gives power to the faint, and to him who has no might he increases strength. Even youths shall faint and be weary, and young men shall fall exhausted; but they who wait for the Lord shall renew their strength; they shall mount up with wings like eagles; they shall run and not be weary; they shall walk and not faint. (Isaiah 40:28-31)

We have all faced times of weakness, when our strength has failed. I've witnessed this and experienced it too. One day several years ago, when forward deployed, I joined hundreds of U.S. Marines in climbing to the summit of Mount Fuji, which stands at 12,388 feet in elevation. Though we were all in reasonably good shape physically, and most of us were fairly young, as we climbed, the higher elevation and thinner air caused some to become faint, weary, and exhausted, so they were unable to reach the summit that day. Though I reached that summit, on many other occasions my own strength has failed me.

I have been so weak physically that I could barely get out of bed or take a few steps while holding on to a walker. I have been spiritually weak too, discouraged and unsure if I could go on. In such times, when reminded of our weakness, God offers us His presence and strength and calls us to come near and lean on Him. Being aware of our weakness and coming to God in faith, we receive the strength He gives today.

For Prayerful Reflection: When have you come to God and received His strength while you were weak? Where are you weak now? What will it mean for you to receive God's strength today?

Bible in a Year: *Deuteronomy 3-4; Mark 10:32-52*

March 8

I CAN *Receive* TODAY . . .
BECAUSE GOD PREPARES US WELL

And David said, "The Lord who delivered me from the paw of the lion and from the paw of the bear will deliver me from the hand of this Philistine." (1 Samuel 17:37)

At times when young David watched over his father's sheep, he faced challenges and dangers, even attacks by a lion or a bear. The Lord was teaching David that he had no reason to fear because God was there and able. God was also preparing David for future occasions when he would need to receive from God what was needed for victory. On one such occasion he defeated the Philistine warrior Goliath in the name and strength of the Lord. Many other victories followed, as David lived what God had taught him. God prepares us too, so we can continually receive from Him what we need in His service.

I was recently reminded of this after finding and listening to a recording of the first sermon I ever preached. It was "Youth Sunday" at our church in early January 1975, when college students were home for the holidays. I was drafted by my peers to preach that day, and I recall the nervousness I felt. I also remember asking God to help me, trusting that He would. And He did. My delivery was definitely unpolished, but God did help me that day. On the recording, my nineteen-year-old voice is heard speaking with passion and authority, for I knew that I was speaking God's Word. My Lord taught me and prepared me to depend on Him for His enabling. God prepares us well for whatever He has in store for us by teaching us to receive His enabling, so we can then step out in faith in His service.

For Prayerful Reflection: When in life have you faced a challenge, a danger, or a daunting task and received from God His enabling? How has God prepared you for whatever you will face today?

Bible in a Year: *Deuteronomy 5-7; Mark 11:1-18*

March 9

I CAN *Receive* TODAY . . .
BECAUSE GOD ANOINTS

Samuel took the horn of oil and anointed him in the midst of his brothers. And the Spirit of the Lord rushed upon David from that day forward. (1 Samuel 16:13)

"I am the vine; you are the branches. Whoever abides in me and I in him, he it is that bears much fruit, for apart from me you can do nothing." (John 15:5)

You have been anointed by the Holy One. But the anointing that you received from him abides in you. (1 John 2:20, 27)

Whenever God calls us to do something for Him, He anoints us to do it and equips us with His life-giving power. Throughout my years of walking with God, this has been a primary lesson He has taught me. As I have depended on Him, God has always anointed me for whatever He called me to do. Without His anointing, it was simply not possible, just as it is impossible for electric lights to shine without receiving electric power. With God's anointing upon us and in us, our lights can shine for Him.

When God set apart and anointed His chosen king, *the Spirit of the Lord rushed upon David from that day forward.* By the power of the Holy Spirit, we are anointed by God today for whatever purpose or task He has for us. How good it is to know that we do not have to worry about whether we can do it!

Jesus said that we become fruitful for Him by abiding in Him, as branches receive their life and fruitfulness from the vine to which they are attached. God has anointed us for fruitfulness today. Our part is to stay connected to Him all through the day by faith and dependence upon Him, thus receiving from Him life and anointing.

For Prayerful Reflection: When have you faced a challenging assignment but depended on God and received His anointing to do it? What is required of you today to stay connected?

Bible in a Year: *Deuteronomy 8-10; Mark 11:19-33*

March 10

I CAN *Receive* TODAY . . .
BECAUSE GOD RESTORES

"I will restore to you the years that the swarming locust has eaten, the hopper, the destroyer, and the cutter, my great army, which I sent among you." (Joel 2:25)

For all have sinned and fall short of the glory of God. (Romans 3:23)

For the wages of sin is death, but the free gift of God is eternal life in Christ Jesus our Lord. (Romans 6:23)

In the 1980s, while working on a doctor of ministry program, I endeavored to write an extensive paper on a biblical theology of marriage and family. The theological framework I applied was creation, brokenness, and restoration, as these primary themes are evident throughout Scripture and in human history. God created us for His glory and for us to be in right relationship with Him and one another. But rebellion and sin brought broken relationships, as evidenced in distance from God and each other. But by great mercy and through His Son, God made a way for our restoration to wholeness in relationship with Him and with each other. Yes, God restores. He has wonderfully done so throughout history, just as He promised – even in the days of the prophet Joel, when many felt so hopeless. Through Jesus Christ, the great miracle of restoration is now freely offered to all.

What is required of us to receive God's restoration in relationship with Him and others? We must see and confess our need of forgiveness and humbly repent of our sin. And God, who loves us so much, will forgive all who repent in faith. And when we have been restored by receiving God's forgiveness, He requires and equips us to forgive others as He has forgiven us, and thereby to be restored with one another.

For Prayerful Reflection: How were you made aware of your brokenness in relationship with God or with someone you love, and of your need for forgiveness and restoration? How can you do this today?

Bible in a Year: *Deuteronomy 11-13; Mark 12:1-27*

March 11

I CAN *Receive* TODAY . . .
BECAUSE GOD HEALS

That evening at sundown they brought to him all who were sick or oppressed by demons. And the whole city was gathered together at the door. And he healed many who were sick with various diseases, and cast out many demons. (Mark 1:32-34)

[Jesus said,] "And proclaim as you go, saying 'The kingdom of heaven is at hand.' Heal the sick, raise the dead, cleanse lepers, cast out demons." (Matthew 10:7-8)

The whole town gathered at Simon's house. They came to see Jesus and to receive from Him healing in body or soul. And that is what He did. Jesus healed people of various injuries and diseases, including healing from spiritual bondage. Imagine being there. It's a pleasant thought, isn't it? What would you see, say, or receive? Jesus Christ is the same today. In His earthly ministry, He often healed people, and He gave His disciples the authority to heal in His name.

Yes, there are mysteries, for God does not always heal in the way or time we want; His perspective is greater than ours. In 2 Corinthians 12, for example, we find the apostle Paul asking the Lord for healing, but God's answer to him then was no, for He had a greater purpose. I have experienced what Paul did in this regard, and perhaps you have too.

But I have also received, seen, and celebrated God's healing, for He is able. Our responsibility and joy is not to deny it, but to come to Jesus in faith and receive the healing He brings today. We are to enjoy the privilege of praying in His name for God to touch and heal those who are broken in body or soul, and thus to see and celebrate the healing God brings.

For Prayerful Reflection: When did you receive or witness God's healing? How willing are you to pray today with faith in Jesus and receive His healing grace?

Bible in a Year: *Deuteronomy 14-16; Mark 12:28-44*

March 12

I CAN *Receive* TODAY . . .
BECAUSE GOD COMFORTS

"I am he who comforts you." (Isaiah 51:12)

"Blessed are those who mourn, for they shall be comforted." (Matthew 5:4)

Blessed be the God and Father of our Lord Jesus Christ, the Father of mercies and God of all comfort, who comforts us in all our affliction, so that we may be able to comfort those who are in any affliction, with the comfort with which we ourselves are comforted by God. (2 Corinthians 1:3-4)

God comforts us. He has often comforted me. We are blessed to receive our Lord's comfort and then to bring it to others. Like children who need to be held close and comforted by a loving parent, so God promises to hold and comfort us. Joni Eareckson Tada, paralyzed from her neck down as a teenager, has received much of God's comfort through the years, and she has passed it on well. She has testified, "You don't have to be alone in your hurt! Comfort is yours. Joy is an option. And it's all been made possible by your Savior. He went without comfort so you might have it. He postponed joy so you might share in it. He willingly chose isolation so you might never be alone in your hurt and sorrow."[4] Amen.

A little girl was sent on an errand by her mother, but was slow in returning. When at last she arrived at home, her mother asked for an explanation on why it took her so long. The little girl said that on her way, she met a friend who was crying because she had broken her doll. "Oh," said the mother, "you stopped to help her fix her doll?"

"No," said the little girl, "I stopped to help her cry."

God comforts us. He joins us in our tears, our struggles, and our pain, and holds us in His loving arms. Our duty is to receive His comfort and then pass it along to others.

For Prayerful Reflection: When and how have you received God's comfort? Today, how could you bring His comfort to others?

Bible in a Year: *Deuteronomy 17-19; Mark 13:1-20*

---
[4] *Christian Reader*, Vol. 32.

March 13

I CAN *Receive* TODAY...
BECAUSE GOD HOLDS ME CLOSE

For I, the Lord your God, hold your right hand; it is I who say to you, "Fear not, I am the one who helps you." (Isaiah 41:13)

"Listen to me, . . . all the remnant of the house of Israel, who have been borne by me from before your birth, carried from the womb; even to your old age I am he, and to gray hairs I will carry you. . . . I will carry and will save." (Isaiah 46:3-4)

"I give them eternal life, and they will never perish, and no one will snatch them out of my hand." (John 10:28).

God always watches over His children – sometimes holding our hand and sometimes carrying us, but always loving us, protecting us, and keeping us close. Consider the trouble little children can stumble into when someone is not keeping an eye on them, carrying them, guiding them, or holding their hand. What happens to a little child's fear when they are held in love? They know and feel that "I am okay, for I am held now." We can know this too, even today.

Through His prophet Isaiah, God reminded the children of Israel who were afraid, even as He has often reminded me in times of trouble or danger, that He was holding them. He holds you too. God reminds His children that He has always carried us; He still carries us, and He will always carry us, until we are old, and then forevermore. Jesus promised all who believe in Him that He has given us eternal life and that we will never perish, for *no one will snatch [us] out of [His] hand.*

How blessed we are to believe and receive the heavenly peace and confident security that comes from knowing we are held by God today and every day. God holds us forever.

For Prayerful Reflection: When have you been afraid or in trouble and heard God's reminder that He is holding you? How can it help you today to know that God is holding you?

Bible in a Year: *Deuteronomy 20-22; Mark 13:21-37*

March 14

I CAN *Receive* TODAY . . .
BECAUSE GOD SEES

[Hagar] called the name of the Lord who spoke to her, "You are a God of seeing," for she said, "Truly here I have seen him who looks after me." (Genesis 16:13)

The Lord looks down from heaven; he sees all the children of man. (Psalm 33:13)

On the Sabbath day we went outside the gate to the riverside, . . . and we sat down and spoke to the women who had come together. One who heard us was a woman named Lydia. . . . The Lord opened her heart to pay attention to what was said by Paul. (Acts 16:13-14)

God sees and watches over His children. Today, right now, God sees you and He sees me. It's an amazing thought, isn't it? We are never outside God's purview. Like Hagar in her loneliest hour, in whatever circumstances we are facing, we can know that God sees us and comes to us. Remember Lydia, whose heart God knew and to whom God sent His servants on that day described in Acts 16; we know that today God sends us in His name. He has brought and still brings the wonderful news of Jesus Christ and of God's great love for us. Like Hagar and Lydia, we know that God sees us today, and we are blessed to receive His great love.

And like Paul, Silas, and Luke who were led by the Lord to go to the riverbank that day, we too can be led by the Holy Spirit to recognize and respond to His divine appointments for us today. We may then bless somebody whom God sees to let them know by our availability, deeds, or words that we do see them, for God sees them, loves them, and comes to them.

For Prayerful Reflection: When have you ever been lonely or troubled but were blessed to know that God sees you? How does it affect you today to know that God sees you? How will this impact your availability to see others in Jesus' name?

Bible in a Year: *Deuteronomy 23-25; Mark 14:1-26*

March 15

I CAN *Receive* TODAY...
BECAUSE GOD SPEAKS

And the Lord came and stood, calling as at other times, "Samuel! Samuel!" And Samuel said, "Speak, for your servant hears." (1 Samuel 3:10)

Long ago, at many times and in many ways, God spoke to our fathers by the prophets, but in these last days he has spoken to us by his Son, whom he appointed the heir of all things, through whom also he created the world. (Hebrews 1:1-2)

The night described in 1 Samuel 3 was life-transforming for Samuel, for it was then that he began to recognize and listen to God's voice. Samuel had been a miracle child, for his mother Hannah, who had long been barren, had fervently prayed for a child and promised God that if He would give her a child, she would consecrate him fully to His service. So as a little boy, Samuel was brought to Eli the priest. He was being raised there to worship and serve the Lord. Young Samuel surely believed in God, but he had no idea yet that God personally speaks.

That night God repeatedly called Samuel's name, and each time Samuel presumed it was Eli who was calling him. Then Eli realized that God was calling Samuel, so he told Samuel to reply to the Lord, *"Speak, for your servant hears."* Thereafter, and for the rest of his earthly life of ministry, Samuel listened to God and served Him.

God has spoken to us through His Son, the Lord Jesus Christ. He speaks to us now by the Holy Spirit and through His inspired Word. Like Samuel, we are greatly blessed to hear God speak and recognize His voice, hearing and heeding His word. God is speaking today. Are we listening?

For Prayerful Reflection: When has God gotten your attention so that you knew He was speaking to you? How can you follow Samuel's example and listen carefully to His word?

Bible in a Year: *Deuteronomy 26-27; Mark 14:27-53*

March 16

I CAN *Receive* TODAY . . .
BECAUSE GOD PROVIDES

For he satisfies the longing soul, and the hungry soul he fills with good things. (Psalm 107:9)

"Bring the full tithe into the storehouse, that there may be food in my house. And thereby put me to the test, says the Lord of hosts, if I will not open the windows of heaven for you and pour down for you a blessing until there is no more need." (Malachi 3:10)

And my God will supply every need of yours according to his riches. (Philippians 4:19)

God promised to always provide for His children's needs. And He has done so in every generation. My grandfather, Pastor Morley Durost, shared sweet testimonies of God's faithful and miraculous provision for him, his sizable family, and his ministry. In sharing these remarkable stories, he wrote these moving words: "I think that the greatest honor God has bestowed on me, aside from making me His son by faith, has been to send me to serve in places where we had to live by faith. If I cannot trust Him to care for me in this world, how can He expect me to trust Him to care for me in the next world? I have learned, and these examples will illustrate, that His promises are absolutely unfailing." Amen.

I wholly affirm this, for in every need of my own life, whether financial or physical, for wisdom or guidance, or for help of any kind, I have asked my God in faith, and He has always provided. If today we are in a place of need, as my grandfather said, we can trust God to provide for us. And when He does, we can receive it in faith, gratitude, and praise.

For Prayerful Reflection: What are your testimonies of God's gracious provision for your needs? How is your assurance of God's promised provision making a difference in your life today?

Bible in a Year: *Deuteronomy 28-29; Mark 14:54-72*

March 17

I CAN *Receive* TODAY . . .
BECAUSE GOD SUSTAINS

Behold, God is my helper; the Lord is the upholder of my life. (Psalm 54:4)

Cast your burden on the Lord, and he will sustain you; he will never permit the righteous to be moved. (Psalm 55:22)

My flesh and my heart may fail, but God is the strength of my heart and my portion forever. (Psalm 73:26)

I can do all things through him who strengthens me. (Philippians 4:13)

Were it not for God's grace to sustain us, we would all be bereft of hope and of life. But God does sustain us, all through our earthly journey. He is the upholder of our life today. Along the way we may at times wonder if we will be able to handle whatever is coming. But we have a God who is with us and who loves us and who sustains us for every situation for each and every day.

Arthur John Gossip was a great preacher in the Church of Scotland. In 1927 while pastoring at Beechgrove Church in Aberdeen, Scotland, he suddenly lost his beloved wife. The following Sunday he preached a powerful sermon titled "When Life Tumbles In, What Then?" His faith held steady even then, just as ours can today, for God sustains and encourages us, even "When Life Tumbles In."

Though our strength may fail us, His cannot and will not. And so today, in faith we can receive God's promise of grace to sustain us every moment and in every circumstance, even when we feel overwhelmed and weak. In faith we can allow God's grace to sustain us today with infused strength, courage, purpose, and peace. God's love sustains us when we are broken.

For Prayerful Reflection: What are your own testimonies of God sustaining you when you were weak or hurting? How does receiving this promise help you today?

Bible in a Year: *Deuteronomy 30-31; Mark 15:1-25*

March 18

I CAN *Receive* TODAY . . .
BECAUSE GOD TRANSFORMS

Do not be conformed to the world, but be transformed by the renewal of your mind, that by testing you may discern what is the will of God, what is good and acceptable and perfect. (Romans 12:2)

And we all, with unveiled face, beholding the glory of the Lord, are being transformed into the same image from one degree of glory to another. For this comes from the Lord who is the Spirit. (2 Corinthians 3:18)

We are all being transformed in some way. Farmers in Zentsuji, Japan, prepare full-grown watermelons for shipment that are square! The melons are placed in tempered-glass cubes while still growing, and in time they take the shape of the container in which they are grown. We are also prone to take on the shape, values, and priorities of the world around us.

This is why the apostle Paul encouraged Christians to *not be conformed to the world, but be transformed by the renewal of your mind* so that we may increasingly *discern what is the will of God.* Referring back to Moses whose face became utterly radiant after he spent prolonged time in the glory of God's presence, Paul said we too *are being transformed into the same image from one degree of glory to another,* and this transformation *comes from the Lord who is the Spirit.*

God will not leave us as we are. God is transforming us. Like clay in the hands of the potter, can't we trust the hands of God? Can we gratefully receive and rejoice in the transformation God is doing in us?

For Prayerful Reflection: What transformation have you seen God do in you or in other Christians you know? How is the reality of God's transforming work impacting you today?

Bible in a Year: *Deuteronomy 32-34; Mark 15:26-47*

March 19

I CAN *Receive* TODAY . . .
BECAUSE GOD RELATES

Then God said, "Let us make man in our image, after our likeness. . . . So God created man in his own image, in the image of God he created him; male and female he created them. (Genesis 1:26-27)

To all who did receive him, who believed in his name, he gave the right to become children of God. (John 1:12)

God created us for relationship with Him. He said, *"Let us make man,"* which declares that He created us relationally, *"in our image, after our likeness."* This means that God created us like Himself, so we might be in relationship with Him. It is rather astounding, isn't it? To think that the infinite God of the universe made us to be in personal relationship with Him! Wow! By God's grace, this is our privilege today, and for all of time and eternity! But though God longs for close relationships with you and me, sin can get in the way.

Relationships are broken. At the dawn of history, God drew a proverbial line in the sand of personal relationship with Him. To paraphrase, He said, "I am God, and you are not. Be in fellowship with me, but know this – on the day you sin *you shall surely die"* (Genesis 2:15-17). Sin puts a barrier between God and us, which can only be removed by the perfect sacrifice of Jesus Christ, the Lamb of God, who takes away the sin of the world. His perfect remedy is applied to us by God's grace through our faith in the Savior (Ephesians 2:8-9). Today our part is to believe in Jesus Christ and turn back to Him in humble repentance. God desires personal relationship with us, and we are so blessed to receive it.

For Prayerful Reflection: What are your earliest memories of personal relationship with God? What does it mean to you to know of God's deep desire for relationship with you and for you to receive it today?

Bible in a Year: *Joshua 1-3; Mark 16*

March 20

I CAN *Receive* TODAY . . .
BECAUSE GOD HEARS

The eyes of the Lord are toward the righteous and his ears toward their cry. When the righteous cry for help, the Lord hears and delivers them out of all their troubles. (Psalm 34:15, 17)

Then he said to me, "Fear not, Daniel, for from the first day that you set your heart to understand and humbled yourself before your God, your words have been heard, and I have come because of your words." (Daniel 10:12)

Whenever God's children cry to Him for help, He hears. The events described in the tenth chapter of the prophetic book of Daniel occurred in a time of world chaos, severe opposition to the people of God, and great distress for Daniel himself. In the midst of such struggles, Daniel knew whom to turn to. For three weeks he fasted, prayed, and cried out to God. Then, an awe-inspiring angel of the Lord appeared to Daniel and declared that he was dearly loved and that from the first day he had cried out to the Lord, God had heard.

God is the same today. He has the same affection for us and the same promise that when we cry out to Him in faith, He hears. God loves us and always listens when we call. Today, let us receive the certainty of this truth.

In his book *Just Like Jesus*,[5] Max Lucado tells of when CBS Anchor Dan Rather asked Mother Teresa what she said during her prayers. She answered, "I listen." So Rather turned the question around and asked her, "Well then, what does God say?" To that Mother Teresa smiled and answered, "He listens." Her point that day was not that we should fail to use words when we pray, but that we must intently desire to hear God, always knowing that God hears us.

For Prayerful Reflection: When have you called out to God, or known that others were interceding for you, and you knew that God heard? How does it affect you today to know that God hears?

Bible in a Year: *Joshua 4-6; Luke 1:1-20*

---
[5] Max Lucado, *Just Like Jesus* (Nashville, TN: Thomas Nelson, 2012), 71.

March 21

I CAN *Receive* TODAY . . .
BECAUSE GOD SEEKS

"For thus says the Lord God: Behold, I, I myself will search for my sheep and will seek them out. As a shepherd seeks out his flock when he is among his sheep that have been scattered, so will I seek out my sheep. . . . I will seek the lost, and I will bring back the strayed, and I will bind up the injured, and I will strengthen the weak." (Ezekiel 34:11-12, 16)

"The Son of Man came to seek and to save the lost." (Luke 19:10)

I was frantic because I could not find my little boy. I had heard Helen call out to me that she was running to the store and would be back in a few minutes. Her departure meant I was solely responsible for keeping an eye on our youngest child, who was then three years old. Taking on this responsibility, I immediately looked for my son, so I could watch him closely.

But I could not find him. I looked all through the house and called his name. Then I looked outside. Because our home was on a river, and he loved following and feeding the ducks, I frantically ran along the river's edge; I looked for him and called his name. I will never forget the painful longing I felt that day nor the great relief I felt when Helen returned from her errand, and little Jonathan was with her.

This was a very small taste of the love and longing God has for each of us, His children. We are precious to Him. He searches for us when we are lost, and doesn't stop until we are found. Today He loves and watches over you. Our part is to be found and gratefully receive His loving care.

For Prayerful Reflection: When have you known that God was calling your name? What has it meant to you to be sought and desired by God? How does it affect you today to receive such loving care?

Bible in a Year: *Joshua 7-9; Luke 1:21-38*

March 22

I CAN *Receive* TODAY . . .
BECAUSE GOD RECONCILES

We implore you on behalf of Christ, be reconciled to God. For our sake he made him to be sin who knew no sin, so that in him we might become the righteousness of God. (2 Corinthians 5:20-21)

To reconcile means to restore to right relationship, to make peace where formerly there was hostility. The Bible speaks of humanity's great need of being reconciled to God. When sin entered this world, and when we sinned, we became alienated from God, for we adopted an attitude of hostility toward Him. This alienation is a great divide we could not bridge on our own. The crucified and risen Christ is the way. He is the bridge from our sin to God's righteousness, from unbelief to belief, from darkness to light, from despair to hope, from fear to peace, from emptiness to fullness, and from death to everlasting life.

With very deep love and a powerful willingness to suffer and lay down His life so we might be restored to right relationship with God, Jesus Christ came. By His sacrificial death and triumphal resurrection, Christ became our reconciler. He became the bridge that brings together Holy God and all who will become God's forgiven and dearly loved children by faith in Him. Today, by faith we can receive this great salvation. Jesus Christ reconciles us and gives us the blessing of leading others to and across this bridge to life through faith in Jesus. We have thus become His agents of reconciliation, for it is all about Jesus. If we have everything but lack Jesus, we really have nothing. But if we have nothing yet have Jesus, we really have everything.

For Prayerful Reflection: What has it meant for you to know that though you were once far from God because of your sin, now and forever through faith in Jesus Christ you are reconciled to God? How is this blessing affecting you today?

Bible in a Year: *Joshua 10-12; Luke 1:39-56*

March 23

I CAN *Receive* TODAY . . .
BECAUSE GOD CONQUERS

No, in all these things we are more than conquerors through him who loved us. For I am sure that neither death nor life, nor angels nor rulers, nor things present nor things to come, nor powers, nor height nor depth, nor anything else in all creation, will be able to separate us from the love of God in Christ Jesus our Lord. (Romans 8:37-39)

At Marine Corps Recruit Depot, Parris Island, where I served as a Chaplain, there is a large and inspiring monument depicting United States Marines raising the flag of victory on the summit of Mount Suribachi. It was the Battle of Iwo Jima, which lasted thirty-five days, from February 19 to March 26, 1945. It included some of the fiercest fighting in the Pacific campaign of World War II. When that flag was raised, the battle was not yet over. When it finally ended, out of more than 18,000 Japanese soldiers, only 216 had survived. And American casualties exceeded 26,000. That battle was won at great cost of life.

The apostle Paul reminds Christians that nothing can ever separate us from God's love, and though intense battles can rage around us, in Jesus Christ we can know the great cost that was paid, the sacrifice that was made, and the blood that was shed for our liberty. By faith in the Lord Jesus Christ, who won the victory for us, we are now *more than conquerors through him who loved us.* How very blessed we are to know that the flag has been raised; the outcome is now certain, the victory is secure, and by God's grace because of Jesus Christ, today and forever we are more than conquerors.

For Prayerful Reflection: What has it meant for you to know that Jesus Christ has already won the victory? How can you receive and reflect this blessing today?

Bible in a Year: *Joshua 13-15; Luke 1:57-80*

March 24

I CAN *Receive* TODAY . . .
BECAUSE GOD CARES

"Can a woman forget her nursing child, that she should have no compassion on the son of her womb? Even these may forget, yet I will not forget you. Behold, I have engraved you on the palms of my hands. (Isaiah 49:15-16)

Humble yourselves, therefore, under the mighty hand of God so that at the proper time he may exalt you, casting all your anxieties on him, because he cares for you. (1 Peter 5:6-7)

God shows that He cares for us, His children, in many ways. Though we might not always notice God's care for us, we should, for He never stops.

When our oldest son Carl was about thirteen years old, he had a neighborhood paper route. Each morning he picked up the newspapers at the head of our driveway, folded them individually, and packed them in his bag for delivery on his bicycle. In inclement weather, when possible, I drove him through his route, so he wouldn't get cold or soaking wet. One wintery morning we woke to a blizzard with strong winds and deep drifting snow. That day the weather was miserable, and there was no way I would allow Carl to go out alone. I helped him prepare and pack his papers, and then we loaded them all onto a sled. In the midst of that blizzard, he and I pulled that sled from house to house along his entire route. Why did I do that? It's obvious, isn't it? It's because he was my son, and I loved him.

Even more so does our God care for you and me. No matter what our circumstances are today, God cares. He always has and always will. And because of His love for us, He will not abandon us. He comes today to help.

For Prayerful Reflection: When have you marveled at how God was showing you His care? What would it mean for you today to cast all your cares upon Him, because He cares for you?

Bible in a Year: *Joshua 16-18; Luke 2:1-24*

March 25

I CAN *Receive* TODAY . . .
BECAUSE GOD ACCOMPANIES US

"It is the Lord who goes before you. He will be with you; he will not leave you or forsake you. Do not fear or be dismayed." (Deuteronomy 31:8)

[God] has said, "I will never leave you nor forsake you." (Hebrews 13:5)

[Jesus said,] "And behold, I am with you always, to the end of the age." (Matthew 28:20)

Wherever we go in this life, God goes with us, and He knows the way. After all, He is our loving Father.

Our daughter, Dr. Amy Hatcher, is a pediatrician now serving in Alaska. We are very proud of her for who she is and for the contributions she makes, caring for precious people, as God's instrument of healing and love. She has often thanked Helen and me for our influence in her life and for being there whenever she has needed us. As her dad, I treasure a particular incident. She was then a senior at Oral Roberts University in Tulsa, Oklahoma, and she had been invited to a medical school interview at the Uniformed Services University of the Health Sciences in Bethesda, Maryland. Wanting her to arrive for her interview rested, energized, and ready to go, I told her I would personally meet her at Ronald Reagan Washington National Airport.

And so, with short-fused planning, that's what I did. I also rented a car, booked a suite at the Navy Bachelor Officer Quarters aboard the National Naval Medical Center, and we arrived safely and on time. Throughout the day of her interview, I was praying, and that evening I was additional eyes and ears as she processed her day. She was later accepted to that institution.

Our heavenly Father does much more for you and me, and He does so every day. God loves each of us, and He never leaves us or forsakes us. What a comforting thought: God accompanies us today.

For Prayerful Reflection: When have you been blessed in realizing God is with you now? How is it impacting you to receive this realization, that God chooses to accompany you today?

Bible in a Year: *Joshua 19-21; Luke 2:25-52*

March 26

I CAN *Receive* TODAY . . .
BECAUSE GOD WELCOMES ME

And [Jesus] took [the apostles] and withdrew apart to a town called Bethsaida. When the crowds learned it, they followed him, and he welcomed them and spoke to them of the kingdom of God and cured those who had need of healing. And taking the five loaves and the two fish, he looked up to heaven and said a blessing over them. Then he broke the loaves and gave them to the disciples to set before the crowd. And they all ate and were satisfied. (Luke 9:10-11, 16-17)

Hospitality is a wonderful gift. To be warmly welcomed into someone's community or home and be shown respect, love, and kindness is a great gift. I've often been the recipient of such kindness, and when tired, in unfamiliar surroundings, or very far from home, such a welcome is a delightful blessing.

God extends such a welcome to you and me today. He opens the door and says, "Please come in. You are welcome here. I am so glad you have come." God meets us where we are and gives us His loving care. The story in Luke 9 illustrates this. The Bible says when the crowds had followed Jesus to Bethsaida, He did not look past them nor turn them away. Rather, *he welcomed them and spoke to them of the kingdom of God and cured those who had need of healing.* Then, with concern for their hunger, Jesus fed them in the event called "the feeding of the five thousand."

How often has God welcomed and memorably blessed you? Now He calls us who have received His welcome to extend it to others also. What a wonderful thought: God welcomes us today.

For Prayerful Reflection: When have you received memorable hospitality? How did it bless you? How are you impacted today by receiving God's welcome and extending His welcome to others?

Bible in a Year: *Joshua 22-24; Luke 3*

March 27

I CAN *Receive* TODAY . . .
BECAUSE GOD KEEPS ME

The Lord is your keeper; the Lord is your shade on your right hand. The Lord will keep you from all evil; he will keep your life. The Lord will keep your going out and your coming in from this time forth and forevermore. (Psalm 121:5, 7-8)

Jude, a servant of Jesus Christ and brother of James, to those who are called, beloved in God the Father and kept for Jesus Christ: May mercy, peace, and love be multiplied to you. (Jude vv. 1-2)

Psalm 121 reminds us that we are on a pilgrimage, and we know where our help comes from. Our help comes from the Lord who promises to keep us all along the way. The word *keep* is primary in this psalm. The Hebrew word is *shamar*, which means "to keep, guard, watch over, attend to carefully." This is what God does for us today and every day, even when our days are hard.

Max Lucado told about a friend of his who had cancer. Well-intentioned Christians had told him, "If you have faith, then you will be healed." But no healing came, only a crisis in faith in that man's life. Max suggested this answer to him: "It's not about you. Your hospital room is a showcase for your Maker. Your faith in the face of suffering cranks up the volume of God's song."[6] That is right. God is our helper throughout our earthly journey. He keeps us.

And through His servant Jude, Jesus reminds us that we will be kept and preserved by God's power from falling away. In this promise we can rest securely.

For Prayerful Reflection: When have you looked to God for help and found that throughout your life journey He has been keeping you? What will it mean for you today to receive and apply this assurance?

Bible in a Year: *Judges 1-3; Luke 4:1-30*

---

[6] Max Lucado, *It's Not About Me* (Nashville, TN: Thomas Nelson, 2004), 126.

March 28

I CAN *Receive* TODAY . . .
BECAUSE GOD FOREORDAINS

We know that for those who love God all things work together for good, for those who are called according to his purpose. For those whom he foreknew he also predestined to be conformed to the image of his Son. . . . And those whom he predestined he also called, and those whom he called he also justified, and those whom he justified he also glorified. (Romans 8:28-30)

This explains how God weaves everything together for good for His children. It flows from His foreknowledge. It is marvelous in this moment of time called "today" to ponder that at the dawn of creation in ancient past, to our conversion and expression of faith in Christ in recent past, and now looking ahead to the day of His return in our glorious future, God intended and knew that you and I would be His.

When William Booth's Salvation Army began making its mark, people started to enlist. Samuel Brengle left a pastorate in the United States to join Booth's Army in England. Accepting his service, General Booth said to Brengle, "You've been your own boss too long." To instill humility, he set Brengle to cleaning boots of other trainees.

Discouraged, Brengle said to himself, "Have I followed my own fancy across the Atlantic to black boots?" But God had a purpose in this. In a vision Brengle saw Jesus bending over the feet of rough fishermen. "Lord," he prayed, "you washed their feet; I will black their shoes."[7]

Yes, there are mysteries in this truth, but we are His today, and He works for our good, even when the day is hard. Paul speaks of our future glorification as though it is already completed. This is our confidence today.

For Prayerful Reflection: What has the foreknowledge of God and His promise to work all things together for your good meant to you thus far? What does it mean for you today?

Bible in a Year: *Judges 4-6; Luke 4:31-44*

---

7 Kent Hughes, *Liberating Ministry from The Success Syndrome* (Carol Stream, IL: Tyndale House Publishers, 1987), 45.

March 29

I CAN *Receive* TODAY . . .
BECAUSE GOD TEACHES

I will instruct you and teach you in the way you should go; I will counsel you with my eye upon you. (Psalm 32:8)

The Lord answered her, "Martha, Martha, . . . one thing is necessary. Mary has chosen the good portion, which will not be taken away from her." (Luke 10:41-42)

"These things I have spoken to you while I am still with you. But the Helper, the Holy Spirit, whom the Father will send in my name, he will teach you all things and bring to your remembrance all that I have said to you." (John 14:25-26)

How blessed we are that God is invested in our education as His children. There are many places in Scripture where God says He will instruct us in the ways we should go, teaching us His way. God the Father promised to teach His children. God the Son, the Lord Jesus Christ, was the embodiment of the Word of God, which He lived and spoke in word and deed. And when Jesus promised the outpouring of God the Holy Spirit, He said the Holy Spirit would be our teacher. And so He is.

The triune God proactively, purposefully, and lovingly teaches us. Our necessary response is to long to learn from God and to desire all that He would teach us. Does this describe your own hunger to learn from Him? This means receiving from God and learning to live just as He has taught us. This requires proactive action, not passive inaction from us. Mary offers a noteworthy example in the story told in Luke 10. Jesus commended her, and now He is calling us to follow her example – taking time, and seizing the opportunity to sit at His feet and learn.

For Prayerful Reflection: When have you known Mary's joy of sitting at His feet, enjoying God's presence, and learning from Him? What does it mean to you today to be taught by God?

Bible in a Year: *Judges 7-8; Luke 5:1-16*

March 30

I CAN *Receive* TODAY . . .
BECAUSE GOD PRUNES

"I am the true vine, and my Father is the vinedresser. Every branch in me that does not bear fruit he takes away, and every branch that does bear fruit he prunes, that it may bear more fruit. Abide in me, and I in you. As the branch cannot bear fruit by itself, unless it abides in the vine, neither can you, unless you abide in me. I am the vine; you are the branches. Whoever abides in me and I in him, he it is that bears much fruit, for apart from me you can do nothing." (John 15:1-2, 4-5)

When I was just eight years old, I memorized chapter 15 of John's Gospel, which is Jesus' teaching. It includes the imagery of God the Father as our gardener, Jesus as our life-giving vine, and each of us as branches, which God fully intends to be fruitful. Though I could not fully understand it then, I liked the picture of God working in my life and of being connected to Jesus.

Many years later Helen and I bought a home with two apple trees in the backyard. When the first year of harvest produced very few apples, I researched pruning apple trees, and I did it. I cut off dead branches and trimmed back others. In the next harvest we had more apples than we could count.

God does this in you and me. He proactively works in us so we might become more fruitful for Him. Our part is twofold today. First, we can welcome His pruning in us, even if it hurts, for we know that He works for our good. Second, we can always remain attached to Jesus in faith, for our life and fruitfulness are in Him.

For Prayerful Reflection: How has God's pruning in your life led to greater fruitfulness for Him? What does it mean for you today to receive the blessings of His pruning and life from Jesus?

Bible in a Year: *Judges 9-10; Luke 5:17-39*

March 31

I CAN *Receive* TODAY . . .
BECAUSE GOD SACRIFICED

All we like sheep have gone astray; we have turned—every one—to his own way; and the Lord has laid on him the iniquity of us all. (Isaiah 53:6)

"The Son of Man will be delivered over to the chief priests and scribes, and they will condemn him to death and deliver him over to the Gentiles to be mocked and flogged and crucified, and he will be raised on the third day." (Matthew 20:18-19)

"Greater love has no one than this, that someone lay down his life for his friends." (John 15:13)

Amazing as it seems, the Son of God sacrificed His life so we might live. Our part is to believe and receive His sacrifice in faith, living forever with gratitude and devotion to Him.

Pastor Bryan Chapell told a story that happened in his hometown. Two brothers were playing on the sandbanks by the river. They ran to the top of a large mound of sand that was not solid, and their weight caused them to sink. When the boys did not return home for dinner, family and neighbors organized a search. They found the younger brother unconscious with his head and shoulders sticking out above the sand. When they cleared the sand to his waist, he awakened. The searchers asked, "Where is your brother?" The child replied, "I'm standing on his shoulders."

With the sacrifice of his life, the older brother had lifted the younger to safety. The sacrificial love of the older brother served as a foundation for the younger brother's life. How much more has the sacrifice of God's Son for you and me on the cross lifted us from inevitable and eternal death, which is the consequence of sin. Christ's sacrificial love is offered to us today. We must receive it in faith.

For Prayerful Reflection: How has Christ's sacrifice affected your love and devotion to Him? What will it mean for you today to acknowledge the sacrifice God made for you?

Bible in a Year: *Judges 11-12; Luke 6:1-26*

12 Themes on Following Jesus

APRIL

Because God . . .
I Can *Pray* Today

April 1

I CAN *Pray* TODAY . . .
BECAUSE GOD INVITES OUR PRAYER

The Lord God took the man and put him in the garden of Eden to work it and keep it. (Genesis 2:15)

And they heard the sound of the Lord God walking in the garden in the cool of the day. (Genesis 3:8)

"Then you will call upon me and come and pray to me, and I will hear you. You will seek me and find me, when you seek me with all your heart. I will be found by you, declares the Lord. (Jeremiah 29:12-14)

Draw near to God, and he will draw near to you. (James 4:8)

If you received an invitation from someone who is famous, and whom you greatly admire, to visit his or her home or go with them for a walk and conversation, what would you do? Would you respond with eagerness? You would not likely ignore it, would you? And if you received multiple invitations, you would be astonished. But what if you received such invitations every single day for the rest of your life?

From the dawn of humanity, God has invited us to come near, to enjoy fellowship with Him, and to pray. Before sin entered the hearts of humanity, this is what our first parents knew. Though sin destroyed sweet fellowship, the Lord Jesus Christ has restored it and made the way for us to draw near. God invites us to come near to Him, to come just as we are, to come anytime and always, and to open our hearts to Him. Our Lord desires close, intimate friendship and conversation with you and with me. Our part is to eagerly answer His invitation today.

For Prayerful Reflection: How have you regarded and answered God's personal invitation to you to come near and pray? What will it mean for you to answer God's invitation to prayer today with a yes?

Bible in a Year: *Judges 13-15; Luke 6:27-49*

April 2

I CAN *Pray* TODAY . . .
BECAUSE GOD HEARS WHEN I PRAY

The Lord has heard my plea; the Lord accepts my prayer. (Psalm 6:9)

And Cornelius said, ". . . a man stood before me in bright clothing and said, 'Cornelius, your prayer has been heard and your alms have been remembered before God.'" (Acts 10:30-31)

"For the eyes of the Lord are on the righteous, and his ears are open to their prayer." (1 Peter 3:12)

Many biblical accounts reveal that God hears when we pray with longing in our hearts for Him and for His will. In Acts 10 we read of Cornelius, a Gentile man who did not yet know the Lord but who prayed with longing for God. In reply God sent a man in bright clothing whose first words to Cornelius were, *"Your prayer has been heard."*

I have often been reminded of this. Several years ago, I was on my way to a hospital to visit a U.S. Navy sailor who had been arrested the previous night for drunk and disorderly conduct. I had learned that his wife had just filed for divorce and that he was in the process of being administratively separated from the Navy for being an alcohol rehab failure. And now due to suicidal thoughts, he was a psychiatric inpatient.

On my way to the hospital, I prayed and asked God for wisdom and for a miracle for this sailor. As I prayed, the Holy Spirit gave me a word of knowledge that this young man had a praying mother. I knew that God was sending me now in answer to his mother's prayers. Tears flowed freely when I met this sailor in his hospital room and asked if he had a praying mother; then a miracle came down.

Our God hears us when we pray today.

For Prayerful Reflection: How and when has God shown you that He hears you when you pray? How is this truth affecting your motivation to pray today?

Bible in a Year: *Judges 16-18; Luke 7:1-30*

April 3

I CAN *Pray* TODAY . . .
BECAUSE GOD TEACHES HOW TO PRAY

Rising very early in the morning, while it was still dark, he departed and went out to a desolate place, and there he prayed. And Simon and those who were with him searched for him, and they found him. (Mark 1:35-37)

Jesus was praying in a certain place, and when he finished, one of his disciples said to him, "Lord, teach us to pray, as John taught his disciples." And he said to them, "When you pray, say: "Father, hallowed be your name. Your kingdom come. Give us each day our daily bread, and forgive us our sins, for we ourselves forgive everyone who is indebted to us. And lead us not into temptation." (Luke 11:1-4)

Jesus' disciples prayed. Like many of us, they had grown up praying. They prayed, for example, when they worshipped, when they needed help, and when they recounted God's blessings. But they had never seen anyone pray like Jesus. Prayer was not an occasional practice for Him. Prayer was His way of life, an essential, treasured time with His Father that occurred every day and throughout the day. When His disciples did not know where Jesus was, and they searched for Him, He was often found praying.

And when Jesus prayed, things happened. Guidance, comfort, and help came, all flowing from sweet fellowship with God. After observing Jesus' prayer life for some time and considering their own prayer life in light of His, they boldly asked Him one day, *"Lord, teach us to pray."* We can share this desire today. We too can long to pray like Jesus, and we can ask Him to teach us. He will do so, for He wants our prayer life to be more than religious observance. He would teach us to pray as a way of life.

For Prayerful Reflection: How are you blessed in knowing that the Lord of all wants to teach you to pray as a way of life? Will you ask Him today to teach you?

Bible in a Year: *Judges 19-21; Luke 7:31-50*

April 4

I CAN *Pray* TODAY . . .
BECAUSE GOD COMMANDS ME TO PRAY

"As for me, far be it from me that I should sin against the Lord by ceasing to pray for you." (1 Samuel 12:23)

"Ask, and it will be given to you; seek, and you will find; knock, and it will be opened to you. For everyone who asks receives, and the one who seeks finds, and to the one who knocks it will be opened. Or which one of you, if his son asks him for bread, will give him a stone? Or if he asks for a fish, will give him a serpent? If you then, who are evil, know how to give good gifts to your children, how much more will your Father who is in heaven give good things to those who ask him!" (Matthew 7:7-11)

God commands His children to pray. This is more than a suggestion, and we cannot safely ignore this. God commands prayer. Near the end of Samuel's life when people were pleading with him to continue praying for them, Samuel said if he should cease praying for them, he would be sinning against the Lord.

By His word and example, Jesus taught us to pray as a way of life. He commanded it, for prayer is as vital to us spiritually as air is to our lungs physically. He has taught us to pray like little children approaching our loving Father, knowing He loves us and desires only our good, and that He loves giving good gifts to His children. We are commanded to pray both for God's glory and for our good. We pray not only because we must; we pray because we can, because we want to, and because God invites us to.

For Prayerful Reflection: To what extent have you seen prayer as both a privilege and a responsibility from the Lord? What would it mean for you to obey the Lord today in living a lifestyle of prayer?

Bible in a Year: *Ruth 1-4; Luke 8:1-25*

April 5

I CAN *Pray* TODAY . . .
BECAUSE GOD REWARDS US AS WE PRAY

"And when you pray, you must not be like the hypocrites. For they love to stand and pray in the synagogues and at the street corners, that they may be seen by others. Truly, I say to you, they have received their reward. But when you pray, go into your room and shut the door and pray to your Father who is in secret. And your Father who sees in secret will reward you." (Matthew 6:5-6)

In Matthew's account of Jesus' teaching on how to pray, our Lord begins by telling His disciples how not to pray. He says we are not to pray like hypocrites who are most concerned with how they outwardly sound or appear to others. Rather, we are to see prayer as heart-to-heart communion with God, and we don't want to miss it. God is our audience and conversation partner. God is the One we seek, enjoy, and trust.

Since fellowship with God is our goal in prayer, the bulk of our prayer life can be in secret. When we pray in this way, enjoying God's fellowship becomes our way of life. Then our Lord's promise is applied: *And your Father who sees in secret will reward you.*

How does God reward us? He rewards us by His presence, by lifting our burdens, and by giving us peace. He rewards us by receiving our praises. He rewards us by hearing our petitions, pouring out grace, and granting favor. He rewards us by hearing and answering our prayers. So we are very blessed today to come apart *and pray to [our] Father who is in secret.*

For Prayerful Reflection: How have you been rewarded by fellowship and prayer time with God? How will you apply this today?

Bible in a Year: *1 Samuel 1-3; Luke 8:26-56*

April 6

I CAN *Pray* TODAY . . .
BECAUSE GOD LOVES IT WHEN HIS CHILDREN PRAY

They were bringing children to him that he might touch them, and the disciples rebuked them. But when Jesus saw it, he was indignant and said to them, "Let the children come to me; do not hinder them, for to such belongs the kingdom of God. Truly, I say to you, whoever does not receive the kingdom of God like a child shall not enter it." And he took them in his arms and blessed them, laying his hands on them. (Mark 10:13-16)

If you have raised or are raising children, perhaps you have known the delight in your heart when you pulled into your driveway or entered your home and your children ran to you with joy. I remember this well, and the memory makes me smile. I now experience a similar joy when grandchildren run to me. This joy is because of love.

It depicts the heart of God when His children run to be near Him, be held by Him, and hear His voice, share His laughter, and love His presence. This happens whenever we, His much-loved children, come near to God and pray.

Three of the four Gospels tell the story of children coming to Jesus and of His disciples trying to stop it. The disciples likely thought children were unimportant or that Jesus had better things to do. But the Bible says Jesus was indignant at their interference. He wants all of us to come to Him as little children with childlike faith and wonder. He wants you and me to come to Him today with childlike trust and dependence. And when we do, having been granted free access to come near anytime, Jesus takes us in His arms, blesses us, and lays His hands upon us. God loves His children to come to Him and pray.

For Prayerful Reflection: When have you known or observed the joy of little children coming to Jesus? What would it mean for you to come to Jesus today and pray with childlike faith and love?

Bible in a Year: *1 Samuel 4-6; Luke 9:1-17*

April 7

I CAN *Pray* TODAY . . .
BECAUSE GOD SURPRISES US AS WE PRAY

"When he calls to me, I will answer him; I will be with him in trouble; I will rescue him and honor him. With long life I will satisfy him and show him my salvation." (Psalm 91:15-16)

"Call to me and I will answer you, and will tell you great and hidden things that you have not known." (Jeremiah 33:3)

When we pray, God may surprise us. Over time we might take for granted God's provision, as the Israelites did who took for granted God's provision of their daily manna. It became an expected thing. But God loves bringing delightful surprises in answer to prayer, so that our awe of Him might keep increasing.

Having walked with God for many decades now, I could easily list a hundred stories of God's surprising answers to prayer in my life. Each one caused my heart to rejoice and my voice to proclaim the goodness of God. One such event happened when I was a twenty-year-old college student. I knew that Helen Richter was to be my wife and life partner, and I was ready to formally propose to her. I had already spoken with her father and received his blessing; I had shopped for a diamond engagement ring, the cost of which was then $300.

I had no money then, and I mentioned this need only to God, asking for precisely $300, so I could affirm my love for Helen and ask her to marry me. We could then formerly announce our engagement. A few days later God surprised me. An envelope was in my college mailbox with a handwritten letter from a woman who had taught me in Sunday school when I was a little boy. She enclosed a check, which she and her husband believed God wanted me to have. It was for $300. I laughed with joy for God's provision.

For Prayerful Reflection: When has God surprised you in answer to prayer? What has God done lately that increased your awe of Him?

Bible in a Year: *1 Samuel 7-9; Luke 9:18-36*

April 8

I CAN *Pray* TODAY . . .
BECAUSE GOD DRAWS US CLOSE WHEN WE PRAY

The Lord is near to all who call on him, to all who call on him in truth. (Psalm 145:18)

Let us then with confidence draw near to the throne of grace, that we may receive mercy and find grace to help in time of need. (Hebrews 4:16)

Draw near to God, and he will draw near to you. (James 4:8)

In Hebrews and in James, when we are invited to *draw near* to God, we could assume it means moving towards a particular location. But this is not the intent of this phrase. The phrase more literally means extreme closeness, which is what God desires for us. God wants us to be extremely close to Him and to never stop moving closer. And as we pursue closeness with God, He promises to draw closer to us.

Praying with a desire to be near God leads toward extreme closeness. It begins in the desires of our heart. This is God's desire too, for He wants us to be close. The question is, What is our desire today?

A married couple was driving down the road with the husband at the wheel and the wife leaning against the passenger door. A young couple then passed by in an old pickup truck with a bench seat. The young woman in the truck was sitting very close to the driver; her head was resting on his shoulder. Observing this, the wife remarked to her husband, "I remember when you and I used to sit that close to each other."

Her husband looked across at her and replied, "Well, which one of us has moved?"

Indeed, if we are not as close to God as we once were, who has moved? Let's remember today the promise of God that when we come, desiring to be near Him, He will draw near.

For Prayerful Reflection: When were you very aware of being close to God as you prayed? How will you draw near to God today?

Bible in a Year: *1 Samuel 10-12; Luke 9:37-62*

April 9

I CAN *Pray* TODAY . . .
BECAUSE GOD STRENGTHENS US AS WE PRAY

My soul melts away for sorrow; strengthen me according to your word! (Psalm 119:28)

"Fear not, for I am with you; be not dismayed, for I am your God; I will strengthen you, I will help you, I will uphold you with my righteous right hand." (Isaiah 41:10)

God strengthens us when we pray, for He reminds us that He is with us now, and we are not alone in our struggle. I have experienced this so many times. I will never forget one painful weekend at Guantanamo Bay, Cuba, when I was serving as the Joint Task Force Command Chaplain. I awoke on a Saturday morning with excruciating pain in my back, so bad that I could barely move. I spent that entire day immobile, resting and hoping that the pain might decrease. By that evening the pain was so intense that I went to the hospital emergency room to seek relief. My immediate concern was that I was scheduled to preach the next morning at Naval Base Guantanamo Chapel, which would be impossible for me to do with this intense pain. At the hospital I was diagnosed with herniated discs, and was prescribed muscle relaxants, then sent to my quarters to rest.

Throughout the night I prayed; I admitted my weakness and asked God for strength. Because I would need a clear mind to preach God's Word, I did not take the medicine Sunday morning. I slowly made my way to the chapel but was in too much pain to stand when the congregation rose to sing. I kept asking God to lift the pain so I could preach His Word. When it was time in the service for the sermon, I rose from my seat, and the pain was instantly gone. I moved freely as I preached with God's anointing that day. Immediately after I finished that sermon, the pain returned in full force, as God again reminded me of my continual dependence on Him, for all of our strength comes from God.

For Prayerful Reflection: When has God strengthened you in answer to prayer? In what areas do you need God's strength as you pray today?

Bible in a Year: *1 Samuel 13-14; Luke 10:1-24*

April 10

I CAN *Pray* TODAY . . .
BECAUSE GOD GIVES HOPE WHEN WE PRAY

"And now, O Lord, for what do I wait? My hope is in you." (Psalm 39:7)

For you, O Lord, are my hope, my trust, O Lord, from my youth. (Psalm 71:5)

Rejoice in hope, be patient in tribulation, be constant in prayer. (Romans 12:12)

Sometimes we need hope, because we have lost it, and our hope is gone. Sometimes we need patience, because our patience is thin. God gives hope and patience when we turn to Him in faith and pray.

In one of Charles Schulz's *Peanuts* comic strips, Snoopy is thinking to himself, "Yesterday I was a dog. Today I'm a dog. Tomorrow I'll probably still be a dog. Oh, there's so little hope for advancement." All of us can be in situations where, like Snoopy, we become locked in hopelessness and see no way out. Whenever this happens, these are times to pray.

When we pray, we shift our focus from our present situation or circumstance to Jesus who can do all things. And as we do this, hope flows in. I have often prayed with or for people in painful or hard situations. As we prayed, God restored hope. And as we waited, God's patience was supplied, and in His time, circumstances were changed for His glory and their good.

Even this week I have heard from various Christian friends in need of hope as they are facing their own illness, the poor health of a loved one, financial struggles, broken relationships, fear and insecurity, or profound grief because of a loved one's death. In all these cases, hope is needed, and it is given as we pray in faith. How very blessed we are to receive God's hope as we pray.

For Prayerful Reflection: When has God met you in hard circumstances and given hope as you prayed? In what areas of your life is God's hope needed today as you pray?

Bible in a Year: *1 Samuel 15-16; Luke 10:25-42*

April 11

I CAN *Pray* TODAY . . .
BECAUSE GOD BLESSES WHEN WE PRAY

About midnight Paul and Silas were praying and singing hymns to God, and the prisoners were listening to them, and suddenly there was a great earthquake, so that the foundations of the prison were shaken. And immediately all the doors were opened, and everyone's bonds were unfastened. (Acts 16:25-26)

I love this biblical story of God's great blessings being poured out as God's people pray. I expect that, like me, you can relate to Paul and Silas's condition, as they had experienced a very hard day. They had been arrested, beaten, chained, and imprisoned. We have had unpleasant days too. Perhaps you have not experienced this degree of struggle, but I can well assume that you have also been misunderstood or treated unfairly. Haven't you also had days that have been so hard as you endured pain of body or soul?

When such days come, this does not necessarily mean God has abandoned us, or that we are outside His will. Paul and Silas were precisely where God wanted them to be, doing exactly what God wanted them to do. They were praying, and praising, and singing, and calling on God. And as they did this, God poured out wonderful blessings. Chains fell off; prison doors swung open; the jailer and his family believed in the Lord Jesus and were baptized that very night. Great blessings come when we pray.

If you have swallowed the false and nonsensical teaching that following Jesus means everything in life should be going well for you without struggle or pain, spit that out. God is far more concerned about making us holy than making us happy. Our times of trial remind us of how blessed we are to know God and to call upon Him. And as we pray, God blesses.

For Prayerful Reflection: When and how has God blessed you as you prayed? In what recent or current struggles is God calling you now to pray?

Bible in a Year: *1 Samuel 17-18; Luke 11:1-28*

April 12

I CAN *Pray* TODAY . . .
BECAUSE GOD IS GLORIFIED WHEN WE PRAY

Not to us, O Lord, not to us, but to your name give glory, for the sake of your steadfast love and your faithfulness! (Psalm 115:1)

"Whatever you ask in my name, this I will do, that the Father may be glorified in the Son." (John 14:13)

"Worthy are you, our Lord and God, to receive glory and honor and power, for you created all things, and by your will they existed and were created." (Revelation 4:11)

When we pray, we glorify God for who He is and for what He has done. Prayer lifts our focus from ourselves or our circumstances to God Himself. As we pray, we confess that our highest desire is not that our will is done but that His will is done so He receives glory.

If we have walked with God for any length of time, we can look back and marvel at how God did just that, intervening time and again with help and mercy in answer to prayer. We have witnessed God being glorified as we prayed. And so, confronting today's challenges and looking ahead to future needs, we can lift all of it before God with confidence that He will be glorified in answer to our prayer.

Hudson Taylor, founder of the China Inland Mission, hung a plaque in his home with two Hebrew words on it: *Ebenezer* and *Jehovah-Jireh.* The first word means "Hitherto hath the Lord helped us," and the second means "The Lord will provide." One word looked back, reminding him of God's past faithfulness, and the other word looked forward, reminding him of God's assurances.[8] As we pray today with such faith, God is glorified.

For Prayerful Reflection: When and how has God taught you to pray for His will and glory? What situations are you confronting today for which you will pray for God to be glorified?

Bible in a Year: *1 Samuel 19-21; Luke 11:29-54*

---

[8] Dr. and Mrs. Howard Taylor, *Hudson Taylor in Early Years: The Growth of a Soul* (London: Morgan & Scott, China Inland Mission, 1911), Chapter 35.

April 13

I CAN *Pray* TODAY . . .
BECAUSE GOD GIVES PEACE WHEN WE PRAY

Do not be anxious about anything, but in everything by prayer and supplication with thanksgiving let your requests be made known to God. And the peace of God, which surpasses all understanding, will guard your hearts and your minds in Christ Jesus. (Philippians 4:6-7)

"Peace I leave with you; my peace I give to you. Not as the world gives do I give to you. Let not your hearts be troubled, neither let them be afraid." (John 14:27)

In a world often filled with chaos, we pray because God gives peace. Prayer is the antidote to our anxiety. In an article of his online series called *The Fax of Life,* Rubel Shelly shared a story told by syndicated columnist Deborah Mathis about a day in her life in Washington, DC. She described passing through busy Union Station and hearing the noisy hubbub of sounds. Then she heard someone singing, What a Friend We Have in Jesus.

She noticed that quarreling stopped, and tense shoulders seemed to relax. As the lone voice sang the remaining verses of Joseph Scriven's lyrics, Deborah Mathis realized she was singing along now, and so were several others. A man said to her, "Nice, huh? I don't even believe in Jesus, but that is nice."

When life for us becomes chaotic, confusing, or cluttered, we are blessed to remember that Jesus has invited us to His peace. Today, what a privilege to carry everything to God in prayer!

For Prayerful Reflection: When were you anxious but received God's peace as you prayed? What will it mean for you today to bring all your burdens and concerns to the Lord in prayer?

Bible in a Year: *1 Samuel 22-24; Luke 12:1-31*

April 14

I CAN *Pray* TODAY . . .
BECAUSE GOD SANCTIFIES WHEN WE PRAY

Have this mind among yourselves, which is yours in Christ Jesus . . . Therefore, my beloved, as you have always obeyed, so now, not only as in my presence but much more in my absence, work out your own salvation with fear and trembling, for it is God who works in you, both to will and to work for his good pleasure. (Philippians 2:5, 12-13)

Every true child of God wants to become more like Jesus. And by God's grace, this happens as we spend time with Him, listen carefully to His Word, and share our hearts with Him in prayer. We can do this as a way of life, conversing often with God. We want and need to talk with Him and listen to Him. The theological term for becoming more Christlike is *sanctification*.

In Philippians 2, Paul says growing in godliness requires intentionality and work. God is not calling the spiritually lost to work hard in order to get saved, for salvation is the free gift of God (Ephesians 2:8-9). But God does call the saved to work hard at seeking Him, desiring obedience, and pursuing sanctification.

Suppose someone said to you, "I am very lonely and need a friend. I will do anything you ask of me if you will please love me." That would be unhealthy, wouldn't it? How much better to hear, "I love you so much that I cannot imagine you asking me to do anything I would not gladly do." This is the way God loves us and how we should want to love Him.

We pray to God who loves us that much. We pray to the One we love and long to honor and please. We pray with a longing to be more like Jesus. And as we pray today, God sanctifies us.

For Prayerful Reflection: Reflecting on your own spiritual growth, how has God been sanctifying you? As you pray today, in what ways do you desire and will you ask to become more like Jesus?

Bible in a Year: *1 Samuel 25-26; Luke 12:32-59*

April 15

I CAN *Pray* TODAY . . .
BECAUSE GOD DEMONSTRATES HOW TO PRAY

Rising very early in the morning, while it was still dark, he departed and went out to a desolate place, and there he prayed. (Mark 1:35)

In these days he went out to the mountain to pray, and all night he continued in prayer to God. And when day came, he called his disciples and chose from them twelve, whom he named apostles. (Luke 6:12-13)

Jesus was praying in a certain place, and when he finished, one of his disciples said to him, "Lord, teach us to pray." (Luke 11:1)

Jesus taught His disciples to pray. His primary method of teaching was to show them by His own prayer life. For Jesus, prayer was far more than a religious practice He adhered to. Prayer was His lifeline to His heavenly Father through which He received encouragement, guidance, and the daily help He needed. Jesus prayed early in the day and throughout the day. He prayed when facing significant decisions like choosing His twelve apostles. He prayed when His heart was heavy. He prayed often, and His disciples took notice of this. So they asked Jesus to teach them. And He did.

My four-year-old grandson Luca loves chess. He will play chess with anyone who is willing. When I was recruited to play several games with him, I was amazed at how well he did. Because Helen has not played chess, she asked Luca to teach her, so they could do this together. She figured that if a four-year-old could play, she should be able to learn. He taught her, and they enjoyed doing this together. Luca won.

Jesus is teaching us to pray so we can do this together. What an awesome privilege!

For Prayerful Reflection: When and why have you ever asked Jesus to teach you to pray? How could it help you today to pray as Jesus prayed?

Bible in a Year: *1 Samuel 27-29; Luke 13:1-22*

April 16

I CAN *Pray* TODAY...
BECAUSE GOD REWARDS PERSISTENCE AS WE PRAY

"Ask, and it will be given you; seek, and you will find; knock, and it will be opened to you. For everyone who asks receives, and the one who seeks finds, and to the one who knocks it will be opened." (Matthew 7:7-8)

[Jesus] told them a parable to the effect that they ought always to pray and not lose heart. (Luke 18:1)

Jesus instructs us to pray with persistence, and He promises that God will hear and answer. I have often seen the proof of this; perhaps you have too. In Matthew 7:7-8, Jesus tells us to *ask, seek,* and *knock*. These words in New Testament Greek are in the present imperative tense, implying persistence. In other words, we are to keep on asking, seeking, and knocking.

In his book *Fresh Wind, Fresh Fire*,[9] Jim Cymbala tells a personal story of his wayward daughter Chrissy; he shared how God answered persistent prayers for her. Following a prolonged period of separation in which his daughter had strayed far from the Lord, fervent prayers were being offered on her behalf. In a Tuesday evening prayer meeting at the church, the Holy Spirit directed the congregation to pause and join in united prayer for Chrissy; so they all prayed.

Thursday morning Chrissy came home. Through her tears she said to her father, "On Tuesday night, Daddy, who was praying for me?... In the middle of the night, God woke me and showed me I was heading toward this abyss. There was no bottom to it.... I was so frightened. I realized how hard I have been, how wrong, how rebellious. At the same time, it was like God wrapped his arms around me and held me tight. He kept me from sliding further, as He said, 'I still love you.'"

Amen. Today, as we press on in prayer, we can all know with confidence that God rewards persistence.

For Prayerful Reflection: When have you seen God reward persistence in prayer? How could it help you today to keep on asking, seeking, and knocking?

Bible in a Year: *1 Samuel 30-31; Luke 13:23-35*

---

[9] Jim Cymbala, *Fresh Wind, Fresh Fire* (Grand Rapids, MI: Zondervan, 1997).

April 17

I CAN *Pray* TODAY . . .
BECAUSE GOD LETS US JOININ
HIS WORK AS WE PRAY

[Be] praying at all times in the Spirit, with all prayer and supplication. To that end, keep alert with all perseverance, making supplications for all the saints, and also for me, that words may be given to me in opening my mouth boldly to proclaim the mystery of the gospel, for which I am an ambassador in chains, that I may declare it boldly, as I ought to speak. (Ephesians 6:18-20)

In the final chapter of his letter to the Ephesians, which Paul wrote from prison, he describes the armor of God, which offers essential protection in spiritual warfare. After listing defensive items that we must all wear, and after describing our primary offensive weapon, which is the Word of God, Paul hones in on prayer, which offensively and defensively allows us to participate with God in His work.

We are encouraged to be *praying at all times,* and to *keep alert with all perseverance, making supplications for all the saints.* Paul then specifically asked the church to pray *also for [him],* that he might have holy boldness as he spoke in Jesus' name. Prayer allows us to participate with God in the work He is doing in various places and through various people. This is too important to ignore.

Does God really need our help to accomplish His work? Not really, as He is all-powerful and in control of all things. But prayer is God's chosen means through which so many things will happen. Prayer, for example, turns hearts toward the love of Jesus. Prayer clears obstacles for God to work. It is not that God is unable to work without our prayers. Rather, He establishes prayer that we may join Him in His work and accomplish His will in this world. What a holy privilege you and I have to pray today!

For Prayerful Reflection: When have you prayed for God to bless someone or to move in a certain way only to hear later what He has done? How will you join in God's work today through prayer?

Bible in a Year: *2 Samuel 1-2; Luke 14:1-24*

April 18

I CAN *Pray* TODAY . . .
BECAUSE GOD GIVES VICTORY OVER EVIL AS WE PRAY

For we do not wrestle against flesh and blood, but against the rulers, against the authorities, against the cosmic powers over this present darkness, against the spiritual forces of evil in the heavenly places. (Ephesians 6:12)

When [Jesus] had entered the house, his disciples asked him privately, "Why could we not cast it out?" And he said to them, "This kind cannot be driven out by anything but prayer." (Mark 9:28-29)

God wants us to be aware of the spiritual battle we are in, and He wants us to know what to do when we are in spiritual warfare. In such situations we must always pray that God will grant us the victory. At various times in my life and ministry, my Lord has taught me this.

One night when I was a young pastor, a young couple rang my doorbell at about 2:00 a.m. They were utterly terrified because strange things were happening in the home to which they had recently moved. They frightfully described apparitions and items, including sharp knives, flying across the room. They were both immobilized by fear.

All I knew to do was pray, so that is what I did. I prayed for discernment, and I led them that night to turn to Jesus in faith. I prayed in His powerful name for a shield of protection over and around them from all powers of darkness, and I promised to come to their home later that day to pray through the house. I assured them that Jesus Christ, who is Lord of all, would put a stop to this. Later that day, when I went to their home with another prayer warrior to pray with me, the peace and power of God came down and dispelled the powers of darkness. Through prayer and in Jesus' name, God gives victory.

For Prayerful Reflection: When have you witnessed the power of God over evil as God's people pray? How does this lesson apply to your prayer life today?

Bible in a Year: *2 Samuel 3-5; Luke 14:25-35*

April 19

I CAN *Pray* TODAY . . .
BECAUSE GOD MAKES PRAYER AVAILABLE

And he told them a parable to the effect that they ought always to pray and not lose heart. (Luke 18:1)

Rejoice always, pray without ceasing, give thanks in all circumstances; for this is the will of God in Christ Jesus for you. (1 Thessalonians 5:16-18)

I thank God whom I serve, as did my ancestors, with a clear conscience, as I remember you constantly in my prayers night and day. (2 Timothy 1:3)

To pray is to be welcomed into the very presence of almighty God and to have conversation with Him. It is to enjoy His presence and acknowledge and lay before Him in repentance our sins, receiving His forgiveness. In prayer we praise Him for who He is and thank Him for what He has given and all He has done. Prayer is lifting our petitions before Him, asking for His mercy, and believing for His answer. To pray is a holy privilege for God's children, and you and I are instructed and blessed to pray always.

What does it mean to pray always? It means to come to God in every situation of life, lean on Him in faith, trust Him, and look to Him for grace and guidance for His glory and our good. When your car careens sideways on the icy or rain-slick road toward an oncoming truck at 60 mph, what do you do? You pray! But what about when the drive is peaceful?

When your doctor comes into your exam room with test results and a worried frown on her face, what do you do? You pray! But what about at your desk when involved in the everyday responsibilities of your job, or when at home preparing dinner with family or reviewing your finances? God has made prayer available to us throughout all of today.

For Prayerful Reflection: What are some examples in your life of praying always? How does this invitation bless you today?

Bible in a Year: *2 Samuel 6-8; Luke 15:1-10*

April 20

I CAN *Pray* TODAY . . .
BECAUSE GOD TEACHES HUMILITY AS WE PRAY

Do nothing from selfish ambition or conceit, but in humility count others more significant than yourselves. Let each of you look not only to his own interests, but also to the interests of others. And being found in human form, he humbled himself by becoming obedient to the point of death, even death on a cross. (Philippians 2:3-4, 8)

Humble yourselves before the Lord, and he will exalt you. (James 4:10)

Humility is a Christlike virtue that God desires in all His children. Prayer develops humility in us, for we are reminded as we approach God's throne that He is God and we are not; we are not in control, God is. This admission humbles us and peels away our pride. Jesus Christ is the greatest example of humility, for though He was God, for our sakes He willingly laid aside the prerogatives of His divinity. Because of His great love for us, He purchased our eternal salvation.

Following Jesus and becoming more like Him means humility replaces pride in us. Our focus becomes less on ourselves and our desires and more on God and His will and on the needs of others. So what is humility, and what makes humble people different? Humility is the opposite of pride and arrogance. In disagreements, pride is concerned with *who* is right, but humility is concerned with *what* is right. Pride and arrogance focus on self. But as Benjamin Franklin said, "A man wrapped up in himself makes a very small bundle." Humility, though, opens us wide to the giving character of God and allows us, even as we pray, to be more Christlike, focusing on the goodness of God and His love and mercies to others.

For Prayerful Reflection: Why is humility so important for God's children? How have you observed or learned it? How might God teach you humility as you pray today?

Bible in a Year: *2 Samuel 9-11; Luke 15:11-32*

April 21

I CAN *Pray* TODAY . . .
BECAUSE GOD BINDS US WITH OTHERS AS WE PRAY

"Again I say to you, if two of you agree on earth about anything they ask, it will be done for them by my Father in heaven. For where two or three are gathered in my name, there am I among them." (Matthew 18:19-20)

And let us consider how to stir up one another to love and good works, not neglecting to meet together, as is the habit of some, but encouraging one another, and all the more as you see the Day drawing near. (Hebrews 10:24-25)

And pray for one another, that you may be healed. (James 5:16)

Prayer not only strengthens our relationship with God, but when we pray with other believers, prayer also strengthens the bonds between us. We are spiritually bound together by our Lord when we join with one another in prayer.

I read about a horse-pull in Canada, in which one horse pulled nine thousand pounds and another pulled eight thousand pounds. We might assume that together they could pull seventeen thousand pounds, but when harnessed together these mighty horses pulled thirty thousand pounds! God's power through His church is greater than the sum of His power in us individually. This becomes evident when God's people join together to pray.

Local churches must offer opportunities for people to request and receive prayer, so no one ever stands alone. This is God's exhortation. Each of us must be bold enough to request prayer when needed and to join with others in prayer, for this allows the power of God to move among us. We are so blessed to pray today, for as we pray, God binds us together.

For Prayerful Reflection: What is so wonderful about praying in faith with other believers? How have you been blessed by this privilege? How can you access this blessing today?

Bible in a Year: *2 Samuel 12-13; Luke 16*

April 22

I CAN *Pray* TODAY...
BECAUSE GOD LETS US HEAR AND HEED AS WE PRAY

"Call to me and I will answer you, and will tell you great and hidden things that you have not known." (Jeremiah 33:3)

"My sheep hear my voice, and I know them, and they follow me." (John 10:27)

In his book *Hearing God's Voice*, Henry Blackaby tells of the first funeral he conducted. It was for a three-year-old, the first child born to a couple in his church and the first grandchild in their extended family. Unfortunately, she was spoiled. While visiting the little girl's home one day, Blackaby observed that she loved ignoring her parents' instructions. When they told her to come, she went the other way. When they told her to sit down, she stood up.

He noticed her parents laughed at this and found her behavior cute. One day their front gate was left open. The parents saw their child leave the yard and head toward the road. To their horror, a car was racing down the street. As she ran out between two parked cars, they screamed at her to stop and turn back. She paused for a second, looked back at her parents, then laughed as she turned and ran into the path of the oncoming car. The parents rushed their little girl to the hospital, but tragically, she died.

God loves us, and He wants His children to grow up in Him, know Him better, love and trust Him more, and come to Him often in prayer. He longs for us to hear and heed His voice. This is not an insignificant matter. It is important for living life as God intends. As we pray, loving, learning, listening, and living as God directs, we are and will be blessed.

For Prayerful Reflection: When have you prayed and known that you heard God, but then proceeded to go your own way? In what area(s) of life are you now praying, earnestly desiring to hear and heed?

Bible in a Year: *2 Samuel 14-15; Luke 17:1-19*

April 23

I CAN *Pray* TODAY . . .
BECAUSE GOD'S SACRIFICE ALLOWS US TO PRAY

The next day [John the Baptist] saw Jesus coming toward him, and said, "Behold, the Lamb of God, who takes away the sin of the world!" (John 1:29)

Let us then with confidence draw near to the throne of grace, that we may receive mercy and find grace to help in time of need. (Hebrews 4:16)

We are blessed to exercise this privilege of prayer, drawing near to God with confidence, because Jesus Christ made the supreme sacrifice for us. He bridged the gap that was between God and us because of our sin. By His perfect sacrifice, we have been set free to know God and to pray. If Christ had not gone to the cross, shed His blood, and died for us, our sin would have kept us forever separated. But our sin is now atoned for, and our life is restored. We are blessed to be God's children today and to pray.

I received this truth while still a young boy. I believed it, and I knew God loved and forgave me, so I was His forever. This realization was wonderful to me, for it meant God loves me, and I can love Him. I sometimes look back with joy for the simple faith I had as a child. I recall getting on my knees, speaking my heart to God, and knowing He heard my prayer and would surely answer. And the wonder of it is that this has been my life since childhood – loving the One who loves me, praying to Him anytime day or night, and always knowing God hears and cares, and He is able. All this is possible because of His sacrifice.

For Prayerful Reflection: When and how did you first grasp the wonderful truth of Christ's sacrifice for you? How does His sacrifice for you impact your prayer life today?

Bible in a Year: *2 Samuel 16-18; Luke 17:20-37*

April 24

I CAN *Pray* TODAY . . .
BECAUSE GOD CHANGES US AS WE PRAY

If any of you lacks wisdom, let him ask God, who gives generously to all without reproach, and it will be given him. (James 1:5)

Humble yourselves, therefore, under the mighty hand of God so that at the proper time he may exalt you, casting all your anxieties on him, because he cares for you. (1 Peter 5:6-7)

Prayer changes us. When we seek God's leading and truth, He gives it. When we lack wisdom and pray for it, God bestows it. When we're anxious, worried, and burdened, and turn to the Lord in prayer, He lightens our load, lifts our worry, dispels anxiety, and changes our experience of life. We want to pray today because when we do, God changes us.

Don't you have countless testimonies of this happening in your life? I do. In March 2011, for example, I was concerned about several things. At that time, while ministering as Conference Minister (Executive Director) of the Conservative Congregational Christian Conference (CCCC), the faith group in which I served, I was also serving as a Chaplain in the U.S. Navy Reserves. I knew I needed God's wisdom then, so I prayed that I might hear from Him. I spent a whole day in fasting and prayer, and as I prayed, I sensed the Holy Spirit telling me that He would soon move me.

I did not expect to hear this, but because I know God answers prayer, and because I only wanted His will and His answer, I was at peace. The next morning, I received a call informing me that I was recalled to active duty in the Navy. I immediately knew that this change was from God. Before changing my location, He first changed my heart. God changes us when we pray.

For Prayerful Reflection: When has God changed you as you prayed? What areas of life are you bringing to the Lord in prayer today with a willingness for God to change you?

Bible in a Year: *2 Samuel 19-20; Luke 18:1-23*

April 25

I CAN *Pray* TODAY . . .
BECAUSE GOD REVEALS HIMSELF AS WE PRAY

"You will seek me and find me, when you seek me with all your heart. I will be found by you, declares the Lord." (Jeremiah 29:13-14)

For now we see in a mirror dimly, but then face to face. Now I know in part; then I shall know fully, even as I have been fully known. (1 Corinthians 13:12)

Oh, taste and see that the Lord is good! Blessed is the man who takes refuge in him! (Psalm 34:8)

God asks us to seek Him, for He wants to be found by us. We know in part who God is, which gives us a desire to know Him even more. Driven by hunger for the life that is found in relationship with God, we seek Him. But we remember that God sought us first. God's very act of creation was one of pursuit, for He created us to know Him. And through Jesus Christ, God has sought to restore us to Himself.

God extends a personal invitation to us to come closer to Him and know Him more. Jesus told His disciples to keep on asking, seeking, and knocking, for in doing so they would receive His good provision. Looking ahead, Jesus prayed for His future believers, including you and me. He promised to make Himself known to us. Clearly God desires personal relationship with us. He has given us a taste of who He is, and we are invited every day to keep on seeking Him. As we do, God increasingly shows Himself to us, and we grow in His love.

For Prayerful Reflection: When have you sought hard after God, thereby learning more of who He is and growing in love for Him? In what ways will you seek God today?

Bible in a Year: *2 Samuel 21-22; Luke 18:24-43*

April 26

I CAN *Pray* TODAY . . .
BECAUSE PRAYER CAN BE OUR WAY OF LIFE

And [Jesus] told them a parable to the effect that they ought always to pray and not lose heart. (Luke 18:1)

And rising very early in the morning, while it was still dark, he departed and went out to a desolate place, and there he prayed. (Mark 1:35)

Train up a child in the way he should go; even when he is old he will not depart from it. (Proverbs 22:6)

Prayer is not merely an activity we can do from time to time, akin to occasional physical exercise. Rather, prayer is a way of life, a continual and necessary source of comfort, renewal, friendship, and strength that we turn to often throughout the day and every day, for we are so blessed to know God and be in communion with Him.

Prayer is analogous to a benefit of marriage or a close friendship. When on our own, we become accustomed to experiencing much of life alone. When tired, angry, frustrated, sad, or confused in sleepless nights or on lonely days, we can try to process all of it on our own. But when we marry, or have a close friend with whom we share life, we are blessed to talk about whatever might be on our hearts – thus, to be understood and to understand. What a great blessing prayer can be!

A lifestyle of prayer means coming to God anytime and all the time. We learn that we're loved and are never alone. Jesus modeled such a lifestyle of prayer. Parents are called to teach and model for their children this privilege of prayer as a way of life.

For Prayerful Reflection: What has a lifestyle of prayer meant to you? What will it mean for you today?

Bible in a Year: *2 Samuel 23-24; Luke 19:1-27*

April 27

I CAN *Pray* TODAY . . .
BECAUSE GOD INVITES US TO PRAY BOLDLY

"Come, everyone who thirsts, come to the waters; and he who has no money, come, buy and eat! Come, buy wine and milk without money and without price. Incline your ear, and come to me; hear, that your soul may live; and I will make with you an everlasting covenant." (Isaiah 55:1, 3)

Let us then with confidence draw near to the throne of grace, that we may receive mercy and find grace to help in time of need. (Hebrews 4:16)

There is something wonderful about receiving an invitation. Knowing we are so cared for and our presence is desired, requested, and sought is a personal and good thing. This perspective applies to prayer, for God desires your presence and invites you to come. We have received His summons to boldly come before His throne of grace through the finished work and sufficient sacrifice of Jesus. We are invited to boldly come anytime, even today.

This invitation from God is broadly offered to all who desire Him, no matter what our status or circumstances are. But please let us notice that this invitation has our name on it. We are thus invited to enter His presence with gladness, not from religious duty.

Further, we are to come not timidly but boldly. It's an astounding image, isn't it? How can we, as sinful mortals, boldly come before God's throne in prayer and approach God with confidence? It is because this is God's *throne of grace*. We can thus boldly pray before God's throne. It is the wonderful grace of Jesus, whose perfect and atoning sacrifice has entirely covered our sin; so we have been made worthy to be in His presence and to pray today.

For Prayerful Reflection: How have you been affected by receiving a personal invitation from God to boldly come to Him in prayer? What will it mean for you today to boldly approach Him in prayer?

Bible in a Year: *1 Kings 1-2; Luke 19:28-48*

April 28

I CAN *Pray* TODAY . . .
BECAUSE GOD OFFERS ESCAPE FROM TEMPTATION AS WE PRAY

"Watch and pray that you may not enter into temptation." (Matthew 26:41)

"No temptation has overtaken you that is not common to man. God is faithful, and he will not let you be tempted beyond your ability, but with the temptation he will also provide the way of escape, that you may be able to endure it. (1 Corinthians 10:13)

Jesus urged His disciples to watch and pray, lest when facing temptation they would sin. We all know what it is to be tempted and to yield to it. Haven't we all experienced some of the bitter agony the apostle Peter knew when *he went out and wept bitterly* (Luke 22:62) after denying three times that he knew the Lord? God calls us to pray so we might escape temptation.

As Paul wrote, the temptations that we face are *common to man;* that is, they are not unique to us. But the good news today is that God has provided for us *the way of escape,* so we are *able to endure it.*

Jesus taught by His example and word that the way to escape must include prayer. When instructing His disciples on prayer, Jesus told them to pray for deliverance from temptation and evil. This required acknowledging the vulnerabilities and spiritual threats they faced – and we face – and asking God for protection and deliverance. Jesus preceded His public ministry with forty days of fasting and prayer in the wilderness, and He concluded it with fervent intercession in the garden of Gethsemane. Our Lord's prayers were answered, for He was victorious over Satan's temptations and over sin and death.

Failing to pray leaves us spiritually weak and exposed; lack of prayer gives increased opportunity and vulnerability for being lured toward sin. But praying as Jesus taught us provides a way to endure and escape.

For Prayerful Reflection: What has God taught you about the correlation between your prayer life and your victory over temptation? What temptations are you facing today for which you will now pray?

Bible in a Year: *1 Kings 3-5; Luke 20:1-26*

April 29

I CAN *Pray* TODAY . . .
BECAUSE GOD INVITES US TO PRAY ANYTIME

But I call to God, and the Lord will save me. Evening and morning and at noon I utter my complaint and moan, and he hears my voice. (Psalm 55:16-17)

And [Jesus] told them a parable to the effect that they ought always to pray and not lose heart. (Luke 18:1)

Pray without ceasing. (1 Thessalonians 5:17)

For God's children, He is always approachable. We are beckoned to come near to God morning, noon, afternoon, evening, and in the darkness of night. God invites us to pray anytime, and He hears us when we do. I have lived this privilege, for I have prayed to my Lord at all times of day and night and in all sorts of situations, and God always assures me that He has heard my cry.

In the years that I served on active duty as a U.S. Navy Chaplain, there were many times when I was forward deployed and far from my family. It was never easy to be away, but my Lord always reminded me that He was with those whom I love, even as He was with me. I knew He would hear and answer my prayers for them. Often when feeling low and sometimes in the darkness of night, I interceded for my family.

I asked God to strengthen and encourage Helen, and He did. I asked God to bring help to her, and He did. I asked God to hold my children close, and I prayed for them often and by name. And God heard and answered my prayers for them. Throughout my days and nights, I prayed too for the servicemen and women whom I was called to serve and for their families, and I often saw God working with evident answers to prayer. How blessed we are today that God invites us to pray anytime.

For Prayerful Reflection: What have you learned about the blessing of praying anytime? What situations or concerns do you face today in which you will want to pray?

Bible in a Year: *1 Kings 6-7; Luke 20:27-47*

April 30

I CAN *Pray* TODAY . . .
BECAUSE GOD LETS US PRAY ANYWHERE

I remember you upon my bed, and meditate on you in the watches of the night. (Psalm 63:6)

"But when you pray, go into your room and shut the door and pray to your Father who is in secret. And your Father who sees in secret will reward you." (Matthew 6:6)

We departed and went on our journey, and they all, with wives and children, accompanied us until we were outside the city. And kneeling down on the beach, we prayed and said farewell to one another. (Acts 21:5-6)

God reminds us that we can pray anywhere. We can pray in a holy sanctuary and in a prison cell. We can pray on a mountaintop and in a deep valley. We can pray when alone in a quiet place and when in a raging battle or walking through a crowd. We can pray in the air, on land, on the sea, and under the sea. We can pray any place God leads us.

I have been blessed to pray in countless places, for I know God is here now, and He hears and will answer. One of my favorite memories was praying in Argentina and Brazil. Along with some friends, Helen and I visited Iguazu Falls, the largest falls in the world. One day after walking along a lengthy path, we came to a spot where we stood under a rainbow, completely surrounded by waterfalls. I was so enthralled at the beauty around me and the majesty of God that I sang and prayed at the top of my lungs, praising God and giving Him glory. Because of the great sound of the water, no one but God heard me. But I knew that God heard. No matter where we are, God invites us to pray.

For Prayerful Reflection: What are some memorable places and occasions when you prayed and knew God heard? Where have you gone, or where might you go today, where you are blessed to pray?

Bible in a Year: *1 Kings 8-9; Luke 21:1-19*

12 Themes on Following Jesus

MAY

Because God . . .
I Can *Praise* Today

May 1

I CAN *Praise* TODAY . . .
BECAUSE GOD IS PRAISEWORTHY

I call upon the Lord, who is worthy to be praised. (Psalm 18:3)

Praise the Lord! Praise God in his sanctuary; praise him in his mighty heavens! Praise him for his mighty deeds; praise him according to his excellent greatness! Let everything that has breath praise the Lord! Praise the Lord! (Psalm 150:1-2, 6)

God is worthy to be praised by all of His creation and by every means, even by me today. After all, were it not for God, would I even be? Would you or I have ever had our first heartbeat or drawn our first breath? Would we have awakened today? Of course not. We owe everything that we are and have to God, and so, *let everything that has breath praise the Lord!* Yes, I will praise God today.

To want to praise God, our senses must be filled with Him. Our observation must be drawn toward Him. Our desires must turn toward Him, as the rivers run to the sea. As long as our focus remains on ourselves, on things that are around us, or on the attractions and problems of this world, we can have no desire or capacity for praising God.

But when in faith we look upward, when we begin to see the majesty of who God is and behold what He has done or marvel at what He is now doing, and when we are at last filled with an awareness of Him, then we cannot help but praise Him. We praise God because He is worthy of our praise! He is worthy of my praise today!

For Prayerful Reflection: When has your heart been so filled with God that you knew He was worthy, and you could not help but praise Him? Why, when, and how will you praise God today?

Bible in a Year: *1 Kings 10-11; Luke 21:20-38*

May 2

I CAN *Praise* TODAY...
BECAUSE GOD IS MY SAVIOR

For unto you is born this day in the city of David a Savior, who is Christ the Lord. And suddenly there was with the angel a multitude of the heavenly host praising God and saying, "Glory to God in the highest, and on earth peace among those with whom he is pleased!" And the shepherds returned, glorifying and praising God for all they had heard and seen, as it had been told them. (Luke 2:11, 13-14, 20)

The shepherds in the fields with their flocks outside Bethlehem that holy night were amazed to hear that God had provided *a Savior, who is Christ the Lord.* This wonderful news prompted thousands of heavenly angels to sing praises to God. After seeing the newborn Christ, the shepherds praised God too. We who believe in the Lord Jesus have much cause for praise today. Our God saves us, not because we could ever earn it, but because of His great grace and love.

In the film *Saving Private Ryan*, soldiers were sent to find Private Ryan and bring him home, because all of his brothers had been killed in the war. It was an act of mercy for his mother's sake. Several soldiers who looked for him were killed, one of whom whispered his dying words to Private Ryan, "Earn this." The final scene of the film is of Private Ryan as an old man in the cemetery of the war-dead asking himself, "Did I earn it? Was I worthy?"

But thanks be to God, we are not required to earn our salvation, for none of us could. Jesus' sacrifice for us was and is wholly sufficient to save us. Our part is to accept His gift of salvation and then seek to honor God every day in the way that we live, not in an effort to "earn this," but because we love Him and He is worthy of our praise.

For Prayerful Reflection: When and to what degree have you shared the angels' and shepherds' praise to God who has provided for you a Savior? How will you praise God today for saving you?

Bible in a Year: *1 Kings 12-13; Luke 22:1-20*

May 3

I CAN *Praise* TODAY . . .
BECAUSE GOD OPENS ACCESS THROUGH PRAISE

Enter his gates with thanksgiving, and his courts with praise! Give thanks to him; bless his name! For the Lord is good; his steadfast love endures forever, and his faithfulness to all generations. (Psalm 100:4-5)

The blood of our Savior provides the way for forgiveness from our sin and a personal relationship with God (Hebrews 10:19). Having received such access by faith, our love and worshipful praise opens a clear and unhindered passage into His presence. Therefore, as the psalmist declared, we are compelled to *enter his gates with thanksgiving, and his courts with praise.* Though access into God's presence and a personal relationship with Him is freely offered through Jesus Christ, we must choose to avail ourselves of this privilege by faith in Jesus, and give Him our love and praise.

A story reported by the Manitoba Historical Society tells of a gift given by the Canadian Pacific Railway to Chief Crowfoot of the Blackfoot nation in southern Alberta.[10] The year was 1886, and the occasion was completion of the Transcontinental Railroad. Chief Crowfoot, who had previously granted permission to lay track across his territory, was presented a lifetime railroad pass. Reportedly, Crowfoot put the pass into a leather pouch and wore it around his neck for the rest of his life, but he never once availed himself of the privileges it spelled out.

It is a great tragedy when Christians do the same thing with the Word of God and the lifetime privilege that we are offered of personally entering God's holy presence through faith in Jesus Christ with a heart of love and praise. Today we are blessed to come to God by faith and with praise!

For Prayerful Reflection: What have you done thus far with the "lifetime pass" you have been given to enter God's presence? What will it mean for you today to *enter his courts with praise*?

Bible in a Year: *1 Kings 14-15; Luke 22:21-46*

---

[10] Betty Woods, "Chief Crowfoot and the Priest Who Became President of the Canadian Pacific Railway," *Manitoba Historical Society* (April 1960, Vol. 5, No. 3).

May 4

I CAN *Praise* TODAY . . .
BECAUSE GOD DWELLS IN OUR PRAISE

My God, my God, why have you forsaken me? Why are you so far from saving me, from the words of my groaning? O my God, I cry by day, but you do not answer, and by night, but I find no rest. Yet you are holy, enthroned on the praises of Israel. In you our fathers trusted; they trusted, and you delivered them. To you they cried and were rescued; in you they trusted and were not put to shame. (Psalm 22:1-5)

Have you experienced times when you felt distant from God, even forsaken and alone? Have you ever felt anguish because your prayers seemed to be unheard and unanswered? Perhaps you are there today. The author of Psalm 22 certainly was. And so was Jesus, when He hung dying for us on a cruel cross of suffering, bearing the judgment of our sins. Jesus prayed from this psalm, *My God, my God, why have you forsaken me?* Our Lord, who endured such intense suffering for us, surely meets us whenever we are weak and our faith wavers, and when we cry out to Him.

This psalm and our Lord Jesus also remind us that though He is always with us, His presence is especially manifest when we offer praise, for God is *enthroned on the praises of Israel*. When we, God's people, lift up our hearts in praise, He is among us, and we know it, for God dwells in the praises of His people! I have learned this lesson in my own times of intense struggle. When I intentionally shift my focus from my pain to His glory and presence and praise Him for His greatness, I become aware that He is here, for God dwells in praise.

For Prayerful Reflection: When have you felt distant from God but then experienced His presence through praise? How could you apply this lesson today?

Bible in a Year: *1 Kings 16-18; Luke 22:47-71*

May 5

I CAN *Praise* TODAY . . .
BECAUSE GOD HAS ORDAINED PRAISE

When the chief priests and the scribes saw the wonderful things that [Jesus] did, and the children crying out in the temple, "Hosanna to the Son of David!" they were indignant, and they said to him, "Do you hear what these are saying?" And Jesus said to them, "Yes; have you never read, 'Out of the mouth of infants and nursing babies you have prepared praise'?" (Matthew 21:15-16)

On the day Jesus entered the city of Jerusalem with every intention of giving His life in suffering and death to atone for our sins and the sins of the world, a remarkable thing happened in the temple that was noticed by the religious elite and by Jesus Himself. Children were crying out their praises to Him. *"Hosanna to the Son of David!"* was their cry, which testified of their love for Jesus and their faith that He was the Christ; they offered Him their adoration and praise!

The chief priests and scribes wanted the little ones to be silenced, but Jesus applauded the children, for their faith and praises were true, as God had ordained and prepared them to give Him praise. This is His intention for all of His children, starting when we are young.

I remember fondly when I was a little boy, sitting around our breakfast table in the morning with my parents and five siblings, singing songs of praise to God. We sang such praises not to entertain but to express our faith and to glorify God, who is worthy to be praised. Throughout the years since then, in various places I have served, I have often witnessed the children of God giving Him praise. It's a wonderful thing to see and hear, for God has ordained praise from His children, even from me and you today.

For Prayerful Reflection: When have you experienced or witnessed the praises of God's children and known that it pleases God? How can you offer childlike praise today?

Bible in a Year: *1 Kings 19-20; Luke 23:1-25*

May 6

I CAN *Praise* TODAY...
BECAUSE GOD CHASES AWAY DESPAIR THROUGH OUR PRAISE

The Spirit of the Lord God is upon me, because the Lord has anointed me to bring good news to the poor; he has sent me to bind up the brokenhearted, to proclaim liberty to the captives, and the opening of the prison to those who are bound; to proclaim the year of the Lord's favor and the day of vengeance of our God; to comfort all who mourn... to grant to those who mourn in Zion . . . the oil of gladness instead of mourning, the garment of praise instead of a faint spirit. (Isaiah 61:1-3

There is no better way to beat the blues than to know Jesus Christ, and to praise God, for this changes our focus from ourselves to Him. Praise because of Jesus Christ produces in us *the oil of gladness instead of mourning, the garment of praise instead of a faint spirit.* On that Sabbath day in the synagogue of Nazareth, Jesus read the first two verses of this text in the scroll of Isaiah, then declared, *"Today this Scripture has been fulfilled in your hearing."* (Luke 4:21)

Because Jesus truly binds up the brokenhearted, proclaims liberty to captives, and sets free those who are bound, we who know Him are blessed recipients of such grace; finding in Him our remedy in despair, our hope in hopelessness, and our comfort in time of mourning. And as the prophet Isaiah declared, when we know and praise God, grief and despair will ultimately be chased away, replaced with *the oil of gladness* and *the garment of praise.*

Have you not found it true that when your heart is heavy, but in faith you choose to trust Jesus and offer God the praise He is due, your spirit is lifted? This is God's grace for us today.

For Prayerful Reflection: When has your heart been heavy, but your spirit was lifted through faith in Jesus and giving praise? In what personal areas of despair, hopelessness, or grief is God calling you today to give Him praise?

Bible in a Year: *1 Kings 21-22; Luke 23:26-56*

May 7

I CAN *Praise* TODAY . . .
BECAUSE PRAISE IS A WEAPON AGAINST THE DEVIL

O Lord, our Lord, how majestic is your name in all the earth! You have set your glory above the heavens. Out of the mouth of babies and infants, you have established strength because of your foes, to still the enemy and the avenger. (Psalm 8:1-2)

And Jesus said to them, "Yes; have you never read, 'Out of the mouth of infants and nursing babies you have prepared praise'?" (Matthew 21:16)

God uses our praise to *still the enemy and the avenger.* Through the seemingly insignificant mouths of babies and infants, even of your mouth and mine, God chooses to reveal His glory. The Greek translation called the *Septuagint,* and more importantly Jesus' words in Matthew 21:16, reveal that the *strength* referred to in Psalm 8 is strength attributed to God in song or praise. When we praise God and declare His majesty, the Enemy is stilled, and the devil flees.

Why is this so? Every day we are involved in spiritual warfare. The devil aims to discourage Christians and causes us to doubt God's truth. The devil's ideas can seem credible in our minds, but they are rooted in unbelief and rebellion. When we accept demonic suggestions, various results can occur, including confusion, discouragement, fear, doubt, and unbelief. But when we choose to praise God, the lies of the Enemy are effectively silenced.

Are you discouraged today? Are you doubting that God is with you, or that He will intervene in your circumstance? Is the fire of your faith being covered today by a wet blanket of unbelief? Then lift your praises to God, for as you do, the lying voice of the Enemy will be stilled.

For Prayerful Reflection: When has your discouraged soul been lifted? When has doubt been silenced as you offered praise to God? In what areas of life have you recently been hearing the devil's lies to you? Will you now choose to give God praise?

Bible in a Year: *2 Kings 1-3; Luke 24:1-35*

May 8

I CAN *Praise* TODAY . . .
BECAUSE GOD IS WORTHY OF MY PRAISE

I call upon the Lord, who is worthy to be praised. (Psalm 18:3)

They cast their crowns before the throne, saying, "Worthy are you, our Lord and God, to receive glory and honor and power, for you created all things, and by your will they existed and were created." (Revelation 4:10-11)

Then I looked, and I heard around the throne and the living creatures and the elders the voice of many angels, numbering myriads of myriads . . . saying with a loud voice, "Worthy is the Lamb who was slain, to receive power and wealth and wisdom and might and honor and glory and blessing!" (Revelation 5:11-12)

For innumerable reasons God is worthy of our praise. God alone deserves heartfelt worship. God is worthy of your praise and mine, for He alone is God. He is worthy of praise because He created all things by His own power and will. God is worthy of praise because in great grace and mercy the Lamb of God, who is the Lord Jesus Christ, died in our place, thus atoning for our sins and purchasing our salvation for time and eternity. All that we are and have and all that we can ever hope for we owe to God, for it is *in him we live and move and have our being* (Acts 17:28). God is worthy of our praise today, tomorrow, and forever.

How can we praise God today? We can praise Him by professing our faith. We can praise Him by participating in works of love, obedience, and service. We can praise Him by prostrating ourselves before Him in heartfelt worship. We can praise God by giving our treasure and ourselves to Him. God is worthy of our worship today.

For Prayerful Reflection: How and why have you praised God? What are some reasons why God is worthy of your praise today?

Bible in a Year: *2 Kings 4-6; Luke 24:36-53*

May 9

I CAN *Praise* TODAY . . .
BECAUSE GOD'S SON IS SOON RETURNING

The twenty-four elders and the four living creatures fell down and worshiped God who was seated on the throne, saying, "Amen. Hallelujah!" And from the throne came a voice saying, "Praise our God, all you his servants, you who fear him, small and great." (Revelation 19:4-5)

And [the angel] said to me, "These words are trustworthy and true. And the Lord, the God of the spirits of the prophets, has sent his angel to show his servants what must soon take place. And behold, I am coming soon." (Revelation 22:6-7)

It is said that a man once asked the Lord what a million years was like to Him. The Lord responded, "It is just a minute in my sight."

"How about a million dollars?" the man asked. "It can't mean more than a penny to you."

"That is right," the Lord said. "A million dollars is but a penny in my sight."

"Then," said the man, "how about giving me a penny?"

"Sure," said the Lord. "In a minute."

Two millennia ago, our Lord told the apostle John, *"Behold, I am coming soon."* It appears that Jesus' understanding of *soon* is different from ours. But He calls us to believe in and expect His soon return.

A few years ago, when in the valley of decision about the next chapter of my life, I had a vivid dream in which my grandfather told me that God's hand remained on me to pastor. At the end, as he prepared to leave, he gave me a hug; then looking at me intently, he said, "Stephen, Jesus is coming very soon."

For so many reasons God is worthy of our praise. Believing in His soon return compels us to praise Him now. We will soon be praising Him in glory, but we should not be satisfied to wait until then.

For Prayerful Reflection: How have you demonstrated your belief in Jesus' soon coming? How does the prospect of praising God soon in a great heavenly assembly influence your praise today?

Bible in a Year: *2 Kings 7-9; John 1:1-28*

May 10

I CAN *Praise* TODAY . . .
BECAUSE GOD IS ALPHA AND OMEGA

And he who was seated on the throne said, "Behold, I am making all things new." Also he said, "Write this down, for these words are trustworthy and true." And he said to me, "It is done! I am the Alpha and the Omega, the beginning and the end. To the thirsty I will give from the spring of the water of life without payment." (Revelation 21:5-6)

"Behold, I am coming soon . . . I am the Alpha and the Omega, the first and the last, the beginning and the end." (Revelation 22:12-13)

Alpha and Omega are the first and last letters of the Greek alphabet. Jesus says He stood beyond and before the universe's beginning, and He will stand at the end as the sovereign source, creator, and sustainer of everything. Our Lord affirms His divine eternity and authority. And when He returns, His children will be gathered before His glorious throne where our thirst will be quenched by drinking deeply from the spring of the water of life, for His grace has made this possible for us.

Is this not cause for praise today? When we are with Him in heavenly glory, we will overflow with praise, for our hearts will greatly rejoice because of who He is and all He has done for us. He is and will forever be our Alpha and Omega, our first and last, our beginning and end. He is the One who places in our hands the cup of His mercy so we may drink deeply from the spring of the living water. Not only will this be the case for us on that day, it is also the case today. Today He is our all in all, and He is worthy of our praise.

For Prayerful Reflection: What does it mean for you that Jesus Christ has been, is now, and will forever be the Alpha and the Omega? How does the expectation of beholding His heavenly glory affect your praise today?

Bible in a Year: *2 Kings 10-12; John 1:29-51*

May 11

I CAN *Praise* TODAY . . .
BECAUSE GOD IS *I AM*

God said to Moses, "I am who I am." And he said, "Say this to the people of Israel: 'I am has sent me to you.'" God also said to Moses, ". . . This is my name forever, and thus I am to be remembered throughout all generations." (Exodus 3:14-15)

Jesus said to them, "Truly, truly, I say to you, before Abraham was, I am." (John 8:58)

From this name *I am*, *Jehovah* or *Yahweh* is derived. This name is used over 6,800 times in the Bible. It is the personal name of God. The *I am who I am* is where we get the Hebrew *YHWH,* which, according to Jewish tradition, was too holy to say out loud, so it was spelled out in four consonants without vowels, making it unpronounceable. Scholars have noted that in the Hebrew, *I am* could also be translated *I will be*. This is because God transcends time.

God is saying, "*I am who I am,* and I will forever be who *I will be*." As the incarnation of God, Jesus declared that He is *I am*. For claiming this, the Jews picked up stones to kill Him. But no one can change who God is or make Him what we want Him to be. Rather, we can believe and trust God for being who He is.

Because God is *I am* forever, He is worthy of our praise for time and eternity. He is worthy of praise for Who He Has Been, Who He Is, and Who He Will Forever Be. How blessed we are that God has revealed Himself to us, and that through Jesus Christ, we can know Him. And so, we are blessed today to give Him our praise.

For Prayerful Reflection: How has knowing the great *I am* been a blessing in your life? How does knowing the great *I am* impact your praise today?

Bible in a Year: *2 Kings 13-14; John 2*

May 12

I CAN *Praise* TODAY . . .
BECAUSE GOD HEALS THE BROKENHEARTED

The Lord is near to the brokenhearted and saves the crushed in spirit. (Psalm 34:18)

Praise the Lord! For it is good to sing praises to our God; for it is pleasant, and a song of praise is fitting. He heals the brokenhearted and binds up their wounds. (Psalm 147:1, 3)

Who among us has never had a broken heart? It is not an issue of whether our heart has been broken, but of what caused our heart to break. It could be a broken relationship, or a failure, or a broken dream, or the death of someone dear. C. S. Lewis suggested that this is an inevitable part of loving. He wrote, "To love at all is to be vulnerable. Love anything, and your heart will certainly be wrung and possibly broken."[11]

But when our heart breaks, we can bring God the broken pieces. Elisabeth Elliot, whose missionary husband Jim was tragically martyred, wrote,

If the only thing you have to offer is a broken heart, you offer a broken heart. Realizing that nothing I have, nothing I am will be refused on the part of Christ, I simply give it to Him as the little boy gave Jesus his five loaves and two small fishes – with the same feeling of the disciples when they said, "What is the good of that for such a crowd?" In almost anything I offer to Christ, my reaction would be, "What is the good of that?" . . . The use He makes of it is none of my business; it is His business and His blessing.[12]

God takes broken hearts and does something good with them. He heals the brokenhearted. This is cause for praise today.

For Prayerful Reflection: When have you brought the pieces of your broken heart to God and seen Him do something good with them? How does God's healing the brokenhearted impact your praise today?

Bible in a Year: *2 Kings 15-16; John 3:1-18*

---

[11] C. S. Lewis, *The Four Loves*, originally published in 1960.
[12] Elisabeth Elliot, *Worldwide Challenge* (January 1978): 39-40.

May 13

I CAN *Praise* TODAY . . .
BECAUSE GOD SETS CAPTIVES FREE

The Lord sets the prisoners free; the Lord opens the eyes of the blind. The Lord lifts up those who are bowed down. (Psalm 146:7-8)

"The Spirit of the Lord is upon me, because he has anointed me to proclaim good news to the poor. He has sent me to proclaim liberty to the captives." (Luke 4:18)

Who among us has not been imprisoned in some way? We have all been imprisoned by sin, and we have all needed a savior who would liberate us with love and mercy. Jesus Christ has done that for you and me. He sets captives free, which gives us great cause for praise.

I have visited people who were imprisoned for their crimes and facing the hard consequences of what they did. I have counseled and prayed with people who humbly owned their sin with true confession. And as they turned to the Lord Jesus in faith, they were blessed to know His grace and the sweet release of His forgiveness. Though consequences remained, and they were still behind bars, Jesus Christ had set them free.

I have visited others who were also imprisoned for their crimes but who refused humble confession and failed to acknowledge their need for a savior. They thus remained both behind bars and in the spiritual bondage of their sin.

I have also been blessed through the years to know many who had been captives to sin, false religions, addictions of various kinds, heartache, or the darkness of despondency, but they met Jesus, and the transformation that then occurred was beautiful and remarkable. Jesus Christ set them free from the chains that bound them. When such deliverance happens, praise results. We want to praise God for His grace in releasing us from bondage and setting us free. Because God sets captives free, today we have cause for praise.

For Prayerful Reflection: From what captivity and chains has God set you free? How is your gratitude for God's deliverance reflected in your praise today?

Bible in a Year: *2 Kings 17-18; John 3:19-36*

May 14

I CAN *Praise* TODAY . . .
BECAUSE GOD RESCUES US FROM ENEMIES

I love you, O Lord, my strength. The Lord is my rock and my fortress and my deliverer, my God, my rock, in whom I take refuge, my shield, and the horn of my salvation, my stronghold. I call upon the Lord, who is worthy to be praised, and I am saved from my enemies. (Psalm 18:1-3)

In this world we all face enemies: enemies of righteousness, holiness, truth, and peace. David testified of how God had rescued him from enemies, for which he gave God praise. Jesus also acknowledged that we face enemies, and He taught us to love and pray for them (Matthew 5:44)

Voice of the Martyrs shared a story from Richard Wurmbrand of a church leader he met while imprisoned in Romania. The man and his family were eating breakfast one morning when police burst into his home. The family had just read Psalm 23. While being arrested, the minister said to the arresting officer, "You are the fulfillment of what we prayed today. We just read that God prepares a table before us in the presence of our enemies. We had a table, but no enemies. Now you have come . . . You are sent by God."

The officer then screamed, "We'll take you to prison . . . where you will die! You will never see your children again!"

The man replied, "We also read of this today, that I pass through the valley of the shadow of death but do not fear it."

"How should you not fear death?" shouted the officer. "Everyone fears death!"

"A shadow of a dog cannot bite you, and a shadow of death cannot kill you. These things are shadows." Though imprisoned, this church leader was praising God who had truly rescued him.[13] We too can praise God today, for He has rescued us from our enemies.

For Prayerful Reflection: From what enemies has God rescued you? How will you express today your own praise for God's deliverance like David did?

Bible in a Year: *2 Kings 19-21; John 4:1-30*

---
13 Adapted from *Voice of the Martyrs* (February 2000).

May 15

I CAN *Praise* TODAY...
BECAUSE GOD SETS ME HIGH UPON A ROCK

One thing I have asked of the Lord, that will I seek after: that I may dwell in the house of the Lord all the days of my life, to gaze upon the beauty of the Lord and to inquire in his temple. For he will hide me in his shelter in the day of trouble; he will conceal me under the cover of his tent; he will lift me high upon a rock. (Psalm 27:4-5)

After expressing his love and longing for God and his desire to be forever in His presence, the psalmist David reflected that he knows when troubles and storms come in his life, he will always be sheltered and kept safe by God, who *will lift [him] high upon a rock*. This is a comforting and compelling picture, for in times of storms that can come to us, God lifts us up and sets us in a safe place, high upon a rock. God shelters us and keeps us safe. So how do we respond when storms come and floodwaters rise? We come to God in faith, seeking Him and giving Him our praise.

When we face fears or feel overwhelmed, when our hearts are troubled or we grieve, like David we can trust God and give Him our praise, for He is setting us high upon a rock. I have frequently experienced such grace, and I know many who are now receiving such strength. Even today I saw sweet evidence of this as I spoke separately with two friends whose wives had recently died. They are each leaning on God in faith, and He is setting them high above the storm. This is reason to praise God today!

For Prayerful Reflection: When have you faced a storm in life and God set you high upon a rock, for which you praised Him? How do such blessings motivate you today toward giving God praise?

Bible in a Year: *2 Kings 22-23; John 4:31-54*

May 16

I CAN *Praise* TODAY . . .
BECAUSE GOD COMFORTS US IN OUR TROUBLES

Blessed be the God and Father of our Lord Jesus Christ, the Father of mercies and God of all comfort, who comforts us in all our affliction, so that we may be able to comfort those who are in any affliction, with the comfort with which we are ourselves are comforted by God. (2 Corinthians 1:3-4)

In these verses the apostle Paul offers praise to God, who is worthy of praise. The One to whom he gives praise is *the God and Father of our Lord Jesus Christ.* This expresses God's relationship with Jesus as His Father and also Jesus' relationship with us, for He holds all authority over us as Lord. The comfort mentioned here for which Paul gives praise is the blessing that comes to all who trust and yield to the lordship of Jesus Christ. As God blesses us with His comfort, He also equips and allows us to pass on to others some of the comfort He has given to us. This is cause for praise today.

I have experienced this, and perhaps you have too. I give God praise for times He has allowed me to come alongside others who are grieving and share the same comfort He gave me in time of grief. I have also been amazed at how God has blessed others suffering from cancer or other trials through blessings I learned and shared from my journey of suffering in my recent book *Walking with God through Deep Valleys,* subtitled *Lessons on Finding Contentment when Life is Hard.*[14] As God comforts us in all our troubles, and as He blesses us to share His comfort with others, this is cause for praise today.

For Prayerful Reflection: When has God comforted you in your troubles or allowed you the blessing of passing on to others what He gave to you? How do these blessings motivate you in giving praise today?

Bible in a Year: *2 Kings 24-25; John 5:1-24*

---

14 Stephen Gammon, *Walking with God through Deep Valleys* (Abbotsford, WI: Aneko Press, 2020).

May 17

I CAN *Praise* TODAY...
BECAUSE GOD DESIRES PRAISE FROM ALL WHO LIVE

Praise the Lord! Praise the Lord, O my soul! I will praise the Lord as long as I live; I will sing praises to my God while I have my being. (Psalm 146:1-2)

Praise the Lord! Praise God in his sanctuary; praise him in his mighty heavens! Praise him for his mighty deeds; praise him according to his excellent greatness! Let everything that has breath praise the Lord! Praise the Lord! (Psalm 150:1-2, 6)

Can you still fog a mirror? To put it another way, are you still breathing? This question is important, for the Word of God says *let everything that has breath praise the Lord!* As long as we live, God deserves and desires our praise. Yes, we can praise Him in His sanctuary. And yes, we can praise Him under His mighty heavens, for *the heavens declare the glory of God, and the sky above proclaims his handiwork* (Psalm 19:1). We can praise God anywhere, for His mighty deeds are many, and His greatness is forever.

In Psalm 146 the psalmist praised God and expressed his intention to *praise the Lord as long as I live.* We are called to do the same – to lift our focus from ourselves and the world to the greatness of God and give Him the praise He is due. We will do this as long as we live and forevermore.

As we praise God today, we enjoy a foretaste of heaven, when it will be our holy privilege to praise God forevermore for His exceeding greatness. If we resist praising God today, doesn't this call into question our desire and readiness to praise Him soon in glory? If we breathe today, we have reason to give God praise!

For Prayerful Reflection: How deep has your commitment been to praise God daily as long as you live? How does praising God today reflect your longing to praise Him forever in heavenly glory?

Bible in a Year: *1 Chronicles 1-3; John 5:25-47*

May 18

I CAN *Praise* TODAY . . .
BECAUSE GOD IS PRAISED BY VAST MULTITUDES

After this I looked, and behold, a great multitude that no one could number, from every nation, from all tribes and peoples and languages, standing before the throne and before the Lamb, clothed in white robes, with palm branches in their hands, and crying out with a loud voice, "Salvation belongs to our God who sits on the throne, and to the Lamb!" (Revelation 7:9-10)

Then I heard what seemed to be the voice of a great multitude, like the roar of many waters and like the sound of mighty peals of thunder, crying out, "Hallelujah! For the Lord our God the Almighty reigns. Let us rejoice and exult and give him the glory." (Revelation 19:6-7)

Go ahead and picture it! Imagine yourself in these amazing scenes depicted in the book of Revelation, as revealed by Jesus to the apostle John. Large, innumerable multitudes of people from every nation, tongue, and tribe worshipping God and praising the author of our salvation! If you have trusted in Jesus Christ as Savior and Lord, we will be together in that glorious throng. Oh, how wonderful it will be!

Perhaps you have been in other great throngs in which the focus and enthusiasm of the crowd drew you. As a lifelong Boston Red Sox fan, I wished that I could have joined the estimated three million fans who gathered on October 30, 2004, for a parade celebrating the team's first World Series championship in eighty-six years. But far greater is the joy we share when we praise God and join with others who praise Him too, celebrating and relishing His great victory over sin and death, for His victory has become ours too.

For Prayerful Reflection: When have you shared great joy in praising God with others? How does anticipating your future presence in the worship scenes depicted in Revelation affect your praise today?

Bible in a Year: *1 Chronicles 4-6; John 6:1-21*

May 19

I CAN *Praise* TODAY...
BECAUSE GOD HIDES ME BENEATH HIS WINGS

He who dwells in the shelter of the Most High will abide in the shadow of the Almighty. I will say to the Lord, "My refuge and my fortress, my God, in whom I trust." For he will deliver you from the snare of the fowler and from the deadly pestilence. He will cover you with his pinions, and under his wings you will find refuge. (Psalm 91:1-4)

I love this image of hiding under God's wings, for we find safety and refuge there. All of us have faced fire, pestilence, flood, or danger of one kind or another; we all have, and we will again. But if we will pause and look back, remembering the times we have run to God in faith and He delivered us, our hearts will overflow again in praise.

I read of a prairie fire that quickly engulfed a farm. When it was over, the farmer who owned the property walked through the ashes of his home and ranch and saw an old hen lying on the ground, burnt to death. Her wings were spread open. In frustration, he kicked the old hen. To his surprise, several baby chicks ran out from under her burnt wings. When that fire came, the hen had draped herself over her little ones and took the fire to save them. How often God has done this for you and me!

Our loving Lord spread out His arms for us on the cross, covering us with His life and blood! Doesn't this fill our hearts with praise today? How blessed we are to know that we can hide under His wings of love and protection. Our Savior is worthy of our praise today!

For Prayerful Reflection: When have you run to God in faith and found protection under His wings? In what ways will God's life-giving protection overflow today with you giving Him your praise?

Bible in a Year: *1 Chronicles 7-9; John 6:22-44*

May 20

I CAN *Praise* TODAY . . .
BECAUSE GOD DELIVERS FROM EVIL

Because you have made the Lord your dwelling place . . . no evil shall be allowed to befall you, no plague come near your tent. "Because he holds fast to me in love, I will deliver him . . . When he calls to me, I will answer him; I will be with him in trouble; I will rescue him and honor him." (Psalm 91:9-10, 14-15)

"Now the salvation and the power and the kingdom of our God and the authority of his Christ have come, for the accuser of our brothers has been thrown down, who accuses them day and night before our God. And they have conquered him by the blood of the Lamb and by the word of their testimony." (Revelation 12:10-11)

The troubling situations listed in Psalm 91 include terror, pestilence, darkness, destruction, and the death of many. These are real dangers from which God promises to protect us. The psalmist declares what we can profess today: *I will say to the Lord, "My refuge and my fortress, my God, in whom I trust."*

When we place our trust in God, we experience His deliverance, for God promises *no evil shall be allowed to befall you*. Is there evil in this fallen world? There surely is, and our Lord teaches us to trust Him and to pray that God will *deliver us from evil* (Matthew 6:13).

Jesus' dying words from the cross were *"It is finished"* (John 19:30). Through His suffering, shed blood, and death, Jesus Christ finished the work of our salvation. This includes His great victory over Satan and evil. Isn't this reason for praise today? It will surely be in heaven, for God protects and delivers His children from evil.

For Prayerful Reflection: When and how has God delivered you from evil? With His final victory in mind, and praying as He taught us, do you believe and will you praise God today for His deliverance?

Bible in a Year: *1 Chronicles 10-12; John 6:45-71*

May 21

I CAN *Praise* TODAY...
BECAUSE GOD IS MY BLESSED REDEEMER

Then I looked, and I heard around the throne and the living creatures and the elders the voice of many angels ... saying with a loud voice, "Worthy is the Lamb who was slain, to receive power and wealth and wisdom and might and honor and glory and blessing!" (Revelation 5:11-12)

The book of Revelation reveals that a major theme of praise in heaven is giving praise to our blessed Redeemer. As we will be singing His praise then, it is good for us to praise Him now. A favorite hymn on this theme was authored by Fanny Crosby, who was born in 1820. Fanny was a blind, brilliant woman of God. She served as a teacher at the New York Institution for the Blind. She knew many portions of the Bible by heart, including all four Gospels, which she had memorized as a child.

One of her hymns reflects the praise that is offered in heaven to Jesus our blessed Redeemer:

> Praise Him! Praise Him! Jesus, our blessed Redeemer!
>   Sing, O Earth, His wonderful love proclaim!
> Hail Him! Hail Him! Highest archangels in glory;
>   Strength and honor give to His holy Name!
> Like a shepherd, Jesus will guard His children,
>   In His arms He carries them all day long.
> Praise Him! Praise Him! Tell of His excellent greatness;
>   Praise Him! Praise Him! Ever in joyful song!

We have very good reason to give God praise today, for He is our blessed Redeemer!

For Prayerful Reflection: To what extent have you grasped that the Lord is your Redeemer, thus causing you to praise Him? How does the promise of praising your Redeemer in heaven affect you today?

Bible in a Year: *1 Chronicles 13-15; John 7:1-27*

May 22

I CAN *Praise* TODAY ...
BECAUSE GOD SOUGHT AND FOUND ME

"What man of you, having a hundred sheep, if he has lost one of them, does not leave the ninety-nine in the open country, and go after the one that is lost, until he finds it? And when he has found it, he lays it on his shoulders, rejoicing. And when he comes home, he calls together his friends and his neighbors, saying to them, 'Rejoice with me, for I have found my sheep that was lost.'" (Luke 15:4-6)

One of my favorite cartoon movies is *Finding Nemo*. Nemo is a little fish, and the story shows the love and determination of his dad, who watched lovingly over Nemo. But one day Nemo disobeyed his father and swam beyond the reef; he was then scooped up by a diver and taken away. Nemo's disobedience caused him to be separated from his father; there was nothing he could do to return home. Nemo ended up in a fish tank in a dentist's office, and his situation seemed hopeless.

But his father loved him so much that it didn't matter to him how big the ocean was. He set out on an incredible adventure to seek and save his son. Eventually, word of his dad's incredible journey reached little Nemo, who was thrilled to learn of his father's love and search for him. Nemo then took a step of faith and jumped out of the fish tank; he went down a drain that led to the ocean. What a great ending when Nemo is saved, home at last with his loving dad.[15]

God has always loved us. He went to great lengths to find us and bring us home. This is cause for praise today and forever.

For Prayerful Reflection: What does it mean to you that God so loved you that He came to seek and save you? How does the realization of His love and of your salvation affect your praise today?

Bible in a Year: *1 Chronicles 16-18; John 7:28-53*

---

[15] *Finding Nemo,* Directed by Andrew Stanton and Lee Unkrich, Produced by Pixar Animation Studios, Released by Walt Disney Pictures, 2003.

May 23

I CAN *Praise* TODAY . . .
BECAUSE GOD DEFENDS ME

O Lord, how many are my foes! Many are rising against me; many are saying of my soul, "There is no salvation for him in God." But you, O Lord, are a shield about me, my glory, and the lifter of my head. I cried aloud to the Lord, and he answered me from his holy hill. I lay down and slept; I woke again, for the Lord sustained me. I will not be afraid of many thousands of people who have set themselves against me all around. (Psalm 3:1-6)

This is the first psalm with a title, which is *"Save Me, O My God."* Humanly speaking, David is in dire straits, but he knows who to turn to, and he models faith for us here. David knows that God was and is his defender. He looks back and recalls the many times and ways God has cared for and defended him, delivering him in times of danger and trouble. Because David knew that God is the same today, despite how dire circumstances may appear, he testifies that he has been able to sleep peacefully.

Have you been in situations when that was not the case for you – when in fact you were so troubled in heart and mind that you were filled with worry and unable to sleep? I have been there, and I expect you have too. By God's grace I have often applied the lessons of this psalm and remembered that God has been, is now, and will always be my defender. He will always be faithful too. So no matter what the chaos of today is, I can praise God. We can know that God will surely see us through.

For Prayerful Reflection: When have you been in dire straits but God defended you and saw you through? How does this promise and truth about God affect your praise today?

Bible in a Year: *1 Chronicles 19-21; John 8:1-27*

May 24

I CAN *Praise* TODAY . . .
BECAUSE GOD IS MY PROVIDER

Abraham lifted up his eyes and looked, and behold, behind him was a ram, caught in a thicket by his horns. And Abraham went and took the ram and offered it up as a burnt offering instead of his son. So Abraham called the name of that place, "The Lord will provide." (Genesis 22:13-14)

And my God will supply every need of yours according to his riches in glory in Christ Jesus. (Philippians 4:19)

As Isaac and Abraham climbed Mount Moriah together, Isaac asked his dad an obvious question: *"Behold, the fire and the wood, but where is the lamb for a burnt offering?" Abraham said, "God will provide for himself the lamb for a burnt offering, my son"* (Genesis 22:7-8).

We read the amazing story of how Abraham was willing to trust God and lay down the life of his son Isaac. Can we then imagine his joy when God spoke and spared Isaac's life? He provided the lamb for the burnt offering! I assure you, Abraham and Isaac both overflowed with praise to God for His gracious provision that day.

God is our provider too, and for this we give Him praise. What needs have you had for which God has provided and for which you gave Him praise today? God provides for all of our needs: food, shelter, protection, clothes, income, rest, relationships, peace, freedom, knowledge, spiritual birth, everlasting life, and more. Because God is our provider, we can give Him praise today.

What is your greatest need? Isn't it a relationship with God? This is ours through faith in Jesus, the Lamb of God, who forgives, restores, and gives everlasting life. When Jesus Christ becomes our first love and highest priority, we seek Him first, and thus experience firsthand God's provision for all our needs. God is my provider, and it is my privilege to give Him praise today.

For Prayerful Reflection: What needs have you seen God wonderfully provide for you for which you gave Him praise? What provisions from God are leading you to praise Him today?

Bible in a Year: *1 Chronicles 22-24; John 8:28-59*

May 25

I CAN *Praise* TODAY . . .
BECAUSE GOD LEADS HIS DEAR CHILDREN ALONG

Thus says the Lord, your Redeemer, the Holy One of Israel: "I am the Lord your God . . . who leads you in the way you should go." (Isaiah 48:17)

As Jesus passed on from there, he saw a man called Matthew sitting at the tax booth, and he said to him, "Follow me." And he rose and followed him. (Matthew 9:9)

God leads His dear children along. And how blessed we are to follow Him wherever and however He leads. When Jesus called His earliest disciples, His call was always *"Follow me."* When they first heard His call, did they have any idea how wonderful this privilege was that Christ was offering to them? They did not, nor do we, but the longer we follow and serve Him, the sweeter He becomes to us.

Have you noticed that when Jesus' disciples were called to follow Him, not one of them asked, "Where are we going?" We who love Him now do not ask this question either, for our desire is to go wherever He leads, no matter where He leads. Our desire is simply to be with Him and to do whatever He bids us do.

I can recall vividly and with joy when at the age of nineteen I clearly heard my Lord call me to follow His leading in my life. By His grace I said yes to His call to follow Him. I have been blessed to do just that, and the joy of it has often stirred praise in my heart for God's great love and for the blessing and clarity of His leading. For this I praise Him today, for lately I have marveled again at His grace in leading me. Because God leads today, we have much cause to give Him praise!

For Prayerful Reflection: When has God answered your prayers and made His direction clear, for which you gave Him praise? How is He leading you now, for which you praise Him today?

Bible in a Year: *1 Chronicles 25-27; John 9:1-23*

May 26

I CAN *Praise* TODAY...
BECAUSE GOD IS MERCIFUL

For the Lord your God is a merciful God. He will not leave you or destroy you or forget the covenant with your fathers that he swore to them. (Deuteronomy 4:31)

You, O Lord, are a God merciful and gracious, slow to anger and abounding in steadfast love and faithfulness. (Psalm 86:15)

And Jesus said, "Father, forgive them, for they know not what they do." (Luke 23:34)

Mercy is giving compassionate treatment towards an offender or adversary who is in one's power or care. Recipients of mercy are receivers of leniency, forgiveness, kindness, and grace. Thanks be to God, who does not treat us as our sins deserve, for God is merciful to us. Even from the cross, in the intensity of His suffering because of my sin and yours, our Lord prayed for us with mercy: *"Father, forgive them, for they know not what they do."*

Imagine having an insurmountable debt, so large you know you could never possibly repay it, and the deserved and inevitable consequence of your debt is lifelong imprisonment until death. If then your debt was suddenly, unexpectedly, and entirely paid for and fully forgiven, wouldn't this fill your heart with overwhelming praise that would burst forth from you like a wellspring of joy? It surely would! Would there ever be a day when you would forget the blessing of receiving such mercy? Is your heart then filled with praise to God today?

In Matthew 18 Jesus told a story that warns us. A certain man was forgiven an astronomical debt, but failed to appreciate it, so he failed to show the mercy of forgiving another. May God help us who are recipients of His mercy to always praise Him and extend His mercy to others.

For Prayerful Reflection: What has it meant to you to be a recipient of God's mercy? How is receiving this blessing reflected in your praise today?

Bible in a Year: *1 Chronicles 28-29; John 9:24-41*

May 27

I CAN *Praise* TODAY . . .
BECAUSE GOD MAKES ALL THINGS NEW

Therefore, if anyone is in Christ, he is a new creation. The old has passed away; behold, the new has come. All this is from God. (2 Corinthians 5:17-18)

And he who was seated on the throne said, "Behold, I am making all things new." (Revelation 21:5)

My wife Helen likes watching those TV shows that show home restoration. You see the home in obvious need of renovation, and at the end you see the remade home. When the family who will live there sees the beautiful change, they cannot help but overflow with joy and praise.

This is what God is doing. He transforms everything. Some of His transformation is dramatic, complete, and immediate, as when we first trusted in Christ and were then born from above, becoming God's own children. We became *a new creation*. But the restoration process continues, as some of His *making all things new* within us happens over time, as we become more and more like Jesus.

Looking ahead in faith to the end of the story, after Christ's glorious return, when we will be with Him and all the saints from all the ages in the glory of heaven, we will then see the completion of God's restoration. Our hearts will overflow with praise, for God will have done just as He has promised: *"Behold, I am making all things new."* Because God has made, is making, and will make all things new, we have very good reason to give Him praise today.

For Prayerful Reflection: What new thing has God done in you? What restorations has God done, is God now doing, or is God yet to do for which you give Him praise today?

Bible in a Year: *2 Chronicles 1-3; John 10:1-23*

May 28

I CAN *Praise* TODAY . . .
BECAUSE GOD GRANTS THE DESIRES OF OUR HEART

Delight yourself in the Lord, and he will give you the desires of your heart. (Psalm 37:4)

"The kingdom of heaven is like treasure hidden in a field, which a man found and covered up. Then in his joy he goes and sells all that he has and buys that field." (Matthew 13:44)

How wonderful to have a God who loves us and is so generous, giving, and good that He grants His children the desires of our hearts! What cause for praise today!

What does this promise and attribute of God really mean? It does not mean that whenever we want something God will give it to us. Imagine if we did this to our children. Would it not lead to their becoming entitled, ungrateful, and self-focused? Just like children, sometimes what we desire would be harmful to us.

The condition of God's promise is *delight yourself in the Lord.* In other words, desire above all the greatest treasure. When we do this, increasingly we long for what is good, for what God desires. Then God *will give you the desires of your heart.*

When we have come to love and follow Jesus, we feel like we have found the greatest treasure of all. And in finding this treasure, we desire it more than anything. We long for God, for His presence, love, and will. When our greatest desire is for the greatest thing and for what He desires, then God gives us what we long for. God gives us the desires of our heart, which is cause for praise today!

For Prayerful Reflection: What desires of your heart has God given to you? What treasures have you found in Jesus Christ, for which you give Him praise today?

Bible in a Year: *2 Chronicles 4-6; John 10:24-42*

May 29

I CAN *Praise* TODAY . . .
BECAUSE GOD IS DESERVING

"Yours, O Lord, is the greatness and the power and the glory and the victory and the majesty, for all that is in the heavens and in the earth is yours. Yours is the kingdom, O Lord, and you are exalted as head above all. And now we thank you, our God, and praise your glorious name." (1 Chronicles 29:11, 13)

Some of the Pharisees in the crowd said to [Jesus], "Teacher, rebuke your disciples." He answered, "I tell you, if these were silent, the very stones would cry out." (Luke 19:39-40)

For from him and through him and to him are all things. To him be glory forever. Amen. (Romans 11:36)

God is forever deserving of praise, even today! Can we picture the scene of the interaction between Jesus and the religious leaders who were incensed because of the praise being offered to God on the day of Jesus' entry into Jerusalem? They said to Him, *"Teacher, rebuke your disciples."* But our Lord's reply was *"If these were silent, the very stones would cry out."* Amen. Whether we choose to praise God or not, He is deserving of praise.

Many Scriptures make this point, for God is the author and creator of everything, and He is the One who gave us life. Infinite majesty and glory are His, and He is the One who extends mercy, grace, forgiveness, and love to us. God is worthy of our praise today.

And there is joy in praising Him. On my prayer walks with my Lord, I often find myself lifting my hands and voice in praise to God, who is worthy of all of this and more. And as I praise Him, my heart often overflows with contentment, adoration, and joy, for praising God is a privilege that deeply satisfies my soul. God is deserving of our praise today.

For Prayerful Reflection: Why is God deserving of your praise, and when have you known joy in praising Him? Will you take time to praise God today, because in your heart He is worthy?

Bible in a Year: *2 Chronicles 7-9; John 11:1-29*

May 30

I CAN *Praise* TODAY . . .
BECAUSE GOD HAS SPOKEN

Ezra opened the book in the sight of all the people, for he was above all the people, and as he opened it all the people stood. And Ezra blessed the Lord, the great God, and all the people answered, "Amen, Amen," lifting up their hands. And they bowed their heads and worshiped the Lord with their faces to the ground. They read from the book, from the Law of God, clearly, and they gave the sense, so that the people understood the reading. . . . And there was very great rejoicing. (Nehemiah 8:5-6, 8, 17)

Have there been times in your life when you heard God speaking, and your heart was filled with praise? This is what happened on the day described in Nehemiah 8. The people of God were in distress because of the chaos in their world and the destruction all around them. Many were afraid. But that day Ezra the priest read from the book of God's Word, and the people listened, understood, and believed it was true. God was speaking, so they lifted their hearts and hands to the Lord in surrender and praise. They bowed before the Lord.

Whenever God speaks, and we have heard Him, we want to give Him praise. There are many times this has been true for me. Several times when in the valley of decision regarding God's plan for me, I desired His will, so I prayed for His leading and opened His Word. In various ways and always by His Word, God has spoken and confirmed His will for me. When I heard His voice and knew His leading, my heart has always overflowed with praise. Because God has spoken, He is worthy of our praise today.

For Prayerful Reflection: When have you heard God speaking to you such that you gave Him your praise? What will it mean for you today to listen carefully to God's Word and to praise Him as He speaks?

Bible in a Year: *2 Chronicles 10-12; John 11:30-57*

May 31

I CAN *Praise* TODAY . . .
BECAUSE I KNOW GOD LOVES ME

[Jesus] said to them, "Cast the net on the right side of the boat, and you will find some." So, they cast it, and now they were not able to haul it in, because of the quantity of fish. That disciple whom Jesus loved therefore said to Peter, "It is the Lord!" (John 21:6-7)

Do you regard yourself as one who is dearly loved by Jesus? I hope you do, for He loves you so. Realizing this fills us with praise. In the gospel penned by John, when referring to himself, he typically did so in the third person. If you were to do this, what phrase would you use to describe yourself? How about adopting John's phrase: *that disciple whom Jesus loved.* One of the first songs my parents taught me and the last song my dad wanted his family to sing with him before he was promoted to heaven was "Jesus Loves Me." Oh yes, He surely does!

One of John's last uses of this phrase in his Gospel was when he described the lakeshore, post-resurrection encounter that happened early one morning. After they had fished all night and caught nothing, someone on shore called out to them and told them to do something that made no sense – to cast their net on the other side of the boat. But this likely sounded familiar to John, for on that memorable day when Jesus first called him to follow and to be a fisher of men, the Lord had given similar instruction, and now He was telling John and the others to cast out their nets again, even though they had fished all night and caught nothing.

So on this glorious morning, when they did as the voice instructed them, their net was suddenly filled with fish. *That disciple whom Jesus loved* was the first one to realize and joyfully proclaim, *"It is the Lord!"* How his heart rejoiced with praise! Recognizing Jesus and His love fills us with praise each day.

For Prayerful Reflection: When and to what extent have you realized that you are a *disciple whom Jesus love[s]*? How does knowing that God loves you impact the praise you offer Him today?

Bible in a Year: *2 Chronicles 13-14; John 12:1-26*

12 Themes on Following Jesus

JUNE

Because God . . .
I Can *Love* Today

June 1

I CAN *Love* TODAY ...
BECAUSE GOD IS LOVE

God said, "Let us make man in our image, after our likeness." (Genesis 1:26)

Beloved, let us love one another, for love is from God, and whoever loves has been born of God and knows God. Anyone who does not love does not know God, because God is love. So we have come to know and to believe the love that God has for us. God is love, and whoever abides in love abides in God, and God abides in him. (1 John 4:7-8, 16)

The Bible says *God is love.* Love is God's essence and is evident in what He does. God therefore gives of Himself to us, for this is love. Love always pursues relationship and gives for that relationship. This is what God has done and is doing today for you and me. He cannot do otherwise, for God is love.

We all inherit various physical traits from our birth parents, which are contained within our family DNA. God, our heavenly Father, is our spiritual parent, so His DNA of love is passed on to us. We are created to love, and we give evidence that we are God's children by demonstrating His traits – especially love.

Why can we love God and the people in our lives who are so dear to us? And why can we love the unlovely and those who are hurt and broken? And why can we even love those who have hurt us? We can love because God is love, and His love has flowed into us and now flows through us to others. We can love because our new birth, which came to us by God's grace and through our faith in Jesus Christ, has resulted in our inheriting the DNA of God's love. We can love today, because God is love, and God is in us!

For Prayerful Reflection: What does it imply for your spiritual character that your heavenly Father is love? How can knowing that God is love and that His love is in you affect the way you love today?

Bible in a Year: *2 Chronicles 15-16; John 12:27-50*

June 2

I CAN *Love* TODAY . . .
BECAUSE GOD COMMANDS LOVING HIM AND PEOPLE

"Teacher, which is the great commandment in the Law?" And [Jesus] said to him, "You shall love the Lord your God with all your heart and with all your soul and with all your mind. This is the great and first commandment. And a second is like it: You shall love your neighbor as yourself. On these two commandments depend all the Law and the Prophets." (Matthew 22:36-40)

"If you love me, you will keep my commandments." (John 14:15)

God commands His children to love, for this is the essence of who He is, and therefore, it is the essence of who we are in Him. God's commands are reduced in simplicity to this: Love God and love people. The fact that God commands this reveals that love is not merely an emotion for us. If love were a feeling, it could not be commanded. Could a parent rightly say to a child, "Go to your room right now and be happy"? Or could a boss say to an employee, "I order you to feel excited about your job or you are fired"?

Feelings cannot be commanded. Love is much more than a feeling. God commands us to love Him and to love others, which is to demonstrably act in love. No matter how we feel on any particular day, with God's help and by His clear command, we are able to act in love toward God, our spouse, our children, our parents, our co-workers, our neighbors, and even our enemies. Obeying God's command means acting in love.

William Booth, founder of the Salvation Army, was quoted as saying, "You cannot warm the hearts of people with God's love if they have empty stomachs and cold feet." This is true. And so, as God has commanded us and as He gives us opportunity today, let us act in His love.

For Prayerful Reflection: What does it mean for you to love God and love people? How might you demonstrate love today in obedience to God's command?

Bible in a Year: *2 Chronicles 17-18; John 13:1-20*

June 3

I CAN *Love* TODAY...
BECAUSE GOD HAS LOVED ME SACRIFICIALLY

"For God so loved the world, that he gave his only Son, that whoever believes in him should not perish, but have eternal life." (John 3:16)

"Greater love has no one than this, that someone lay down his life for his friends." (John 15:13)

God shows his love for us in that while we were still sinners, Christ died for us. (Romans 5:8)

When it comes to expressing love, actions do speak louder than words. The Bible is full of words about God's sacrificial love for us, which He has put into powerful action.

Some years ago, a young mom was making her way on foot across the hills of South Wales, carrying her infant son. A blinding blizzard overtook them, and the mother never reached her destination. Searchers found her lifeless body with the baby snuggled beneath her, warm and alive. She had taken off her outer clothing and scarf and wrapped them all around the boy; then she covered him with her own body. That little baby was David Lloyd George, who in time became the British prime minister. He owed his life to his mother's sacrificial love.[16] Every loving parent says, "Of course, my child, that is what I would do."

Our God has sacrificially loved you and me like this. God's only Son, the Lord Jesus Christ, gave His own life for us upon the cross, so that we might be saved. God paid the highest price imaginable, so we receive the fullness of His life and love for us. We can thus experience a personal relationship with God today and for eternity. We can love today because God has sacrificially loved us.

For Prayerful Reflection: How have you experienced God's sacrificial love for you? How can you sacrificially love today?

Bible in a Year: *2 Chronicles 19-20; John 13:21-38*

---

[16] *Today in the Word* (January 1998).

June 4

I CAN *Love* TODAY . . .
BECAUSE GOD SHOWS ME HOW TO LOVE

Jesus, knowing that the Father had given all things into his hands, and that he had come from God and was going back to God, rose from supper. He laid aside his outer garments, and taking a towel, tied it around his waist. Then he poured water into a basin and began to wash the disciples' feet and to wipe them with the towel that was wrapped around him. [Then Jesus said,] "For I have given you an example, that you also should do just as I have done to you. By this all people will know that you are my disciples, if you have love for one another."
(John 13:3-5, 15, 35)

On His last night with His disciples before His crucifixion, Jesus emphasized His love and instructed us to love one another as He has loved us. He demonstrated what love looks like by washing His disciples' feet. Washing someone's dirty feet might seem like a weird task, but in those days it was necessary, for people wore sandals, and most of their travel was done by walking. So feet became very dirty. Washing dirty feet was considered the task of a lowly servant.

But on the night of Jesus' betrayal and arrest, He gathered with His disciples for that intimate observance of the Passover Feast, in which He instituted the observance we call Holy Communion. The Bible says Jesus knew that He had all of God's authority and power and that He would soon be returning to God in heaven. He also knew that He was about to show the depth of God's love for humanity by dying for us on the cross.

But that evening, what did Jesus do? He showed us how to love like a lowly servant. Humbly, tenderly, up close, and personally, Jesus washed the dirty feet of His disciples. And when He finished, He told us to love one another like that.

For Prayerful Reflection: What are some ways God has shown His love for you? How can you love like that today?

Bible in a Year: *2 Chronicles 21-22; John 14*

June 5

I CAN *Love* TODAY . . .
BECAUSE GOD IS THE SOURCE OF LOVE

Beloved, let us love one another, for love is from God, and whoever loves has been born of God and knows God. Anyone who does not love does not know God, because God is love. Beloved, if God so loved us, we also ought to love one another. (1 John 4:7-8, 11)

Need love? God has an infinite supply. Several years ago in New Orleans, Louisiana, while crossing the Mississippi River on a ferry, I marveled at the size and power of that river; I thought of all the waters that had fed into it, and I praised God. Helen and I are now living in Minnesota, which contains the headwaters of the Mississippi. At a spot where the water is about eighteen inches deep, one can cross the river on foot. Between Minnesota and the Gulf of Mexico, waters enter this river from an enormous, far-ranging river basin. No wonder the river is so huge. In Minnesota, we have over ten thousand lakes, including the deepest lake in North America. It is estimated that in Lake Superior there is enough water to cover all of North and South America in a foot and a half of water.

Where does it all come from? Creator God is the source of it all, and the source of all love. Paul prayed that Christians would be *rooted and grounded in love, [having] strength to comprehend with all the saints what is the breadth and length and height and depth* of God's love (Ephesians 3:17-18). Sometimes we can see it deep and wide. Other times perhaps we wade through it. But we can always know that the supply is unending. God's river of life and love always flows and welcomes us to see it and to enter His love, knowing there is an infinite supply. We who are so deeply loved by God can now love in His name.

For Prayerful Reflection: When have you experienced the deep, deep love of God for you? Reflecting on His infinite supply, how can you love extravagantly today?

Bible in a Year: *2 Chronicles 23-24; John 15*

June 6

I CAN *Love* TODAY . . .
BECAUSE GOD WILL NEVER STOP LOVING ME

In all these things we are more than conquerors through him who loved us. For I am sure that neither death nor life, nor angels nor rulers, nor things present nor things to come, nor powers, nor height nor depth, nor anything else in all creation, will be able to separate us from the love of God in Christ Jesus our Lord. (Romans 8:37-39)

Give thanks to the God of heaven, for his steadfast love endures forever. (Psalm 136:26)

As a sports fan, I admire players and teams who give their all in pursuit of victory. With determination such athletes practice and train, so when their best is needed, they are prepared. Through my years of serving in the military, I saw the same concept as troops practiced, exercised, drilled, and trained, and then did it some more in pursuit of excellence, so that if conflicts came, they were ready.

God's Word reminds followers of Jesus Christ that though we all face battles in life, *we are more than conquerors*. How is this so? It's *through him who loved us.* In other words, because of God's great and never-ending love for us, His victory is coming. It comes because we are on His team, and He is leading now. In the battles of this life, ultimate victory is assured because of who Jesus Christ is, what He has done for us, and because nothing will ever separate us from His love.

Perhaps you have known the pain of promised love that has become broken love. Such pain is very deep. But we can be assured today that this cannot and will not happen with God. He deeply loves us today, *for his steadfast love endures forever.* And because His love never stops, we can keep on loving too.

For Prayerful Reflection: If you have experienced the pain of broken love, how has this affected your trust in God's love for you? As you reflect on God's enduring love, how will you keep on loving?

Bible in a Year: *2 Chronicles 25-27; John 16*

June 7

I CAN *Love* TODAY . . .
BECAUSE GOD LIVES IN ME AND LOVES THROUGH ME

I have been crucified with Christ. It is no longer I who live, but Christ who lives in me. And the life I now live in the flesh, I live by faith in the Son of God who loved me and gave himself for me. (Galatians 2:20)

The fruit of the Spirit is love, joy, peace, patience, kindness, goodness, faithfulness, gentleness, self-control. (Galatians 5:22-23)

It is God who works in you, both to will and to work for his good pleasure. (Philippians 2:13)

The Bible says that when we put our trust in Jesus Christ as our Savior and Lord, our old sinful self (the way we were) dies, because we *have been crucified with Christ*. So remarkable is this spiritual transformation that the apostle Paul said, *It is no longer I who live, but Christ who lives in me*. Think about that for a moment. When you put your trust in Jesus Christ, you invited Him in, and He gladly moved in. This means Christ lives in you now, not as a guest but as Lord of your home and heart.

Among other things, this means that today you are able to love, and you will love, for Christ enables you. This is the character of your Lord *who loved [us] and gave himself for [us]*. Because God lives in you and loves you now, His character will increasingly be seen in you. The *fruit of the Spirit*, which is the nature of God, will therefore increasingly become your nature. And what is the first spiritual fruit mentioned by Paul in Galatians 5? It is love. When you cannot easily love, what you can do is ask Jesus Christ who lives in you to love through you. He can and will love through you today.

For Prayerful Reflection: What has it meant for you to have Jesus Christ, the Lord of love, living in you? What will it mean for you today to allow Christ to love through you?

Bible in a Year: *2 Chronicles 28-29; John 17*

June 8

I CAN *Love* TODAY . . .
BECAUSE GOD'S LOVE IS GIVEN, NOT EARNED

But God, being rich in mercy, because of the great love with which he loved us, even when we were dead in our trespasses, made us alive together with Christ—by grace you have been saved—and raised us up with him and seated us with him in the heavenly places in Christ Jesus, so that in the coming ages he might show the immeasurable riches of his grace in kindness toward us in Christ Jesus. For by grace you have been saved through faith. And this is not your own doing; it is the gift of God.
(Ephesians 2:4-8)

None of us deserve God's love, nor could we ever earn it, yet He loves us. God loves us so much that He paid the highest price imaginable to offer us forgiveness and eternal life with Him. No one could earn such grace, no matter what our actions are or how religious we are. *But God, being rich in mercy, because of the great love with which he loved us* has made us alive forever through Jesus Christ. God's love is a priceless gift to be received and forever treasured.

Sometimes we can be very hard on ourselves, for we all fall short. We say, think, or do things that we are ashamed of. We can determine to do better, but in time we fall short again. So we can struggle with believing that God really loves us. When we regard ourselves that harshly, we will do the same toward others and struggle to forgive and love.

The answer to this is to know that God truly loves you and me, not because we have earned it, but because of His grace. When we accept this truth, we can then forgive as we have been forgiven, and we can love as we have been loved.

For Prayerful Reflection: To what degree have you accepted that no matter how you've fallen short, God really loves you? What will it mean for you today to extend love to others as Christ has to you?

Bible in a Year: *2 Chronicles 30-31; John 18:1-18*

June 9

I CAN *Love* TODAY . . .
BECAUSE GOD ALWAYS ABOUNDS IN LOVE FOR US

You, O Lord, are a God merciful and gracious, slow to anger and abounding in steadfast love and faithfulness. (Psalm 86:15)

The steadfast love of the Lord never ceases; his mercies never come to an end; they are new every morning; great is your faithfulness. (Lamentations 3:22-23)

No matter what the changing circumstances of our lives are, God's love for us continues, steadfast and true. The story is told of the renown nineteenth-century English preacher and Bible teacher Charles Spurgeon, who was walking one day with his friend through the English countryside and noticed a weather vane on the roof of a barn that had no rooster on top, simply the words *God is Love*. Spurgeon said to his friend that he thought this was an inappropriate place for such a message, for he said, "Weather vanes are changeable, but God's love is constant."

His friend said, "I don't agree with you, Charles. You misunderstood the meaning. That sign indicates a truth about God's love. Regardless of which way the wind blows, God is love. When we yield ourselves wholly to the Lord, we can see God's love in all kinds of storms and circumstantial winds of favor or opposition" (source unknown).

Amen. The wonder of God's love for us never fails or ends, no matter the circumstances. When I was diagnosed with cancer and in my darkest days, the love of God remained steadfast and ever faithful. When life has been challenging and hard, filled with grief, uncertainty, or pain, God's love has always been sweet and constant. If and when your life is tough or difficult, please look up and see the evidence of God's great love for you. The wind of God's love is still blowing today, and it covers you.

For Prayerful Reflection: When and how in difficult circumstances have you been reminded of God's love for you? How does this reminder bless you today?

Bible in a Year: *2 Chronicles 32-33; John 18:19-40*

June 10

I CAN *Love* TODAY . . .
BECAUSE GOD DELIGHTS IN THOSE HE LOVES

He brought me out into a broad place; he rescued me, because he delighted in me. (Psalm 18:19)

The Lord your God is in your midst, a mighty one who will save; he will rejoice over you with gladness; he will quiet you by his love; he will exult over you with loud singing. (Zephaniah 3:17)

In the days of the prophet Zephaniah, things were very dark. Many Israelites had abandoned God, and there was so much sin and injustice in the land. Zephaniah's message was largely of doom, the ultimate consequence of sin. But then through this prophet, God offered a message of hope to those who would hear and believe – that God in great mercy would take away their punishment and forgive their sins.

We can imagine the comfort received by the people who heard and believed this message. Though God's judgment for sin is wholly justified, in merciful love He offers salvation and hope. His love is so deep it cannot be contained. God even bursts into singing.

I love this image of God holding us in His arms, quieting us by His love, and singing over us. Having raised children and now having grandchildren, this image touches me. When you have a child who is hurting, afraid, or in danger, you want to hold them close, don't you? You want to hug them, tell them you love them, and let them know everything is going to be okay. Sometimes you may even want to sing a song of joy, life, and love over them.

God reminds all who see and love Him as our heavenly Father that He holds us like that. He loves and takes delight in us. When we are in God's arms, we are right where He wants us to be. Our privilege today is to let Him hold us, to let Him love us, to enjoy the song, and to love Him in return.

For Prayerful Reflection: When and how in difficult circumstances have you been reminded of God's great love for you? How is this reminder blessing you today?

Bible in a Year: *2 Chronicles 34-36; John 19:1-22*

June 11

I CAN *Love* TODAY . . .
BECAUSE GOD HAS MADE ME HIS CHILD

See what kind of love the Father has given to us, that we should be called children of God; and so we are. (1 John 3:1)

We are dearly loved children of God. We have heard before the beautiful phrase *children of God*, but today let's take some time to let it sink in afresh. God, our heavenly Father, calls and regards you and me as His very own children. When we enter into personal relationship with God through faith in Jesus Christ, we become God's own child. As His dearly loved children, God delights in us. Wanting the best for us, God desires to fill us with love, joy, and blessing.

For many years my sister Marilee has been involved in His Hands Ministries, a Christian organization whose ministries include coordinating sponsorships for precious children in various nations, so they can be provided the necessities of life: love, food, shelter, clothing, education, and medical care. A few years ago, I partnered with this ministry to support some dear children in Myanmar, as our Lord vividly reminded me when I visited them that each one of them is His dearly loved child.

Many years earlier I had come to further understand our Lord's sentiment toward His children when Helen and I loved a little boy and adopted him as our son. We still love him and always will. Likewise, God loves you and me, for we are His dearly loved children today, and we will be forever. Did we earn His love? No. But in faith and deep gratitude we can receive it. And we who have been so loved by God are enabled, taught, and blessed by Him to love today, even as He has loved us.

For Prayerful Reflection: When did you first realize that you really are God's own child? How has this realization blessed you? How does being God's child affect the way you love today?

Bible in a Year: *Ezra 1-2; John 19:23-42*

June 12

I CAN *Love* TODAY . . .
BECAUSE GOD'S LOVE IS THE PERFECT MODEL

> *"A new commandment I give to you, that you love one another: just as I have loved you, you also are to love one another. By this all people will know that you are my disciples, if you have love for one another."*
> (John 13:34-35)

My son Jonathan, who is also a dad now, once said to me, "Dad, you showed me how to be a good and loving father." What treasured words to hear – though I know and confess again that I certainly have not always loved as my heavenly Father has loved me. Yet He still loves me, and He loves you too. I pray that you may know in your soul today that God loves you very much, for He has shown His love to you, and He shows it over and over again.

Shortly before Jesus was to die for you and me, while sharing the Passover observance with His disciples, Jesus wanted them to hear and see the depth of His love for them. He expressed this in the treasured gifts of the Lord's Supper, vivid reminders of His broken body and shed blood for you and me. He also tenderly expressed His love to each of them and served them individually by washing their feet. And then what did He say? Jesus said that the way He has loved us is how we are to love each other.

Jesus Christ is the perfect model of love. He not only calls us to love, but He also demonstrates how to love by loving us first. God enables us to love today, as we walk in personal relationship with Him and share with others the love we have received.

For Prayerful Reflection: What are some ways God has demonstrated His love for you? What might it look like for you to do as our Lord has instructed – to love as He has loved you?

Bible in a Year: *Ezra 3-5; John 20*

June 13

I CAN *Love* TODAY . . .
BECAUSE GOD'S LOVE EXPELS FEAR

There is no fear in love, but perfect love casts out fear. For fear has to do with punishment, and whoever fears has not been perfected in love. We love because he first loved us. (1 John 4:18-19)

A young couple, much in love, were about to get married in church. The pastor heard that the bride was very nervous, so he sent the best man to find her and read to her a verse that would encourage her and to tell her he would be preaching on it in the wedding. The verse was 1 John 4:18, which says, *There is no fear in love, but perfect love casts out fear.* The best man was unfamiliar with Scripture, so he did not know the difference between John's Gospel and the first letter of John. When he found the bride, he told her the pastor said this was an appropriate verse for her and that he was going to preach on it in the wedding. Then he read John 4:18, which says, *"For you have had five husbands, and the one you now have is not your husband."*

Humor is good medicine, but fear is not. Fear debilitates, distracts, derails, and discourages us. And we may all experience it at times. But *perfect love casts out fear,* for we know that no matter what happens today, we are loved, and that assurance brings us peace. God wants us to know today that nothing can ever dissuade Him from loving us.

I recall being nervous on my wedding day too. But when I held Helen's hand and looked into her eyes to make my vows, I saw her love, and the nervousness and fear were gone. Our Lord holds our hand today and lovingly looks upon us. We can let go of our fears today; because of His love, we can love.

For Prayerful Reflection: When have you felt afraid but looked to God in faith, and His love dispelled your fear? What will it look like for you to let go of your fears today and to rest in His perfect love?

Bible in a Year: *Ezra 6-8; John 21*

June 14

I CAN *Love* TODAY . . .
BECAUSE GOD'S LOVE HAS VERY DEEP ROOTS

> *That Christ may dwell in your hearts through faith—that you, being rooted and grounded in love, may have strength to comprehend with all the saints what is the breadth and length and height and depth, and to know the love of Christ that surpasses knowledge, that you may be filled with all the fullness of God.* (Ephesians 3:17-19)

Roots are important, for they are what secures living plants and trees and are the means through which life-giving water and nutrients are received. Some plants and trees have shallow roots, so they are more prone to fall in high winds or to shrivel or die in times of drought. Others have much deeper roots, so they stand strong in times of storm and find deep moisture in times of drought.

Tumbleweeds, for example, put down just one shallow root, so they are easily uprooted and blown about as the winds may blow. Oak trees, though, put down deep, strong roots; when the storm winds blow, they stand strong. God's love for us today is deep and strong. The apostle Paul therefore prayed that we, *being rooted and grounded in love, may have strength to comprehend . . . the breadth and length and height and depth, and to know the love of Christ that surpasses knowledge.*

Faith in Jesus Christ includes having deep spiritual roots that are growing ever deeper into God's love. He loves us, not in a shallow way that cannot support us in times of storm, but in a far deeper and stronger way than we have thus far comprehended. With the deep roots of God's love, we can stand today, no matter what comes.

For Prayerful Reflection: When have you been enabled to stand strong in a time of storm because of God's deep love for you? What does it mean for you today to be deeply *rooted and grounded* in God's love?

Bible in a Year: *Ezra 9-10; Acts 1*

June 15

I CAN *Love* TODAY . . .
BECAUSE GOD'S LOVE KEEPS ME SAFE

Let all who take refuge in you rejoice; let them ever sing for joy, and spread your protection over them, that those who love your name may exult in you. For you bless the righteous, O Lord; you cover him with favor as with a shield. (Psalm 5:11-12)

If you've ever taken a course in psychology, you have likely heard of Abraham Maslow who in 1943 introduced a theory of motivation based on a hierarchy of human needs. He suggested that people are motivated to fulfill basic needs before moving on to more advanced ones. He posited that immediately above basic physiological needs, our next felt need is for safety and security. We all long to be safe.

God knows this need and wants all of His children to be and to feel safe and secure in His loving care. His love protects us like a shield, and He comforts us with His presence. Being in God's love is a place of ultimate safety. When we run to God for protection, He surrounds us with the strong shield of His love.

I thought about this some years ago while in military service in South Korea. As the threat of war has been longstanding, South Korean and U.S. troops are deeply dug in, with security a primary focus. While there I entered a reinforced underground bunker, deep beneath a granite mountain that is purportedly secure enough to survive a nuclear attack. Security is available under that mountain, no matter what war may rage outside.

God's love is our mountain of safety today. Think about that for a while. Experience the security that you have because God's love covers you. Allow His love to flood your heart and mind with peace today.

For Prayerful Reflection: When in the face of danger have you known safety in the deep love of God? What does it mean for you to be covered today by a shield and mountain of God's love?

Bible in a Year: *Nehemiah 1-3; Acts 2:1-21*

June 16

I CAN *Love* TODAY...
BECAUSE GOD'S LOVE IS VAST

Your steadfast love, O Lord, extends to the heavens, your faithfulness to the clouds. (Psalm 36:5)

As high as the heavens are above the earth, so great is his steadfast love toward those who fear him; as far as the east is from the west, so far does he remove our transgressions from us. (Psalm 103:11-12)

These quoted psalms are from David who surely pondered the vastness of God's love and the expressions of His love that are revealed in His faithfulness and forgiveness. David said the vastness of God's steadfast love *extends to the heavens.* I picture David doing what you and I have done: looking up into the magnificent night sky, pondering the expanse of it, and marveling at the power and love of God.

Today we are able to view incredible pictures of the universe taken from the Hubble Space Telescope as it orbits the earth. One such image is of a very small slice of the sky, reportedly revealing just one thirteen-millionth of the whole, yet it contains an estimated ten thousand galaxies. We simply cannot fully comprehend the vastness of God's creation or of God.

But today let us ponder the vastness of God's love. His love is as high as the heavens are above the earth, and His forgiveness which flows from His love is as infinite as the distance from east to west. We know that we could travel east indefinitely and never ever arrive at west. God's vast love for us is offered today with the glory of His forgiveness. It is ours through faith by believing in the Lord Jesus Christ. And through confession and repentance of our sins, we who are blessed recipients of God's vast supply of love are wonderfully blessed today to bring and give His great love to others.

For Prayerful Reflection: When and how has God opened your mind and heart to the vastness of His love? How does this insight help you own His love for you and extend His love to others?

Bible in a Year: *Nehemiah 4-6; Acts 2:22-47*

June 17

I CAN *Love* TODAY . . .
BECAUSE GOD ADOPTED ME IN LOVE

Blessed be the God and Father of our Lord Jesus Christ, who has blessed us in Christ with every spiritual blessing in the heavenly places, even as he chose us in him before the foundation of the world, that we should be holy and blameless before him. In love he predestined us for adoption to himself as sons through Jesus Christ, according to the purpose of his will, to the praise of his glorious grace. (Ephesians 1:3-6)

Though it is certainly possible to have a child without intending to do so, it is not possible to accidentally adopt a child. Adopting a child requires intentionally choosing to love, cherish, and care for that child from that moment onward, even for life. My experience with adoption taught me much about God's love for us. That day when Helen and I adopted our son is seared forever in my memory and heart. Standing in the court that day, holding that precious child in my arms, with tears of joy in my eyes and love in my heart, Helen and I affirmed our intention to adopt him as our own, and from that moment on he was ours.

When God adopted you and when He adopted me, it was no accident. He chose to love, cherish, and care for us from that moment on and forever. We are God's children today, and He delights in us.

Let's ponder today how the eternal God of the universe loves us so personally and chooses each of us to be His own child. Have you fully accepted God's deep love for you? Do you dearly love Him too? And because of His great love, does your heart not overflow today with love for others?

For Prayerful Reflection: What have been the effects on your life of knowing that God chose you to be His dearly loved child? How does your adoption by God contribute to how you love others today?

Bible in a Year: *Nehemiah 7-9; Acts 3*

June 18

I CAN *Love* TODAY . . .
BECAUSE GOD GAVE HIS OWN SON FOR ME

"For God so loved the world, that he gave his only Son, that whoever believes in him should not perish but have eternal life. For God did not send his Son into the world to condemn the world, but in order that the world might be saved through him. (John 3:16-17)

It can be hard to understand without being a parent that the love parents feel for their children is among the deepest kind of love any human can possibly have for another. Loving parents cannot conceive of any reason they would willingly allow their child to die. They would rather die than allow their child to die, because their child's life is more important to them than their own.

But God so loves us that He willingly gave His Son to be rejected and mistreated and to die in judgment for our sins? Why would our heavenly Father sacrifice His Son whom He has forever loved? It is because of His great love for us and for all the people of the world. *God so loved the world, that he gave his only Son.* That is why.

What does this tell you about the depth of God's love for you today? He loves you so much *that he gave his only Son.* What wondrous love is this! Our loving heavenly Father gave His only Son so that we who believe in Him could be forgiven of all our sin today and *not perish but have eternal life,* which means living today, tomorrow, and forever with God as His own dear children. Though such love is beyond our full understanding, it beckons us to love God deeply today and then to love others deeply, as He has loved us.

For Prayerful Reflection: What does Father God's sacrifice of His Son, the Lord Jesus, tell you about God's love for you? How is the realization of His love for you affecting your life and love today?

Bible in a Year: *Nehemiah 10-11; Acts 4:1-22*

June 19

I CAN *Love* TODAY . . .
BECAUSE GOD LOVES US EVEN WHEN WE REBEL

For one will scarcely die for a righteous person—though perhaps for a good person one would dare even to die—but God shows his love for us in that while we were still sinners, Christ died for us. (Romans 5:7-8)

Have you messed up, sinning again and feeling shame? Are you wondering if God can really love the likes of you? Today's good news is that no matter how you may have failed Him, or how far from God you may now feel, He still loves you and still desires a close, personal relationship with you.

One of the great joys and challenges of my life has been being a parent. From the time we first expect a child and the moment we first see or hold them, we love our children. We love them always – when they're sweet and good and when they are not. If a child should ever say, "I hate you!" or if they should reject us and say, "You're not my parent," of course it hurts. But loving parents will never stop loving their children.

In times when we have rebelled against God by our unbelief, unloving actions, or unrighteous behavior, or in times of fury if we should ever say to God, "I hate you," God replies, "I love you." *God shows his love for us in that while we were still sinners, Christ died for us.*

Recognizing our sin is God's grace to us, for we are then blessed to come again in faith to our heavenly Father through Jesus Christ, confessing our sin and turning from it in humble repentance. Today we are blessed to receive the grace of God's forgiveness and the embrace of His love. Because God loves us and always will, even when we rebel, we can rest in His love and offer His love to others who are sinners too.

For Prayerful Reflection: When have you rebelled against God and then experienced His forgiveness and love? How does the realization of His unending love for you affect the way you love today?

Bible in a Year: *Nehemiah 12-13; Acts 4:23-37*

June 20

I CAN *Love* TODAY . . .
BECAUSE GOD'S LOVE LETS ME GROW

For the love of Christ controls us, because we have concluded this: that one has died for all, therefore all have died, and he died for all, that those who live might no longer live for themselves but for him who for their sake died and was raised. (2 Corinthians 5:14-15)

And may the Lord make you increase and abound in love for one another and for all, as we do for you. (1 Thessalonians 3:12)

God loves us just the way we are, but He loves us too much to allow us to stay as we are. He wants us to grow up in Him. Parents understand this, for we too love our children just as they are, but we also want them to grow up. I am blessed with four grandsons whose current ages are nine, six, five, and two. I love them just as they are. But how awful it would be if ten years from now they still acted like the ages they are today. Loving our children, we want them to grow and mature.

God wants the same for you and me. He wants us to spiritually grow until we *no longer live for [ourselves] but for him.* He wants to see His children continue to mature spiritually to *make [us] increase and abound in love for one another and for all.* Is this happening in you? To accomplish this, God does what loving parents do. God allows us into situations where our faith and endurance are tested, and our comfort zone is stretched, so that we learn to trust Him more; thus, we develop the heart of a servant and express His love even more. Today God is allowing us to grow.

For Prayerful Reflection: When has God put you in a challenging place, thus allowing your love to grow? In what ways might God, in love, allow you to grow today?

Bible in a Year: *Esther 1-2; Acts 5:1-21*

June 21

I CAN *Love* TODAY . . .
BECAUSE GOD BOUGHT ME WITH JESUS' BLOOD

You were ransomed from the futile ways inherited from your forefathers, not with perishable things such as silver or gold, but with the precious blood of Christ, like that of a lamb without blemish or spot. (1 Peter 1:18-19)

Do you not know that your body is a temple of the Holy Spirit within you, whom you have from God? You are not your own, for you were bought with a price. So glorify God in your body. (1 Corinthians 6:19-20)

How precious are you to God? How much does He love you? In the Scriptures we are reminded of the extraordinary price God paid to redeem us from our sinful condition. God loves us so much that He purchased us, *not with perishable things such as silver or gold, but with the precious blood of Christ, like that of a lamb without blemish or spot.* We are dearly loved indeed.

In his address at the 2017 National Prayer Breakfast, Dr. Barry Black, Chaplain of the U.S. Senate and a former Chief of Chaplains of the U.S. Navy, said, "The value of an object is based on the price someone is willing to pay." Referencing the above quoted verses in 1 Peter, he said when it dawned on him that God was willing to give His Son Jesus for him, then "no one could ever make me feel inferior again." Amen.

God loves me. Let each of us reflect today on this personal assurance. Let us allow this recognition to stir our hearts with love for Him. Let it move our soul today toward adoring worship, rousing our will to obey Him, drowning the fiery flames of our fears, silencing the nagging shouts of self-condemnation, and impressing upon us the wonderful truth of our inestimable worth to God.

For Prayerful Reflection: What has been the impact in your life of God's indisputable love for you? How could this perspective shape the way you relate to others today?

Bible in a Year: *Esther 3-5; Acts 5:22-42*

June 22

I CAN *Love* TODAY . . .
BECAUSE GOD THE HOLY SPIRIT HELPS ME LOVE

"I will ask the Father, and he will give you another Helper, to be with you forever, even the Spirit of truth . . . You know him, for he dwells with you and will be in you." (John 14:16-17)

God's love has been poured into our hearts through the Holy Spirit who has been given to us. (Romans 5:5)

But the fruit of the Spirit is love. (Galatians 5:22)

God calls us to love in ways we cannot possibly do on our own. I mean, how could anyone love their enemies, or lovingly treat someone who's rude or unkind, or lovingly pray for those who have caused their suffering? But Jesus did pray like this from the cross, as did the Lord's servant Stephen while being martyred: *"Lord, do not hold this sin against them"* (Acts 7:60). We are equipped in this way today, as the Holy Spirit helps us to love.

Jesus promised to give us *another Helper, to be with you forever, even the Spirit of truth.* This means *God's love has been poured into our hearts through the Holy Spirit who has been given to us.* And the fruit of the Holy Spirit is love. Inviting and allowing the Holy Spirit to help us to love, we are supernaturally enabled to do so, which is evidenced in our actions.

In *Mere Christianity, Book 2* of C. S. Lewis's eight-volume set, he says love transcends feelings and is evidenced in actions. He said we shouldn't waste time worrying about whether or not we feel love for our neighbor. Rather, in Jesus' name we are to act in love, for then we come to love.

God's love flows out of us by God the Holy Spirit who indwells us, stirs us, and enables us to act in love. Our part today is to demonstrate God's love with the help of the Holy Spirit.

For Prayerful Reflection: When have you been surprised by demonstrations of God's love in action? How might you, with the Holy Spirit's help, put love into action today?

Bible in a Year: *Esther 6-8; Acts 6*

June 23

I CAN *Love* TODAY . . .
BECAUSE GOD CARES FOR PEOPLE IN ANGUISH

I will rejoice and be glad in your steadfast love, because you have seen my affliction; you have known the distress of my soul, and you have not delivered me into the hand of the enemy; you have set my feet in a broad place. Be gracious to me O Lord, for I am in distress. (Psalm 31:7-9)

When [Jesus] saw the crowds, he had compassion for them, because they were harassed and helpless, like sheep without a shepherd. (Matthew 9:36)

When life becomes hard, we might feel alone or feel like no one cares. But God cares for people who are in anguish. He cares about us in our sadness, struggle, anguish, or pain. God cares because of His love. After first looking back on ways God previously cared for him, David considered his current trials and declared, *I will rejoice and be glad in your steadfast love, because you have seen my affliction.* Jesus vividly demonstrated such care for people in anguish, as He had compassion and ministered in love. God does the same for you today and blesses you to do the same in His name.

God does not promise to immediately fix all of our problems. As we all know, in this broken world we experience suffering and sorrow. He promises in love that a day is coming when we will be with Him in eternity, and all sin and anguish will be gone forever.

But God does not simply say, "It's going to get better someday." Because of His compassion and love, God comes to us today; He meets and loves us in times of anguish; He fills us with His love, so that in His name we can meet and love people in their pain.

For Prayerful Reflection: When and how has God demonstrated His love for you in times of anguish? How might you demonstrate His love in His name to someone in anguish today?

Bible in a Year: *Esther 9-10; Acts 7:1-21*

June 24

I CAN *Love* TODAY . . .
BECAUSE GOD'S MERCIES ARE NEW TODAY

The steadfast love of the Lord never ceases; his mercies never come to an end; they are new every morning; great is your faithfulness. (Lamentations 3:22-23)

I will recount the steadfast love of the Lord, the praises of the Lord, according to all that the Lord has granted us, and the great goodness to the house of Israel that he has granted them according to his compassion, according to the abundance of his steadfast love. (Isaiah 63:7)

Mercy in the Bible is God's withholding of just punishment. The particular Hebrew word used by Jeremiah in Lamentations 3:22 has to do with tender love, great and tender mercy, or pity. The same word when used in Isaiah 63:7 is translated *compassion*. God has pity on His suffering children. His mercies are extended to us today.

Jeremiah's declaration that God's mercies are *new every morning* flows into the statement that follows: *Great is your faithfulness.* Because God is faithful today as He has always been, His mercies toward His people are unfaltering. Though His people were facing great trials, being in exile in far-off Babylon, God's covenant with Abraham's descendants would still be kept. His mercy and faithfulness were bright rays of hope shining through the smoke of Jerusalem's ruins, and that hope still shines in love today over this broken world.

The dawning of each new day is for us a symbol of God's light breaking through the darkness and His mercies overpowering our troubles. Each new day is a fresh demonstration of God's grace, a new beginning in which gloom must flee away. The mercies of God keep coming in a host of manifestations, as they are new every morning. God's love for you means His mercies are extended to you today.

For Prayerful Reflection: After a dark night in your life, how did God demonstrate His mercies to you? How might you, in love, demonstrate God's mercy to someone today?

Bible in a Year: *Job 1-2; Acts 7:22-43*

June 25

I CAN *Love* TODAY . . .
BECAUSE GOD DEMONSTRATES HIS LOVE THROUGH ME

In this is love, not that we have loved God but that he loved us and sent his Son to be the propitiation for our sins. Beloved, if God so loved us, we also ought to love one another. No one has ever seen God; if we love one another, God abides in us and his love is perfected in us. (1 John 4:10-12)

The fruit of the Spirit is love, joy, peace, patience, kindness, goodness, faithfulness, gentleness, self-control. (Galatians 5:22-23)

When we love as God loves us, people will see in us a glimpse of God, who is love. It can be difficult for people to comprehend God, but when we love in His name, they can taste of His love. Lamentably, Christians are sometimes known more for judgment than for love. If we desire to help others know who God is, we can do so by loving them.

Many years ago, Helen and I spent a night with new friends in Florida. In the morning they served us freshly squeezed orange juice, which they had just made from the fruit of their backyard tree. It was sweet and delicious, and they could serve it to us because this fruit was readily available to them. The Bible says we can do the same with the fruit of the Spirit, which God has planted and made available to us. And the very first fruit that is listed is love, because it is the primary characteristic of God.

God loves you, and He has planted His love in you. As you allow God's love to grow within you, it will be like a fruit-producing plant. You cannot consume it all yourself. It is your responsibility, blessing, and joy to serve the fruit of God's love to others today.

For Prayerful Reflection: What are some ways you have received the fruit of God's love through others? How could you demonstrate the fruit of God's love to someone today?

Bible in a Year: *Job 3-4; Acts 7:44-60*

June 26

I CAN *Love* TODAY . . .
BECAUSE GOD ALLOWS US TO REMAIN IN HIS LOVE

But you, beloved, building yourselves up in your most holy faith and praying in the Holy Spirit, keep yourselves in the love of God, waiting for the mercy of our Lord Jesus Christ that leads to eternal life. (Jude vv. 20-21)

Sometimes you can find yourself in a place you do not want to leave. It might be a particularly beautiful vacation where you are having a wonderful time. Or perhaps it's a family reunion where many whom you dearly love have gathered, and you wish you could freeze the day so it doesn't end. Perhaps it's a long-awaited event that has finally arrived, and you are filled with gratitude and joy.

A number of years ago when our Lord blessed me with a glorious picture of heaven, I knew in my soul and with more joy than I can describe that there in the Lord's presence is where I belong, where I long to be, and where I never want to leave. This is of course our confident hope and joy, for we who belong to God through faith in Jesus Christ will be with Him forever. But praise be to God, we need not wait until then.

Jude reminds us that God allows us to remain in His love today and every day. He says as we are *waiting for the mercy of our Lord Jesus Christ that leads to eternal life,* we are invited by God to *keep [ourselves] in the love of God.* Right now, we are in God's love. God loves us wonderfully, dearly, deeply, tenderly, and tangibly. Believe it, because it is true. And the great news for us today is that we never have to leave. In faith we can remain here and keep ourselves always in the love of God.

For Prayerful Reflection: When have you ever been in a place you didn't want to leave? How does it bless you today to know that you can always remain in God's love?

Bible in a Year: *Job 5-7; Acts 8:1-25*

June 27

I CAN *Love* TODAY . . .
BECAUSE GOD PROTECTS HIS OWN

How precious is your steadfast love, O God! The children of mankind take refuge in the shadow of your wings. (Psalm 36:7)

"When you pass through the waters, I will be with you; and through the rivers, they shall not overwhelm you; when you walk through the fire you shall not be burned, and the flame shall not consume you. For I am the Lord your God, the Holy One of Israel, your Savior. . . . Because you are precious in my eyes, and honored, and I love you." (Isaiah 43:2-4)

Having spent much of his youth watching over his dad's sheep, David had considerable life experience outdoors, so he had surely seen baby birds beneath their mother's wings. In time of wind, rain, or danger, he had seen those baby birds take refuge under the wings of their mother bird. As he reflected on this image and heard God's voice, David saw himself and the children of humankind running to God in times of storm, taking refuge under the shadow of His wings. He pondered that God invited and allowed us to do this, as He protected us. Then David worshipfully proclaimed, *How precious is your steadfast love, O God!*

The prophet Isaiah also heard God's loving promise to protect His own. Whether we face raging fire, rising flood, or any other hardship or danger, God is the One we can run to, and whenever we do, He protects us. Why does God say He does this? It is *"because you are precious in my eyes, and honored, and I love you."* Do you need protection today? God covers you now because of His protective love for you. Because of this, you are free and enabled by God to love today.

For Prayerful Reflection: When have you faced a storm, running in faith to God and finding shelter under His wings? How does your experience of God's loving protection affect your love for others today?

Bible in a Year: *Job 8-10; Acts 8:26-40*

June 28

I CAN *Love* TODAY . . .
BECAUSE GOD FIRST LOVED ME

We love because he first loved us. If anyone says, "I love God," and hates his brother, he is a liar; for he who does not love his brother whom he has seen cannot love God whom he has not seen. And this commandment we have from him: whoever loves God must also love his brother. (1 John 4:19-21)

God takes the first step in loving us. And now *we love because he first loved us.* The effectual love of God for us changes our hearts so we can love. His example of loving us moves us to love others. God's love for us, our love for Him, and our love for others are interconnected. If we have received God's love, we will love God, and we will love others. The Bible says we cannot rightly say we love God whom we have not seen if we do not love those whom we do see.

I often pray for divine appointments in which I can show God's love. A recent one happened for me in a Walmart parking lot when we were far from home. In the middle of the lot, I saw a woman crying and I prayerfully approached her. Through tears she told me her name, she said that her husband had left her and their children, and with no money for rent, they had been evicted. She did not know what to do.

Though traveling and not knowing local resources, I could still love her. So I listened, cared, counseled, gave her money for that day's needs, and we prayed. She needed a hug, so I gave her one. I wished that I could have done more, but in love I did what I could, and we both knew that God was there. Wherever we are today, we can love because God has first loved us.

For Prayerful Reflection: What has it meant for you to love others as God has first loved you? Would you ask God today for divine appointments, so you might love someone as God has loved you?

Bible in a Year: *Job 11-13; Acts 9:1-21*

June 29

I CAN *Love* TODAY . . .
BECAUSE GOD PUT LOVE IN MY WARDROBE

Put on then, as God's chosen ones, holy and beloved, compassionate hearts, kindness, humility, meekness, and patience, bearing with one another and, if one has a complaint against another, forgiving each other; as the Lord has forgiven you, so you also must forgive. And above all these put on love, which binds everything together in perfect harmony. (Colossians 3:12-14)

What's in your closet? I recently went through my closet and found clothes I used to wear that no longer fit. I prefer saying, "They shrunk in the closet," but what really happened is that I'm larger than I used to be. They do not fit anymore, so I have removed them from my closet.

We are urged to do something similar regarding the life we live in Jesus Christ and the characteristics we now wear as His followers. In Colossians 3:8 Paul tells Christians to get rid of the various sins we used to walk in and to *put them all away*. He then teaches us to put on the qualities God has placed in our wardrobe, which are available to us now. These include *compassionate hearts, kindness, humility, meekness, and patience*, plus forbearance and forgiveness. And what is the primary garment we are always to wear? It is love.

Perhaps you have some favorite garments you like to wear. God has given us the favorite garment of His love. It is a conscious choice for us, though, to put it on every day. It's a choice to wear and bear the precious love of God in every interaction all through the day. Let us choose to wear God's love today.

For Prayerful Reflection: What garments hanging in your spiritual closet need to be removed now? What lovely garments has God blessed you to wear? What will it mean for you today to *put on love*?

Bible in a Year: *Job 14-16; Acts 9:22-43*

June 30

I CAN *Love* TODAY . . .
BECAUSE GOD HAS LOVED ME EXTRAVAGANTLY

"Everyone to whom much was given, of him much will be required, and from him to whom they entrusted much, they will demand the more." (Luke 12:48)

By this we know love, that he laid down his life for us, and we ought to lay down our lives for the brothers. But if anyone has the world's goods and sees his brother in need, yet closes his heart against him, how does God's love abide in him? Little children, let us not love in word or talk but in deed and in truth. (1 John 3:16-18)

Our Lord taught us that *everyone to whom much was given, of him much will be required.* If we believe this, it is good to ponder a bit on how much we have received and in particular, how blessed we have been by the wonderful love of God. God has loved us extravagantly, and we are thus enabled and compelled to lavishly love as we have been loved.

I read of a certain medieval monk who had announced that he would be preaching the following Sunday evening on "The Love of God." As shadows fell and the light ceased to come in through the cathedral windows, the congregation gathered. In the darkness of the altar, the monk lit a candle and carried it to the crucifix. First, he illumined the crown of thorns, next the two wounded hands, then the wounded feet, and then the marks of the spear wound. In the hush that fell, he blew out the candle and left the cathedral. There was nothing more to say.

God has loved us extravagantly. What then is required of those who have been so loved? May God help us to love lavishly today, even as He has loved us.

For Prayerful Reflection: How extravagantly has God loved you, and how has this affected your desire to love? What might it mean for you today to love lavishly, even as God has loved you?

Bible in a Year: *Job 17-19; Acts 10:1-23*

12 Themes on Following Jesus

JULY

Because God . . .
I Can *Listen* Today

July 1

I CAN *Listen* TODAY . . .
BECAUSE GOD WANTS ME TO KNOW HIM

Thus says the Lord: "Let not the wise man boast in his wisdom, let not the mighty man boast in his might, let not the rich man boast in his riches, but let him who boasts boast in this, that he understands and knows me, that I am the Lord who practices steadfast love, justice, and righteousness in the earth. For in these things I delight, declares the Lord." (Jeremiah 9:23-24)

"And this is eternal life, that they know you, the only true God, and Jesus Christ whom you have sent." (John 17:3)

When I first met Helen, she intrigued me, and I was drawn to her. The more I spent time with her, the more I wanted to spend time with her. And amazingly to me, she wanted to spend time with me, so we might know each other. One of the first things I noticed about her, which has never changed, is that she insisted that we openly communicate. She wanted us to talk about anything and everything; she wanted us to be real with each other. The more I got to know her, the more I wanted the same.

This is God's desire for each of us. God wants us to be open in communication with Him. God knows us and wants us to know Him. Toward this end God speaks to us; and yes, we *can* hear His voice. You and I are invited to enjoy an amazing privilege of personal relationship with God through faith in Jesus Christ. As all personal relationships are established and maintained through open communication, it is vitally important that we learn to honestly share what is on our heart, and to hear and listen to God's voice, so our relationship with Him may deepen.

For Prayerful Reflection: How did you learn that God wants a personal relationship with you, and what has this meant to you? What will it mean for you today to listen to God, and to share your heart with Him?

Bible in a Year: *Job 20-21; Acts 10:24-48*

July 2

I CAN *Listen* TODAY . . .
BECAUSE GOD IS SPEAKING

And he called the name of the place Massah and Meribah, because of the quarreling of the people of Israel, and because they tested the Lord by saying, "Is the Lord among us or not?" (Exodus 17:7)

"Hear, O my people, while I admonish you! O Israel, if you would but listen to me!" (Psalm 81:8)

"Inattentional blindness occurs when someone fails to perceive an unexpected stimulus in plain sight, purely as a result of a lack of attention."[17] I read of a case study in which researchers clipped money on a tree branch across a walking trail. The branch was about at head height so no one would miss it, and about four hundred passersby were observed. Ninety-four percent of them did not see the money, as their attention was focused on their running, music, or cell phones. Inattentional blindness prevents us from noticing what is happening around us.

This applies to seeing what God is doing and hearing what He is saying. God is moving and speaking, but we too easily miss it. The events described in Exodus 17 are an example of this. God had answered His people's troubled pleas from Egypt, leading them by pillars of cloud and fire. He parted the sea for them, delivered them from thirst, and provided their daily bread. But in a time of trial, they were so focused on a problem that they neither saw nor heard God, and they even asked, *"Is the Lord among us or not?"*

God is here and is speaking today. In faith we can look up and listen. And when we do, we are again amazed at His faithfulness and blessed to hear His voice again.

For Prayerful Reflection: When were you too preoccupied to see or hear what God was doing or saying? As God speaks today, how can you remove distractions to give Him your full attention?

Bible in a Year: *Job 22-24; Acts 11*

---

[17] "Inattentional Blindness," WIKIPEDIA: *The Free Encyclopedia, https://tinyurl.com/a48j7c4v* (May 24, 2021).

July 3

I CAN *Listen* TODAY...
BECAUSE GOD IS HERE NOW

Now Moses was keeping the flock of his father-in-law, Jethro, the priest of Midian, and he led his flock to the west side of the wilderness and came to Horeb, the mountain of God. And the angel of the Lord appeared to him in a flame of fire out of the midst of a bush. He looked, and behold, the bush was burning, yet it was not consumed. And Moses said, "I will turn aside to see this great sight, why the bush is not burned." When the Lord saw that he turned aside to see, God called to him out of the bush, "Moses, Moses!" And he said, "Here I am." (Exodus 3:1-4)

This remarkable story describes a day that changed the course of history for Moses, for the people of Israel, and for us. On that amazing day, God appeared to Moses and spoke to him and dramatically revealed *"I am"* (v. 14). *I am* is always here, but that day, Moses grasped that God is personal, God speaks, and God was with him then.

This unexpected encounter occurred on a day that started out like many others. For forty years Moses had been living in Midian as a shepherd, watching his father-in-law's flock. Sure, Moses believed in God, but it was from a distance, not up close and personal. He never expected that God would actually come to him or speak to him by name or call him into His service. Yet God did just that. I praise God today, for He has done the same for me.

As Moses realized that day, God wants us to realize that He is here now, revealing Himself, speaking to us, and calling us to carefully listen and in faith to say yes to Him.

For Prayerful Reflection: When have you in faith been astounded to realize that God is here now and is speaking to you? As God speaks today, what does it mean for you to truly listen?

Bible in a Year: *Job 25-27; Acts 12*

July 4

I CAN *Listen* TODAY . . .
BECAUSE GOD'S WORD IS FOR MY GOOD

"But my people did not listen to my voice; Israel would not submit to me. So I gave them over to their stubborn hearts, to follow their own counsels. Oh, that my people would listen to me, that Israel would walk in my ways!" (Psalm 81:11-13)

To clearly hear God's voice, we must pay close attention to His Word, for it is always for our good. We must read God's Word and prayerfully tune in to the frequency of heaven to hear the voice of God and then to act upon it. It is always to our detriment when we disregard His Word.

The story is told of a loyalist spy who during the Revolutionary War appeared at the headquarters of Hessian Commander Colonel Johann Rall. He carried an urgent message that General George Washington and his Continental Army had secretly crossed the Delaware River that morning and were now advancing on Trenton, New Jersey, where the Hessians were encamped. The spy was denied an audience with the commander, so he wrote his message on a piece of paper. A porter took the note to the Hessian colonel, who was involved in a poker game, so he stuffed the unread note into his pocket. Later that day the Hessian army was captured, which gave the colonists their first major victory of the war.[18] Have we ever done that with a message sent from God?

On this Independence Day in the USA, God reminds us that His message to us is too important to ignore, for it is always for our good. Ultimate freedom is only found in receiving God's Word and living by it. Are we listening today, grateful for God's grace to speak and lead us in the way of His will?

For Prayerful Reflection: Why does God long for you to carefully listen to Him? How can you ensure that you are carefully listening to God today?

Bible in a Year: *Job 28-29; Acts 13:1-25*

---
18   *Today in the Word* (October 1991), 21.

July 5

I CAN *Listen* TODAY . . .
BECAUSE GOD IS SPEAKING IN A WHISPER

> *[God] said, "Go out and stand on the mount before the Lord." And behold, the Lord passed by, and a great and strong wind tore the mountains and broke in pieces the rocks before the Lord, but the Lord was not in the wind. And after the wind an earthquake, but the Lord was not in the earthquake. And after the earthquake a fire, but the Lord was not in the fire. And after the fire the sound of a low whisper. And when Elijah heard it, he wrapped his face in his cloak and went out and stood at the entrance of the cave. And behold, there came a voice to him and said, "What are you doing here, Elijah?"* (1 Kings 19:11-13)

Have you ever been in a place where you really needed to hear from God, and you hoped He would speak in a remarkable way that would remove all doubt for you? I have been there, as was Elijah. He knew God was able, because he had recently seen the Lord send down fire from heaven on Mount Carmel. But now Elijah was afraid and running for his life. And God spoke, didn't He?

But it was not through wind, fire, an earthquake, or another earth-shattering way. Elijah had to learn, as do we, to be quiet enough in God's presence to hear His still small voice. God speaks by His Word and through the Holy Spirit, directing us and aligning our thoughts with His. Listening means pausing the torrential flow of our own words so that we might hear His. Like Elijah on that day, when we are still enough to listen, we hear God's voice today.

For Prayerful Reflection: When have you been still and heard God speaking? What practical things could you do today to help quiet the noise in your heart to better hear the quiet whisper of God?

Bible in a Year: *Job 30-31; Acts 13:26-52*

July 6

I CAN *Listen* TODAY . . .
BECAUSE GOD CALLS ME

And the Lord called again, "Samuel!" and Samuel arose and went to Eli and said, "Here I am, for you called me." But he said, "I did not call, my son; lie down again." Now Samuel did not yet know the Lord, and the word of the Lord had not yet been revealed to him. And the Lord came and stood, calling as at other times, "Samuel! Samuel!" And Samuel said, "Speak, for your servant hears." (1 Samuel 3:6-7, 10)

As Samuel learned, it is important to hear and answer when God calls us. I see myself in this biblical story. Like Samuel, I was raised in the faith, where people worshipped God. Like him, I believed in God too. And like Samuel, I needed to learn firsthand how personal God is and that He even calls me by name. God wants all of us to hear, answer, and obey when He calls us. As in Samuel's example, may we not ignore His call.

Danish philosopher Soren Kierkegaard told of a goose that was wounded and landed in a barnyard with some chickens. He played and ate with the chickens, and after a while he thought he was a chicken. One day geese flew over, honking in the sky. Kierkegaard said, "Something stirred within the breast of this goose. Something called him to the skies. He began to flap the wings he hadn't used, and he rose a few feet into the air. Then he stopped and settled back again into the mud of the barnyard. He heard the cry but settled for less."[19] We miss God's best when we hear but disregard God's call.

For Prayerful Reflection: When and how did you first become aware that God speaks personally to you? What could it mean for you to pray like Samuel today, *"Speak, for your servant hears"*?

Bible in a Year: *Job 32-33; Acts 14*

---

[19] Illustration from *sermoncentral.com*, March 2, 2001, *https://www.sermoncentral.com/sermon-illustrations/1649/call-by-mark-roper.*

July 7

I CAN *Listen* TODAY . . .
BECAUSE GOD REDIRECTS

Now as he went on his way, he approached Damascus, and suddenly a light from heaven shone around him. And falling to the ground, he heard a voice saying to him, "Saul, Saul, why are you persecuting me?" And he said, "Who are you, Lord?" And he said, "I am Jesus, whom you are persecuting. But rise and enter the city, and you will be told what you are to do." (Acts 9:3-6)

Saul of Tarsus was devout: a lifelong student of the Scriptures, a disciplined follower of Rabbi Gamaliel, a Pharisee, and now a passionate warrior against what he regarded as heresy. Saul was doing the best he knew how in going the right way, but he was going the wrong way. And in great grace, God came to Saul, called him by name, and redirected him in the way he should go.

When we are off course, going a way that is wrong for us but that we think is right, we need what Saul needed that day. We need in God's mercy a fresh encounter with Him so that we might hear His voice and allow Him to change and redirect us in the right way. I have been there, haven't you?

Like Saul, I have arrogantly thought I knew what was best, when I did not. But here is a truth I have lived, and every disciple of Jesus Christ is blessed to live: whenever we are going the wrong way, God does not leave us unchallenged on our perilous path. God intervenes and calls us by name, so that like Saul, we might hear Him, repent of our waywardness, and change our course to the way that He leads us. That day Saul's life was wonderfully changed. Today may be such a day for us.

For Prayerful Reflection: When were you going the wrong way but God intervened to redirect you? What are some implications of knowing that when you are off course, God speaks to redirect you?

Bible in a Year: *Job 34-35; Acts 15:1-21*

July 8

I CAN *Listen* TODAY . . .
BECAUSE GOD SPEAKS IN OUR EXILE

I, John, your brother and partner in the tribulation and the kingdom and the patient endurance that are in Jesus, was on the island called Patmos on account of the word of God and the testimony of Jesus. I was in the Spirit on the Lord's day, and I heard behind me a loud voice like a trumpet saying, "Write what you see in a book and send it to the seven churches." (Revelation 1:9-11)

The apostle John was now an old man in exile. In AD 95 he was banished to the island of Patmos by the Roman Emperor Domitian. Patmos is a volcanic, treeless, rocky island measuring about six miles by thirty miles in size, and located twenty miles off the western coast of modern Turkey. Criminals whom the Romans did not want to escape were sentenced to Patmos, a lonely and isolated place. Being sentenced there was regarded as a sentence of death by loneliness.

But in John's exile our Lord was there too, speaking to him, giving him the company of a myriad of angels, and opening his spiritual eyes and ears to the revelations described in the last book of the New Testament. How wonderful for John and us that God met him, was with him, and spoke to him in his exile.

We too can face isolation and loneliness. Though we may feel alone, we are not alone, for our Lord is with us everywhere and always. God comes. He meets us, loves us, and speaks with us. Like John, we are blessed by God's presence. My part and yours is to open our hearts wide to believe He is with us today and to open our eyes and ears to see and listen.

For Prayerful Reflection: When has your Lord met you as you faced isolation or loneliness? What are some implications for you today of knowing that God speaks in your times of exile?

Bible in a Year: *Job 36-37; Acts 15:22-41*

July 9

I CAN *Listen* TODAY . . .
BECAUSE GOD OPENS HIS WORD TO US

> *[Jesus] said to them, "O foolish ones, and slow of heart to believe all that the prophets have spoken! Was it not necessary that the Christ should suffer these things and enter into his glory?" And beginning with Moses and all the Prophets, he interpreted to them in all the Scriptures the things concerning himself. They said to each other, "Did not our hearts burn within us while he talked to us on the road, while he opened to us the Scriptures?"* (Luke 24:25-27, 32)

The local congregation Helen and I now fellowship with is called Emmaus Church. The name is taken from the resurrection story told in Luke 24. Some years ago, the fellowship of churches and ministers in which I served (CCCC) planted a local church in Philadelphia with an innovative name based on this story. It is called Seven Mile Road Church, as the journey from Jerusalem to Emmaus was about seven miles long.

The two men described in this passage were downcast and filled with confusion. Along the way they encountered the risen Christ. As they continued walking down this road together with Jesus, He spoke to them and showed them from the Scriptures how it all pointed to Him. In the end, these men who had been filled with doubt became filled with faith in Jesus. God does the same today.

On the road to Emmaus while walking with them, Jesus opened their minds to the truth of His Word. They later said their hearts burned within them as they listened to the Lord. We are blessed to walk with God today. We too can listen carefully as He opens His Word to us, and as we do, like those disciples on the road to Emmaus, we are changed.

For Prayerful Reflection: When and how has God met you when you were downcast and He opened your mind to His truth? What does it mean for you to listen carefully to the Lord today?

Bible in a Year: *Job 38-40; Acts 16:1-21*

July 10

I CAN *Listen* TODAY . . .
BECAUSE GOD WELCOMES ME TO SIT WITH HIM

As they went on their way, Jesus entered a village. And a woman named Martha welcomed him into her house. And she had a sister called Mary, who sat at the Lord's feet and listened to his teaching. But Martha was distracted with much serving. And she went up to him and said, "Lord, do you not care that my sister has left me to serve alone? Tell her then to help me." But the Lord answered her, "Martha, Martha, you are anxious and troubled about many things, but one thing is necessary. Mary has chosen the good portion, which will not be taken away from her."
(Luke 10:38-42)

I can relate to Martha. Can you? We are often consumed by well-meaning busyness. Our busy lifestyles and responsibilities can keep us going full speed much of the time. And when we're busy, we can resent anyone that we think is not pulling their share of the load. Martha wasn't frivolously wasting her time. She had guests in her home, including Jesus, and she was focused on serving them well. Though well intentioned amidst her busyness, she was missing the opportunity of a lifetime.

I do not want to do that. But I know I have been there, busily serving God while failing to spend much focused time with Him. Mary shows us how important it is to take the time to lay aside our activity for a while, just to be with Jesus, to sit with Him, and to listen. He welcomes us to do so today. And when we do, like Mary, we are blessed.

For Prayerful Reflection: In this story, do you relate more to Martha or to Mary? Why? What does it mean for you today that Jesus invites and welcomes you to sit with Him for a while and to listen?

Bible in a Year: *Job 41-42; Acts 16:22-40*

July 11

I CAN *Listen* TODAY . . .
BECAUSE GOD INVITES CHILDREN TO COME

And they were bringing children to him that he might touch them, and the disciples rebuked them. But when Jesus saw it, he was indignant and said to them, "Let the children come to me; do not hinder them, for to such belongs the kingdom of God." (Mark 10:13-14)

See what kind of love the Father has given to us, that we should be called children of God; and so we are. (1 John 3:1)

I love that God sees us as His children and invites us to come to Him, even to run into His open arms. What a beautiful picture – little ones running to Jesus, loving Him, laughing, jumping on His lap, touching His face, and maybe pulling on His beard! Contrary to the perceptions of our Lord's disciples who presumed He had better things to do than this, Jesus wanted the children to come to Him.

As my own children are now in their thirties, it has been a while since my own little ones ran into my arms and climbed on my lap with laughter, kisses, and love. But I do remember it well and treasure the memories. In recent years I have relived and enjoyed this treasure through my grandchildren who are all dear to me. The youngest one who is now two runs to Grandpa with arms outstretched and enters my embrace with laughter and love. He sits on my lap and listens as I read to him. He puts his hands on my face and plays with my beard. The joy this gives me reflects the joy we give to our heavenly Father, when as His children we run to Him, sit with Him, love Him, and listen to Him.

For Prayerful Reflection: Can you see yourself as God's own child running to Him with open arms, giving Him joy as you do? What will it mean for you to come near to God today as His child and to listen?

Bible in a Year: *Psalm 1-3; Acts 17:1-15*

July 12

I CAN *Listen* TODAY . . .
BECAUSE GOD SPEAKS THROUGH HIS WORD

Your word is a lamp to my feet and a light to my path. (Psalm 119:105)

We also thank God constantly for this, that when you received the word of God, which you heard from us, you accepted it not as the word of men but as what it really is, the word of God. (1 Thessalonians 2:13)

All Scripture is breathed out by God and profitable for teaching, for reproof, for correction, and for training in righteousness, that the man of God may be complete, equipped for every good work. (2 Timothy 3:16-17)

The Bible is God's provision to equip us for doing His will. For this to happen we must believe and receive it for what it is – the very Word of God. We must listen, learn, and let God's Word guide us. When I think about this, I inevitably recall a night when I was with U.S. Marines, sleeping on my mat in an area covered with sharp rocks. When I awoke and crawled outside, I saw nothing, for it was as dark as dark can be. Without a light to show the way, I would have surely been injured. I was very glad that night that I had a flashlight. God knows our need today, and He provides His light to show the way.

The Bible is an essential part of walking with God. We must not neglect or ignore it, for it is a primary means by which He speaks personally, powerfully, and today. Our part is to develop a life practice of reading, meditating on, memorizing, learning, loving, listening to, and living out God's Word. This is how His Word becomes for us *a lamp to [our] feet and a light to [our] path.*

For Prayerful Reflection: When in a time of darkness and confusion has God showed you the way by His Word? How will you be listening today as God speaks to you through His Word?

Bible in a Year: *Psalm 4-6; Acts 17:16-34*

July 13

I CAN *Listen* TODAY . . .
BECAUSE GOD SPEAKS THROUGH GIFTED TEACHERS

Having gifts that differ according to the grace given to us, let us use them: if prophecy, in proportion to our faith; if service, in our serving; the one who teaches, in his teaching; the one who exhorts, in his exhortation; the one who contributes, in generosity; the one who leads, with zeal; the one who does acts of mercy, with cheerfulness. (Romans 12:6-8)

There are varieties of gifts, but the same Spirit; and there are varieties of service, but the same Lord; and there are varieties of activities, but it is the same God who empowers them all in everyone. (1 Corinthians 12:4-6)

God gives many different gifts to His church through members of His body, including us. When God gives such gifts, they are not to be hoarded by individuals but are always to be passed along to others. Each of us is responsible before God for using the gifts He entrusts to us for the glory of God and for the blessing and good of others.

What do you do when given a gift by somebody? You accept it gratefully and treasure it, don't you? Helen and I have received many treasured gifts through the years from people who are dear to us, and we are very grateful. God has given us countless gifts. The Bible says one of the gifts He gives to His church is teaching. God anoints some with a spiritual gift to open His Word and pass it along in a way people can understand and apply it. In this way God feeds His children. Our part is to thank God for those He has gifted in this way and to appreciate, listen to, learn, and live what God teaches us.

For Prayerful Reflection: How have you been blessed of God through persons to whom He has entrusted a gift of teaching? How can you show appreciation today for a teacher whom God has gifted?

Bible in a Year: *Psalm 7-9; Acts 18*

July 14

I CAN *Listen* TODAY . . .
BECAUSE GOD TEACHES THROUGH DIFFICULTIES

David said to Saul, "Your servant used to keep sheep for his father. And when there came a lion, or a bear, and took a lamb from the flock, I went after him and struck him and delivered it out of his mouth. And if he arose against me, I caught him by his beard and struck him and killed him. Your servant has struck down both lions and bears, and this uncircumcised Philistine shall be like one of them, for he has defied the armies of the living God." (1 Samuel 17:34-36)

Sometimes life isn't easy. David knew this well. Speaking to King Saul, David recounted difficulties he faced as a shepherd, including attacks by lions and bears. In these trials God taught David how to lean on Him in difficulties and receive His help to endure and triumph. Because David learned what God taught him then, he was prepared to face the Philistine army and the giant warrior Goliath. I too have learned much from God through difficulties. I have learned that God is ever faithful, and in Him I have all I need.

The story is told of a World War I soldier who was tired of the war and wished he could run away and go home. Then one night he was lost in the dark and came across what he thought was a road sign. He climbed the sign and lit a match to read it. In that moment he was looking into the face of Jesus, for he had climbed a roadside crucifix. He remembered how the Lord endured the pain of the cross and did not turn from it. Though we cannot run from all difficulties, we can always run to Jesus who is with us now and who grants us courage to face today with Him.

For Prayerful Reflection: What has God taught you through difficulties? How can you apply the lessons He has taught you?

Bible in a Year: *Psalm 10-12; Acts 19:1-20*

July 15

I CAN *Listen* TODAY . . .
BECAUSE GOD EMPOWERS BY THE HOLY SPIRIT

"These things I have spoken to you while I am still with you. But the Helper, the Holy Spirit, whom the Father will send in my name, he will teach you all things and bring to your remembrance all that I have said to you." (John 14:25-26)

"But you will receive power when the Holy Spirit has come upon you, and you will be my witnesses in Jerusalem and in all Judea and Samaria, and to the end of the earth." (Acts 1:8)

Northfield, Minnesota, where I now live, was established in 1855 on the Cannon River, largely because the river and the waterfall offered a ready and continual supply of power, first to operate a sawmill and then a gristmill. The need for water and power applies to us all.

Jesus Christ established His church alongside the living water of new life in relationship with Him through faith and by the steady supply of power available to us by the Holy Spirit. As our Lord was about to ascend to heaven, where He now intercedes for us and from where He will soon return, He made an incredible promise that remains true today. He promised that the Holy Spirit will *teach [us] all things* and will give us the power needed to *be [his] witnesses.*

How blessed we are today to be recipients of such a gift and to live each day with the Holy Spirit indwelling and empowering us. How are we best helped by this gift of God? As the Holy Spirit has been given to teach us, today we can seek, listen, learn, and yield to Him, and then by His power we can be a witness for the Lord Jesus Christ.

For Prayerful Reflection: What has the Holy Spirit taught you about learning from Him and receiving His power? How will you listen today and by the power of the Holy Spirit be a witness for Jesus?

Bible in a Year: *Psalm 13-15; Acts 19:21-41*

July 16

I CAN *Listen* TODAY . . .
BECAUSE GOD SPEAKS
THROUGH HIS CREATION

"Ask the beasts, and they will teach you; the birds of the heavens, and they will tell you; or the bushes of the earth, and they will teach you; and the fish of the sea will declare to you. Who among all these does not know that the hand of the Lord has done this? In his hand is the life of every living thing and the breath of all mankind." (Job 12:7-10)

The heavens declare the glory of God, and the sky above proclaims his handiwork. (Psalm 19:1-2)

Have you heard? God is speaking through His creation. As an artist speaks through his or her handiwork, God reveals Himself in the wonders He has made. Looking upward toward the heavens, the psalmist could hear God declaring His glory. The galaxies show God's fingerprints. The sun echoes God's radiance. The immeasurable nature of space shows the infinite nature of God's person.

Flowers, gemstones, and tropical fish eloquently shout the beauty of God and the brilliance of His glory. Snowflakes reflect the purity of God's holiness, His grace to cover sin, and the sheer endlessness of His creativity. The lion, tiger, and bear hint at His strength and fearlessness, and the soaring eagle exhibits the graceful moving of God far above all things. The trees point upward toward heaven, and the wind speaks God's power to move heaven and earth. The birds show God's care for all His creatures. And every newborn baby affirms the miracle of life, which is of God. God is speaking through His creation.

It is good for us to hear what God is saying through His creation. Are you listening today?

For Prayerful Reflection: When and how has God taught you through His creation? What have you learned? What will it mean for you to listen today to what God is saying through what He has made?

Bible in a Year: *Psalm 16-17; Acts 20:1-16*

July 17

I CAN *Listen* TODAY . . .
BECAUSE GOD SPEAKS IN DREAMS AND VISIONS

"'In the last days it shall be, God declares, that I will pour out my Spirit on all flesh, and your sons and your daughters shall prophesy, and your young men shall see visions, and your old men shall dream dreams; even on my male servants and female servants in those days I will pour out my Spirit, and they shall prophesy.'" (Acts 2:17-18, quoting Joel 2:28-29)

Is it any wonder that God may speak to His children in dreams and visions? After all, God created us and knows us far better than we know ourselves. God is best qualified to know how to communicate with each of us in ways we will hear. In his book *The Five Love Languages,* Gary Chapman suggests that there are five emotional love languages, and we must learn to speak the love language of our spouse.[20] This makes sense to me, as we want to communicate to those we love in ways they can hear.

On the day of Pentecost, Peter quoted the prophet Joel who foretold that when the Holy Spirit is poured out, God's children would see visions and dream dreams. In the Bible God communicated in this way to Jacob, Solomon, Joseph, Peter, John, Paul, and others. When God spoke in this way, they knew He was speaking. My Lord has at times met me in this way with His message always consistent with His Word. I met a man who had been Muslim but now follows Jesus after encountering Him in a vision. Around the world, this is happening today.

God initiates dreams and visions through which He speaks. Our part is to prayerfully listen and receive what God says, however He speaks.

For Prayerful Reflection: Has God ever met you through a dream or vision? If so, what did you hear? To what extent are you open to hear Him today through whatever means He chooses?

Bible in a Year: *Psalm 18-19; Acts 20:17-38*

---

[20] Gary Chapman, *The Five Love Languages: The Secret to Love That Lasts* (Chicago: Northfield Publishing, 1992).

July 18

I CAN *Listen* TODAY . . .
BECAUSE GOD SPEAKS IN SURPRISING WAYS

And the donkey said to Balaam, "Am I not your donkey, on which you have ridden all your life long to this day? Is it my habit to treat you this way?" And he said, "No." Then the Lord opened the eyes of Balaam, and he saw the angel of the Lord standing in the way, with his drawn sword in his hand. And he bowed down and fell on his face. (Numbers 22:30-31)

Sometimes God speaks to us in surprising ways. In Balaam's case, it was through his donkey. While going to a place God did not want him to go, to do a task God did not want him to do, Balaam was riding his donkey. On the way, the donkey saw the angel of the Lord and would not proceed. When Balaam began beating his donkey, God spoke through the donkey. God speaks through any means He chooses – through a donkey, a burning bush, or other ways that may surprise us.

In 1989 I entered a worship service while wrestling with whether to become an active-duty U.S. Navy Chaplain, something I had never considered doing before. This required a contract for a minimum of three years. No one there knew I was struggling with this matter. At one point the preacher paused as though listening, pointed in the direction where I was sitting, and said, "God wants to know if you are willing to see the next three years of your life as a window of time. Are you willing to do something for God you have never considered doing before?" God spoke to me that day, for this was the very question I had been asking. God speaks in surprising ways. Our part is always to listen and then say yes to Him.

For Prayerful Reflection: In what surprising ways has God spoken to you? Will you prayerfully determine to listen when God speaks today through any means He chooses and say yes to Him?

Bible in a Year: *Psalm 20-22; Acts 21:1-17*

July 19

I CAN *Listen* TODAY . . .
BECAUSE GOD SPEAKS WORDS OF LOVE

"And he arose and came to his father. But while he was still a long way off, his father saw him and felt compassion, and ran and embraced him and kissed him. And the son said to him, 'Father, I have sinned against heaven and before you. I am no longer worthy to be called your son.' But the father said to his servants, 'Bring quickly the best robe, and put it on him, and put a ring on his hand, and shoes on his feet. And bring the fattened calf and kill it, and let us eat and celebrate. For this my son was dead, and is alive again; he was lost, and is found.' And they began to celebrate." (Luke 15:20-24)

Can you relate to the young man in Jesus' parable? He had made a mess of things. He'd been foolish and had sinned egregiously, and now he faced the consequences. He was rightly ashamed. In his trouble he remembered his father. He imagined a conversation in which he would humbly confess his sin, beg his father's forgiveness, and plead for crumbs of mercy. The best he hoped for was a well-deserved tongue-lashing with the allowance to be his slave.

Because we are sinners, living with the consequences of our transgressions, we might feel unworthy to approach our Father in heaven and hope for nothing more than a crumb of mercy. But Jesus says the Father longs for us, and with compassion He runs to us, embraces and kisses us, and speaks words of joyful welcome and love that we would never have heard if we had not come home to Him. Our Lord longs for each of us in this way. He loves us, and we can hear Him say so, as in faith we approach and listen today.

For Prayerful Reflection: What surprising words of love has God said concerning you? What will it mean to approach Him today, confessing your sin and need, and hearing His words of love spoken to you?

Bible in a Year: *Psalm 23-25; Acts 21:18-40*

July 20

I CAN *Listen* TODAY . . .
BECAUSE GOD SPEAKS THROUGH MY CIRCUMSTANCES

And the Lord appointed a great fish to swallow up Jonah. And Jonah was in the belly of the fish three days and three nights. Then Jonah prayed to the Lord his God from the belly of the fish, saying, "I called out to the Lord, out of my distress, and he answered me; out of the belly of Sheol I cried, and you heard my voice." (Jonah 1:17-2:2)

We might yearn for God to speak to us audibly, and we think we would then know for sure what He desires of us and then we would do it. "How wonderful and easy that would be," we might say. But though God spoke this clearly to Jonah, he did not heed God's voice, did he? Rather, Jonah ran from God's word and will, foolishly thinking he could run from God.

But mercifully, God was still there, even as He remains with us. And God kept speaking to Jonah through his circumstances: first in the storm at sea, then in being swallowed by a great fish, then when a vine grew up to shade him, and then again when the vine withered. In these circumstances God was speaking His truth and drawing Jonah to Himself.

I have developed a life practice of asking my Lord about my circumstances, saying, "Lord, what are you saying through all of this?" God is sure to answer this prayer. Rather than being stubborn like Jonah and wanting to go our own way, it is good for us to prayerfully consider our life circumstances and ask the Lord what He is saying through all of this.

For Prayerful Reflection: When has God spoken to you in and through your circumstances? Will you ask and prayerfully consider what the Lord might be saying to you through today's circumstances?

Bible in a Year: *Psalm 26-28; Acts 22*

July 21

I CAN *Listen* TODAY . . .
BECAUSE GOD SPEAKS THROUGH WISE COUNSEL

To know wisdom and instruction, to understand words of insight, to receive instruction in wise dealing, in righteousness, justice, and equity; to give prudence to the simple, knowledge and discretion to the youth— Let the wise hear and increase in learning, and the one who understands obtain guidance. The fear of the Lord is the beginning of knowledge; fools despise wisdom and instruction. (Proverbs 1:2-5, 7)

When we seek godly counsel, we can hear God speak. Such counsel aligns with and complements Holy Scripture. When we seek wise and godly mentors in the Lord, we are not asking them to hear from God for us, but rather to prayerfully discern and confirm if what we have heard from the Lord is correct.

Haven't we all at times arrogantly presumed we knew what we were doing, only to discover later that we were foolish indeed? This has happened to me and likely to you too, for our experience is limited, and our wisdom is partial. But thanks be to God, His wisdom is complete and unlimited.

God extends His wisdom as revealed in His Word. Because our perception of His wisdom can be easily clouded by our personal desires, when we are unsure, it is good to seek confirmation of His will from wise counselors who can pray with us, who know the Lord and His Word, and who know us well.

In major decisions and times of struggle, I have often sought such counsel from wise men or women of God who love and listen to Him. And God has used them to affirm His wisdom and point me toward His will. By grace I have also been privileged to pray, listen, and share God's wise counsel with others.

For Prayerful Reflection: What poor decisions have you made in your own limited wisdom? What matters are you facing today in which you need God's wisdom and should listen to wise counsel?

Bible in a Year: *Psalm 29-30; Acts 23:1-15*

July 22

I CAN *Listen* TODAY . . .
BECAUSE GOD SPEAKS THROUGH PEACE

Put on then, as God's chosen ones, holy and beloved, compassionate hearts, kindness, humility, meekness, and patience, bearing with one another and, if one has a complaint against another, forgiving each other; as the Lord has forgiven you, so you also must forgive. And above all these put on love, which binds everything together in perfect harmony. And let the peace of Christ rule in your hearts, to which indeed you were called in one body. And be thankful. (Colossians 3:12-15)

These verses remind us of what followers of Jesus Christ are to be like in this world today: how we are to act toward one another and be a witness in this world. All these qualities and behaviors reflect the One we are following – Jesus Christ. The only possible way we can do this is through Christ who lives in us and among us.

Of these listed qualities of our Lord that are also to be in us, we focus today on peace. He is, after all, the Prince of Peace and the One who brings His peace to all who come to Him in faith. In today's Scripture the apostle Paul tells us to *let the peace of Christ rule in your hearts.* This is therefore a decision for each of us; we must allow it to be so. The word that is here translated *rule* means "to reign." To reign includes being the authority, and thus the one who ultimately decides. This suggests that if peace is lacking in a decision, it is not of the Lord. In Christ, we should not proceed without His peace.

God speaks through His peace. As we seek Jesus Christ and desire Him and His will, He meets us in peace. Let us seek God by listening for and receiving His peace, thus letting Him *rule in [our] hearts* today.

For Prayerful Reflection: When has the lack of peace caused you to pause, seek, and listen until God brought His peace? What will it mean for you today to let the peace of Christ rule in your heart?

Bible in a Year: *Psalm 31-32; Acts 23:16-35*

July 23

I CAN *Listen* TODAY . . .
BECAUSE GOD SPEAKS IN OUR THOUGHTS

Behold, he who forms the mountains and creates the wind, and declares to man what is his thought, who makes the morning darkness, and treads on the heights of the earth—the Lord, the God of hosts, is his name! (Amos 4:13)

And her husband Joseph, being a just man and unwilling to put her to shame, resolved to divorce her quietly. But as he considered these things, behold, an angel of the Lord appeared to him in a dream, saying, "Joseph, son of David, do not fear to take Mary as your wife, for that which is conceived in her is from the Holy Spirit." (Matthew 1:19-20)

Where do our thoughts come from, and can God speak through them? The prophet Amos declared that the God of the universe who made all things, makes His ways known in and through our thoughts. After learning that Mary, his betrothed, was with child, Joseph thought much about these things. And as he did, God spoke and redirected him.

Yes, we must be careful because we live in a sinful world, and we are all born with a sinful nature, so every thought that we have is not of God. We can think up some things on our own or think thoughts that have been fed to us by this depraved world. We must prayerfully judge to discern if our thoughts are in fact of God. When they are, they will align with truth revealed in Scripture. When our thoughts contradict the character and truth of God, those thoughts are not of Him.

But God, who created our minds, can surely give to us thoughts that are of Him and point us toward His will and truth. Our part then is to prayerfully listen to what God is saying as we think on these things.

For Prayerful Reflection: What thoughts has God given you that pointed you toward Him and His will? What could it mean for you today to do as Joseph did and think on things, wanting to honor God?

Bible in a Year: *Psalm 33-34; Acts 24*

July 24

I CAN *Listen* TODAY . . .
BECAUSE GOD SPEAKS UNIQUELY TO ME

When they got out on land, they saw a charcoal fire in place, with fish laid out on it, and bread. Jesus said to them, "Bring some of the fish that you have just caught." So Simon Peter went aboard and hauled the net ashore, full of large fish, 153 of them. And although there were so many, the net was not torn. Jesus said to them, "Come and have breakfast." Now none of the disciples dared ask him, "Who are you?" They knew it was the Lord. (John 21:9-12)

God hears, answers, stands with us, and tells us the right way to go. He has done this for me. When 1996 began, Helen and I were facing a decision on whether I should remain on active duty as a Navy Chaplain. I had been recently promoted and was to report next to an aircraft carrier, but we wanted to hear from God whether this was indeed His will for us or if He would be leading us back to local church life. Two days later God connected me with a local church for which I had long been praying.

Several months later, early on the day that I was to meet again with the pastoral search team, I read John 21, the account of Jesus' resurrection appearance on the lakeshore. My attention was strangely drawn to *153*, the precise number of fish the disciples had caught that day. The Holy Spirit let me know this number would be important to me that day, even though I could not imagine why.

Later when I met with the search team, they said they were agreed that I was the person God would have to be their senior pastor. When I asked how they came to this conclusion, the committee chair said they had looked at 153 candidates, and I was the first and only one they agreed on. That word was uniquely intended by God for me and confirmed the way that He would have me go.

For Prayerful Reflection: When has God spoken a word that you knew without a doubt was for you? How might you listen today as God speaks uniquely to you?

Bible in a Year: *Psalm 35-36; Acts 25*

July 25

I CAN *Listen* TODAY . . .
BECAUSE GOD WANTS ME TO HEAR, THEN DO

Elisha sent a messenger to [Naaman], saying, "Go and wash in the Jordan seven times, and your flesh shall be restored, and you shall be clean." But Naaman was angry and went away, saying, "Behold, I thought that he would surely come out to me and stand and call upon the name of the Lord his God, and wave his hand over the place and cure the leper." But his servants came near and said to him, "My father, it is a great word the prophet has spoken to you; will you not do it?" . . . So he went down and dipped himself seven times in the Jordan, according to the word of the man of God, and his flesh was restored like the flesh of a little child, and he was clean. (2 Kings 5:10-11, 13-14)

Naaman needed a touch from God, for he suffered from leprosy. So he journeyed from Syria to Israel to seek God's help through the prophet Elisha. For Naaman to receive God's blessing he had to listen and then obey the Lord. Speaking through Elisha, God told Naaman to go to the Jordan River and wash seven times. This made no sense to Naaman; he thought he knew better, so he was not going to obey the Lord. But his servants intervened and told him to do as God said. When Naaman obeyed, he was healed.

It is always good to seek the Lord when we are in need. It is not good to disregard what God says. As we seek Him and trust that He knows best, we must listen carefully. And then, like Naaman, we must do what the Lord requires of us. Have we not learned that God blesses when we hear and then do?

For Prayerful Reflection: When did God give you guidance that made no sense to you, and you resisted doing it? Are you desiring today to hear and do whatever God requires, no matter how He leads?

Bible in a Year: *Psalm 37-39; Acts 26*

July 26

I CAN *Listen* TODAY . . .
BECAUSE GOD CALLS ME TO A LISTENING WAY OF LIFE

"Listen to me, you who pursue righteousness, you who seek the Lord: look to the rock from which you were hewn, and to the quarry from which you were dug. Look to Abraham your father and to Sarah who bore you; for he was but one when I called him, . . . Give attention to me, my people, and give ear to me, my nation." (Isaiah 51:1-2, 4)

God seeks people who will desire and seek Him and therefore listen to Him, not occasionally, but as a way of life. Isaiah used a word picture that can help us grasp this. He tells those who know and seek the Lord to *look to the rock from which you were hewn, and to the quarry from which you were dug.* God calls us to remember from whom we came. Abraham and Sarah heard from God a seemingly impossible promise, that in their old age He was going to give them a son, and through that child a nation of innumerable descendants. Despite their circumstances, they listened and believed God.

God calls me to be like that, and He calls you too. He calls us into lifelong relationship with Him in which we become accustomed to seeking and listening to Him. And when we hear Him, we believe, and we are changed by His Word. This way of life flows out of personal relationship with God that includes a devotional life like this: opening and studying His Word often, praying often, fasting at times as God may direct, spending time in fellowship and service with other believers, living in His presence, waiting on the Lord, and following wherever He leads us. When this is our way of life, we are blessed to hear from and listen to the Lord and share life with Him as with a friend close by.

For Prayerful Reflection: When and how did you realize God was inviting you to a lifestyle of personal relationship with Him? What has God said today that He calls you now to hear and believe?

Bible in a Year: *Psalm 40-42; Acts 27:1-26*

July 27

I CAN *Listen* TODAY . . .
BECAUSE GOD SPEAKS THAT I MIGHT OBEY

Therefore we must pay much closer attention to what we have heard, lest we drift away from it. For since the message declared by angels proved to be reliable, and every transgression or disobedience received a just retribution, how shall we escape if we neglect such a great salvation? It was declared at first by the Lord, and it was attested to us by those who heard, while God also bore witness by signs and wonders and various miracles and by gifts of the Holy Spirit distributed according to his will. (Hebrews 2:1-4)

It is conceivable for someone to hope to hear from God but have no desire to obey if His word is not to our liking. Whenever this happens, we cannot and will not hear God. If we have no interest in trusting Him and obeying Him, we cannot hear and will not listen to Him.

Have there been times in your life when you knew you were wrong, and in a futile attempt to remove feelings of guilt you asked God to speak? I have been there and have learned that God does not clearly speak to those with disobedient hearts, because our spiritual ears have become plugged. To hear the Lord clearly, we must have a yearning within us to love and trust and obey Him.

As an example, a Christian considering marriage with an unbeliever should know what the Bible says about not being unequally yoked with unbelievers. If that believer still intends to disregard what God has said, then they are foolish to be asking God what to do. We cannot ignore God's Word, hoping we might hear something more to our liking. God speaks today so that I might listen, hear, and obey.

For Prayerful Reflection: When did you ever ask God for guidance, without really wanting it? What has God said to you today that He is calling you now to hear and obey?

Bible in a Year: *Psalm 43-45; Acts 27:27-44*

July 28

I CAN *Listen* TODAY . . .
BECAUSE GOD HEALS THAT I MIGHT HEAR

"Blessed are the pure in heart, for they shall see God." (Matthew 5:8)

"He who has an ear, let him hear what the Spirit says to the churches." (Revelation 2:7, 11, 17, 29; 3:6, 13, 22)

Seeing and hearing God is not automatic, even for the children of God. It is possible to be in God's presence, as He reveals Himself and speaks life-giving truth, but not see or hear Him. Jesus said that this is a heart issue.

A few years ago, I began having chest pains. It happened more than once. I went to a heart specialist. Heart catheterization revealed a coronary artery blockage, and angioplasty removed the blockage. After that I changed my lifestyle and began taking prescribed medicines, which resolved the problem.

When we have difficulty seeing God's presence and hearing His voice, it is a heart issue. Whatever is blocking us from wholehearted devotion must be removed. This miracle happens when we come to God, the Great Physician. By faith in Christ, with repentance and receiving His forgiveness, He becomes our first love, and His will becomes our first priority. When God heals us spiritually, we can hear Him.

I was initially shocked when hospitalized for chest pains and when I was told I had a blockage. But how thankful I was for the care I received. How much more do I thank God for the times He rightly diagnosed and revealed the condition of my spiritual heart, and in mercy removed the dangerous blockage of sin that held me back. God is here now to heal our spiritual hearts so we can see, listen, and hear Him today.

For Prayerful Reflection: What spiritual blockages has God revealed and healed in you? What spiritual obstacles could be holding you back from hearing God today? Will you bring these to Him?

Bible in a Year: *Psalm 46-48; Acts 28*

July 29

I CAN *Listen* TODAY . . .
BECAUSE GOD IS MY GOOD SHEPHERD

The Lord is my shepherd; I shall not want. He makes me lie down in green pastures. He leads me beside still waters. He restores my soul. (Psalm 23:1-3)

"I am the good shepherd. I know my own and my own know me. My sheep hear my voice, and I know them, and they follow me." (John 10:14, 27)

I love the image of the Lord as my shepherd. He knows all of us and cares for us in every way. Jesus said that like sheep who recognize their shepherd, we know Him. We can hear and recognize His voice and gladly follow wherever He leads. Are we learning to listen carefully to His voice?

A preacher was teaching a children's Sunday school class about Psalm 23 and spent a lot of time talking about sheep. He pointed out that the children in the class who loved Jesus were like sheep of the flock. Then he asked, "If you are the sheep, then who is the shepherd?"

In that church preachers were referred to as *pastors,* which is another word for *shepherd,* so he thought the children would say he was the shepherd of the flock. But one little boy replied, "Jesus is the shepherd."

This answer, while entirely true, startled the preacher a little, and he then asked, "Well then, who am I?"

The same little boy replied, "I guess you must be a sheepdog."

Having been a pastor, I find that reply humorous. But all of us, pastors included, have a Good Shepherd to follow, and that means staying near to Jesus so we will hear His voice, listening carefully, and then following wherever He leads us.

For Prayerful Reflection: What has it meant to you to be part of Jesus' flock? What disciplines are you practicing today to ensure you do not wander off but that you hear, listen, and follow your Lord?

Bible in a Year: *Psalm 49-50; Romans 1*

July 30

I CAN *Listen* TODAY . . .
BECAUSE GOD'S WORD IS GUARANTEED

"For as the rain and the snow come down from heaven and do not return there but water the earth, making it bring forth and sprout, giving seed to the sower and bread to the eater, so shall my word be that goes out from my mouth; it shall not return to me empty, but it shall accomplish that which I purpose, and shall succeed in the thing for which I sent it." (Isaiah 55:10-11)

"For I am the Lord; I will speak the word that I will speak, and it will be performed." (Ezekiel 12:25)

Helen and I just replaced the air conditioner in our home, which is now warrantied, fully guaranteed for ten years, so if it should stop working in that time, it will be repaired or replaced. When we buy any appliance, or anything electronic, it always comes with a guarantee for a certain period of time.

God offers us a better guarantee. His promise is not for a particular season; it is timeless. God guarantees to be my God and yours forever, to protect us, keep us, walk with us, and guide us through life for time and eternity. God guarantees to never leave us nor forsake us. We can always count on Him. But to understand His guarantee, we must spend time with Him and learn of His trustworthiness; we must learn to love Him more and to listen to Him daily.

As we live this way, we learn that God's Word is always true, for He is fully dependable. His Word is guaranteed. As I learn that I can count on Him, I want to hear and know Him more. So today I will listen.

For Prayerful Reflection: What has it meant to you to know that God's Word is fully guaranteed? What guaranteed promises of God are especially meaningful to you today, and why?

Bible in a Year: *Psalm 51-53; Romans 2*

July 31

I CAN *Listen* TODAY . . .
BECAUSE GOD SPEAKS TO HIS FRIENDS

"You are my friends if you do what I command you. No longer do I call you servants, for the servant does not know what his master is doing; but I have called you friends, for all that I have heard from my Father I have made known to you." (John 15:14-15)

Jesus calls His disciples *friends*. As Israel Houghton beautifully says in his song, "Friend of God," "It's amazing." What do good friends do? They spend time together, and they talk. Jesus says this is what He does with us. We can hear Him, listen to His heart, and share ours with Him.

In this friendship we might not always hear clearly, or we might wrongly presume God is not hearing us. A man who'd been married to his wife for forty years became frustrated at her not answering when he spoke to her. He suspected her hearing was going, but she would not admit it.

So he decided to conduct a test. When she did not know he was there, he stood behind her chair across the room and said, "Honey, can you hear me?" She didn't respond. He moved a little closer and asked again. She still didn't respond, so he moved closer still. He did this a fourth time, and this time he was right behind her.

At this she spun around in her chair and said with aggravation, "For the fourth time, yes, I can hear you!"

Our friend Jesus always hears us when we call. If ever our communication with God feels lacking, the problem is not on His end, it's on ours. Admitting this is a first step to healing, as God enables us to listen and hear.

For Prayerful Reflection: What has it meant to you to be a friend of God? How will you live this privilege today as you listen to your Lord and friend and share with Him your own heart?

Bible in a Year: *Psalm 54-56; Romans 3*

12 Themes on Following Jesus

AUGUST

Because God . . .
I Can *Rest* Today

August 1

I CAN Rest TODAY . . .
BECAUSE GOD RESTED

Thus the heavens and the earth were finished, and all the host of them. And on the seventh day God finished his work that he had done, and he rested on the seventh day from all his work that he had done. So God blessed the seventh day and made it holy, because on it God rested from all his work that he had done in creation. (Genesis 2:1-3)

After creating, God rested. Why? It is not because God was exhausted, as we can often be. He was not tired after all He had accomplished, for God's power, strength, and endurance are infinite. Rather, God's rest suggests focus on the purpose of His creation. All that God made was now His dwelling place and sanctuary. *So God blessed the seventh day and made it holy, because on it God rested from all his work that he had done in creation.* God's Sabbath rest focused on the purpose of all creation, which was, and is, and always will be for His glory. This is why we can rest today, keeping our focus on God, the glorious One who is the power and reason for all things.

In the creation account in Genesis, the seventh day is the only day that does not conclude with the refrain, *and there was evening and there was morning*. This could suggest that the seventh day continues, for we are still focusing on the One who does all things for His glory. In God we find our rest.

God created us in His own image, so as God rested, it is important to our spiritual walk to rest too. In rest, God lets us renew, fixing our focus again on the One who has made all things, including us, for His glory.

For Prayerful Reflection: How has reflecting on God's creation of all things affected your own worship and rest? What will it mean for you today to rest as God rested?

Bible in a Year: *Psalm 57-59; Romans 4*

August 2

I CAN Rest TODAY . . .
BECAUSE GOD RESTORES ME AS I REST

He restores my soul. (Psalm 23:3)

"Come to me, all who labor and are heavy laden, and I will give you rest. Take my yoke upon you, and learn from me, for I am gentle and lowly in heart, and you will find rest for your souls. For my yoke is easy, and my burden is light." (Matthew 11:28-30)

Our Lord restores us when we come to Him for rest; He renews our strength and replenishes our depletion. He restores our soul. God knows when we are exhausted and running on fumes, weighed down by life's burdens. He knows when we need rest, and in such times, He invites us to come to Him.

Some of us see little good in rest. We prefer pressing on with our heavy workloads, foolishly believing that we do not need rest and that we will accomplish more by continual activity. Have you learned the foolishness of this perspective as I have? God has made us for rest, through which He restores us.

One woodsman challenged another to an all-day tree-chopping contest. The challenger worked incessantly and stopped only for a brief lunch break. But the other man had a leisurely lunch and took several rest breaks during the day. At the end of the day, the challenger was surprised to see the other fellow had chopped substantially more wood than he had. "I don't get it," he said. "I saw you resting, while I kept working, yet you chopped more wood than I."

The winning woodsman replied, "But you did not notice that when I rested, I was sharpening my ax."

Rest is restorative. God promises that when we come to Him for rest, He will renew and restore us.

For Prayerful Reflection: When has your burden been lightened and your ax sharpened when you came to God tired and carrying a heavy load? How can God restore you today as you rest in Him?

Bible in a Year: *Psalm 60-62; Romans 5*

August 3

I CAN Rest TODAY...
BECAUSE GOD COMMANDS ME TO REST

"Remember the Sabbath day, to keep it holy. Six days you shall labor, and do all your work, but the seventh day is a Sabbath to the Lord your God. On it you shall not do any work. . . . For in six days the Lord made heaven and earth, the sea, and all that is in them, and rested on the seventh day. Therefore, the Lord blessed the Sabbath day and made it holy." (Exodus 20:8-11)

One of God's Ten Commandments is to *remember the Sabbath day, to keep it holy*. On the Sabbath, in addition to holy worship, we are commanded to rest. Why do we need teaching and commandments regarding rest? It is because we are all sinfully prone to self-centeredness and restlessness, which precludes us from true worship or from remembering that God is the source of our own life and of all things.

We are prone to find self-worth in the achievement of our labors rather than in the person of God. Our hopes therefore become centered in what we accomplish rather than in what God has accomplished for us. So to our shame, we may disregard God's command of Sabbath rest.

A lady who was angry at her pastor said, "I called and I dropped by to see you Tuesday, but you were not there."

The minister said, "I'm sorry, but Tuesday is my day off."

"Your day off?" she said self-righteously. "The devil never takes a day off!"

To this the pastor replied, "You are absolutely right, and I suppose if I did the same thing, I would become like him." For many good reasons God commands us to rest.

For Prayerful Reflection: When have you ever failed to rest, thus experiencing why God lovingly commands us to do so? How can you shift focus from yourself to the Lord by resting in Him?

Bible in a Year: *Psalm 63-65; Romans 6*

August 4

I CAN Rest TODAY...
BECAUSE GOD GIVES ME A LONGING FOR HIS REST

My heart is in anguish within me; the terrors of death have fallen upon me. Fear and trembling come upon me, and horror overwhelms me. And I say, "Oh, that I had wings like a dove! I would fly away and be at rest." (Psalm 55:4-6)

The Psalms do not always present life as it ought to be, but as it is. And real life includes anguish and pain. Psalm 55 is such a psalm. The psalmist was betrayed by someone close to him, and his heart was filled with anguish to the point of fearing death. Perhaps you have experienced something like this or another circumstance that overwhelmed you in sorrow or pain. I have been there.

The psalmist's response here can be ours too, as we also long for rest that is available in God alone. God gives us this longing. Several times in my life, when I was overwhelmed by anguish and sorrow and saw no way to ease my own pain, I prayed to God who put a longing for Him in my heart. And in Him I found rest.

The psalmist portrayed his longing by saying, *"Oh, that I had wings like a dove! I would fly away and be at rest."* This desire is God Himself calling us to fly to Him for His rest. Busyness and ferocious effort will not relieve pain or give us rest. Resting in God brings rest and relief.

The Chinese pictograph for *busy* is comprised of two characters: one is the character for heart, and the other is the character for killing. When our heart is dying, continued busyness is not the answer. Rather, the answer is coming to our Lord to rest in Him.

For Prayerful Reflection: When were you overwhelmed and heard God call you to come to Him for rest? What would it mean for you today to be real with God about your struggles and fly to Him for rest?

Bible in a Year: *Psalm 66-67; Romans 7*

August 5

I CAN Rest TODAY . . .
BECAUSE GOD GIVES REST TO HIS BELOVED

Unless the Lord builds the house, those who build it labor in vain. Unless the Lord watches over the city, the watchman stays awake in vain. It is in vain that you rise up early and go late to rest, eating the bread of anxious toil; for he gives to his beloved sleep. (Psalm 127:1-2)

The theme of Psalm 127 is that without God's blessing, human toil and striving is ultimately fruitless. Building a house, raising a family, working the fields, laboring in our occupations and employment, and all our many endeavors are all part of life, and we must of course be diligent in them. But we must trust God to make them all work well, which brings us to the rest God gives to His beloved.

We may presume that success requires our heroic efforts, so we toss and turn with the pressure of thinking we must try harder and give more than we have or can. But God who loves us does not want His beloved children struggling under such a heavy burden. God wants us to trust fully in Him and know He is with us in this, and that His presence and blessing bring success. Living this way is rest.

Nineteenth-century theologian and preacher A. B. Simpson expressed this truth poetically when he wrote,

> Once my life was full of effort;
> Now 'tis full of joy and zest;
> Since I took His yoke upon me,
> Jesus gives to me His rest.

Yes, God gives rest to His beloved, even to us today.

For Prayerful Reflection: When have you lacked rest because of self-imposed demands to try harder and give more? What will it mean for you today to rest in God who loves you and in whom success is found?

Bible in a Year: *Psalm 68-69; Romans 8:1-21*

August 6

I CAN Rest TODAY . . .
BECAUSE GOD MAKES ME SAFE ENOUGH TO REST

Answer me when I call, O God of my righteousness! You have given me relief when I was in distress. Be gracious to me and hear my prayer! In peace I will both lie down and sleep; for you alone, O Lord, make me dwell in safety. (Psalm 4:1, 8)

There arose a great storm on the sea, so that the boat was being swamped by the waves; but he was asleep. And they went and woke him, saying, "Save us Lord; we are perishing." (Matthew 8:24-25)

In this storm-filled, stress-inducing world, where do we find safety and rest? In Psalm 4, the psalmist acknowledges the deep distress he has known; then he tells us what he did and what God did for him. In distress he called to the Lord, and what did God do? The psalmist testified, *In peace I will both lie down and sleep; for you alone, O Lord, make me dwell in safety.* When storms rage around us and we turn to God in faith, He is with us and blesses us with peace and safety; so in Him we find our rest.

Jesus demonstrated this. While His disciples battled a storm, Jesus slept. He was physically exhausted after a long day, and He slept peacefully. Was He nervous about this storm? Clearly not. And because Jesus was with His disciples, and because today He is with us, do we have reason to worry? We too can call out to God today, knowing His presence, experiencing His power, and receiving His rest.

Perhaps each of us could prayerfully consider this today: do I have more faith in the power of the storm or in the power of God who is with me to bless me, protect me, and give me His rest?

For Prayerful Reflection: When have you, like the psalmist, called on God in your distress and received His peace and rest? What might be the effect for you today of trusting God more than the power of the storm?

Bible in a Year: *Psalm 70-71; Romans 8:22-39*

August 7

I CAN Rest TODAY . . .
BECAUSE GOD CREATED ME WITH A NEED FOR REST

"Six days you shall do your work, but on the seventh day you shall rest; that your ox and your donkey may have rest, and the son of your servant woman, and the alien, may be refreshed." (Exodus 23:12)

And [Jesus] said to them, "The Sabbath was made for man, not man for the Sabbath." (Mark 2:27)

God gave us the Sabbath as a gift for our physical and spiritual refreshment. Just as we are made to worship as a way of life, so we are made to rest. We know this too. We know what happens if we operate a cell phone or tablet all day long, or if an animal is continually burdened with a heavy load. Breakdowns happen. Batteries die. Exhaustion sets in. Efficiency is lost. This is true of each of us, for we were made by God with a need for rest, and without it our effectiveness is lost.

So why have I sometimes felt lazy or selfish when resting? Anne Morrow Lindbergh made such an observation: "If one sets aside time for a business appointment, a trip to the hairdresser, [or] a social engagement, . . . that time is accepted as inviolable. But if one says: I cannot come because that is my hour to be alone [i.e., to rest], one is considered rude, egotistical or strange. What a commentary on our civilization: when being alone is considered suspect; when one has to apologize for it."[21]

Concerning our rest, others may misunderstand, or we may even harshly judge ourselves. But from God's Word we learn that, in fact, regular time for solitude and rest is a precious and necessary gift from God Himself to recharge our batteries and restore our souls.

For Prayerful Reflection: What lessons have you learned concerning your own need for rest? What are some implications for you today and this week in knowing that God has made you with a need for rest?

Bible in a Year: *Psalm 72-73; Romans 9:1-15*

---

21 Anne Morrow Lindbergh, *Gift from the Sea* (New York: Pantheon Books, 1975), 50.

August 8

I CAN Rest TODAY . . .
BECAUSE GOD KNOWS MY FRAME

He knows our frame; he remembers that we are dust. (Psalm 103:14)

That evening they brought to him many who were oppressed by demons, and he cast out the spirits with a word, and healed all who were sick. And when he got into the boat, his disciples followed him. And behold, there arose a great storm on the sea, so that the boat was being swamped by the waves; but [Jesus] was asleep. (Matthew 8:16, 23-24)

God knows our frame, which includes our propensity to fatigue and our need for rest. In His humanity, even Jesus experienced this. Matthew 8 describes a busy day for our Lord as He ministered late into the night, compassionately caring for people and healing injuries and illnesses. After this long day and being utterly exhausted, He climbed into a boat and fell sound asleep. Another such day is described beginning in Matthew 4:23, as Jesus ministered to huge crowds in Galilee and then taught them in what we call the Sermon on the Mount.

Jesus wonderfully demonstrated God's compassion and power that day, and He imparted God's truth. But have we paused to reflect on His humanity in all this, and how He too must have faced exhaustion? This is imaginatively depicted in Season 2 Episode 3 of the dramatic series called *The Chosen*. After a very long day of ministry, Jesus stumbled into camp exhausted, so tired He didn't want conversation, only sleep. His mother ministered to Him; she washed his sore and filthy feet and prepared Him for rest.

God knows our human frame and so our need for rest. He helps us find rest in Him today and provides opportunities for us to help others who need rest also.

For Prayerful Reflection: How has God reminded you that He knows your frame and your need for rest? What opportunities has God given you, or might He give you today, to assist somebody in need of rest?

Bible in a Year: *Psalm 74-76; Romans 9:16-33*

August 9

I CAN Rest TODAY...
BECAUSE GOD'S PRESENCE BRINGS REST

> *Moses used to take the tent and pitch it outside the camp, far off from the camp, and he called it the tent of meeting.... When Moses entered the tent, the pillar of cloud would descend and stand at the entrance of the tent, and the Lord would speak with Moses... face to face, as a man speaks to his friend.... And [God] said [to Moses], "My presence will go with you, and I will give you rest."* (Exodus 33:7, 9, 11, 14)

Moses had a huge responsibility, and he knew that he could not possibly do it without God's help. So he didn't try. Rather, he lived the same privilege that is now afforded to us. Moses often entered a quiet place to be in God's presence and to seek His face. Moses called it *the tent of meeting.* And what happened there? Moses and God met together face to face. There God heard Moses, and Moses heard God speaking to him with reassurance and direction. And there, God lifted the burden and gave him rest.

In 2003 when I was called to serve as Conference Minister of the CCCC, I knew the responsibility was bigger than me, and that I needed to often meet with God for direction, help, and rest. As Helen and I and our teenage son Jonathan looked for the home God intended for us, amazingly we found one with a built-in prayer chapel in its lowest level. As I stood there tearfully beholding this, Jonathan put his hand on my shoulder and said, "This is for you, Dad." And it was.

We are greatly blessed to enter God's presence in faith each day to meet with Him, hear His voice, and receive His peace and rest.

For Prayerful Reflection: To what extent are you entering a *tent of meeting* to meet with God, enjoy His presence, and receive His guidance and rest? How will you be answering this invitation today?

Bible in a Year: *Psalm 77-78; Romans 10*

August 10

I CAN Rest TODAY . . .
BECAUSE GOD GIVES REST IN PEACE

The righteous man perishes, and no one lays it to heart; devout men are taken away, while no one understands. For the righteous man is taken away from calamity; he enters into peace; they rest in their beds who walk in their uprightness. (Isaiah 57:1-2)

I heard a voice from heaven saying, "Write this: Blessed are the dead who die in the Lord from now on." "Blessed indeed," says the Spirit, "that they may rest from their labors, for their deeds follow them!" (Revelation 14:13)

In a time of great national turmoil, Isaiah saw a trend toward fewer righteous people; and when people of faith died, most failed to see what it meant or that God was welcoming the righteous into His peace and rest. A similar message is conveyed in the book of Revelation, where faithful followers of God who have endured, obeyed the Lord, and kept faith in Jesus are blessed in death with *rest from their labors*. The Bible says when we die in Christ, we are going to be with Him forever and experience the full measure of His rest and peace. But already by His grace and through faith we can have a measure of His rest now.

Two little children walked to a neighborhood florist to buy a Mother's Day arrangement for their mom. When they presented it to her, she was thrilled at their thoughtfulness but mystified by their gift. It was a small wreath with a ribbon that said "REST IN PEACE." They said, "We thought this was perfect for you, Mom, because you're always asking for a little peace so you can rest." Well, aren't we all?

Through Jesus Christ, we will rest in peace when He calls us home to heaven. But even now, even today, He gives rest in peace as we trust in Him.

For Prayerful Reflection: What comfort have you received from God's promise of rest in peace in heaven? How are you experiencing this today?

Bible in a Year: *Psalm 79-80; Romans 11:1-18*

August 11

I CAN Rest TODAY . . .
BECAUSE GOD IS GRANTING A SABBATH REST

If Joshua had given them rest, God would not have spoken of another day later on. So then, there remains a Sabbath rest for the people of God, for whoever has entered God's rest has also rested from his works as God did from his. Let us therefore strive to enter that rest, so that no one may fall by the same sort of disobedience. (Hebrews 4:8-11)

When Joshua at last led the people of Israel into the land promised to Abraham, they had been wandering in the wilderness for forty years. What sort of rest were the people longing for then? They longed for the rest they would find when they would be physically settled into their new communities and homes. The rest they were seeking was entirely on this side of glory.

They did enter that promised land, and they settled in. This was God's blessing to His people, even as God has abundantly blessed us on this side of heaven. But God had in mind a Sabbath rest far greater than what we can know for a few years in this life. The Bible says God also has in store a Sabbath rest that will be glorious and complete, in which we will strive no more, for at last we will be where God wants us to be forever – in His holy presence knowing the full measure of His rest.

The writer of Hebrews says to *strive to enter that rest,* but that does not say we can earn our salvation, for it is entirely of God's grace through Christ (Ephesians 2:8-9). Striving now for such rest is to depend fully on the grace of God and love Him, live in obedience to Him, and receive His Sabbath rest.

For Prayerful Reflection: In what ways have you already received God's Sabbath rest? How will you today *strive to enter that rest*?

Bible in a Year: *Psalm 81-83; Romans 11:19-36*

August 12

I CAN Rest TODAY . . .
BECAUSE GOD GIVES PEACE IN TIMES OF TROUBLE

"Peace I leave with you; my peace I give to you. Not as the world gives do I give to you. Let not your hearts be troubled, neither let them be afraid." (John 14:27)

"I have said these things to you, that in me you may have peace. In the world you will have tribulation. But take heart; I have overcome the world." (John 16:33)

In 2018, besides my physical trials of developing hypogammaglobulinemia and multiple myeloma, I was dealing with grief and loss. In the recent past my brother David had suddenly died. A few months later my father died, and my mom was approaching death. Though dealing with these trials was difficult, I was leaning on my Lord who was walking with me through all of it; He was sustaining me. By God's grace I was given a good measure of His peace, and I came to realize that others were noticing.

Following a medical appointment one day, a nurse friend who had been observing me for some time asked me a personal question. She wanted to know how I was able to be calm and peaceful while dealing with such trials. The answer I gave her is the same one Jesus gave His disciples: Jesus gives me His peace, which does not depend on circumstances, but comes from knowing, loving, and trusting Him.

When by faith we believe that God is with us in all of life, even in the dark nights and hard trials, we are blessed to receive His peace through it all. Our part is to come to Him in faith today, surrender ourselves to Him again, trust Him for the outcomes, and choose to let go and rest in Him.

For Prayerful Reflection: When and how have you experienced God's peace in time of trouble? In what current trials is God calling you to rest in Him?

Bible in a Year: *Psalm 84-86; Romans 12*

August 13

I CAN Rest TODAY . . .
BECAUSE GOD DISPLACES ANXIETY WITH PEACE

Rejoice in the Lord always; again I will say, rejoice. . . . The Lord is at hand; do not be anxious about anything, but in everything by prayer and supplication with thanksgiving let your requests be made known to God. And the peace of God, which surpasses all understanding, will guard your hearts and your minds in Christ Jesus. (Philippians 4:4-7)

Anxiety is hard to live with. CBS News told the story of Sergei, a Latvian prison convict. With ten months left to serve in his seven-year burglary sentence, he decided to escape. But even after years of freedom, Sergei could not relax. "Worry over being caught was proving too stressful," he said. He worked several jobs and moved into an apartment with his girlfriend, but Sergei was constantly looking over his shoulder. In a move that surprised prison officials, Sergei showed up at the minimum-security facility and turned himself in, five years after escaping.[22]

Anxiety is a prison of its own that robs us of peace. From prison the apostle Paul told Christians how we can release our anxiety and receive God's peace in its place. This requires making a decision to shift our focus from the prison of our anxiety to the freedom of faith in Christ. Paul showed us how to do this.

We are to rejoice in the Lord, in who He is, for thus we joyfully shift our focus from the cause of our anxiety to God Himself. And we are to pray and lift before almighty God our various petitions, including the things that cause us worry; we are to do this with thanksgiving. Then it happens. God displaces our anxiety and replaces it with His peace. So in Jesus Christ, we find rest.

For Prayerful Reflection: When have you struggled with escaping anxiety, and when did God swap out your anxiety for His peace? In what trials today is God calling you to rest in Him?

Bible in a Year: *Psalm 87-88; Romans 13*

---
[22] "Man Picks Jail Over Girlfriend," CBSnews.com, https://ssnet.org/blog/guilty-refuge/ (February 22, 2005).

August 14

I CAN Rest TODAY . . .
BECAUSE GOD MAKES US RESTLESS WITHOUT HIM

For God alone, O my soul, wait in silence, for my hope is from him. He only is my rock and my salvation, my fortress; I shall not be shaken. On God rests my salvation and my glory; my mighty rock, my refuge is God. Trust in him at all times, O people; pour out your heart before him; God is a refuge for us. (Psalm 62:5-8)

"Come to me, all who labor and are heavy laden, and I will give you rest." (Matthew 11:28)

Restlessness is an inability to rest or relax. The cause can be anxiety or boredom, but the result is the same: we lack rest. I am sure that you, like me, have had bouts of restlessness. When this happens, we long for an answer, something that can satisfy our longing. The Bible makes it clear that ultimately God alone can do this for us.

David confessed this in Psalm 62 and determined in deep longing to wait on God, putting his trust in the One who promises to be our refuge. Jesus invites us to come to Him like this for our rest.

Aurelius Augustinus (Saint Augustine) had spent his life battling the bondages of sexual temptation and philosophical pride. But he was never satisfied. Then in God's time and great mercy, Augustine learned that God made him and us with a longing for Him and only He can satisfy our restless souls. At the age of thirty-one, Augustine's life was transformed by the power of God through His Word. Years later as bishop of Hippo, Augustine testified of God, "You have made us for yourself, and our heart is restless until it rests in you."[23]

This is true of you and me today. We are restless without Him. But in Christ we receive His peace.

For Prayerful Reflection: When have you known restlessness, and what did God teach you about finding your rest in Him? What is God teaching you today about your restless longings?

Bible in a Year: *Psalm 89-90; Romans 14*

---
23 Saint Augustine, *St. Augustine's Confessions*, Book 1, Chapter 1.

August 15

I CAN Rest TODAY . . .
BECAUSE GOD KEEPS THE WATCH

He will not let your foot be moved; he who keeps you will not slumber. Behold, he who keeps Israel will neither slumber nor sleep. (Psalm 121:3-4)

It is a wonderful thing to know that God is watching over us always, 24/7, every moment of every day. Believing this allows us to trust God to do it well, and that lets us feel safe today and able to rest in Him.

Throughout my twenty-seven years of service as a Navy Chaplain, both active duty and reserves, I attended and participated in innumerable retirement ceremonies for sailors wrapping up their Navy careers. Often, near the conclusion of such ceremonies, a poem entitled "The Watch" is read. In every Navy Command, at all hours of day or night, sailors stand watch and keep an eye on things; they stand guard, run the ship, and protect everyone in their charge. "The Watch" includes these words: "For 27 years this Sailor has stood the Watch. While some of us were in our bunks at night, this Sailor stood the Watch."[24]

Trusting those who stand the watch allows us to rest. The psalmist says this is true of God – *He . . . will not slumber.* Indeed, *he . . . will neither slumber nor sleep.* God keeps the watch. The implications of this for us today are many. We can trust Him wholly. We can know that God is armed and ready to protect us from all attacks. We can know that God knows the way and is steering us toward our destination. We can know that God will ensure that we are safe under His care, so we can rest in His peace. Have you experienced this wonderful truth? You can today, for God is keeping watch over you.

For Prayerful Reflection: When has it especially blessed you to know God was keeping watch over you and over those whom you love? How does this knowledge affect you today?

Bible in a Year: *Psalm 91-93; Romans 15:1-13*

---

[24] "The Watch," *https://pdf4pro.com/view/the-watch-retirement-ceremony-welcome-to-the-343f4.html.*

August 16

I CAN Rest TODAY . . .
BECAUSE GOD'S SALVATION INCLUDES PEACE AND REST

For God alone my soul waits in silence; from him comes my salvation. He alone is my rock and salvation, my fortress; I shall not be greatly shaken. (Psalm 62:1-2)

For if while we were enemies we were reconciled to God by the death of his Son, much more, now that we are reconciled, shall we be saved by his life. (Romans 5:10)

We rightly love the promise of heaven, for it is our destination through faith in Jesus Christ. His victory over sin and death assures all who believe in Him of the great treasure of everlasting life. But this future reality is certainly not all there is to our salvation. God's salvation includes His influence and blessing in every area of our lives today, including our need for peace and rest.

Two artists attempted to paint a picture of peace. The first painted an idyllic scene of a still harbor with a graceful sailboat passing by. Overhead the sky is blue and dotted with light, fluffy clouds. And on the shore children play in the shallows, making castles in the sand. It is a picture of peace.

The second artist's picture reflects an even clearer image of the blessings of salvation that are ours on this side of heaven. A wild and rocky shore is depicted. Angry billows burst in lofty clouds of spray. The sky is black with storm clouds, and waves tower and toss. But far up on a rocky precipice, hidden in the cleft of a rock and sheltered from the wind, sits a bird, safe and secure in her nest, looking out with a calm and serene eye at all the turmoil raging beneath. This is a picture of the peace God brings to us today.

For Prayerful Reflection: When have you experienced God's peace and rest while a storm raged around you? How could you point someone today toward knowing His peace?

Bible in a Year: *Psalm 94-96; Romans 15:14-33*

August 17

I CAN Rest TODAY...
BECAUSE GOD IS MY SHELTER
IN TIME OF STORM

The Lord is a stronghold for the oppressed, a stronghold in times of trouble. (Psalm 9:9)

For you have been a stronghold to the poor, a stronghold to the needy in his distress, a shelter from the storm and a shade from the heat. (Isaiah 25:4)

In this world, dangerous storms can occur at any time. And when they come, we need a shelter. We call some storms *natural disasters,* like torrential rains, powerful hurricanes, blinding blizzards, destructive tornadoes, raging fires, volcanic eruptions, and rising floods. Over my lifetime I have witnessed the effects of all of these. When storms come, we need a refuge.

Even more threatening are the spiritual storms that can overwhelm us with pain from relationship loss, emotional injury, deep depression, and discontent; we experience fearful uncertainties due to our poor health or that of someone we dearly love, profound grief, and even lost hope. When such raging storms come, we need a refuge, a shelter in the time of storm. I have experienced such storms, as I expect you have. Even today there are many on my heart who are enduring raging storms, and for them I am praying. I testify to you today that I have experienced and seen firsthand the blessing of entering God's refuge in the time of storm. God holds us close, keeps us safe, and lets us rest in His love.

If you are in a storm today, or when you find yourself in one in days to come, by grace run in faith to the Lord and enter the shelter of His love.

For Prayerful Reflection: In what storms of life have you sought the Lord and found safety in Him? What storms are you facing today in which you now hear God inviting you to enter His refuge?

Bible in a Year: *Psalm 97-99; Romans 16*

August 18

I CAN Rest TODAY . . .
BECAUSE GOD GIVES ME REST AS I TRUST IN HIM

You keep him in perfect peace whose mind is stayed on you, because he trusts in you. Trust in the Lord forever, for the Lord God is an everlasting rock. (Isaiah 26:3-4)

Do not be anxious about anything, but in everything by prayer and supplication with thanksgiving let your requests be made known to God. And the peace of God, which surpasses all understanding, will guard your hearts and minds in Christ Jesus. (Philippians 4:6-7)

Everyone attempts to rest, but not everyone can rest when they want to. Have you at times tossed and turned at night as you tried to find sleep but to no avail? Or have you ever taken a much-needed vacation, only to find yourself worried and unable to relax? Why can we desperately desire rest but find our minds ruminating on things that bother us: our problems, regrets, concerns, and whatever stresses us out? God wants to give us rest as we trust in Him.

For us, this requires faith; we must keep our minds stayed on Him rather than continually spinning our wheels in the mud of worry. There is good reason why Paul urged us to admit our anxieties and in faith *by prayer and supplication with thanksgiving let your requests be made known to God*. For then, *the peace of God, which surpasses all understanding, will guard your hearts and minds in Christ Jesus*.

In this way, God gives rest to His children. This is why I treasure my childhood memories of kneeling beside my bed at bedtime, lifting before God every concern on my heart, entrusting it all to Him, and then enjoying His rest. This practice has been for me, and can be for you today, a way of life.

For Prayerful Reflection: When have you tossed and turned with worry and then given it to God and received His rest? What burdens are you facing today that you want to entrust to God now as you keep your mind stayed on Him?

Bible in a Year: *Psalm 100-102; 1 Corinthians 1*

August 19

I CAN Rest TODAY . . .
BECAUSE GOD REPLENISHES WEARY SOULS

I love the Lord, because he has heard my voice and my pleas for mercy. Because he inclined his ear to me, therefore I will call on him as long as I live. Return, O my soul, to your rest; for the Lord has dealt bountifully with you. (Psalm 116:1-2, 7)

"For I will satisfy the weary soul, and every languishing soul I will replenish." At this I awoke and looked, and my sleep was pleasant to me. (Jeremiah 31:25-26)

God's promise to replenish the weary souls of His people is precious, for we all know what it is to be weary. We know what it is to be physically or emotionally exhausted, even thinking we cannot possibly take another step. Sometimes the burdens we have long carried have worn us down, and we are weary indeed. Recalling such times, the psalmist determined to come again to God to find rest in Him. And the prophet Jeremiah passed along to the people who were enduring much heartache in exile that God has indeed promised, *"I will satisfy the weary soul, and every languishing soul I will replenish."*

I remember the day I returned home more physically tired than I had ever been. The previous night I had marched twenty-five miles with my battalion of infantry Marines, carrying my fully loaded pack. My feet were bleeding, my back was screaming in pain, my body was aching, and I was utterly exhausted. When I arrived home, my dear wife Helen was there, loving and caring for me in ways only she could. She tenderly cared for me, as the loving hands of God.

How often God does this for us. When our souls are weary, He lovingly nurses, nurtures, and replenishes us. Letting God do this for us means releasing to Him our burdens and receiving His touch.

For Prayerful Reflection: When has God met you in great weariness and replenished your soul? In what ways might you be God's hands of love today for another weary soul?

Bible in a Year: *Psalm 103-104; 1 Corinthians 2*

August 20

I CAN Rest TODAY...
BECAUSE GOD OFFERS REST IN WORSHIP

"If it seems slow, wait for it; it will surely come; it will not delay... but the righteous shall live by his faith. ... But the Lord is in his holy temple; let all the earth keep silence before him." (Habakkuk 2:3-4, 20)

Habakkuk had a tough assignment: he was to prophesy of the Babylonian invasion that was soon coming as a consequence of the people's rebellion against God. The prophet's heart was heavy as he carried this burden; he cried out to God in a search for understanding. At first, he was very troubled. But in the end, he was a changed person; he had learned to wait and trust in God who works in and through our struggles for His glory and our good.

Here we find insight for acquiring God's rest in troubling times. Habakkuk teaches us that such rest can be found in faith and in worship. God's rest is found by entering into His holy presence, stilling our busy minds, and being silent before Him; this is not the time to explain to God all the things that bother us, but to simply recognize and enjoy His presence in this moment and give Him our heartfelt worship.

I can recall so many times in my life when, like Habakkuk, my heart was very troubled. Sometimes it was because of grief, or worry, or the weight of heavy responsibility. Sometimes it was inner turmoil because of crisis, conflict, or confusion. Sometimes I have found myself screaming out for God to come now and do something. But when I have paused enough to listen and recognize His presence, I could hear the quiet voice of God inviting me to enter into His holy temple and be very still, simply realizing who He is and that He is here. When I have thus worshipped Him, God has given me His rest.

For Prayerful Reflection: When have you found rest in worshipping God in time of trouble? What does it mean for you today to take some time to be silent before Him?

Bible in a Year: *Psalm 105-106; 1 Corinthians 3*

August 21

I CAN Rest TODAY . . .
BECAUSE GOD PROVIDES NEEDED REST STOPS

The people grumbled against Moses, saying, "What shall we drink?" And he cried to the Lord, and the Lord showed him a log, and he threw it into the water, and the water became sweet. . . . Then they came to Elim, where there were twelves springs of water and seventy palm trees, and they encamped there by the water. (Exodus 15:24-25, 27)

Did you ever as a child, or later as a parent, take a long road trip? If you did as a child, can you recall incessantly asking, "Are we there yet? How much longer? I'm hungry! I'm thirsty! I need to go to the bathroom! So-and-so just hit me!" And if you were the parent on this road trip, you fielded all of this! If you think you had it hard, consider Moses, who was responsible for about two million people, many of whom complained incessantly.

Today's verses remind us that God is the One who cares for us along our way and that He knows and provides what we need. On this life journey, we need rest stops: places to pause, refuel, rest, and refresh. Whenever a rest stop is needed, it is unwise and unkind to drive by without stopping. God knows where the rest stops are and when we need them, and for our sake He pulls in.

But it does us no good unless we take advantage of them. What rest stops does God provide? He offers us quiet times, like you are enjoying right now. He gives us opportunities to pause our frenetic activity, just to be still in His presence and hear His voice. He gives us other opportunities like Bible studies, small groups, retreats, and worship gatherings where our souls can be refreshed and we can find rest.

For Prayerful Reflection: What rest stops has God provided in your life that have especially blessed you? What rest stops is God offering you today, and what will it mean for you to take full advantage of them?

Bible in a Year: *Psalm 107-109; 1 Corinthians 4*

August 22

I CAN Rest TODAY . . .
BECAUSE GOD IS HOLDING ME AS HIS CHILD

O Lord, my heart is not lifted up; my eyes are not raised too high; I do not occupy myself with things too great and too marvelous for me. But I have calmed and quieted my soul, like a weaned child with its mother; like a weaned child is my soul within me. O Israel, hope in the Lord from this time forth and forevermore. (Psalm 131)

The above quoted verses are an entire psalm. The theme of Psalm 131 is having a calm and quieted soul with God like a weaned child with its mother. We can know today that we are being held by God. When we know in faith that this is true, when we feel God's love and enjoy His closeness and embrace, and when we therefore trust God to take care of our big worries, then we are indeed *calmed and quieted* in our soul.

I testify to this truth today. Do you? I can think of many times through the years when as a child I was nervous, troubled, or afraid, and in faith I trusted God to hold me; His calm settled upon me like a warm blanket. Speaking of warm blankets, many times when I've been hospitalized and feeling poorly, a nurse brought me a warm blanket, which always reminded me of the love and warm embrace of God.

But as the psalmist said – experiencing this calm is a choice we make. We can choose to trust Him and to rest in His arms. We can choose to enjoy His closeness and embrace. We can choose to feel safe and to rest in God today.

For Prayerful Reflection: When in time of trouble have you felt like a child being held in God's loving arms? What will it mean for you today to choose to trust Him and to rest in His embrace?

Bible in a Year: *Psalm 110-112; 1 Corinthians 5*

August 23

I CAN Rest TODAY . . .
BECAUSE GOD IS WITH ME IN THE LIONS' DEN

> *Then, at break of day, the king arose and went in haste to the den of lions. As he came near to the den where Daniel was, he cried out in a tone of anguish. The king declared to Daniel, "O Daniel, servant of the living God, has your God, whom you serve continually, been able to deliver you from the lions?" Then Daniel said to the king, "O king, live forever! My God sent his angel and shut the lions' mouths, and they have not harmed me."* (Daniel 6:19-22)

Daniel's deliverance in the lions' den teaches us about God's deliverance in our lives too. Daniel had been sentenced to die in a den of hungry lions. Darius, king of the Medo-Persian Empire, was frantic with worry for Daniel, whom he greatly admired, but who had been convicted and sentenced because of his faithfulness to God. Throughout that night Daniel was surrounded by lions but was unharmed, so in the morning he proclaimed to the king, *"My God sent his angel and shut the lions' mouths, and they have not harmed me."*

Daniel rested much better than Darius did that night, for God kept him safe. Though we might not face literal lions, we all confront trials and dangers. And when God is with us in those dangerous dens, He keeps us safe, and we are able to rest in Him.

In August 2018, I became very ill with bacteremia, a serious blood infection that required six weeks of intravenous antibiotics, of which a few weeks were done at home. God's loving angel for me was Helen. She took care of everything, so I could rest. This is what God does for us today.

For Prayerful Reflection: In what "lions' den" has God taken care of you, so that you could safely rest? What will it mean for you to trust Him for your safety today, so you can rest?

Bible in a Year: *Psalm 113-115; 1 Corinthians 6*

August 24

I CAN Rest TODAY . . .
BECAUSE GOD GOES WITH US INTO THE STORM

> *When evening had come, he said to them, "Let us go across to the other side." And leaving the crowd, they took him with them in the boat, just as he was. . . . And a great windstorm arose, and the waves were breaking into the boat, so that the boat was already filling. But he was in the stern, asleep on the cushion. And they woke him and said to him, "Teacher, do you not care that we are perishing?" And he awoke and rebuked the wind and said to the sea, "Peace! Be still!" And the wind ceased, and there was a great calm.* (Mark 4:35-39)

I keep returning to this story, for there are so many lessons in it that God brings to my mind. Notice the Lord Himself pointed His disciples into the storm, but through it all, He was with them, for *they took him with them in the boat.* The same is true for all of us who know, love, and follow the Lord Jesus. When storms arise, He knows, and He is right there with us in the boat.

Notice too that Jesus was not worried at all. His disciples were, but Jesus was not. So He peacefully slept. This is the only place in the gospels that mentions Jesus sleeping. This tells us that the Prince of Peace was and is perfectly at peace even in a storm, for He is Lord of all. Jesus took a nap in the storm, being fully aware that He was precisely where He belonged. Because our Lord is with us in the boat today, no matter what storms we may encounter, we can share His peace and thus His rest.

For Prayerful Reflection: What storms have you encountered in which you knew Jesus was with you in the boat? How are you affected by knowing that no matter what comes today, God is with you and brings you peace and rest?

Bible in a Year: *Psalm 116-118; 1 Corinthians 7:1-19*

August 25

I CAN Rest TODAY . . .
BECAUSE GOD FIGHTS MY BATTLES

> *"O our God, . . . we are powerless against this great horde that is coming against us. We do not know what to do, but our eyes are on you." And he said, "Listen, all Judah and inhabitants of Jerusalem and King Jehoshaphat: Thus says the Lord to you, 'Do not be afraid and do not be dismayed at this great horde, for the battle is not yours but God's.'" And the fear of God came on all the kingdoms of the countries when they heard that the Lord had fought against the enemies of Israel. So the realm of Jehoshaphat was quiet, for his God gave him rest all around.* (2 Chronicles 20:12, 15, 29-30)

Perhaps you have been in a situation like Jehoshaphat was in. He faced a grave threat, and he and his people were *powerless against this great horde*. He did not know what to do. But really, he did know, for he turned to the Lord. And God told him precisely what He has told me and what He tells you – that we do not need to be afraid or dismayed, *for the battle is not yours but God's*.

Jehoshaphat led the people to pray; then he led them to praise and sing with faith that God would surely see them through this battle. God won that victory, and for the king and his people, *God gave him rest all around*.

When we face circumstances that seem overwhelming or battles that seem unwinnable, may God help us hear and believe as Jehoshaphat did that He is with us now. He fights this battle for us. In faith we can know that the ultimate outcome is certain, so today we can rest in God.

For Prayerful Reflection: What overwhelming battles have you faced that God fought for you and won a victory for you? What battles are you facing today in which you will now trust, and praise, and pray?

Bible in a Year: *Psalm 119:1-88; 1 Corinthians 7:20-40*

August 26

I CAN Rest TODAY . . .
BECAUSE GOD BESTOWS REST IN QUIETNESS

The Lord of hosts is with us; the God of Jacob is our fortress. "Be still, and know that I am God." (Psalm 46:7, 10)

For thus said the Lord God, the Holy One of Israel, "In returning and rest you shall be saved; in quietness and in trust shall be your strength." But you were unwilling. (Isaiah 30:15)

Sinful human nature being what it is, we are prone to think we know best; so we do whatever we want. Adam and Eve, the patriarch and matriarch of humanity, thought they knew better than God did, so they ate forbidden fruit. Every small child at some point says no to parental authority and chooses the words of Frank Sinatra to "do it my way." This is the philosophy of this world and of self, but it is not God's way for us.

In the 1520s, after the Diet of Worms at which Martin Luther was charged with heresy, ex-communicated, and declared an outlaw, he penned the hymn "A Mighty Fortress Is Our God," which he based on Psalm 46. This psalm reminded Luther, and reminds us today, that through all trials and tribulations, God is our mighty fortress, and in Him we find peace and rest.

To enter this mighty fortress and know God's rest requires our quietness before Him; we must *"be still, and know that I am God."* Rather than continuing blindly on the way of our own choosing, He promises that *"in quietness and in trust shall be your strength."* Sadly, Isaiah said of his initial hearers, *But you were unwilling.* May that never be said of us. Let us choose today to quietly trust God and rest in Him.

For Prayerful Reflection: When were you ever unwilling to rest in quietness before God but went your own way instead? In what area(s) of life today do you need and choose to *"be still, and know that I am God"*?

Bible in a Year: *Psalm 119:89-176; 1 Corinthians 8*

August 27

I CAN Rest TODAY...
BECAUSE GOD CALLS ME TO COME AWAY WITH HIM

The apostles returned to Jesus and told him all that they had done and taught. And he said to them, "Come away by yourselves to a desolate place and rest a while." For many were coming and going, and they had no leisure even to eat. And they went away in the boat to a desolate place by themselves. (Mark 6:30-32)

The twelve apostles had been sent out by Jesus to minister in His name and with His authority. This was a foretaste of what their lives would be as lifelong servants of the Lord. He sent them out two by two, for our Lord desires us to serve Him alongside others who love Him. Then, after a glorious but apparently exhausting season, they had all returned, understandably excited about *all that they had done and taught.* Jesus was glad to see them and hear their wonderful testimonies, but He also saw that they were tired and needed rest.

So Jesus invited them and now invites us to *"come away by yourselves to a desolate place and rest a while."* Through the years I have often heard this invitation. Some of the highlights of my life have come from setting aside time to get away with my Lord. I have had special times of daily devotion with Him, and there have been many overnighters, sometimes for several days. It takes preparation to make this happen, but how blessed I have been in doing so! With many demands in our lives, even in days of much fruitfulness as the apostles had known, we all need times to come apart with Jesus for a while, and in His presence to rest, listen, and be renewed.

For Prayerful Reflection: When were you tired and heard God inviting you to come apart with Him and rest? What decisions or steps could you take today that would allow you to come apart with your Lord?

Bible in a Year: *Psalm 120-122; 1 Corinthians 9*

August 28

I CAN Rest TODAY . . .
BECAUSE GOD RELIEVES ME OF MY WORRIES

What then shall we say to these things? If God is for us, who can be against us? (Romans 8:31)

Humble yourselves, therefore, under the mighty hand of God so that at the proper time he may exalt you, casting all your anxieties on him, because he cares for you. (1 Peter 5:6-7)

Our first piece of furniture was an old rocking chair. Helen and I were engaged to be married and prayerfully planning for our future. As we drove by an antique barn in rural Maine, we saw an antique rocking chair, painted blue, so we pulled in. The seat was missing, and the dealer said it was well over a century old. I bought that old chair, stripped off the paint, and freshly stained it; once the new, caned seat was applied, that old rocking chair was reborn. It is still my favorite piece of furniture, for in it I remember from where we have come, the faithfulness of God, and how my Lord reclaimed me for Himself. I also remember the old adage I have often quoted: "Worry is like a rocking chair. It gives you something to do, but doesn't get you anywhere."

In that rocking chair, and in life, God has invited me to bring worries, anxieties, and cares to Him. When I do, He lifts them from me and lets me know, "I've got this." Worry is our distress about future uncertainties, caused by real or imagined threats to ourselves or people we care about. We feel vulnerable, unsafe, or alone, so we rock and ruminate and get nowhere. But God wants us to get somewhere by casting our anxieties upon Him. We can pray and trust and give them to Him today. And as we do, our Lord gives peace and rest.

For Prayerful Reflection: When have you ever been stuck, rocking and ruminating on worries? What will it mean for you today to cast *all your anxieties upon him, because he cares for you*?

Bible in a Year: *Psalm 123-125; 1 Corinthians 10:1-18*

August 29

I CAN Rest TODAY . . .
BECAUSE GOD GIVES REST TO THOSE WHO RETURN

Thus said the Lord God, the Holy One of Israel, "In returning and rest you shall be saved; in quietness and in trust shall be your strength." But you were unwilling, and you said, "No!" (Isaiah 30:15-16)

Thus says the Lord: "Stand by the roads, and look, and ask for the ancient paths, where the good way is; and walk in it, and find rest for your souls. But they said, 'We will not walk in it.'" (Jeremiah 6:16)

God is so gracious to offer peace and rest to all who hear His invitation and in faith return to Him to follow His way. In the days of Isaiah and later in Jeremiah's time, though many had forsaken God, He called people to repent of waywardness and sin, change course, and return to Him, for in so doing, He promised salvation and rest.

God spoke through Jeremiah and urged people to *ask for the ancient paths, where the good way is; and walk in it, and find rest for your souls.* But the typical answer then and now was no.

Such an answer is foolishness, isn't it? Don't we all desire safety and peace in this life? Don't we all desire rest for our souls? God knows we do, and He offers it to us from His heart of mercy and love. But to receive God's grace by returning to that *ancient path*, we must regret whatever path of disobedience we are on and repent of it, which is to change course and come home to Him.

As we do this, God saves us and gives to us His rest. And in quietness and trust we receive His strength today.

For Prayerful Reflection: When were you ever lost and on the wrong road but then heard God calling you back to the right road where you found rest in Him? What will it mean for you today to return to God and receive His rest?

Bible in a Year: *Psalm 126-128; 1 Corinthians 10:19-33*

August 30

I CAN Rest TODAY...
BECAUSE GOD SUSTAINS ME IN EVERY WAY

O Lord, how many are my foes! Many are rising against me; many are saying of my soul, "There is no salvation for him in God." But you, O Lord, are a shield about me, my glory, and the lifter of my head. I cried aloud to the Lord, and he answered me from his holy hill. I lay down and slept; I woke again, for the Lord sustained me. I will not be afraid of many thousands of people who have set themselves against me all around. (Psalm 3:1-6)

Though we have known trouble in our days, none of us have known the kind of trouble King David was facing when he penned this psalm. An attempted coup was underway. Several times David uses the word *many* to describe the foes coming against him. Many were convinced that David's reign was over, and they wanted him dead. The greatest heartache was that this attack was being led by his own son Absalom. The anguish David knew exceeded any I have ever known.

But in the midst of this, we notice David's faith. Let it speak to us today that we might respond in the same way. David *cried aloud to the Lord, and he answered.* In the midst of such chaos and pain, David said, *I lay down and slept; I woke again, for the Lord sustained me.* There was for David an oasis of safety, provision, and peace in the center of it all, for God was sustaining him.

Our Lord does the same for all His children who do as David did. Crying out to God, committing ourselves to Him, and entrusting our circumstances to Him allows us to rest in faith in Him. This is our privilege today.

For Prayerful Reflection: When have you found a measure of rest in the midst of chaos as you called upon God? How is God sustaining you in your current circumstances?

Bible in a Year: *Psalm 129-131; 1 Corinthians 11:1-16*

August 31

I CAN Rest TODAY . . .
BECAUSE GOD ALWAYS KEEPS HIS PROMISES

God said to Noah, "I have determined to make an end of all flesh. . . . Make yourself an ark of gopher wood. Make rooms in the ark, and cover it inside and out with pitch." Noah did this; he did all that God commanded him. Then the Lord said to Noah, "Go into the ark, you and all your household, for I have seen that you are righteous before me in this generation. Take with you . . . animals, . . . male and female, to keep their offspring alive on the face of all the earth. And Noah did all that the Lord had commanded him. (Genesis 6:13-14, 22; 7:1-3, 5)

In every generation, season, and circumstance God keeps His promises, for He is forever trustworthy. Noah's life is an early example of this. In perfect righteousness, God determined to destroy humanity for its wickedness and rebellion against Him. But in the midst of the destruction, He would save for Himself a faithful remnant.

God told Noah what He would do and then gave him a seemingly ridiculous assignment – to build an ark over five hundred feet long, nearly ninety feet wide, and fifty feet high, with a volume of more than 1.5 million cubic feet. It took a very long time, but Noah did it. The Bible says, *Noah walked with God* (Genesis 6:9), which means he believed and obeyed. He built the ark, stocked it with enormous amounts of food for the animals and for his family, and led the animals in. Then, along with his family, Noah entered that ark.

This is how we can know God's rest amidst the turmoil of this world. Like Noah, we can walk with God, doing whatever He gives us to do, and in faith enter the ark of His promise. Here we find our rest in Him.

For Prayerful Reflection: What has God called you to do that requires you to believe His promise? How does Noah's example speak to your entering God's rest today?

Bible in a Year: *Psalm 132-134; 1 Corinthians 11:17-34*

12 Themes on Following Jesus

SEPTEMBER

Because God . . .
I Can *Testify* Today

September 1

I CAN Testify TODAY . . .
BECAUSE GOD TELLS ME TO TESTIFY

> *Jesus came and said to them, "All authority in heaven and on earth has been given to me. Go therefore and make disciples of all nations, baptizing them in the name of the Father and of the Son and of the Holy Spirit, teaching them to observe all that I have commanded you. And behold, I am with you always, to the end of the age."* (Matthew 28:18-20)

These words of Jesus are called the Great Commission. These are His final words before ascending into heaven. Speaking to His disciples, He gives this command. Is He making it optional? No, He makes it an imperative. This is a direct command from the Head of the Church, the commander of heaven's armies, the King of Kings, the Lord of Lords, and our supreme authority. He tells us to go in His name and make disciples for Him by teaching and testifying of who He is and what He has taught and done for us.

Would He command us to do something we are incapable of doing? That would be cruel. But our Lord is loving and good. So whatever God calls us to do, He equips us to do it – even to bear witness for Him. Having served in the military for twenty-seven years, I can tell you with certainty that when given a direct order by the highest-ranking senior officer, no committed soldier, sailor, airman, marine, coastguardsman, or Space Force guardian would intentionally disregard or disobey the order. We just wouldn't do it.

Jesus, our Lord and King, has told us to be His witnesses. So can you? Can I? Yes, we can testify of Jesus Christ, even today.

For Prayerful Reflection: How seriously have you taken Jesus' command to testify for Him? How willing are you to listen, learn, and obey this command from your Lord?

Bible in a Year: *Psalm 135-136; 1 Corinthians 12*

September 2

I CAN Testify TODAY...
BECAUSE GOD HAS GIVEN ME A STORY TO TELL

As he was getting into the boat, the man who had been possessed with demons begged him that he might be with him. And he did not permit him but said to him, "Go home to your friends and tell them how much the Lord has done for you, and how he has had mercy on you." And he went away and began to proclaim in the Decapolis how much Jesus had done for him, and everyone marveled. (Mark 5:18-20)

This man had an amazing story to tell of God's deliverance and blessing in His life. The Bible says he lived among the tombs and no one could help him. He was imprisoned in deep bondage and possessed by a legion of demons. So many demons left him that they entered and destroyed an entire herd of pigs numbering over two thousand. This man may have been possessed by a larger number of demons than anyone before or after him in order to show that Jesus can set anyone free, no matter how hopeless it may seem or no matter the size of the chains that bind us.

When Jesus delivered this man from the powers of darkness that had bound him for so long, the man was overjoyed in his freedom and longed to follow and serve the Lord who had set him free. So he begged Jesus to let him follow Him. But Jesus' initial direction to this man is also direction to us who have met Him and been set free by Him. He calls us to go and *tell them how much the Lord has done for [us]*. As God gave that man a story to tell, He gives us one also.

For Prayerful Reflection: What is your story of what God has done for you? Who are some people in your life to whom your Lord would have you tell the story?

Bible in a Year: *Psalm 137-139; 1 Corinthians 13*

September 3

I CAN Testify TODAY...
BECAUSE GOD'S LOVE COMPELS ME

We make it our aim to please him. For the love of Christ controls us, because we have concluded this: that one has died for all, therefore all have died; and he died for all, that those who live might no longer live for themselves but for him who for their sake died and was raised.
(2 Corinthians 5:9, 14-15)

What motivates us to testify of Jesus? Is it not His love? We who have received and experienced the incredible love of God, who truly grasp the reality of His love for us when He suffered and died in our place on that cross for our sins, are now therefore deeply motivated to love Him in return. So as Paul said, we now *make it our aim to please him.*

The English Standard Version Bible expresses the beginning phrase of 2 Corinthians 5:14 as *the love of Christ controls us.* Other translations have *Christ's love compels us* or *the love of Christ constraineth us.* In other words, we who have received the wonderful love of Jesus Christ are now motivated by His love in all we do. This includes desiring to pass Christ's love on to others by testifying of Him.

Billy Sunday (1862–1935) was a professional baseball player who became an evangelist. His compelling desire was to tell of Jesus and His love. On his way to a particular city, he wrote a letter to the mayor and asked for names of individuals there who had a spiritual problem and needed help and prayer. In return, the evangelist received from the mayor a city telephone book. Indeed.

Every person whom we know needs God's love and needs to learn of Jesus. If Christ's love compels us, then through our own life and witness, we will be bringing His love into our world today.

For Prayerful Reflection: How has Christ's love compelled you lately? Who are some people in your life to whom you could demonstrate and speak of God's love?

Bible in a Year: *Psalm 140-142; 1 Corinthians 14:1-20*

September 4

I CAN Testify TODAY . . .
BECAUSE GOD GAVE JESUS AS THE ONLY WAY

Whoever believes in [Jesus] is not condemned, but whoever does not believe is condemned already, because he has not believed in the name of the only Son of God. The Father loves the Son and has given all things into his hand. Whoever believes in the Son has eternal life; whoever does not obey the Son shall not see life, but the wrath of God remains on him. (John 3:18, 35-36)

Jesus said to him, "I am the way, and the truth, and the life. No one comes to the Father except through me." (John 14:6)

When taking a trip, if you follow a map or use a Global Positioning System (GPS) device, you have a choice of routes to your destination. Many believe there are also several options for reaching the destination of knowing God and entering heaven. One local pastor emphasized this by saying, "We all have a piece of the truth. It's arrogant and rude for any of us to suggest our way is better or more right than any other."

But what does God say? God says Jesus Christ is the only way to forgiveness, salvation, and everlasting life, for He alone, by His sacrificial and atoning death and triumphal resurrection, can cleanse us of our sins and make us worthy to be in the presence of God. Jesus is indeed the only way to everlasting life. And because this is true, when we believe it, we are obliged to testify of Him, and we will.

The late Episcopal Bishop Sam Shoemaker sadly observed that "In the Great Commission, the Lord has called us to be . . . fishers of men," but "we have become merely keepers of the aquarium."[25] God help us. Because believing that Jesus is the only way, we must testify of Him today.

For Prayerful Reflection: How convinced are you that Jesus is the only way to everlasting life? How are you demonstrating your conviction?

Bible in a Year: *Psalm 143-145; 1 Corinthians 14:21-40*

---

25 Emory A. Griffin, *The Mind Changers: The Art of Christian Persuasion* (Wheaton, IL: Tyndale House Publishers, Inc., 1976), 151.

September 5

I CAN Testify TODAY . . .
BECAUSE GOD WASHES ME CLEAN

We have all become like one who is unclean, and all our righteous deeds are like a polluted garment. (Isaiah 64:6)

Do you not know that the unrighteous will not inherit the kingdom of God? . . . But you were washed, you were sanctified, you were justified in the name of the Lord Jesus Christ and by the Spirit of our God. (1 Corinthians 6:9, 11)

I think the dirtiest I have ever been was the long day I spent on an endurance course with infantry Marines. We crawled hundreds of yards through mud and sludge. At the end of the day, our clothes were in tatters, and we were hosed down with a fire hose. We were so dirty.

The Bible says we are all filthy sinners before God. Sin cannot be allowed in God's presence, for it contradicts and opposes His holiness. This is why Satan was cast from heaven after rebelling against God, and why Adam and Eve and all of humanity were cast from Eden. What a mess humanity is in!

Yet, because we were made for relationship with God, we do long to be clean before Him. Blaise Pascal described this longing as a "God-shaped vacuum" within us. Because God designed us to enjoy fellowship with Him for time and eternity, we long for it. But no matter how hard we try or how religious we become, we all fall short, and sin remains.

Our only hope was for God to do what we could not possibly do: wash us clean, forgive us, and give us everlasting life. This is the gospel of Jesus Christ, for He is the one and only way God has provided for us to be made clean. His victory over sin and death washes away my sin, paving the way for me to live today and every day in right relationship with God. Because of such grace, I can testify today.

For Prayerful Reflection: How were you blessed from being washed clean through Jesus Christ? How might this grace be presented to someone struggling with self-condemnation or guilt?

Bible in a Year: *Psalm 146-147; 1 Corinthians 15:1-28*

September 6

I CAN Testify TODAY...
BECAUSE GOD USES UNLIKELY PEOPLE

The woman left her water jar and went away into town and said to the people, "Come, see a man who told me all that I ever did. Can this be the Christ?" They went out of the town and were coming to him. Many Samaritans from that town believed in him because of the woman's testimony,... And many more believed because of his word. They said to the woman, "It is no longer because of what you said that we believe, for we have heard for ourselves, and we know that this is indeed the Savior of the world." (John 4:28-30, 39, 41-42)

In her book, *Miracles in West Africa: God's Wonders Among the Worodougou,* Carolyn Ainley Pinke tells of her ministry and that of her husband Bruce among the Worodougou people in Côte d'Ivoire.[26] When they arrived in 1976, no Christians lived among that people group, but God began gathering a people who would believe and follow Jesus. Among these was an unlikely woman named Nochee, who was changed by Jesus; she then shared the gospel with everyone she could. And God built His church.

The woman whom Jesus met at the well in Sychar was another unlikely candidate. She was despised by her community and afraid of the people. But when she met Jesus, she testified to everyone she could of what He did for her. Because of her testimony, people came to see for themselves, and many more came to believe.

God uses unlikely people like us to simply share what He has done for us. God then accomplishes the miracle of drawing people to Himself. Nochee and the woman of Sychar may have seemed like unlikely candidates, but God chose and used them. Today this privilege is ours.

For Prayerful Reflection: What story do you have to tell of what God has done for you? How privileged do you consider yourself today to share the good news of Jesus?

Bible in a Year: *Psalm 148-150; 1 Corinthians 15:29-58*

---

26 Carolyn Ainley Pinke, *Miracles in West Africa: God's Wonders Among the Worodougou* (2019).

September 7

I CAN Testify TODAY...
BECAUSE GOD DOESN'T WANT ANYONE TO PERISH

"The master said to the servant, "'Go out to the highways and hedges and compel people to come in, that my house may be filled.'" (Luke 14:23)

This is good, and it is pleasing in the sight of God our Savior, who desires all people to be saved and to come to the knowledge of the truth. (1 Timothy 2:3-4)

Each Wednesday at 1:00 p.m., a loud siren blares in our neighborhood. An emergency warning system is tested, which is designed to warn when a destructive tornado is on the ground, so residents may take shelter immediately. At times I have been annoyed with this loud siren. I have wondered what the real chances of a tornado hitting here were. But last night we received a tornado warning via text message, which let us know a tornado was on the ground nearby. Such warnings are given so no one will perish.

Far greater is the threat of the sudden destruction that is coming upon this world by the judgment of God because of sin. From this destruction, there is only one escape: we are saved through repentance of sin and faith in the Lord Jesus Christ who gave His sinless life for our salvation. The warning of coming judgment because of sin is hard for some to hear, but it must be given, as well as the wonderful news of the safety that can be found in the Lord Jesus.

Since by His grace God does not want anyone to perish, those who love Him will not perish. So today we can testify about God's warning and of His deep love and promise of where grace is found.

For Prayerful Reflection: How freely have you shared God's desire that no one should perish? How might your life and conversation reflect God's loving desire today?

Bible in a Year: *Proverbs 1-2; 1 Corinthians 16*

September 8

I CAN Testify TODAY . . .
BECAUSE GOD'S SON WILL RETURN WHEN ALL NATIONS HAVE HEARD

"And this gospel of the kingdom will be proclaimed throughout the whole world as a testimony to all nations, and then the end will come." (Matthew 24:14)

"They will deliver you over to councils, and you will be beaten in synagogues, and you will stand before governors and kings for my sake, to bear witness before them. And the gospel must first be proclaimed to all nations." (Mark 13:9-10)

Jesus said a distinct indicator of the nearness of His return is when the gospel is *proclaimed throughout the whole world as a testimony to all nations.* *"Then,"* He said, *"the end will come."* God's love will reach every tongue, tribe, and people, and every nation of people will be represented in heaven. Jesus promises, therefore, that the gospel of His love and salvation through faith in Him is going to be brought to all nations. He was not referring to the definition of *nation* as we use it today with recognized geographical boundaries. The Greek word used in the gospel is *ethne,* from which we get the word *ethnic,* meaning "a unique people group."

Jesus commissioned His church to testify of the good news of the gospel to all people groups; then He will return. How can we join in this mission from our Lord today? We can offer prayers and financial support for some who are strategically bringing the good news of Jesus to unreached people groups, or we can go ourselves if God calls us. We can also pray for persecuted believers around the world, and we can look for opportunities to build relationships with people from ethnic groups where few know the Lord. We can love them by showing in word and deed the good news of Jesus.

For Prayerful Reflection: Why does our Lord commission us to testify to every nation? How does this directive affect you? How will you join today in God's desire for people of every ethnic group?

Bible in a Year: *Proverbs 3-5; 2 Corinthians 1*

September 9

I CAN Testify TODAY . . .
BECAUSE GOD OPENS EYES TO SEE

They said to him, "Then how were your eyes opened?" He answered, "The man called Jesus made mud and anointed my eyes and said to me, 'Go to Siloam and wash.' So I went and washed and received my sight." . . . "One thing I do know, that though I was blind, now I see." (John 9:10-11, 25)

Mary Magdalene went and announced to the disciples, "I have seen the Lord." (John 20:18)

God opens eyes to see. Just imagine the testimony of that man who had always been blind, until he met the Lord Jesus. Thereafter he joyfully testified that *"though I was blind, now I see."* And on Easter morning, Mary Magdalene's eyes were opened to see Jesus, after which she testified, *"I have seen the Lord."* We can do today as they did and testify of what God has shown us and pray that by grace God may open the eyes of many to see what they cannot yet see.

Some years ago Christopher Chabris and Daniel Simons conducted an experiment at Harvard University that became infamous in psychology circles. Their book *The Invisible Gorilla* popularized it. They filmed students passing basketballs while moving in a circular fashion. In the middle of the short film, a woman dressed in a gorilla suit walked into the frame, beat her chest, and walked out. The sequence took nine seconds in the short video. Viewers were instructed to count the number of passes made by players wearing white shirts. But the researchers only wanted to see if viewers would notice something they weren't looking for. Half of the test group did not see the gorilla.

As we testify of what God has shown us, let's pray that God helps us see what we are missing and that He opens more and more eyes to perceive His truth.

For Prayerful Reflection: What spiritual truths were you unable to see until God opened your eyes? How might you testify today of wonderful things God has blessed you to see?

Bible in a Year: *Proverbs 6-7; 2 Corinthians 2*

September 10

I CAN Testify TODAY . . .
BECAUSE GOD CAUSES ME TO GROW

> *We have not ceased to pray for you, asking that you may be filled with the knowledge of his will in all spiritual wisdom and understanding, so as to walk in a manner worthy of the Lord, fully pleasing to him, bearing fruit in every good work and increasing in the knowledge of God.* (Colossians 1:9-10)
>
> *I pray that the sharing of your faith may become effective for the full knowledge of every good thing that is in us for the sake of Christ.* (Philemon 1:6)

Paul's prayers for the church, including Christian friends like Philemon, were that they would grow spiritually and increasingly *walk in a manner worthy of the Lord, fully pleasing to him.* He prayed for increased effectiveness in sharing their faith in Jesus. God has designed us to grow spiritually as we testify of Him.

It requires faith on our part to step out and testify of Christ, especially if there is any hostility from those who hear us. Because faith and obedience are required to do this, God rewards us by giving us the words we need and reminding us of Scriptures and spiritual truths that are needed. After having such conversations with others, I sometimes marvel that God would use me to communicate such wonderful things to others. It is because God is with us, He increases our faith, meets our need, and matures us spiritually as we testify of Him.

I have had many such experiences through the years, as I testified of Christ to those who did not yet know Him; sometimes I testified to some who were antagonistic toward the gospel. But through such experiences, God helped me grow spiritually, and in mercy He drew some to Himself. If we wish to grow spiritually, testifying of Jesus is a wonderful way God provides for us to do this.

For Prayerful Reflection: How have you grown spiritually through testifying of the Lord? Will you ask God now to help you grow spiritually as you step out in faith to testify of Him?

Bible in a Year: *Proverbs 8-9; 2 Corinthians 3*

September 11

I CAN Testify TODAY...
BECAUSE GOD EDIFIES OTHERS
WHEN I TESTIFY

> *And they rose that same hour and returned to Jerusalem. And they found the eleven and those who were with them gathered together, saying, "The Lord has risen indeed, and has appeared to Simon!" Then they told what had happened on the road, and how he was known to them in the breaking of the bread.* (Luke 24:33-35)

Hasn't your heart been blessed from hearing testimonies of faith shared by those who know Him? Surely there was joy among our Lord's disciples who were all edified by testifying of what the risen Lord had done for them.

One of my more memorable experiences of this was years ago in a mountain village in Nepal. A pastor friend and I had traveled there to offer Bible teaching to Nepalese pastors and church leaders who had hiked for days to be there. All of them had personal testimonies of how God opened their eyes to the truth of the gospel and how they then boldly shared the good news of Jesus. Many told of suffering for Jesus through rejection or physical abuse for testifying of Christ. I heard testimonies of imprisonment and torture, miraculous healings and demonic deliverances, and the faithfulness of God in drawing people to Himself.

And I cannot forget the U.S. Navy sailor with whom I had prayed for miraculous healing of his wife who was dying in a far-off hospital in Cameroon. At the very moment we prayed, God touched his wife and healed her. Thereafter, every time I saw that young man, he testified of what God had done. When we share our stories of Jesus and His love, we are blessed, God is glorified, and others are edified.

For Prayerful Reflection: What is your testimony of what God has done for you? How might you edify someone today by sharing some of your story of Jesus and His love?

Bible in a Year: *Proverbs 10-12; 2 Corinthians 4*

September 12

I CAN Testify TODAY . . .
BECAUSE GOD USES MY TRIALS

> *The jailer called for lights and rushed in, and trembling with fear he fell down before Paul and Silas. Then he brought them out and said, "Sirs, what must I do to be saved?" And they said, "Believe in the Lord Jesus, and you will be saved, you and your household." And they spoke the word of the Lord to him and to all who were in his house. And he took them the same hour of the night and washed their wounds; and he was baptized at once, he and all his family. . . . And he rejoiced along with his entire household that he had believed in God.* (Acts 16:29-34)

We can be quite sure that neither Paul nor Silas had volunteered to go to that Philippian jail. They had been beaten, chained, and imprisoned. But see what God did through their trials! As Paul and Silas leaned on the Lord, singing praises in the night of their struggle, God did something remarkable for His glory and the honor of His name. Other prisoners heard and saw them demonstrate their faith in Jesus, as did the jailer. And before that night was over, the jailer and his entire family were saved, and much praise was given to God.

I too have marveled at how the Lord uses my trials for His glory and my struggles to help somebody. From my journey with cancer and my walk with God through it all, my Lord blessed me to testify of His help in my book *Walking with God through Deep Valleys: Lessons on Finding Contentment When Life Is Hard*,[27] which He is using to help many others. God brings good even from our trials. When you testify of what God has done for you, He may use your testimony to bless others.

For Prayerful Reflection: How has God used your trials to bless you or others? How might you edify someone today by testifying of God's help in a time of trial?

Bible in a Year: *Proverbs 13-15; 2 Corinthians 5*

---

[27] Stephen Gammon, *Walking with God through Deep Valleys: Lessons on Finding Contentment When Life Is Hard* (Abbotsford, WI: Aneko Press, 2020).

September 13

I CAN Testify TODAY . . .
BECAUSE GOD GIVES ME WHAT I NEED

Then [Jesus] opened their minds to understand the Scriptures, and said to them, "Thus it is written, that the Christ should suffer and on the third day rise from the dead, and that repentance for the forgiveness of sins should be proclaimed in his name to all nations, beginning from Jerusalem. You are witnesses of these things. And behold, I am sending the promise of my Father upon you. But stay in the city until you are clothed with power from on high." (Luke 24:45-49)

When we are on our way to a particular place or assignment, perhaps to do something challenging, momentous, or fun, what do we do? We prepare, don't we? We carefully consider what we are going to need along the way and upon arrival at where we are going, and then we pack. Think of how important this practice has been in your life.

I remember preparing to go to summer camp for a week when I was nine years old. My mother made sure I had packed every single thing I might need, and I was so thankful. I think too of preparations I made for military deployments, or geographic moves for a new assignment, or a mountain climb. Would we foolishly do any of these things without being prepared?

God has given us an important and exciting assignment – to be His witnesses and testify of Him wherever He leads us. God has packed our bags, ensuring we have what we will need. We have the Holy Scriptures, which is the truth of God. We have the Holy Spirit, who is the presence of God in and with us who empowers us to testify of Jesus in a way that may draw others to Him.

For Prayerful Reflection: When and how have you seen God giving what you needed to be His witness? What has God given you to help you testify of Him today?

Bible in a Year: *Proverbs 16-18; 2 Corinthians 6*

September 14

I CAN Testify TODAY...
BECAUSE GOD CHANGES ME

If anyone is in Christ, he is a new creation. The old has passed away; behold, the new has come. All this is from God, who through Christ reconciled us to himself and gave us the ministry of reconciliation.
(2 Corinthians 5:17-18)

When we meet Jesus Christ and put our trust in Him, we are changed. This becomes part of our testimony. The apostle Paul, who had been a zealous persecutor of the church, became a powerful voice for the gospel of Jesus. The Philippian jailer, who had once guarded Christian prisoners, became a devoted follower of Christ and with his family were among the first members of the church in Philippi. They testified of what Jesus Christ had done for them.

When we turn in faith to Jesus, God changes us too. We are then entrusted by Him with *the ministry of reconciliation,* which means we testify of Christ and how through faith in Him we are reconciled to God and changed for our good and His glory.

When I was a young man preparing for pastoral ministry, my grandfather shared with me in personal conversations, and also in his writing of several testimonies for the blessing and benefit of his family, stories of persons he had known whose lives were troubled in one way or another, but when they met Jesus Christ, they were changed. They became effective witnesses for Him. God does this in every generation.

What about in your life? Consider the ways God has changed you for His glory and your good; for by His grace, this is part of your testimony now. Just yesterday, when I shared part of my story with somebody of what Christ has done for me, my Lord met them and drew them closer to Himself. This is our holy privilege.

For Prayerful Reflection: What are some ways God has changed you or is still changing you? How might God use portions of your testimony to help and bless someone today?

Bible in a Year: *Proverbs 19-21; 2 Corinthians 7*

September 15

I CAN Testify TODAY . . .
BECAUSE GOD HAS MADE ME A WITNESS

> *That which was from the beginning, which we have heard, which we have seen with our eyes, which we looked upon and have touched with our hands, concerning the word of life . . . that which we have seen and heard we proclaim also to you, so that you too may have fellowship with us; and indeed our fellowship is with the Father and with his Son Jesus Christ.* (1 John 1:1, 3)

I was subpoenaed for jury duty, an obligation I take seriously, because justice requires responsibility. I also took it seriously on the occasion when I was called as a trial witness. Before testifying I was required to swear to tell the truth and nothing but the truth. Trial witnesses are not allowed to postulate or imagine. They are to tell the truth of what they have seen and heard.

The apostle John used a similar picture to portray our task in Christ. He declared that the testimony of Jesus he was proclaiming was indeed what he had heard, seen, and touched. John was, after all, a close disciple and dearly loved friend of Jesus throughout His ministry, and an eyewitness of Jesus' death, burial, resurrection, and ascension.

We are also called to testify of what we have witnessed, though we have not physically heard or seen Jesus like John did, nor have we touched His physical body. We have often seen our Lord in faith, however. We have heard Him by the voice of the Holy Spirit and have spiritually touched Him. He has often met us, and we have enjoyed being in His presence. Haven't we known great joy in loving and serving Him? Our God-given responsibility today and every day is to testify to the truth we know.

For Prayerful Reflection: What is your testimony of having seen, heard, and been touched by God? To what extent do you see being a faithful witness of Jesus Christ as your God-given responsibility?

Bible in a Year: *Proverbs 22-24; 2 Corinthians 8*

September 16

I CAN Testify TODAY . . .
BECAUSE GOD HAS DIVINE APPOINTMENTS FOR ME

An angel of the Lord said to Philip, "Rise and go toward the south to the road that goes down from Jerusalem to Gaza." . . . And he rose and went. And there was an Ethiopian, a eunuch. . . . And the Spirit said to Philip, "Go over and join this chariot." So Philip ran to him. . . . Then Philip opened his mouth, and . . . told him the good news about Jesus. (Acts 8:26-27, 29-30, 35)

We are his workmanship, created in Christ Jesus for good works, which God prepared beforehand, that we should walk in them. (Ephesians 2:10)

We can testify because God prepares divine appointments. Did Philip arrange this encounter with the Ethiopian eunuch? Did he plot, plan, or prepare for it? He did not. Rather, he listened, recognized, and responded to God's leading, wherever and however He led. From that divine appointment, this man of Ethiopia heard and believed the gospel of Jesus; he was saved unto everlasting life.

The Bible teaches that we *are his workmanship, created in Christ Jesus for good works, which God prepared beforehand, that we should walk in them.* In other words, God prepares divine appointments for you and me. Our part is to recognize and respond to each one. Over the years I have often prayed toward this end, and I could spend the rest of today describing divine appointments He has given me. We cannot convince anyone of the love or truth of Christ with our own wisdom or eloquence, but God can. God prepares people for divine appointment encounters and conversations. When we pray with availability, the Holy Spirit lets us know this is an opportunity to show His love, speak His truth, or point someone to the mercy of God.

For Prayerful Reflection: What are some divine appointments you knew God prepared for you? What might it mean for you to pray with availability to respond to opportunities God provides today?

Bible in a Year: *Proverbs 25-26; 2 Corinthians 9*

September 17

I CAN Testify TODAY...
BECAUSE GOD'S LIGHT SHINES IN ME

Jesus [said], "I am the light of the world. Whoever follows me will not walk in darkness, but will have the light of life." (John 8:12)

"You are the light of the world. A city set on a hill cannot be hidden. Nor do people light a lamp and put it under a basket, but on a stand, and it gives light to all in the house. In the same way, let your light shine before others, so that they may see your good works and give glory to your Father who is in heaven." (Matthew 5:14-16)

Light conquers darkness. This world was dark because of sin, but then came Jesus. Philip Bliss described it in his hymn:

The whole world was lost in the darkness of sin,
The Light of the world is Jesus!
Like sunshine at noonday, His glory shone in;
The Light of the world is Jesus![28]

Of Himself Jesus says, *"I am the light of the world."* He also says to us who love Him, *"You are the light of the world."* Like lanterns carrying His flame, we bring His light into this dark world by our lives, love, words, and witness. We are not the source of the light, Christ is. His light shines through us today.

A little boy had forgotten his lines in a Sunday school presentation, but his mother was in the front row to prompt him. She formed the words on her lips, but it didn't help. Her son's memory was blank. She leaned forward and whispered the cue, *"I am the light of the world."* Loudly and with much feeling, he then said, "My mom is the light of the world!" Yes, Jesus is the Light of the World, and we are His light sent into the world today.

For Prayerful Reflection: What are some ways God's light has shined through others for you? What could it mean for you today to *let your light shine before others*?

Bible in a Year: *Proverbs 27-29; 2 Corinthians 10*

---
28 Philip Bliss, "The Light of the World is Jesus," Public Domain, 1875.

September 18

I CAN Testify TODAY . . .
BECAUSE GOD ALONE VACCINATES

Behold, a Canaanite woman from that region came out and was crying, "Have mercy on me, O Lord, Son of David; my daughter is severely oppressed by a demon." Then Jesus answered her, "O woman, great is your faith! Be it done for you as you desire." And her daughter was healed instantly. (Matthew 15:22, 28)

As by the one man's disobedience the many were made sinners, so by the one man's obedience the many will be made righteous. (Romans 5:19)

Where could this mother go? Her much-beloved daughter was demon possessed, under the controlling influence of evil and darkness. The situation seemed hopeless. Then somebody told her about Jesus, about who He was and what He could do. She knew then that He was her only hope. So she went to Him, determined to not take no for an answer. Seeing her faith, Jesus delivered her daughter that day. He is still bringing hope where there is no hope, and healing where there is no cure. Christ alone offers a life-saving "vaccination" against evil and sin by His amazing grace and righteousness.

We know about vaccinations, don't we? COVID-19 vaccines, for example, now protect hundreds of millions of people from this dangerous virus. The stem cell transplant, which I received last year as cancer treatment, erased my immune system so it could be "born again." I then lost the protection from every vaccination I had ever received, but these are now being reintroduced into my body, for which I am grateful. I recently received six vaccine shots on the same day, each of which provides protection from a serious illness, and I blessed the ones who provided these for me. How much more should we bless our God.

Our Lord reminds us that He blesses us to testify of Him and share the good news of His freely offered victory over sin, evil, and death. Today we can deliver His vaccination of hope and healing.

For Prayerful Reflection: What spiritual threat is God protecting you from? Could you share with someone who is hopeless except for what only Jesus can do?

Bible in a Year: *Proverbs 30-31; 2 Corinthians 11:1-15*

September 19

I CAN Testify TODAY . . .
BECAUSE GOD'S TRUTH IS WHOLLY TRUE

"My judgment is true, for it is not I alone who judge, but I and the Father who sent me." (John 8:16)

"If you abide in my word, you are truly my disciples, and you will know the truth, and the truth will set you free." (John 8:31-32)

"I am the way, and the truth, and the life. No one comes to the Father except through me." (John 14:6)

In the 1992 film *A Few Good Men*, there is a memorable line about truth. In the courtroom, Navy Attorney Lieutenant Kaffee yells to the witness, Marine Colonel Jessep, "I want the truth!"[29]

The colonel screams back, "You can't handle the truth!" In the story, Colonel Jessep ultimately has his own distorted view of what is right and true.

This is an all-too-common problem. In our culture many view themselves as the ultimate determiner of what is true and often believe that absolute truth is implausible. This allows them to disregard any "truths" they do not approve of. Persons who hold to objective and timeless truth like the Word of God are often regarded as narrow-minded and are viewed with contempt. Postmodern relativists believe that truth is relative and each culture or individual can define for themselves what is truth.

But the eternal God is the arbiter of truth, and Jesus Christ is the embodiment of it. We who know Jesus Christ can and must testify of the truth of God that we have come to know. We would be callous and unloving not to do so. We can testify today that we have experienced and are experiencing today the sweet promise of God that His truth sets us free.

For Prayerful Reflection: What happened when you accepted the truth of Jesus and of God's Word? How might you respectfully and lovingly testify of God's truth to someone who doesn't yet believe?

Bible in a Year: *Ecclesiastes 1-3; 2 Corinthians 11:16-33*

---
[29] Aaron Sorkin, *A Few Good Men* (Castle Rock Entertainment, 1992).

September 20

I CAN Testify TODAY...
BECAUSE GOD CHANGES LIVES THROUGH TESTIMONY

On the day I called, you answered me; my strength of soul you increased. Though I walk in the midst of trouble, you preserve my life; you stretch out your hand against the wrath of my enemies, and your right hand delivers me. (Psalm 138:3, 7)

The Psalms are worship anthems, often with a testimony of what God has done. In the Psalm quoted today, David testifies to what God did in His life. Jim Cymbala shares a story of what God did through the power of a testimony.[30]

After a powerful choir anthem, Pastor Jim was prompted by the Holy Spirit; he changed the order of service and invited the young soloist to tell his personal testimony of how God set him free from addiction to crack cocaine. After this, Pastor Jim felt led to extend an altar call, and dozens came forward in surrender to Christ. Later that week a man from Texas called and shared his story of visiting New York City with his teenage son who had been raised in the Christian faith but walked away from God. He brought his son to the church service that morning, though they intended to leave early to catch a flight.

When the young soloist shared his powerful testimony, and Pastor Jim then shared the gospel of Jesus, that teenage son headed for the altar and surrendered his life to Jesus Christ. The dad said, "When he came back to the seat, he was a different person." God changed that worship service and that boy through the power of personal testimony. We are blessed to testify of what God has done for us.

For Prayerful Reflection: What testimonies have you heard through which God changed your life? What testimony do you have of what God has done for you?

Bible in a Year: *Ecclesiastes 4-6; 2 Corinthians 12*

---

30   Jim Cymbala, *Fresh Faith: What Happens When Real Faith Ignites God's People* (Grand Rapids, MI: Zondervan, 2003), 78-82.

September 21

I CAN Testify TODAY...
BECAUSE GOD IS PRESENT IN THE VALLEY OF DEATH

Even though I walk through the valley of the shadow of death, I will fear no evil, for you are with me; your rod and your staff, they comfort me. You prepare a table before me in the presence of my enemies; you anoint my head with oil; my cup overflows. Surely goodness and mercy shall follow me all the days of my life, and I shall dwell in the house of the Lord forever. (Psalm 23:4-6)

But [Stephen], full of the Holy Spirit, ... said, "Behold, I see the heavens opened, and the Son of Man standing at the right hand of God." (Acts 7:55-56)

Death is common to all. None will escape. Many who are terrified of death are intrigued by testimonies of those who have no fear of it and even more so by those who joyfully anticipate it because of faith in God's promises. A commonly read Scripture at funeral services is Psalm 23, in which David testifies of his own lack of fear when walking *through the valley of the shadow of death.* Why? *For you [God] are with me.* And as Stephen was being stoned to death because of faith in Jesus, the mob expected to see his terror and hear his screams. But instead, Stephen was seeing the glory of heaven and Jesus.

I have often beheld such peace and joy when followers of Jesus have approached death. I have peace about my own mortality, and I joyfully anticipate seeing my Lord very soon. In this world where death continually happens, and fear of it is rampant, we who know Jesus Christ are blessed to testify of Him to others, for He is the reason for our hope.

For Prayerful Reflection: What effect is your faith in Jesus having on reflections about your own death? How might God use your testimony to help somebody who is fearful of death?

Bible in a Year: *Ecclesiastes 7-9; 2 Corinthians 13*

September 22

I CAN Testify TODAY . . .
BECAUSE GOD PREPARES ME

[Jesus] called the twelve together and gave them power and authority over all demons and to cure diseases, and he sent them out to proclaim the kingdom of God and to heal. (Luke 9:1-2)

In your hearts honor Christ the Lord as holy, always being prepared to make a defense to anyone who asks you for a reason for the hope that is in you. (1 Peter 3:15)

Preparation is needed to be effective at many things in life. This is why we attend school, why athletes train, why military commanders drill, why musicians rehearse, and why apprentices learn their trades by working alongside masters in the field. Effective parents, teachers, coaches, musicians, commanders, and trade professionals take seriously their responsibilities to prepare those who will follow them.

God is preparing us as His witnesses. When Jesus sent out the Twelve to proclaim the kingdom of God, He gave them what they needed. Prior to His ascension, Jesus promised the Holy Spirit to His followers to prepare and empower them (and us) to be His witnesses.

The apostle Peter was determined that every disciple of Jesus should always be *prepared to make a defense to anyone who asks you for a reason for the hope that is in you.* He explained how such preparation begins. He said, *In your hearts honor Christ the Lord as holy.* The New International Version translates this as *in your hearts revere Christ as Lord,* and the *New Living Translation* has *worship Christ as Lord of your life.* God's preparation for us to be effective as His witnesses begins with us setting Jesus Christ as Lord of all in our lives. When we have done this, we will not stay silent about Him.

For Prayerful Reflection: What preparations has God led you through for being His witness? How is revering Jesus Christ as Lord of your life influencing your witness for Him today?

Bible in a Year: *Ecclesiastes 10-12; Galatians 1*

September 23

I CAN Testify TODAY . . .
BECAUSE GOD SAYS DON'T BE ASHAMED

"Everyone who acknowledges me before men, I also will acknowledge before my Father who is in heaven, but whoever denies me before men, I also will deny before my Father who is in heaven." (Matthew 10:32-33)

I am not ashamed of the gospel, for it is the power of God for salvation to everyone who believes. (Romans 1:16)

Do not be ashamed of the testimony about our Lord, nor of me his prisoner, but share in suffering for the gospel by the power of God. . . . I am not ashamed, for I know whom I have believed, and I am convinced that he is able to guard until that day what has been entrusted to me. (2 Timothy 1:8, 12)

Nobody enjoys suffering or experiencing a hard time because of who they are or what they do or believe. The temptation can be real, therefore, for Christians to deny knowing Christ or to keep their mouths closed when given an opportunity to speak of Him. Of course, we don't want persecution. But Jesus warned that *"whoever denies me before men, I will also deny before my Father who is heaven."* This sobering truth means the eternal consequence of refusing to testify of Christ will be much worse than the persecution and suffering we feared.

The apostle Paul, who suffered greatly for the sake of the gospel, encouraged the Christians in Rome and also young Pastor Timothy to not be ashamed of the gospel of Christ but to testify of Him, even if suffering should result. All around this world, Christians are boldly declaring their faith in the Lord, often at great cost. We are called and blessed to join them today, for God says *do not be ashamed*.

For Prayerful Reflection: When have you experienced the temptation to be ashamed of the gospel? Will you pray with availability today and ask for opportunities to testify of the Lord?

Bible in a Year: *Song of Solomon 1-3; Galatians 2*

September 24

I CAN Testify TODAY . . .
BECAUSE GOD LETS ME SPEAK OF HIS LOVE

"Know therefore that the Lord your God is God, the faithful God who keeps covenant and steadfast love with those who love him and keep his commandments, to a thousand generations." (Deuteronomy 7:9)

"A new commandment I give to you, that you love one another: just as I have loved you, you also are to love one another." (John 13:34)

We love because he first loved us. (1 John 4:19)

God has repeatedly shown and told us of His love for us. We who are recipients of God's love are called and blessed to keep passing it on as long as we have life, by showing and telling of God's love, by our love.

A few days before my dad died, he was carried by ambulance from the hospital to the nursing home where my mom resided. For the first time in several weeks, they lived again in the same room. One of those evenings I was with them, and with the bathroom door open while I rinsed my mom's dentures, I heard this brief and touching conversation:

Dad: "Marjorie?"
Mom: "Yes dear?"
Dad: "I love you!"
Mom: "I love you too, dear!"

They had spent a lifetime giving and receiving love with each other, and they kept speaking it until the end. I was a blessed recipient of their love, and through them I was a recipient of God's love. We who have been so loved by God are blessed to receive it, to love Him in return, and to testify of God's great love to others. His love is too wonderful for us to remain silent.

For Prayerful Reflection: How have you heard God telling you of His love for you? Why do you as a recipient of God's great love want to testify of His love to others in what you say and do?

Bible in a Year: *Song of Solomon 4-5; Galatians 3*

September 25

I CAN Testify TODAY...
BECAUSE GOD BRINGS FAITH FROM HEARING

> *If you confess with your mouth that Jesus is Lord and believe in your heart that God raised him from the dead, you will be saved. For with the heart one believes and is justified, and with the mouth one confesses and is saved. For the Scripture says, "Everyone who believes in him will not be put to shame." How then will they call on him in whom they have not believed? And how are they to believe in him of whom they have never heard? And how are they to hear without someone preaching? So faith comes from hearing, and hearing through the word of Christ.*
> (Romans 10:9-11, 14, 17)

Having one's sins forgiven and receiving God's gift of everlasting life requires believing in Jesus, that He is Savior and Lord and is risen from the dead. In Romans 10 the apostle makes the excellent point that since believing in Jesus is required for salvation, it is absolutely critical that people are told of the good news of Jesus Christ. This is where we come in.

If you have been raised in the Christian faith, as I was, or have been around the church for some time, you might have little awareness of how many people have never heard a clear presentation of the gospel of Christ. In my twenty-seven years as a military chaplain, I saw this often. I met so many who knew nothing about Jesus and who had not once in their lives been invited to a church or a Christian fellowship. This is tragic.

Faith comes from hearing, and hearing requires people like us to testify of Jesus. We would be wise to prayerfully consider today our availability and willingness to speak of Him as He provides opportunity.

For Prayerful Reflection: Who told you of Jesus, contributing to your belief, salvation, and spiritual growth? What level of responsibility have you accepted for testifying of Jesus so that others may hear?

Bible in a Year: *Song of Solomon 6-8; Galatians 4*

September 26

I CAN Testify TODAY . . .
BECAUSE GOD IS GLORIFIED
IN MY TESTIMONY

As he passed by, he saw a man blind from birth. And his disciples asked him, "Rabbi, who sinned, this man or his parents, that he was born blind?" Jesus answered, "It was not that this man sinned, or his parents, but that the works of God might be displayed in him." (John 9:1-3)

When Samuel arrived in Bethlehem to anoint the chosen king, God taught him a principle we would do well to remember today: *"The Lord sees not as man sees: man looks on the outward appearance, but the Lord looks on the heart"* (1 Samuel 16:7). Our Lord's perspective is greater and better than ours.

Another example of this is seen in the gospel story of a man who was born blind. While Jesus' disciples noticed only the outward appearance of the man's blindness and struggle, our Lord saw what God was doing and was going to do through this man and his situation, all for His glory.

Our own life testimonies are about more than outward appearances: more than the struggles, trials, and heartaches. God would have our focus transcend these things, so that we might see and therefore testify of how God has brought glory to His name through the blindness and other trials that we have endured. For the man in this gospel account, what a testimony he had to tell of how God brought glory to His name through his life.

My own testimony is similar, for I have so many stories to tell of how through various trials and hard circumstances, God brought glory to His name, and for this I give Him the praise. May God be glorified through your testimony and mine, for surely, He has done great things.

For Prayerful Reflection: How has God been glorified even through the trials in your life? What opportunities may God give you to share portions of your testimony with somebody today?

Bible in a Year: *Isaiah 1-2; Galatians 5*

September 27

I CAN Testify TODAY...
BECAUSE GOD TOUCHED ME

The neighbors and those who had seen him before as a beggar were saying, "Is this not the man who used to sit and beg?" Some said, "It is he." Others said, "No, but he is like him." He kept saying, "I am the man." So they said to him, "Then how were your eyes opened?" He answered, "The man called Jesus made mud and anointed my eyes and said to me, 'Go to Siloam and wash.' So I went and washed and received my sight." (John 9:8-11)

This is one of many gospel accounts of Jesus touching somebody who was powerfully changed and who then testified to all who listened about what Christ had done for them. This is our privilege too. Bill Gaither expressed the testimony of God's touch in the song "He Touched Me." The lyrics include:

> He touched me, Oh He touched me,
> And oh, the joy that floods my soul!
> Something happened and now I know,
> He touched me and made me whole.[31]

The man in John 9 had been blind his entire life. Then Jesus touched him, put mud on his eyes, and told him where to wash. And when he did as the Lord instructed, he could see. Can you imagine it?

When I received my first pair of glasses as a child, I was so excited, because now I could see clearly. This man's excitement and joy must have been off the charts, for he was seeing for the very first time. Of course he testified of what God had done for him. That is what we can do. What Christ has done for you is part of your testimony now. Isn't it too good to keep to yourself?

For Prayerful Reflection: What is your own testimony of God touching and changing you? What opportunities might God give you to share with somebody today what He has done?

Bible in a Year: *Isaiah 3-4; Galatians 6*

---
[31] Quoted with permission.

September 28

I CAN Testify TODAY . . .
BECAUSE GOD REVEALS HIS MAJESTY TO ME

We did not follow cleverly devised myths when we made known to you the power and coming of our Lord Jesus Christ, but we were eyewitnesses of his majesty. For when he received honor and glory from God the Father, and the voice was borne to him by the Majestic Glory, "This is my beloved Son, with whom I am well pleased," we ourselves heard this very voice borne from heaven, for we were with him on the holy mountain. (2 Peter 1:16-18)

By the time he had written this, Peter had followed Jesus for nearly forty years. Writing in 2 Peter 1:13-14 that he would soon be departing this life, Peter clearly believes this epistle is his final discourse. From prison in Rome, the apostle is imparting reminders to the church about what he has taught on how to faithfully live for Christ according to the true revelation of God. He especially discredits false teaching and affirms God's revealed truth. When we speak of Jesus, we too are affirming God's truth.

Peter shares some personal testimony, for *we were eyewitnesses of his majesty* (see Luke 9:28-36). He describes seeing Jesus in the fullness of heavenly glory and hearing the voice of God the Father confirming that Jesus is His beloved Son. As Peter is now approaching his promotion to heaven, the glorious revelation of Christ's majesty is wonderful comfort indeed. Peter therefore testified of this, so that others would believe in His majesty too.

Though we have not yet seen the glory as Peter saw it, God has surely revealed His majesty to us. I have seen His glory in many ways: hearing His voice and experiencing His presence. I have worshipped Him in awe and wonder. Have you? As God reveals His majesty to us, we are blessed to testify of Him.

For Prayerful Reflection: How has God revealed His majesty to you? What testimonies could you share of God opening your spiritual eyes and ears to behold Him in His glory?

Bible in a Year: *Isaiah 5-6; Ephesians 1*

September 29

I CAN Testify TODAY...
BECAUSE GOD SACRIFICED FOR ME

"Greater love has no one than this, that someone lay down his life for his friends." (John 15:13)

Therefore be imitators of God, as beloved children. And walk in love, as Christ loved us and gave himself up for us, as a fragrant offering and sacrifice to God. (Ephesians 5:1-2)

God says that all who have experienced the sacrificial love of God are to be imitators of Him, not doing so out of obligation but as His beloved children. While serving as a pastor and military chaplain, I often asked God to fill me with His love so I might love those He called me to serve, even as He loves me.

One of my favorite stories of this is told in *Sea of Glory* by Ken Wales and David Poling.[32] This is the true story of four chaplains who were with their troops aboard the U.S.A.T. Dorchester, when in the early hours of February 3, 1943, the ship was torpedoed by a German submarine. As the ship was sinking, panicked soldiers jumped for overcrowded lifeboats, and others dove into the water. When the life jackets ran out, all four chaplains removed their own and gave them away, so others might live. One survivor said, "It was the finest thing I have seen or hope to see this side of heaven."

If you had survived because of being a recipient of one of those life jackets, what would the effect be on you? Would you not be forever grateful? Would you not often tell this story of sacrificial love? Friends, this is our story in Jesus Christ. God's Son laid down His life to save you and me. So, with love, we testify today.

For Prayerful Reflection: Pondering God's sacrificial love for you, what is in your heart for Him? What does it mean for you to be an *imitator of God* in loving Him and others and in testifying of His love?

Bible in a Year: *Isaiah 7-8; Ephesians 2*

---

[32] Ken Wales and David Poling, *Sea of Glory: A Novel Based on the True WWII Story of the Four Chaplains and the U.S.A.T. Dorchester* (Nashville: Broadman & Holman, 2001).

September 30

I CAN Testify TODAY . . .
BECAUSE GOD HAS GIVEN ME ETERNAL LIFE

If we receive the testimony of men, the testimony of God is greater, for this is the testimony of God that he has borne concerning his Son. Whoever believes in the Son of God has the testimony in himself. Whoever does not believe God has made him a liar, because he has not believed in the testimony that God has borne concerning his Son. And this is the testimony, that God gave us eternal life, and this life is in his Son. (1 John 5:9-11)

The gospel that we believe and the message that we bear are not based only on human testimony. God confirms His truth to us. We believe not only because our minds and outward senses say so, but also because God the Holy Spirit has touched and changed us on the inside, affecting our whole being. When God confirms His truth to us, we know it. John adds that when we refuse to believe what God reveals, we have *made him a liar.*

The fruit of believing God's testimony includes receiving the priceless gift of eternal life in Christ. Recipients of this wonderful gift are now blessed to open the way for others. Father William Bausch told of a boy who arrived very early at school one morning and waited patiently at the door. Next to arrive was a lady who was surprised this youngster had arrived so early. "It's locked," the boy said as the teacher tried the door. She began fumbling for her keys, and the boy brightened up. "You're a teacher!" he said.

"How do you know that?" she asked.

The boy then said, "You have the key."

We who know the Lord Jesus have the key to everlasting life. Testifying of Him opens a door for others to enter too.

For Prayerful Reflection: Who opened the door for you by testifying of Jesus? What does God's gift of eternal life mean to you today? How can you testify of it to others?

Bible in a Year: *Isaiah 9-10; Ephesians 3*

12 Themes on Following Jesus

OCTOBER

Because God . . .
I Can *Serve* Today

October 1

I CAN Serve TODAY...
BECAUSE GOD IS THE MASTER SERVANT

"Whoever would be great among you must be your servant, and whoever would be first among you must be slave of all. For even the Son of Man came not to be served but to serve, and to give his life as a ransom for many." (Mark 10:43-45)

God designed us to serve. Part of being created in God's own image is being made to serve. Because of our sin nature, we can often resist this, preferring others to serve us. But our maker, the infinite and eternal God of heaven and earth, reminds us that He has served us. It is good to allow this startling truth to have its effect on us today.

Jesus, the glorious and everlasting Son of God, said that He entered humanity *not to be served but to serve*. And how did He serve? Ultimately, by giving *his life as a ransom for many*. On the cross of Calvary, the Son of God supremely served us by suffering and dying, giving His life to pay our ransom. Let's hit the pause button in our minds for a moment and reflect on this. Could there be any higher act of serving than this? Jesus Christ did this for you and me.

To ransom a person is to deliver them from bondage by paying the price of redemption. The one who is redeemed is forever grateful to the redeemer. Our God did this for us by the suffering and sacrificial death of Jesus Christ, *the Lamb of God, who takes away the sin of the world* (John 1:29). The master servant sets us free. Because we owe Him our life and freedom, surely and gladly, we want to serve Him. This is our great privilege today.

For Prayerful Reflection: How are you changed by believing Jesus Christ came to serve and ransom you? How does His sacrifice for you affect your availability and intention to serve God and others today?

Bible in a Year: *Isaiah 11-13; Ephesians 4*

October 2

I CAN Serve TODAY...
BECAUSE GOD ENABLES ME TO LIVE AS HIS SERVANT

Let love be genuine. Abhor what is evil; hold fast to what is good. Love one another with brotherly affection. Outdo one another in showing honor. Do not be slothful in zeal, be fervent in spirit, serve the Lord. (Romans 12:9-11)

Loving Jesus means serving Him by serving others, no matter what their responses may be. One pastor's wife learned this lesson. Her husband, Pastor Dunn, had finished his lengthy sermon and concluded the service. His wife Gladys approached a sleepy-looking gentleman sitting nearby to welcome him. She extended a hand in greeting and said, "Hello, I'm Gladys Dunn."

To this he replied, "You're not the only one!" Gladys smiled then served him anyway, by caring for him and making him feel welcome.

God calls and enables us to live today as His servants. As Christ works within us, we are made servants by nature. Richard Foster said, "When we choose to serve, we are still in charge. We decide whom we will serve and when we will serve. And if we are in charge, we will worry a great deal about someone stepping on us, that is, taking charge over us. But when we choose to be a servant, we give up the right to be in charge, ... we surrender the right to decide who and when we will serve. We become available and vulnerable."[33]

God brings people into our lives whom He dearly loves and calls us to serve in His name. We do not do this for earthly rewards or for a particular result, but for the joy of serving God. We therefore cannot walk away from those He calls us to serve. We are to love and serve them as though they were Jesus Christ Himself.

For Prayerful Reflection: Have you regarded yourself as a servant by nature, ready and willing to serve? What might it mean for you today to love and serve someone as though they were Jesus Christ Himself?

Bible in a Year: *Isaiah 14-16; Ephesians 5:1-16*

---

[33] Richard J. Foster, *Celebration of Discipline: The Path to Spiritual Growth* (San Francisco: Harper & Row, 1978), 132.

October 3

I CAN Serve TODAY...
BECAUSE GOD ELEVATES SERVANT LEADERSHIP

Do nothing from selfish ambition or conceit, but in humility count others more significant than yourselves. Let each of you look not only to his own interests, but also to the interests of others. (Philippians 2:3-4)

God intends servant leadership to attract people to Himself. But when we fail to serve in the character of Christ, we can repel people from Him instead. A woman interviewed a prospective servant and asked, "Are you able to serve company?"

The applicant replied, "Yes, ma'am, both ways."

The woman looked puzzled and asked, "What do you mean, 'both ways'?"

"So they'll come again or stay away." The way we serve makes a difference.

Cheryl Bachelder, former CEO of Popeyes Louisiana Kitchen, turned her company around with a focus on serving. She chronicled the story of Popeyes' success in her book *Dare to Serve: How to Drive Superior Results by Serving Others*.[34] As a committed Christian, Bachelder says she keeps Philippians 2:3 on her calendar because it reminds her of how she wants to lead her family and her business. She says the words on counting others more significant than ourselves remind her that we all have an inner two-year-old that sometimes kicks and screams when we don't get what we want.

This is sad but true. We need God's inner transformation if we are to become servant leaders who are more focused on the needs of others than on our own interests. Jesus says that when we humble ourselves before Him, He blesses us and helps us reflect Him in the way we lead and serve others.

For Prayerful Reflection: Where have you observed or experienced servant leadership that reflects the Lord? What might it look like for you to *in humility count others more significant than [yourself]*?

Bible in a Year: *Isaiah 17-19; Ephesians 5:17-33*

---

34 Cheryl Bachelder, *Dare to Serve: How to Drive Superior Results by Serving Others* (Oakland, CA: Berrett-Koehler Publishers, Inc., 2015).

October 4

I CAN Serve TODAY...
BECAUSE GOD SEES ALL I DO AS SERVICE TO HIM

Whatever you do, work heartily, as for the Lord and not for men, knowing that from the Lord you will receive the inheritance as your reward. You are serving the Lord Christ. (Colossians 3:23-24)

The little drummer boy wanted to do something for Jesus, so he played his drum. That image reminds us that we can all serve God by offering Him whatever we do in loving service. Serving coffee is a small example. A pastor and a young boy in a congregation were discussing this, because the boy noticed that after the service each week many stayed for coffee and conversation. As someone served the pastor a cup, he asked the little boy if he knew why they served coffee. The boy said, "Is it to get the people awake before they drive home?" The boy's funny answer was a nice try, wasn't it?

Paul said we can serve God in whatever we do. This implies that if we're ever doing something that we know cannot honor the Lord, we should stop and find something else that we can do for Him. You might be wondering how to apply this lesson, for the things you do day by day seem earthly and unspiritual. But the whole world, including all our days and moments, ultimately belongs to God, and they are intended for His glory.

A man asked Martin Luther how he could serve God. Luther asked him, "What is your work now?"

The man said, "I'm a shoemaker."

To the cobbler's surprise, Luther replied, "Then make good shoes and sell them at a fair price."[35] May our daily prayer be "All for you, Lord."

For Prayerful Reflection: What does it mean to serve God in all you do? What might it look like for you to do everything that you do for Him today?

Bible in a Year: *Isaiah 20-22; Ephesians 6*

---

35 Tullian Tchividjian, "Our Calling, Our Spheres," *Christianity Today: Leadership Journal*, Summer 2010, www.christianitytoday.com/pastors/2010/summer/ourcallingspheres.html (June 2021).

October 5

I CAN Serve TODAY . . .
BECAUSE GOD IS GREATER
THAN HIS SERVANTS

Truly, truly, I say to you, a servant is not greater than his master, nor is a messenger greater than the one who sent him. If you know these things, blessed are you if you do them. (John 13:16-17)

Representing Jesus involves making sacrifices to serve with love, for He who is greater than we are gave everything for us. Following Jesus includes sacrificially serving in His name. Chinese church leader Watchman Nee, who suffered greatly for the gospel, taught about demonstrating Jesus Christ in the way we love and serve.

He told of a Christian who owned a rice paddy next to one owned by a communist man. The Christian irrigated his paddy by pumping water from a canal, using one of those leg-operated pumps that make the user appear to be seated on a bicycle. Every day after the Christian had pumped enough water to fill his field, the communist came out, removed some boards that kept the water in the Christian's field, and let the water flow down into his own field; that way he didn't have to pump. This continued day after day. The Christian prayed, "Lord, if this keeps up, I'm going to lose all my rice, maybe even my field. I've got a family to care for. What can I do?"

In answer, God put a thought in his mind. So the next morning he arose in the predawn hours and started pumping water into the field of his neighbor. Then he replaced the boards and pumped water into his own rice paddy. In a few weeks both fields of rice were doing well, and the communist was converted.[36]

May God guide us today in following His example of loving, sacrificial service.

For Prayerful Reflection: When have you seen others sacrificially serving like Jesus? What might it look like for you to do the same today?

Bible in a Year: *Isaiah 23-25; Philippians 1*

---

36 Dr. Paul Faulkner, *Making Things Right When Things Go Wrong: Ten Proven Ways to Put Your Life in Order* (West Monroe, LA: Howard Publishing Company, Inc, 1996).

October 6

I CAN Serve TODAY...
BECAUSE GOD GIVES ME OPPORTUNITY

Do not be deceived: God is not mocked, for whatever one sows, that will he also reap. And let us not grow weary of doing good, for in due season we will reap, if we do not give up. So then, as we have opportunity, let us do good to everyone, and especially to those who are of the household of faith. (Galatians 6:7, 9-10)

In his autobiography *Just As I Am*, Billy Graham described a conversation he had with President Kennedy on the gospel of Jesus.[37] Sometime later, after the 1963 National Prayer Breakfast, the president asked if he could come back to the White House with him so they could talk, but Graham told him he wasn't feeling well and asked if they could do this another time. The president said, "Of course." But there was no other time, for later that year Kennedy was assassinated. Graham said that missed opportunity still haunted him.

But haven't we all missed opportunities? Haven't you at times become *weary of doing good,* being tired, weak, distracted, or bored, and missed divine appointments God had prepared for you to serve Him and someone He loves? I know your answer is yes, for so is mine. This is why we are encouraged by our Lord to be looking for the opportunities He provides, so we might be faithful in each one. This is why my Lord has taught me to often pray, "Lord, help me to recognize and respond to each divine appointment you have for me today. Help me to serve and honor you in each one."

Doing this requires active service. Thomas Edison once observed, "Opportunity is missed by most people because it is dressed in overalls and looks like work." May God help us to respond favorably to every opportunity for service He has prepared for us today.

For Prayerful Reflection: When have you rightly discerned a divine appointment and gladly responded in service? What keeps you from looking for and then responding to God-given opportunities to serve?

Bible in a Year: Isaiah 26-27; Philippians 2

---
37 Billy Graham, *Just As I Am: The Autobiography of Billy Graham* (San Francisco: HarperOne, 1997).

October 7

I CAN Serve TODAY...
BECAUSE GOD GAVE HIS LIFE FOR ME

"Whoever would be great among you must be your servant, and whoever would be first among you must be your slave, even as the Son of Man came not to be served but to serve, and to give his life as a ransom for many." (Matthew 20:26-28)

What the incarnate Son of God did for us is earth shattering and life changing. Let it sink into your soul. Ponder again that the Lord of the universe cares so much for you that He intentionally and lovingly entered humanity in service to bring life and hope to you. He laid down His life for you.

Jesus said He would do this and then did it; He gave *his life as a ransom for many*. He now enables and desires us who love Him to follow Him in selfless service. This is contrary to our former nature, for we were sinfully prone to primarily consider what is in it for us. But a life transformed by the sacrificial love of God becomes inclined and pleased to follow Him now in selfless service.

One example of this was Damien, a nineteenth-century Belgian priest who moved to Kalawao on the island of Molokai, Hawaii, which was a quarantined leper colony. For sixteen years he lived and served among the lepers because he believed it was what Jesus would do. He learned their language, bandaged and embraced bodies no one else would touch, and preached to lonely hearts. He organized schools, bands, and choirs. He built homes for shelter and two thousand coffins so that when the lepers died they could be buried in dignity. And in time, he too became a leper and died.

We can give our lives in service to others today for the sake of Christ who laid down His life for us.

For Prayerful Reflection: How astounded are you today by the service and sacrifice of the Lord for you? What is Jesus Christ saying to you about following Him today in selfless service?

Bible in a Year: *Isaiah 28-29; Philippians 3*

October 8

I CAN Serve TODAY . . .
BECAUSE GOD WASHES MY FEET

When he had washed their feet and put on his outer garments and resumed his place, he said to them, "Do you understand what I have done to you? You call me Teacher and Lord, and you are right, for so I am. If I then, your Lord and Teacher, have washed your feet, you also ought to wash one another's feet. For I have given you an example, that you also should do just as I have done to you." (John 13:12-15)

Let's picture this scene again. The Messiah and Son of God is taking a towel and a basin of water. He lovingly kneels before you – lifting, touching, and washing your dirty feet, then drying them with a towel. Is this not personal, humbling, and amazing? Doesn't it move you? And when He is finished, our Lord commissions you to do for others what He has done for you. Our question today is, Are we doing it? Are we getting close to people, following Christ's example of humble service?

I came to more fully understand this call of service in the summer of 1976. At the end of that summer, I married Helen and began my final year of college. After that, I attended three years of seminary and then continued with a lifetime of pastoral ministry. But that summer I learned to humbly serve.

Working as a home health aide, I visited homes of men who needed help. They were all ill, and many were dying. In various ways I "washed their feet." I bathed and dressed them and did whatever needed doing – up close, personal, and extremely humbling. But I kept hearing my Lord remind me that He loves these men, and in His name, I was showing them His love. We are blessed to humbly serve today, for we have a God who washes feet.

For Prayerful Reflection: How has God loved and tenderly cared for you? What opportunities is He giving you to humbly and personally serve someone in need?

Bible in a Year: *Isaiah 30-31; Philippians 4*

October 9

I CAN Serve TODAY . . .
BECAUSE GOD CAME AS A SUFFERING SERVANT

All we like sheep have gone astray; we have turned—every one—to his own way; and the Lord has laid on him the iniquity of us all. He was oppressed, and he was afflicted, yet he opened not his mouth; like a lamb that is led to the slaughter, and like a sheep that before its shearers is silent, so he opened not his mouth. (Isaiah 53:6-7)

As was foretold by Isaiah, our Lord came to us as a servant and suffered for our sins. And we who love and follow Him may be required to suffer in His name as we serve Him and those whom He calls us to serve.

Some years ago, while ministering in Bulgaria, I met Pastor Christo Kulichev, a Congregational pastor who was arrested and imprisoned in 1985 for the crime of preaching the gospel in the church that he served. The previous week the committee who ran the village had appointed a new pastor loyal to the Communist party. So when Pastor Kulichev preached the Word that week, he was immediately arrested and imprisoned. But Jesus Christ was with him in his suffering and imprisonment, and he counted it a privilege. He later said that God was better served by his presence in prison than if he had been free. His story is told in *Imprisoned for Christ*.[38]

If suffering is required in your service to God, do not curse the suffering. Rather, thank God and pray that the Lord who came to be a suffering servant for our sake may by His grace bless and use your suffering for His glory and draw others to Him.

For Prayerful Reflection: How are you blessed in knowing Jesus Christ endured suffering for you? What will it mean to offer your suffering to God for His glory and to bless others?

Bible in a Year: *Isaiah 32-33; Colossians 1*

---

38 Michael P. Halcomb and Christo Kulichev, *Imprisoned for Christ* (Carol Stream, IL: Tyndale House Publishers, 2001).

October 10

I CAN Serve TODAY...
BECAUSE GOD'S GOSPEL IS ADORNED IN SERVICE

Whatever you do, work heartily, as for the Lord and not for men, knowing that from the Lord you will receive the inheritance as your reward. You are serving the Lord Christ. (Colossians 3:23-24)

Submitting to one another out of reverence for Christ.... Husbands should love their wives as their own bodies. (Ephesians 5:21, 28)

Living as Christians and proclaiming God's Word must always be dressed in loving acts of service. This is true in marriages and in families, in our Lord's church, and in the world. Being married or having a family means proactively serving them in love. When Helen and I married, expressing our love for each other, we included in our wedding vows our shared aim: "that together we might better serve God and others." As followers of Jesus Christ, we continue with this as our desire. We serve God by serving each other and people He loves.

A wealthy American traveler was visiting a hospital in Southeast Asia. As he walked through the corridors, he saw a young missionary woman who wore the garments of a nurse. She was cleaning the sores of a sick and dirty elderly man who'd been found lying in a gutter. The rich traveler said to the nurse, "I wouldn't do that for a million dollars."

She answered quietly and with conviction, "Neither would I."

Money cannot purchase extravagant love for Jesus or a desire to serve in His name. Like Mary, whose story of devotion to Jesus is told in John 12, her life was broken and spilled out for the love of God.

Living the gospel of Jesus means wearing garments of service in our families, in the church, and anywhere He sends us.

For Prayerful Reflection: When have you witnessed the gospel of Jesus in loving acts of service? How will you demonstrate God's love in acts of service today?

Bible in a Year: *Isaiah 34-36; Colossians 2*

October 11

I CAN Serve TODAY . . .
BECAUSE GOD MAKES LEADERS WHO SERVE

He asked them, "What were you discussing on the way?" But they kept silent, for on the way they had argued with one another about who was the greatest. And he sat down and called the twelve. And he said to them, "If anyone would be first, he must be last of all and servant of all." (Mark 9:33-35)

What we proclaim is not ourselves, but Jesus Christ as Lord, with ourselves as your servants for Jesus' sake. (2 Corinthians 4:5)

Jesus' disciples had been arguing about which of them was the greatest, presumably thinking they might soon be in a position where others would serve them. Knowing their thoughts, Jesus taught them that the greatest leaders lead by serving.

A theme verse in my life has been 2 Corinthians 4:5 in which Paul affirmed that his message and goal were not about him but about Jesus Christ as Lord. He regarded himself *as your servant for Jesus' sake.* The hymn "Blest be the Tie that Binds" illustrates this. The author was John Fawcett, a Baptist preacher who had served a small country church in 1722, but had been invited to shepherd a larger, more prestigious church in London.

After preaching his farewell sermon, his family's possessions were packed. The tears of his parishioners who helped them load the carts touched John and his wife. She said, "I cannot bear this! I know not how to go."

"Nor I," he replied, "nor will we go. Unload the wagon and put everything in the place it was before." They stayed and served that flock for fifty-four years.[39] We can lead today by faithfully serving where God plants us.

For Prayerful Reflection: How have you received or lived the Lord's vision of servant leadership? What will it mean for you to lead today by faithfully serving where God has planted you?

Bible in a Year: *Isaiah 37-38; Colossians 3*

---
[39] E. E. Ryden, *The Story of Christian Hymnody* (Rock Island, IL: Augustana Book Concern, 1959).

October 12

I CAN Serve TODAY...
BECAUSE GOD GIFTS US TO SERVE

As each has received a gift, use it to serve one another, as good stewards of God's varied grace: whoever speaks, as one who speaks oracles of God; whoever serves, as one who serves by the strength that God supplies—in order that in everything God may be glorified through Jesus Christ. To him belong glory and dominion forever and ever. Amen.
(1 Peter 4:10-11)

Haven't we all at one time or another received a gift that we stuck in a box and stored on a shelf but never used? It happens, doesn't it? Do we even wonder what the giver would think if they knew we never used what they gave us? What of the gifts God has given us? Surely we know God is not pleased when we fail to appreciate or use the gifts that He has given us. Our Lord made this clear in His parable of the talents as told in Matthew 25.

The apostle Peter says God has given gifts to every follower of Jesus Christ. These are anointed passions and abilities from God Himself. And what does God intend for us to do with the gifts He gives? He says we are to *use [them] to serve one another, as good stewards of God's varied grace.* So whatever passion or ability God has given you, He desires and expects you to use it to serve. Are you doing so?

May our goal be to make a positive difference through service. If we ask God to show us how, He will. Mother Teresa, who personified servanthood, encouraged others by saying, "Let no one ever come to you without leaving better and happier." May our aim today be to serve others with the gifts God has given us.

For Prayerful Reflection: What passions and gifts has God given you that you have not been using much lately? How might you make a positive difference today by serving others as God has gifted you?

Bible in a Year: *Isaiah 39-40; Colossians 4*

October 13

I CAN Serve TODAY . . .
BECAUSE GOD IS MY SUPREME EXAMPLE

"This is my commandment, that you love one another as I have loved you." (John 15:12)

Have this mind among yourselves, which is yours in Christ Jesus, who, though he was in the form of God, did not count equality with God a thing to be grasped, but emptied himself, by taking the form of a servant, being born in the likeness of men. And being found in human form, he humbled himself by becoming obedient to the point of death, even death on a cross. (Philippians 2:5-8)

Being loved by God like this allows and enables us to love and serve like Jesus. A great example of this is Dawson Trotman, founder of The Navigators, who visited Taiwan on one of his overseas trips. During the visit he hiked with a Taiwanese pastor back into one of the mountain villages to meet with some of the national Christians. The roads and trails were wet, and their shoes became very muddy.

Later, someone asked this Taiwanese pastor what he remembered most about Dawson Trotman. Without hesitation the man replied, "He cleaned my shoes." How surprised this humble national pastor must have been to arise in the morning and realize that the visiting Christian leader had arisen before him and cleaned the mud from his shoes. Such a spirit of servanthood marked Dawson Trotman throughout his Christian life. He died as he lived, giving his life to rescue someone from drowning.[40]

As our Lord in humility *emptied himself, by taking the form of a servant,* so can we who follow Him. We can do so at our home, in our neighborhood, in the church, and anywhere He sends us in His name.

For Prayerful Reflection: When and how have you experienced someone loving and serving you like this? In what ways could you, like Jesus, in humility, love and serve someone today?

Bible in a Year: *Isaiah 41-42; 1 Thessalonians 1*

---
[40] Jerry Bridges, "Loving by Serving," *Discipleship Journal,* May/June 1985.

October 14

I CAN Serve TODAY . . .
BECAUSE GOD SENDS ME WHERE HE GOES

In the beginning was the Word, and the Word was with God, and the Word was God. He was in the beginning with God. All things were made through him, and without him was not any thing made that was made. And the Word became flesh and dwelt among us. (John 1:1-3, 14)

"If anyone serves me, he must follow me; and where I am, there will my servant be also." (John 12:26)

Forty years later I still remember a sermon that I preached one Christmas Eve, which I titled "The Visited Planet." How astounding, earth shattering, and life changing to believe and know that the infinite God of heaven and earth, the Creator of all things by the power of His Word, came to be with us. He came out of love for us, the ones that He made in His image. God revealed Himself to us and laid down His life to save us. This is the incarnation of God.

In our sinful condition we could not approach God, for He is holy, sinless, and pure. So in love and great mercy, God came to us. Through the incarnation of Jesus Christ, God came to be with us.

And now we who love and follow Him are sent in His name and with His anointing to bring God's presence to people. As a military chaplain, I was often reminded of my calling to incarnational ministry, for I went in His name wherever the troops were. I experienced many holy encounters in places I would not have previously imagined. This is true of all Christians, for our Lord says, *"If anyone serves me, he must follow me; and where I am, there will be my servant be also."*

For Prayerful Reflection: How amazed are you at the incarnation of God? How does this bless you? Where and to whom might the Lord be sending you to serve in His name today?

Bible in a Year: *Isaiah 43-44; 1 Thessalonians 2*

October 15

I CAN Serve TODAY . . .
BECAUSE GOD MADE ME HIS SERVANT

Mary said, "Behold, I am the servant of the Lord; let it be to me according to your word." (Luke 1:38)

I have made myself a servant to all, that I might win more of them. To the weak I became weak, that I might win the weak. I have become all things to all people, that by all means I might save some. I do it all for the sake of the gospel, that I may share with them in its blessings. (1 Corinthians 9:19, 22-23)

When introducing ourselves, after we have given our name, we may begin with mentioning our profession; if we mention our Christian faith at all, it may come nearer the end of our introductions. But Mary and Paul saw themselves first as servants of God.

I treasure the memory of young Helen introducing herself to me. She said, "I am a Christian who happens now to be a student majoring in social work." Her primary identity was not in her studies or in her profession but in her relationship with Christ. Is this true of you? Being a follower of Jesus means our relationship with Him is primary; loving and serving Him is and will be our first ambition. Thus, we serve people in His name.

Howard Hendricks described sitting on a plane that was delayed for takeoff; he noticed how gracious one of the flight attendants was as she dealt with irritated passengers. Later he told the flight attendant how amazed he was at her poise. She replied that she didn't work for the airline company but for Christ, and before going to work each day, she prayed to be a good representative for Him.[41] We are God's servants today.

For Prayerful Reflection: Is your primary identity in your relationship with Christ? If so, how has this affected your ambition? What might happen if you prayed to be a good representative for Christ today?

Bible in a Year: *Isaiah 45-46; 1 Thessalonians 3*

---

[41] Lorne Sanny, "The Right Way to Respond to Authority," *Discipleship Journal,* March/April 1982.

October 16

I CAN Serve TODAY...
BECAUSE GOD BLESSES US TO SERVE THE LEAST OF THESE

> *"Then the righteous will answer him, saying, 'Lord, when did we see you hungry and feed you, or thirsty and give you drink? And when did we see you a stranger and welcome you, or naked and clothe you? And when did we see you sick or in prison and visit you?' And the King will answer them, 'Truly, I say to you, as you did it to one of the least of these my brothers, you did it to me.'"* (Matthew 25:37-40)

Who are *the least of these,* and what does it mean to serve them? In Jesus' parable, *the least of these* refers to the most vulnerable and needy. Jesus commends His followers for their compassionate care of people who are in need, including the hungry, thirsty, strangers, naked, sick, or imprisoned. Jesus says that when we care for and serve these, we are doing it to Him.

We might think that the opposite of love is hate, but this passage suggests that the opposite of love is indifference. It is failing to notice the pain of others or to care. It is not allowing the circumstances of hurting people to affect our own comfort. We might not always be able to help, but love begins with sharing another's pain.

One of the most beautiful examples of serving *the least of these* in Jesus' name was Mother Teresa, who devoted herself to caring for the poorest of the poor in Calcutta, India. She lived and taught that faith in action is love, and love in action is service. She said, "Not all of us can do great things, but we can do small things with great love." God blesses us to notice, love, and serve *the least of these.*

For Prayerful Reflection: How have you blessed and served *the least of these*? How might God have you notice, love, and serve *the least of these* today?

Bible in a Year: *Isaiah 47-49; 1 Thessalonians 4*

October 17

I CAN Serve TODAY . . .
BECAUSE GOD FREES US TO SERVE

This is the will of God, that by doing good you should put to silence the ignorance of foolish people. Live as people who are free, not using your freedom as a cover-up for evil, but living as servants of God.
(1 Peter 2:15-16)

God frees us from our sin, spiritual bondage, and self-focus, so we can serve. Doug Nichols, a missionary in India, was studying the language when he contracted tuberculosis and was sent to a sanatorium to recuperate. Praying that God would bring good from this, he took tracts and gospel booklets with him, but no one was interested. He was often awakened at night with sounds of coughing, including his own. One night he noticed an old man attempting to sit on the edge of the bed, but he was too weak; he fell back on the bed and sobbed. After a while a stench permeated the ward, because the old man had been unsuccessful at getting to the restroom.

Doug said the nurses were angry, for they had to clean up the mess. One nurse even slapped him, and the man curled into a ball and wept. The next night when the old man tried to get out of bed, Doug got up and carried the man to the restroom; he then carried him back to his bed. The old man kissed Doug on the cheek.

In the morning Doug awakened to a steaming cup of tea served by another patient, and people began taking his gospel booklets. Over the next several days, several acknowledged trust in Christ as Savior as a result of reading the good news. All this resulted from serving a man needing the bathroom.[42] God has freed us to serve Him today.

For Prayerful Reflection: In what sense has God freed you to live as His servant? What opportunities might God be affording you today to humbly serve someone in need?

Bible in a Year: *Isaiah 50-52; 1 Thessalonians 5*

---
42 Harold J. Sala, *Heroes: People Who Made a Difference in Our World* (Uhrichsville, OH: Barbour Publishing, Inc., 1998), 29-31.

October 18

I CAN Serve TODAY . . .
BECAUSE GOD GIVES FERVOR FOR SERVICE

Let love be genuine. Abhor what is evil; hold fast to what is good. Love one another with brotherly affection. Outdo one another in showing honor. Do not be slothful in zeal, be fervent in spirit, serve the Lord. (Romans 12:9-11)

Here Paul fleshes out what it means to live a life that is pleasing to God. Loving service is the theme. Genuine love is more than feeling or sentimentalism; it is fervent, good, and evident in service to others. In fellowship with God, our spiritual batteries are charged, so we can lovingly serve in the name of Jesus. We are enabled and responsible to step out in faithful, fervent service.

A waitress named Chelsea demonstrates such fervor for service. The day after Helen and I arrived at our new hometown in Minnesota, we visited a local restaurant for breakfast. Chelsea was our server that day, and in addition to serving breakfast, she served us spiritually. Rightly discerning that we were weary of soul and body, for we still bore the effects of my cancer, she asked questions that reflected her love and God's. She then asked if she might pray for us, which she did at our breakfast table for God's glory and our blessing.

A few months later another friend described being in the post office on a challenging day when her husband was ill, and a young woman approached with loving concern and asked if she could help in any way. Then this woman prayed with her. Hearing this, we asked if that young woman's name was Chelsea. It was. God gives spiritual fervor today, not just for our sake, but also so we can see and respond to opportunities He gives us to serve others in His name.

For Prayerful Reflection: When were you blessed to be on the receiving end of loving Christian service? What might it mean for you to *be fervent in spirit, serv[ing] the Lord*?

Bible in a Year: *Isaiah 53-55; 2 Thessalonians 1*

October 19

I CAN Serve TODAY ...
BECAUSE GOD LOVES THROUGH ME

Now you are the body of Christ and individually members of it.
(1 Corinthians 12:27)

Through love serve one another. (Galatians 5:13)

If anyone has the world's goods and sees his brother in need, yet closes his heart against him, how does God's love abide in him? Little children, let us not love in word or talk but in deed and in truth. (1 John 3:17-18)

God intends to love people through us. Being the incarnation of God, Jesus Christ was the living, breathing personification of love. We can see it in the way He loved His disciples, had compassion on the hungry and hurting, embraced outcasts and sinners, and wept near Lazarus's grave. Supremely, our Lord showed His love for all people by dying on the cross as the atoning sacrifice for our sins.

But now we are the body of Christ. The church and every individual member, including you and me, are His body to embody and express His love in this world in personal and tangible ways. God intends to love people through us today. He teaches that whenever we serve people in love, we are doing His work. In our acts of loving service, people can see and receive God's love.

We can do this when we allow God's love to permeate us. We might be compared to a dry sponge intended to do good. When hard and brittle, we are of little use until dampened. If ever we attempt to love or serve from our own dry heart, we will fail. But when the moisture of God's love has saturated us through daily fellowship with Him, then we are made pliable, ready for God to do His works of loving and serving through us.

For Prayerful Reflection: What are some ways that God has been loving people through you? How pliable are you today in God's loving hands to *through love serve one another*?

Bible in a Year: *Isaiah 56-58; 2 Thessalonians 2*

October 20

I CAN Serve TODAY . . .
BECAUSE GOD RAISED JESUS

When they had finished breakfast, Jesus said to Simon Peter, "Simon, son of John, do you love me more than these?" He said to him, "Yes, Lord; you know that I love you." He said to him, "Feed my lambs." (John 21:15)

One Sunday morning a pastor listened to a radio station as he dressed for church. Suddenly he heard, "It's Easter, and it doesn't make any difference if Christ be risen or not . . . ."
Shocked, the pastor, A. H. Ackley, shouted, "It's a lie! He is risen!"
His wife said, "Why don't you write a song about it?"
Led by the Spirit of God, he wrote,

> I serve a risen Savior, He's in the world today.
> I know that He is living, whatever men may say.

When we truly and deeply know this, we want to serve our risen Lord by serving His people. A biblical illustration of this is seen in the conversation between Simon Peter and Jesus as described in John 21. Not long before this conversation, Peter had sinned by denying that he knew Jesus and running away in shame. But on this day, Peter had no doubt that Jesus Christ was alive, for he was there – living, breathing, eating, and speaking. Peter's heart was filled with boundless joy and love for his Lord.
Three times Jesus asked Peter, *"Do you love me?"*
Each time Peter said, *"You know that I love you."*
What did Jesus say to Peter and what does He say to you and me? Jesus commissioned Peter to *"feed my lambs," "tend my sheep,"* and *"feed my sheep."* Jesus Christ commissioned Peter, and He commissions you and me to serve Him by serving His flock. Our risen Lord loves and cares for His people today through us as we serve them in His love.

For Prayerful Reflection: How has your belief in Jesus' resurrection affected your desire to serve Him? What might it mean for you today to obey the Lord by feeding one or more of His lambs?

Bible in a Year: *Isaiah 59-61; 2 Thessalonians 3*

October 21

I CAN Serve TODAY...
BECAUSE GOD NOTICES PEOPLE

[Jesus] entered Jericho and was passing through. And behold, there was a man named Zacchaeus. He was a chief tax collector and was rich. And he was seeking to see who Jesus was, but on account of the crowd he could not, for he was small in stature. So he ran on ahead and climbed up into a sycamore tree to see him, for he was about to pass that way. And when Jesus came to the place, he looked up and said to him, "Zacchaeus, hurry and come down, for I must stay at your house today." (Luke 19:1-5)

The local church that Helen and I attend honored and blessed the high school graduates. The youth pastor shared praises to God for many ways that God had blessed him and the church through these graduates. In this context he quoted one teen who had said with gratitude, "Thanks for noticing me." Though that might seem a small thing, it is not. To lovingly care for those whom God loves, we must first notice them and then care enough to serve them.

Throughout the Gospels we see Jesus doing this. For example, while passing through Jericho on His way to Jerusalem, where He would die for our sins, Jesus noticed and served Bartimaeus, a man who had been blind from birth; Jesus restored his sight. Jesus also noticed and served Zacchaeus, a sinful but spiritually hungry man who came to repentance that day, and his life was changed forever by Jesus. Jesus notices and serves hurting people. In His name, this is our call and privilege, so that people might be changed and say to Him and perhaps to us, "Thanks for noticing me."

For Prayerful Reflection: How have you experienced being noticed by Jesus? Will you ask the Lord to help you notice people today that He sees and that you can serve in His name?

Bible in a Year: *Isaiah 62-64; 1 Timothy 1*

October 22

I CAN Serve TODAY...
BECAUSE GOD HELPS ME SERVE ONLY HIM

It is the Lord your God you shall fear. Him you shall serve and by his name you shall swear. (Deuteronomy 6:13)

Jesus answered him [the devil], "It is written, 'You shall worship the Lord your God, and him only shall you serve.'" (Luke 4:8)

God designed us to serve Him by serving others, even when it is hard. Because this is God's purpose for us, He helps us do it. Jesus affirmed this intention when in the face of the devil's temptation, He quoted this Scripture: *"It is written, 'You shall worship the Lord your God, and him only shall you serve.'"* As our Lord conquered that temptation, today He helps us do what we otherwise could not do – serve only God. We serve God when in His name we care for those He gives us to serve.

How wonderful that God helps us do what we could not do on our own. At various times in life there are things that we should do and that we want to do, but we cannot do them because our strength is insufficient. But God gives us what we need. I was reminded of this recently when riding my new e-bike. I have been riding bicycles since I was a boy, but advancing age, reduced stamina, and decreased mobility have kept me from riding. My e-bike fits me well, and it provides the assistance I need when climbing hills or pedaling long stretches. I can do it now, because I have the help I need.

We know that God gives us what we need today to serve only Him, even while climbing steep hills of serving by caring for people He loves.

For Prayerful Reflection: What does it mean to serve God only? What help do you need from God today to serve Him by serving people? How does He provide that help?

Bible in a Year: *Isaiah 65-66; 1 Timothy 2*

October 23

I CAN Serve TODAY . . .
BECAUSE GOD FLIPS MY DEFINITION OF *GREAT*

> *A dispute also arose among them, as to which of them was to be regarded as the greatest. And he said to them, "The kings of the Gentiles exercise lordship over them, and those in authority over them are called benefactors. But not so with you. Rather, let the greatest among you become as the youngest, and the leader as one who serves. For who is the greater, one who reclines at table or one who serves? Is it not the one who reclines at table? But I am among you as the one who serves."* (Luke 22:24-27)

The disciples argued over which of them was the greatest, presuming such designation would bring greater prestige and service from others. But Jesus flipped their definition of *greatness* upside down. He said greatness in God's eyes is seen in serving others. Following Jesus means being His arms to comfort, His eyes to see, and His ears to hear persons in need of help. It is being His feet on missions of mercy and His hands to demonstrate care.

Only two months before Martin Luther King Jr. died, he said in a sermon, "Every now and then I think about my own funeral. . . . If you get somebody to deliver the eulogy, tell him not to talk too long. . . . Tell him not to mention I have a Nobel Peace Prize; that isn't important. Tell him not to mention that I have . . . other awards; that's not important. . . . I'd like somebody to mention that day that Martin Luther King Jr. tried to give his life serving others. . . . I want you to say that I tried to love and serve humanity." Excerpts of this recorded sermon were played at King's funeral.[43] May all followers of Jesus be known by the greatness of their service.

For Prayerful Reflection: How has following Jesus affected your definition of true greatness? What are some ways you can humbly serve the Lord by serving someone today?

Bible in a Year: *Jeremiah 1-2; 1 Timothy 3*

---

43 Dagmawi Woubshet, "Revisiting One of King's Final and Most Haunting Sermons," *The Atlantic* (April 1, 2018), www.theatlantic.com/entertainment/archive/2018/04/revisiting-martin-luther-king-jrs-most-haunting-sermon/ 556277/ (July 7, 2021).

October 24

I CAN Serve TODAY...
BECAUSE GOD FILLS ME WITH HIMSELF

By the grace given to me I say to everyone among you not to think of himself more highly than he ought to think, but to think with sober judgment, each according to the measure of faith that God has assigned. Love one another with brotherly affection. Outdo one another in showing honor... serve the Lord. (Romans 12:3, 10-11)

[Jesus] emptied himself, by taking the form of a servant. (Philippians 2:7)

If we are full of ourselves, we can be disinclined to care for and serve others. But this changes when God enters our hearts and fills us with Himself. This is why Jesus modeled and taught a view of greatness in God's sight that is contrary to our natural perception. It's also why the apostle Paul urged Christians toward attitudes and behaviors that reflect God's heart of love and service. When Jesus Christ lives in us such that we are filled with His compassion and love, we can and will love and humbly serve.

President Ulysses S. Grant was once on the way to a reception in his honor when he was caught in a rain shower and ended up sharing his umbrella with a stranger who was also headed to the reception. The stranger, who did not recognize him, said to Grant, "I have never seen President Grant, and I'm merely going to satisfy a personal curiosity. Between you and me, I always thought that Grant was a much overrated man."

Grant replied, "That is my view also." Such humility in leaders is noteworthy.

Servant leaders are not conceited, but in humility they gladly serve. When Jesus Christ is living in us, we can comprehend and live in this humility, for He *emptied himself, by taking the form of a servant.* Having been filled by God, we can serve for Him today.

For Prayerful Reflection: What are some ways you have been emptied and then filled by Jesus Christ? How does being filled by Jesus Christ help you serve others?

Bible in a Year: *Jeremiah 3-5; 1 Timothy 4*

October 25

I CAN Serve TODAY . . .
BECAUSE GOD HELPS ME SAY NO, SO I CAN SAY YES

[Jesus] saw a man called Matthew sitting at the tax booth, and he said to him, "Follow me." And he rose and followed him. (Matthew 9:9)

Jesus said to him, "If you would be perfect, go, sell what you possess and give to the poor, and you will have treasure in heaven; and come, follow me." When the young man heard this he went away sorrowful, for he had great possessions. (Matthew 19:21-22)

A question we must often ask in life is, If I say yes to this, what will I be saying no to? We can learn the hard way the importance of this question, for if we say yes too often or to things that distract from what is best, we can become overworked and tired, and important things can be neglected. To say yes to things that matter most, we must learn when to say no. For every decision made regarding what we will do, there are consequences of what we now will not do.

Materially speaking, Matthew had it good. He was a tax collector, which brought financial rewards and other benefits. But one day Jesus came and said, *"Follow me."* Saying yes to this opportunity would mean saying no to what he had known. Matthew said yes to Jesus and thereafter served the Lord.

Another young man came to Jesus inquiring about eternal life. He too was offered a phenomenal opportunity, but he understood that saying yes meant saying no to some things he desired more. For both of these young men their choices brought consequences. This is true of us too. We cannot say yes to everything. But with God's help we can say no as needed, so we can say yes to His best.

For Prayerful Reflection: How have you learned the importance of saying no, so you can say yes? How does this apply in your current life of service?

Bible in a Year: *Jeremiah 6-8; 1 Timothy 5*

October 26

I CAN Serve TODAY...
BECAUSE GOD USES SERVANT LEADERS AS EXAMPLES

I exhort the elders among you, as a fellow elder and a witness of the sufferings of Christ, as well as a partaker in the glory that is to be revealed: shepherd the flock of God that is among you, exercising oversight, not under compulsion, but willingly, as God would have you; not for shameful gain, but eagerly; not domineering over those in your charge, but being examples to the flock. (1 Peter 5:1-3)

As a servant leader, the apostle Peter followed the example of Jesus and urged other Christian leaders to do the same. As he wrote this portion of his epistle, I wonder if Peter was not recalling the events described in John 13 when our Lord and Master knelt with basin and towel and washed his dirty feet. After doing this, Jesus told Peter and the other apostles – and through them He is telling us – *"I have given you an example, that you also should do just as I have done to you"* (John 13:15).

It was Jesus' example that powerfully demonstrated what servant leadership is. Then Peter showed what his Lord taught him about service; he urged all Christian leaders to do the same.

Having served over forty years as a shepherd of the church, I have learned much about following and demonstrating Jesus' example of serving. On several opportunities to speak at services for ordination or installation of a local church pastor, and with the picture in mind of Jesus humbly washing dirty feet, I have given a towel to the pastor as a reminder and symbol of his call to lead by humbly serving.

Thanks be to God for leaders who serve. Like Peter, let us prayerfully determine to follow Jesus today in servant leadership.

For Prayerful Reflection: What are some good examples you have seen of servant leadership? What will it look like for you to take up the towel of servant leadership?

Bible in a Year: *Jeremiah 9-11; 1 Timothy 6*

October 27

I CAN Serve TODAY . . .
BECAUSE GOD HEALS TO SERVE

When Jesus entered Peter's house, he saw his mother-in-law lying sick with a fever. He touched her hand, and the fever left her, and she rose and began to serve him. (Matthew 8:14-15)

There was in Joppa a disciple named Tabitha, which, translated, means Dorcas. She was full of good works and acts of charity. In those days she became ill and died. . . . Peter put them all [the widows] outside, and knelt down and prayed; and turning to the body he said, "Tabitha, arise." And she opened her eyes, and when she saw Peter she sat up. (Acts 9:36-37, 40)

These women had two things in common. They both had servant hearts, and they both were raised up, ultimately, by Jesus. The Gospels don't reveal much about Peter's mother-in-law, but it appears she lived in Capernaum, for on the day Jesus came to Peter's house, she was there, *lying sick with a fever.* Jesus went to her; then *He touched her hand, and the fever left her.* After Jesus healed her, what did she do? Immediately *she rose and began to serve him.* When Jesus healed her, it was her joy to serve Him.

Some years later Peter was traveling from town to town ministering in Jesus' name. In the town of Joppa, a dear woman named Tabitha became ill and died. The Christians there heard that Peter was in nearby Lydda, so they sent messengers to fetch him. When he arrived in Joppa, through their tears, the believers described to him the servant heart of Tabitha and showed him garments she had made. After praying in Jesus' name, Peter said, *"Tabitha, arise."* And Tabitha came back to life. We know what she then did: she served. I personally attest that when God heals you, you want to serve Him!

For Prayerful Reflection: From what has God healed you? How has it affected your devotion to Him? How is His touch in times past influencing your desire to serve today?

Bible in a Year: *Jeremiah 12-14; 2 Timothy 1*

October 28

I CAN Serve TODAY . . .
BECAUSE GOD REWARDS FAITHFUL SERVICE

> *"He who had received the five talents came forward, bringing five talents more, saying, 'Master, you delivered to me five talents; here, I have made five talents more.' His master said to him, 'Well done, good and faithful servant. You have been faithful over a little; I will set you over much. Enter into the joy of your master.'"* (Matthew 25:20-21)

There is an apocryphal allegory of heaven and hell attributed to various sources, including C. S. Lewis, which portrays heaven and hell as having identical banquet rooms with nice chairs, a huge table, plenty of guests, and a limitless supply of sumptuous food. But the food can only be eaten with forks that are over three feet long. The scene in hell is anger, frustration, and fighting as people scramble to feed themselves, but they cannot. But in heaven, instead of chaos or conflict, there is great joy and laughter, because the diners are not focused on feeding themselves; they are patiently feeding each other.

The lesson of this allegory speaks of today, for God designed us to serve Him by serving one another; when we do, there is much blessing and reward. But when we do not serve, there is judgment and loss. In this parable of Jesus as recorded in Matthew's Gospel, He says God always rewards faithful service. He blesses those who go beyond self-focus and aim to serve God by serving others. By His grace, those who do so are assured of being wonderfully at home in heaven.

If you have known the great joy of serving God and others while on your earthly journey, you have already received rich blessings, and you are assured of a great reward when you reach heaven's glory, for God has promised this to you.

For Prayerful Reflection: What rewards are you receiving now from serving God and others? How deep is your longing to hear the Lord say to you, *"Well done, good and faithful servant"*?

Bible in a Year: *Jeremiah 15-17; 2 Timothy 2*

October 29

I CAN Serve TODAY . . .
BECAUSE GOD JUDGES UNFAITHFUL SERVICE

> *"Master, I knew you to be a hard man, reaping where you did not sow, and gathering where you scattered no seed, so I was afraid, and I went and hid your talent in the ground. Here, you have what is yours.' But his master answered him, 'You wicked and slothful servant! . . . cast the worthless servant into the outer darkness. In that place there will be weeping and gnashing of teeth.'"* (Matthew 25:24-26, 30)

In this parable Jesus affirms that God blesses and rewards His faithful servants. He also teaches that God judges those who fail to live as servants of God. The man in Jesus' parable had lived his life without regard to God, pretending that his life was his alone and that he had no responsibility to God. But imagining something does not make it so. Because God is God, and because God holds everyone accountable to Him, the day is coming when we will all give account.

Though we might wish it was not so and therefore ignore this truth, doing so is foolishness, akin to burying our heads in the sand like an ostrich. So what is our Lord's message in this portion of His Word? Isn't it that we would understand that He is God, and we are not? Isn't it that we would all gratefully see ourselves as His servants, living daily to honor Him? Isn't it that we would aim to please Him, expressing His truth and reflecting His love in how we serve Him and those He calls us to serve?

Because of God's grace, trusting in Jesus means we do not need to be afraid. But in love He warns all who are denying His truth and failing to live in faithful service to Him.

For Prayerful Reflection: What are some implications of knowing that He is God and you are not? What might it look like for you to live today as God's faithful servant?

Bible in a Year: *Jeremiah 18-19; 2 Timothy 3*

October 30

I CAN Serve TODAY...
BECAUSE GOD HAS DONE GREAT THINGS

And Samuel said to the people, "Do not be afraid; you have done all this evil. Yet do not turn aside from following the Lord, but serve the Lord with all your heart. And do not turn aside after empty things that cannot profit or deliver, for they are empty. Only fear the Lord and serve him faithfully with all your heart. For consider what great things he has done for you." (1 Samuel 12:20-21, 24)

In Samuel's last formal address to Israel, the prophet reviews and reminds the people of the great things God has done and of the implications of His greatness. He reviews some history of God's amazing works on behalf of His people, including the miraculous exodus from bondage in Egypt and His leading them into this promised land. Then Samuel reminded them and warned them that *they forgot the Lord their God* (1 Samuel 12:9).

It is very sad that this happens, but it does. Samuel wanted the people of God to remember the great things God had done and for this to move all of them to *serve the Lord with all [their] heart*. Looking back and ahead, Samuel declared that trouble comes whenever we forget God. Rather than consciously rebelling against God like Israel, we might simply forget about Him; we might live day after day with little remembrance of who God is or what He has done. When that happens, we inevitably fail to serve Him faithfully.

So today, let us remember God. Let us remember the salvation He has wrought for us; let us remember the many great things He has done for us. And in remembering, let us heed Samuel's good exhortation to *only fear the Lord and serve him faithfully with all your heart.*

For Prayerful Reflection: What great things has God done that you have not remembered lately? How does remembering what God has done affect your desire to faithfully serve Him today?

Bible in a Year: *Jeremiah 20-21; 2 Timothy 4*

October 31

I CAN Serve TODAY...
BECAUSE GOD INVITES ME TO CHOOSE

"Now therefore fear the Lord and serve him in sincerity and in faithfulness. Put away the gods that your fathers served beyond the River and in Egypt, and serve the Lord. And if it is evil in your eyes to serve the Lord, choose this day whom you will serve. . . . But as for me and my house, we will serve the Lord." (Joshua 24:14-15)

When approaching the end of life, it is natural to look back in review of what we have seen and experienced, and for people of faith to remember what God has done and the blessings we have known. I did this when facing my own mortality while battling cancer. This is what Joshua did near the end of his life. Israel was settling in the land of promise, and Joshua knew he would soon breathe his last. His prayerful reflections were not only for himself; they were also for Israel and for us, so that they and we might choose to follow and serve the Lord.

Being aware of our own sinful nature and proclivity to serve ourselves and our various idols rather than the God who made us, Joshua laid the choice before us, for we all personally choose whom we will serve. Neither our parents nor our leaders can choose for us. God invites us to choose well, as Joshua said, *"Choose this day whom you will serve."* Then he announced again the decision he had made long ago and reaffirmed on that day: *"But as for me and my house, we will serve the Lord."*

God invites and enables us to choose well today. Choosing to obey Him involves serving Him in any way He chooses for us. It includes loving Him and doing all that we do for Him as we serve people in His name.

For Prayerful Reflection: What does it mean to choose to serve the Lord? What will making this choice look like for you today?

Bible in a Year: *Jeremiah 22-23; Titus 1*

12 Themes on Following Jesus

NOVEMBER

Because God . . .
I Can *Give* Today

November 1

I CAN Give TODAY . . .
BECAUSE GOD GIVES GOOD GIFTS

"If you then, who are evil, know how to give good gifts to your children, how much more will your Father who is in heaven give good things to those who ask him!" (Matthew 7:11)

If any of you lacks wisdom, let him ask God, who gives generously to all without reproach, and it will be given him. (James 1:5)

God loves giving good things to His children. As a dad and as a grandpa, I can relate to this, for I too love giving good gifts to my children and grandchildren. But God's gifts to us are far more priceless than we can grasp, for they are heavenly and eternal and of far greater worth than gold, diamonds, or any other earthly treasure. Jesus taught that God wants us to come to Him daily and in faith, asking and believing for His good gifts.

An old story tells about how the University of Chicago once received a huge grant from the heiress of a major department store. Because she had been a student at Northwestern, administrators of that school went to visit her and asked why she had not made such a gift to her alma mater. Her answer was simple: "The people at the University of Chicago asked. You did not." God blesses with us with good gifts when we come to Him in faith, asking and believing for His blessings.

Because God blesses us with good gifts, we are blessed to bring His offer of grace to others and to give good gifts in His name. For God's sake, for our sake, and for the sake of many whom God loves, let us come to our heavenly Father, asking and believing. And wherever He sends us in His name, let us give to others in faith from what we have wonderfully received.

For Prayerful Reflection: What good gifts has your heavenly Father given you? What might it mean for you to pass along God's good gifts to someone today?

Bible in a Year: *Jeremiah 24-26; Titus 2*

November 2

I CAN Give TODAY...
BECAUSE GOD GIVES OUT OF LOVE

"For God so loved the world, that he gave his only Son, that whoever believes in him should not perish but have eternal life." (John 3:16)

"Greater love has no one than this, that someone lay down his life for his friends." (John 15:13)

We love because he first loved us. (1 John 4:19)

Love is the ultimate motivator for giving and for all of life. Love desires only the best for another. Love cares more for another's well-being than our own pleasure or comfort. Love focuses on another's good. We know about love, and we can receive it because God, our Creator, has first loved us. And from His love, God has given so much. Because *God so loved the world, ... he gave his only Son.* Jesus loved us so much that He *[laid] down his life for his friends.* Having received such love from our God, we can love others in the same way He has loved us.

Mother Teresa of Calcutta powerfully lived such a life of love. She taught that "love is a one-way street. It always moves away from self in the direction of the other. Love is the ultimate gift of ourselves to others. When we stop giving, we stop loving; when we stop loving, we stop growing. Unless we grow, we will never attain personal fulfillment; we will never open out to receive the life of God. It is through love we encounter God."[44]

Amy Carmichael, another missionary in India who also powerfully loved in the name of our Lord, rightly observed that "one can give without loving, but one cannot love without giving." Yes, God enables us today to give out of love – His love and ours.

For Prayerful Reflection: How has God's giving affected your motivation to be giving to others? What are some ways you could express God's love and your love through giving today?

Bible in a Year: *Jeremiah 27-29; Titus 3*

---

[44] Mother Teresa, *Where There Is Love, There Is God: A Path to Closer Union with God and Greater Love for Others,* editor Brian Kolodiejchuk (New York: Doubleday, 2012), 26.

November 3

I CAN Give TODAY . . .
BECAUSE GOD LOVES AND GIVES TO THE UNLOVELY

While we were still weak, at the right time Christ died for the ungodly. For one will scarcely die for a righteous person—though perhaps for a good person one would dare even to die—but God shows his love for us in that while we were still sinners, Christ died for us. (Romans 5:6-8)

We find it easier to love and give to adorable people, those we like or who impress us and with whom we feel some affinity. But God lifts us to a higher and broader standard of love and of giving. As the apostle Paul reminded us concerning our Lord: *God shows his love for us in that while we were still sinners, Christ died for us.* His love extends to the unlovely, even to you and me today. Because this is so, we too can love and give to the unlovely.

Mother Teresa of Calcutta, who was prolifically quoted, often said things beyond people's expectations that reflected God's wisdom. Once when visiting Phoenix, Arizona, to speak at the opening of a home for the destitute, she was interviewed by the largest radio station in town. During a commercial break, the announcer asked Mother Teresa if there was anything he could do for her. He expected her to request a donation or media help to raise money for the new facility. Instead, she looked him in the eye and said, "Yes, there is. Find someone nobody else loves and love them." This challenge is ours today.

Because God loves and gives to the unlovely, I can too. And so can you. May God help us today in His name and on His behalf to love and give to the unlovely, even to someone nobody else seems to love.

For Prayerful Reflection: When did you hear God calling you to notice, love, and give to someone who was unlovely? How might you do this today in the name of Jesus?

Bible in a Year: *Jeremiah 30-31; Philemon*

November 4

I CAN Give TODAY...
BECAUSE GOD GIVES PRICELESS TREASURES

"The kingdom of heaven is like treasure hidden in a field, which a man found and covered up. Then in his joy he goes and sells all that he has and buys that field." (Matthew 13:44)

"We cannot but speak of what we have seen and heard." (Acts 4:20)

God wants all of us to discover the great treasure of knowing and loving Him and to know great joy when we do. After we have found this treasure and know this joy, what then? As Peter and John were threatened to remain quiet about Jesus, their reply reflects all who know the Lord: *"We cannot but speak of what we have seen and heard."* We simply cannot keep to ourselves what God has given us.

I heard of a man who had stolen an enormous amount of money, but then he was captured. The money wasn't with him, so they asked where he hid it. Because the man spoke another language, they sent for an interpreter. When the interpreter came, the authorities said, "Ask him where he hid the money." The interpreter asked the thief this question in his own language, and the thief replied. The authorities asked the interpreter, "What did he say?"

The interpreter said, "He's not telling!"

The authorities shouted, "Tell him we want to know where the money is, and we want to know now!"

The interpreter kept asking the question to the thief and then said, "He said he's not telling!" In time the thief was convicted. The interpreter found and kept the money for himself. Though we would look upon that interpreter with disgust, have we ever done the same with God's great treasure?

God has blessed us. And today He calls and enables us to freely give what He has given us.

For Prayerful Reflection: What was it like for you to discover the treasure of knowing and loving God? How might you freely give today from what God has given you?

Bible in a Year: *Jeremiah 32-33; Hebrews 1*

November 5

I CAN Give TODAY ...
BECAUSE GOD BLESSES IN PROPORTION TO WHAT WE SOW

"Give, and it will be given to you. Good measure, pressed down, shaken together, running over, will be put into your lap. For with the measure you use it will be measured back to you." (Luke 6:38)

Whoever sows sparingly will also reap sparingly, and whoever sows bountifully will also reap bountifully. (2 Corinthians 9:6)

Have you noticed that when you buy a box of cereal it says something like this: "Contents packed by weight, not by volume"? Because the contents can settle a lot, when you open the box, it doesn't look full. Jesus promises that when we give, we receive blessings back, and there is no worry about settling.

If you have ever planted a vegetable garden, you know the larger the garden and the more you plant, the greater the harvest will be. The apostle Paul says this is so regarding planting seeds of faith in the kingdom of God. Jesus and Paul were not primarily focusing on financial blessings, though we do sometimes receive them. The most important blessings we can gain are knowing and pleasing God now. The future abundance is in store for us in His eternal kingdom, because this world is only our temporary home.

A biblical principle teaches that whoever gives is going to receive more in return. So whoever sows sparingly is going to reap sparingly, but whoever sows bountifully will reap bountifully. These principles are timeless and true, for God blesses in proportion to our giving. He leads us and blesses us today with the great privilege of giving and sowing for Him. May God lead and help us give for His glory and our good and for the good of those He will bless.

For Prayerful Reflection: When have you experienced God's blessing in proportion to what you sowed? How might God lead you to give or sow today for His glory and to bless someone?

Bible in a Year: *Jeremiah 34-36; Hebrews 2*

November 6

I CAN Give TODAY...
BECAUSE GOD GIVES ME WHAT I NEED

God said, "Behold, I have given you every plant yielding seed that is on the face of all the earth, and every tree with seed in its fruit. You shall have them for food. And to every beast of the earth and to . . . everything that has the breath of life, I have given every green plant for food." And it was so. (Genesis 1:29-30)

If a brother or sister is poorly clothed and lacking in daily food, and one of you says to them, "Go in peace, be warmed and filled," without giving them the things needed for the body, what good is that? (James 2:15-16)

Hasn't God given what we have needed? Don't we know that our strength, health, provision, fellowship, peace, purpose, hope, and even our life all come from God who gives what we need? And we who are recipients of these gifts are now blessed to be God's instruments of giving to others. The grace of giving what we have received brings honor to God and meets the needs of people He loves. But like God, we must actually give.

Some years ago, one of the Ad Council's effective public service campaigns was called "Don't Almost Give." One ad showed a homeless man curled up in a ball, lying on top of a pile of rags, and covered with a ratty sheet. The narrator says, "This is Jack Thomas. Today someone almost bought Jack something to eat. Someone almost brought him to a shelter. Someone almost gave him a warm blanket." Then, after a pause, the narrator says, "And Jack Thomas? Well, he almost made it through the night."

Almost giving doesn't cut it. Because God actually gives me what I need, I am blessed to actually give.

For Prayerful Reflection: What is on your list of gifts that God has given to you? How could you imitate God by actually giving to meet somebody's need?

Bible in a Year: *Jeremiah 37-39; Hebrews 3*

November 7

I CAN Give TODAY . . .
BECAUSE GOD EXPECTS ME TO GIVE

> "When you give to the needy, sound no trumpet before you, as the hypocrites do . . . that they may be praised by others. Truly, I say to you, they have received their reward. But when you give to the needy, do not let your left hand know what your right hand is doing, so that your giving may be in secret. And your Father who sees in secret will reward you." (Matthew 6:2-4)

Jesus' point here is that our giving should be done in secret, not to draw attention or praise to ourselves. This is why it is good to give anonymously when possible, so that praise can be directed toward God rather than toward us.

But did you notice that Jesus does not say here *if* you give? Twice He says, *"When you give."* This is His expectation of us. In the United States, we can appreciate living in a democracy in which, at least in theory, everyone gets a say in what happens. But the Lord's church is not governed this way. As believers in Jesus Christ, we are part of God's kingdom, which is not a democracy. A divine and loving King makes the rules and has power to enforce them. One of His rules addresses giving: *when you give.*

This concerns the lordship of Jesus. Some are running toward His lordship, and others are running away from it. One who rightly heard that being a Christian means following Jesus' rules now said to a preacher, "I can't stand your message. All I ever hear from you Christians is give, give, give."

The preacher thought a minute and said, "That's about the best description of Christianity I have ever heard!" God, who gives us everything through Jesus Christ, blesses us and expects us to give as we have received.

For Prayerful Reflection: Why did Jesus say, "When you give . . ."? How does this reflect His lordship? In this regard, have you been running toward or away from His lordship?

Bible in a Year: *Jeremiah 40-42; Hebrews 4*

November 8

I CAN Give TODAY...
BECAUSE GOD FREELY GIVES HIS BEST

"You received without paying; give without pay." (Matthew 10:8)

He who did not spare his own Son but gave him up for us all, how will he not also with him graciously give us all things? (Romans 8:32)

When Jesus sent His disciples out in His name to preach His good news and minister His power and love, He reminded them that as they had freely received from Him, they were to freely give. In other words, as we have been recipients of His love and grace, we are to be generous distributors of it.

In Paul's joyful conclusion to his teaching on the real opposition of Satan and of unbelievers, he says in Romans 8 that because God is for us, which He demonstrated by not sparing His Son, we can know with certainty that we will overcome. We should have no doubt of this because God gave and will always give His best. As Jesus taught, being recipients of His gifts allows us to be generous givers.

I have often witnessed generous giving from grateful recipients of God's grace. When my teenage son had an opportunity and desire to serve on a summer mission trip and funds were immediately needed, a dear woman wrote a personal check for the full amount and gave it with much joy. When a Christian children's home needed funds for a permanent home, God stirred the children in the local church I was serving to wash cars and raise funds, and many people gave generously. I have seen and known the joy of generous giving by many recipients of God's generosity, and I have gladly joined in. We who have received God's best are blessed and glad to freely give from what we have received.

For Prayerful Reflection: How have you witnessed generous giving by grateful recipients of God's grace? What needs has God presented to you lately to which you could freely give as you have received?

Bible in a Year: *Jeremiah 43-45; Hebrews 5*

007# November 9

I CAN Give TODAY . . .
BECAUSE GOD HAS DELIVERED ME

For you have delivered my soul from death, my ears from tears, my feet from stumbling; I will walk before the Lord in the land of the living. What shall I render to the Lord for all his benefits to me? I will lift up the cup of salvation and call on the name of the Lord, I will pay my vows to the Lord in the presence of all his people. (Psalm 116:8-9, 12-14)

Psalm 116 is a hymn of personal thanksgiving for God's deliverance and care with a decision and reminder that declaring it outwardly and worshipping Him publicly is a fitting tribute, for thus is God glorified, and others can be blessed. We who have received God's touch and deliverance are able to give Him our praise and give others the good news of His grace.

In 2018 when I was in the Providence VA hospital and miserably sick, during a dark night, I called upon my Lord because I thought I was going to die. God sent an unlikely messenger named Joe. Joe was a veteran with severe dementia who had wandered from his room. He sat down at the foot of my bed and asked, "How are you today?" I told him that I was very sick. Joe then got up, leaned over the foot of my bed, and said, "Yes you are, but you are going to be just fine!" In that moment I knew that my God had sent him to me. Twice that day my Lord sent me a nurse; each one asked if they could pray over me. One even sang a song of worship to the Lord for me.

Because so many times God has delivered us as He did the psalmist, we can give Him our praise and worship, and we can gladly give others what we have received.

For Prayerful Reflection: When and how has God delivered you? What has God given you that you might pass along to others?
Bible in a Year: *Jeremiah 46-47; Hebrews 6*

November 10

I CAN Give TODAY...
BECAUSE GOD GAVE HIMSELF

Jesus looked up and saw the rich putting their gifts into the offering box, and he saw a poor widow put in two small copper coins. And he said, "Truly, I tell you, this poor widow has put in more than all of them. For they all contributed out of their abundance, but she out of her poverty put in all she had to live on." (Luke 21:1-4)

I appeal to you therefore, brothers, by the mercies of God, to present your bodies as a living sacrifice, holy and acceptable to God, which is your spiritual worship. (Romans 12:1)

Jesus teaches that God measures gifts not by their size but based on how great the sacrifice was and how sincere and selfless the heart of the giver was. Why does God measure gifts this way? Because though God needs nothing, He desires our sincere love and full devotion; He did not give to us merely a token of His love. As astounding as it may be, God gave Himself for us and to us.

So, how will grateful recipients of such extravagance respond? Worshipful giving is more than simply offering something to God. For those who have received the mercies of God, giving that pleases Him begins with offering ourselves to Him *as a living sacrifice, holy and acceptable.* This is pleasing to God, for it is our *spiritual worship.* We who love Jesus are recipients of God's mercies, so we are blessed to place ourselves on His altar in worship. We are not dead sacrifices, but living ones, giving ourselves to Him again and again every day.

By the mercies of God, who gave Himself for us, we can give ourselves to Him today and so give of ourselves to others in His great name.

For Prayerful Reflection: Why do you think God desires your full love and devotion? Will you give it to Him today? If so, what might it look like?

Bible in a Year: *Jeremiah 48-49; Hebrews 7*

November 11

I CAN Give TODAY...
BECAUSE GOD GIVES ME TIME

You know the time, that the hour has come for you to wake from sleep. For salvation is nearer to us now than when we first believed. The night is far gone; the day is at hand. So then let us cast off the works of darkness and put on the armor of light. Let us walk properly as in the daytime. . . . But put on the Lord Jesus Christ. (Romans 13:11-14)

As time is a gift entrusted to us by God, with an eye on the future we can give time to God and bless others. To remain focused primarily on the past is to miss out on the present and on the future that is coming. And to live only for the present is to be unconnected with what has happened and uninvested in what will come. But God, who created time, transcends it, for the past, the present, and the future are all His. The apostle therefore urged Christians to look beyond the present, and with an eye on the future that God intends, to live life today being wholly devoted to God. This allows us to gladly give of the time He has entrusted to us.

In his book *The Present Future*, Reggie McNeal says, "We think we are headed toward the future. The truth is the future is headed toward us. And it's in a hurry."[45] So when the apostle says that we *know the time*, he is saying that it is not enough for us as Christians to simply pass time while going through the motions of faith. God, who has gifted us with time, encourages us to invest and give it for God's glory, for the blessing of others, and for the sake of His preferred future.

For Prayerful Reflection: What does it mean to *know the time*? How does that affect the way Christians are to live? What will it mean for you today to give time for God's glory and to bless others?

Bible in a Year: *Jeremiah 50; Hebrews 8*

---

45 Reggie McNeal, *The Present Future: Six Tough Questions for the Church* (Hoboken, New Jersey: John Wiley & Sons, Inc., 2009), xiii.

November 12

I CAN Give TODAY...
BECAUSE GOD SHOWS THE BLESSEDNESS OF GIVING

"In all things I have shown you that by working hard in this way we must help the weak and remember the words of the Lord Jesus, how he himself said, 'It is more blessed to give than to receive.'" (Acts 20:35)

These are the last recorded words of Paul given in person to the elders at Ephesus. He had summoned them to Miletus for a final in-person meeting before he boarded the ship to complete his journey to Jerusalem, where he knew he would face arrest and hardship. His final message to these Christians whom he loved was to encourage them to follow the example he had set for them, which included working hard and giving of themselves in Jesus' name to help those who were weak. And he quoted Jesus, who said, *"It is more blessed to give than to receive."*

These words of Jesus quoted by Paul were not recorded in any of the four Gospels; this reminds us that Jesus said and did much more than was written down (see John 20:30-31). But this saying of Jesus was widely known, for He had taught and shown by His words and example the blessedness of giving.

Why is this true? When we give, we emulate God who has graciously given us all things. And when we give like God, we discover that we are keeping what is of greatest value. Take love, for example, for this is the greatest motivation for giving. Doesn't God show us that the love we give is the love we keep? The way to retain love and even grow love is to give it away. So God is showing and calling you and me to the blessedness of giving.

For Prayerful Reflection: How has God taught you that it is indeed more blessed to give than to receive? What have you ever given away that by God's grace you were thus blessed to keep?

Bible in a Year: *Jeremiah 51-52; Hebrews 9*

November 13

I CAN Give TODAY . . .
BECAUSE GOD GIVES PEACE

"Peace I leave with you; my peace I give to you. Not as the world gives do I give to you. Let not your hearts be troubled, neither let them be afraid." (John 14:27)

Because this world is so full of distress and anxiety, most people spend a considerable part of their lives searching for peace. We want to feel safe, accepted, and whole. Jesus knew this, and He knew that He would soon be crucified, then risen, and then ascended into heaven. And Jesus knew that His disciples at that time and His disciples today would long for and search for peace.

Some people hope that such peace can be found when comfortable conditions are achieved, shiny new things are acquired, or affirmation and acceptance are received from people that we long to please. But life teaches us that this sort of peace cannot possibly endure, because circumstances continually change, and troubles constantly come. But God, through Jesus Christ, gives true peace. He says, *"My peace I give to you."*

This is a different sort of peace, for it is God's peace. He freely gives it to us when we fully trust in Him. God gives to us this invaluable peace which He bought and paid for with the exorbitant price of Christ's perfect sacrifice on the cross. We who trust in His redeeming work are covered with His peace even today, for we know that nothing can ever separate us from His love. Therefore, our hearts are neither troubled nor afraid, and we encounter Christians who, though going through great trials, still have and demonstrate the peace of God. Because of this, we can have God's peace, carry it, and give it to troubled souls in this troubled world.

For Prayerful Reflection: How have you experienced God's peace in this troubled world? What are some ways you might bring and give God's peace to someone today?

Bible in a Year: *Lamentations 1-2; Hebrews 10:1-18*

November 14

I CAN Give TODAY...
BECAUSE GOD GIVES LIFE

Then Job arose and tore his robe and shaved his head and fell on the ground and worshiped. And he said, "Naked I came from my mother's womb, and naked shall I return. The Lord gave, and the Lord has taken away; blessed be the name of the Lord." (Job 1:20-21)

Have you ever known anyone who chose to be born, had personal input into their formation in their mother's womb, or decided where they would enter this world, into what family, or with what characteristics? Of course not, for God alone creates life. So on the day Job experienced great heartache and loss in the tragic death of his children, he testified as he worshipped God, saying, *"The Lord gave, and the Lord has taken away; blessed be the name of the Lord."*

I have known just a little of what Job knew, for in the early years of our marriage, Helen and I lost two children who were born prematurely but died. The first was a son born in 1979, and the second a daughter born in 1980. Our hearts were filled with deep sorrow, but like Job, we leaned on God. And as God later blessed Job with more children, in time He also blessed Helen and me with three precious children. I am especially grateful and mindful of God's gift of life today, for this is our daughter Amy's birthday. I vividly recall the deep gratitude and praise I gave to God that day when she was born, and which I have often given for her since then, and for our other children and grandchildren. I thank God who gave them life.

Because God gives us life, we are greatly blessed to give Him our praise today and offer His life to others through faith and relationship with the Lord Jesus.

For Prayerful Reflection: When have you been able to say, *"The Lord gave, and the Lord has taken away; blessed be the name of the Lord"*? How could you bring God's life to someone today?

Bible in a Year: *Lamentations 3-5; Hebrews 10:19-39*

November 15

I CAN Give TODAY . . .
BECAUSE GOD DESIGNED ME TO GIVE

> *As for the rich in this present age, charge them not to be haughty, nor to set their hopes on the uncertainty of riches, but on God, who richly provides us with everything to enjoy. They are to do good, to be rich in good works, to be generous and ready to share, thus storing up treasure for themselves as a good foundation for the future, so that they may take hold of that which is truly life.* (1 Timothy 6:17-19)

If we regard giving as a good-to-do but elective activity rather than a must-do and essential activity, then we are disregarding how God made us and we are living dangerously. To be spiritually healthy, we must give. For this reason, Paul urged Christians who have been blessed to *be generous and ready to share,* so that we *may take hold of that which is truly life.*

Charles Haddon Spurgeon illustrated this lesson when he compared giving to the function of our physical heart, which does not store up the blood it receives. While it pumps blood in, it also sends it out. The blood continually circulates and never becomes stagnant. Spurgeon said the whole human system lives by giving, and if its members ever refuse to give to the whole, the whole body becomes poverty-stricken and dies. So God has designed us to be giving: to accumulate, we must also scatter; to be happy, we must make others happy; and to receive good and become spiritually vigorous, we must do good and seek the spiritual welfare of others.[46]

As God has designed us to give even as He has given to us, may we do so today, honoring Him and blessing others.

For Prayerful Reflection: Have you tended to regard giving as good-to-do or as essential-to-do? Why? Why has God designed you to give? How could you do so today?

Bible in a Year: *Ezekiel 1-2; Hebrews 11:1-19*

---

[46] Charles Haddon Spurgeon, *The Quotable Spurgeon* (Wheaton, IL: Harold Shaw Publishers, Inc., 1990).

November 16

I CAN Give TODAY . . .
BECAUSE GOD GIVES JOYFULLY

Each one must give as he has decided in his heart, not reluctantly or under compulsion, for God loves a cheerful giver. (2 Corinthians 9:7)

Looking to Jesus, the founder and perfecter of our faith, who for the joy that was set before him endured the cross, despising the shame, and is seated at the right hand of the throne of God. (Hebrews 12:2)

I heard about a panhandler who asked a woman for money; she dug in her purse and handed him a dollar bill. She then admonished him, "I'll give you a dollar, not because you deserve it, but because it pleases me."

"Thank you, ma'am," he replied, "but while you're at it, why not make it a ten and thoroughly enjoy yourself!"

The truth is, joyful giving emanates from love. God, whose very essence is love, generously and joyfully gives. Jesus Christ, the incarnation of God, loved us so much that He gave more than our finite minds can completely fathom. Our Lord selflessly gave His own sinless and perfect life; He endured the cross and despised the shame of it. The Bible says He gave us this inestimably great gift *for the joy that was set before him.*

Because God has done this for us, giving sacrificially and with joy, He grants us to know some of His joy by giving sacrificially in His name. I have known this kind of joy, have you? I have known a measure of God's joy when giving to a person, a need, a ministry, or a cause that honors Him and that blesses somebody in His name. This gift is worth much more than what we have given. Because God gives to me joyfully, I can know the blessing of giving with His joy today.

For Prayerful Reflection: What joy has the Lord received by enduring the cross for you? When have you known great joy from giving, and how might you know it again today?

Bible in a Year: *Ezekiel 3-4; Hebrews 11:20-40*

November 17

I CAN Give TODAY . . .
BECAUSE GOD BECAME POOR FOR ME

I say this not as a command, but to prove by the earnestness of others that your love also is genuine. For you know the grace of our Lord Jesus Christ, that though he was rich, yet for your sake he became poor, so that you by his poverty might become rich. (2 Corinthians 8:8-9)

Paul encouraged Christians to give lovingly in grateful remembrance of how God in Jesus Christ *became poor, so that you by his poverty might become rich.* Indeed, because God willingly became poor for me, I can now give of myself and of His grace to others.

One of the most impactful speakers I ever heard was Corrie Ten Boom; with her family she had hid Jews from the Nazis and was therefore sentenced to a concentration camp. She described one Christmas when she and other Christians had placed some meager handmade decorations on trees to celebrate Christ's birth. She said that under those same trees were thrown lifeless bodies of fellow prisoners who had died that day.

That Christmas Corrie heard a little child pleading for her mommy. Knowing one of the bodies beneath a tree was the child's mother, Corrie went to the child's bunk and softly told her that Mommy cannot come now. She asked the child if she could tell her about the One who came that first Christmas and would come to be with her now. Corrie told the child how God gave His Son in love and how Jesus suffered, then died for us, and rose again. She explained that now He is in heaven preparing a safe, beautiful home for her and everyone who loves Him. And in those holy moments, that little girl trusted in Jesus and soon thereafter, she was in His arms.

No matter what our circumstances are, we have much to give because God became poor for us.

For Prayerful Reflection: How am I blessed today by knowing that Jesus became poor for my sake? How does this affect my giving and sharing with others?

Bible in a Year: *Ezekiel 5-7; Hebrews 12*

November 18

I CAN Give TODAY . . .
BECAUSE GOD THROUGH CHRIST HAS SAVED ME

"Brothers, what shall we do?" And Peter said to them, "Repent and be baptized every one of you in the name of Jesus Christ for the forgiveness of your sins." . . . And they devoted themselves to the apostles' teaching and the fellowship, to the breaking of bread and the prayers And all who believed were together and had all things in common. And they were selling their possessions and belongings and distributing the proceeds to all, as any had need. (Acts 2:37-38, 42, 44-45)

On the day of Pentecost when the church was born, the good news was heard and believed; the Holy Spirit confirmed it, and people asked Peter, *"What shall we do?"*

Peter's first direction was, *"Repent and be baptized every one of you in the name of Jesus Christ for the forgiveness of your sins."* Because God through Jesus Christ has saved us, this is where we begin.

And then what? For those who by faith belong to God now, there are things we will naturally want to do because of our love for the One who saved us. This includes devoting ourselves *to the apostles' teaching* (God's Word), *and the fellowship* (Christian community), *to the breaking of bread* (hospitality and Holy Communion), *and the prayers* (a lifestyle of prayer in fellowship with God).

The early church was also known for their generosity with one another, even *selling their possessions and belongings and distributing the proceeds to all, as any had need.* The Bible says they were all doing this. Why? It was because Jesus was their first love. He had saved them from their sins, which meant more to them than all earthly possessions. Regarding themselves now as stewards of what belongs to God, they generously and gladly gave. Is this not our reasonable response too?

For Prayerful Reflection: What has been your response to being saved by God through Jesus Christ? How has receiving the gift of salvation affected your propensity and attitude toward giving?

Bible in a Year: *Ezekiel 8-10; Hebrews 13*

November 19

I CAN Give TODAY . . .
BECAUSE GOD GIVES GREAT GRACE THROUGH GIVING

Now the full number of those who believed were of one heart and soul, and no one said that any of the things that belonged to him was his own, but they had everything in common. And with great power the apostles were giving their testimony to the resurrection of the Lord Jesus, and great grace was upon them all. There was not a needy person among them, for as many as were owners of lands or houses sold them and brought the proceeds of what was sold and laid it at the apostles' feet, and it was distributed to each as any had need. (Acts 4:32-35)

When the church gives and loves like this, people are drawn to God, for they are seeing in living color the love and grace of God. No wonder the Bible says of the early church, *And the Lord added to their number day by day those who were being saved* (Acts 2:47). Luke records that *great grace was upon them all.* A primary evidence of His grace among them was that the church demonstrably showed God's concern for the poor; it gave, so no one had any need.

Through Moses God revealed His gracious intent to provide for the poor, for He said, *"'You shall open wide your hand to your brother, to the needy and to the poor, in your land'"* (Deuteronomy 15:11). God cares for all who are poor, needy, weak, infirmed, or burdened in any way, so He gives to all who call upon Him in faith. And whenever we generously give to express God's loving concern, His grace falls upon us, for we have become His instruments of grace to others.

For Prayerful Reflection: How have you experienced or seen God's grace to care for those in need? When have you received great grace through giving and being His instrument of grace to others?

Bible in a Year: *Ezekiel 11-13; James 1*

November 20

I CAN Give TODAY...
BECAUSE GOD ENCOURAGES THROUGH GIVING

Thus Joseph, who was also called by the apostles Barnabas (which means son of encouragement), a Levite, a native of Cyprus, sold a field that belonged to him and brought the money and laid it at the apostles' feet. (Acts 4:36-37)

God knows we all need encouragement. We all need to be reminded that we are loved and cared for. We need to know that with God's presence and with the support He provides us through others, we can do whatever we are called to do. God our Father encourages His dear children, so that we do not become or remain despondent, disillusioned, or discouraged. God encourages us by speaking to our hearts through His Word, by hearing us as we pray, and by showing His love for us in many ways, such as sending people to us who care, and giving us precisely what we need when we need it.

One person in the early church who embodied God's gift of encouragement was Joseph. So great was this gift in him that the apostles renamed him Barnabas, *which means son of encouragement.* His character of encouragement shows up several times in Acts, as he introduced Paul, the former persecutor and newly converted follower of Jesus, to the circle of apostles. He accompanied Paul as his first missionary companion and later stood up for John Mark who had lost Paul's trust. Barnabas's gift of encouragement was also seen when he *sold a field that belonged to him and brought the money and laid it at the apostles' feet.*

Have you ever been personally encouraged by receiving a gift of God through someone who, like Barnabas, generously gave? Have you also considered that God may desire to encourage somebody today through your generous giving?

For Prayerful Reflection: How have you experienced or witnessed God's encouragement through generous giving? How might God encourage someone today through your giving?

Bible in a Year: *Ezekiel 14-15; James 2*

November 21

I CAN Give TODAY . . .
BECAUSE GOD SEES EVERY GIVER'S HEART

> *But a man named Ananias, with his wife Sapphira, sold a piece of property, and with his wife's knowledge he kept back for himself some of the proceeds and brought only a part of it and laid it at the apostles' feet. But Peter said, "Ananias, why has Satan filled your heart to lie to the Holy Spirit and to keep back for yourself part of the proceeds of the land?" When Ananias heard these words, he fell down and breathed his last. And great fear came upon all who heard of it.* (Acts 5:1-3, 5)

God sees the heart of every giver. In a church in which people were generously giving to glorify God and care for one another, Ananias and Sapphira's deceit and greed stood in sharp contrast. God commended Christians who were *of one heart and soul* (Acts 4:32) and who gave so *there was not a needy person among them* (Acts 4:34). Ananias and Sapphira likely wanted the sort of appreciation Barnabas received because of his generosity, so they too sold some property and brought a portion of the proceeds to the apostles; they pretended they were giving it all, but they were lying – lying to the Holy Spirit.

Giving to God and others in His name is our freewill choice. And when we give, it is to be an act of worship intended to honor God and bless others, not to gain praise for ourselves or to be patted on the back for what we did. Our relationship with and love for God is to be the foundation of our life: why we do what we do and why we give as we give. Because God always sees our heart, He requires honesty toward Him and integrity toward each other, so He can bless us as we give.

For Prayerful Reflection: Why does God care about where your heart is when you give? How could you ensure your heart is in the right place for generous giving?

Bible in a Year: *Ezekiel 16-17; James 3*

November 22

I CAN Give TODAY . . .
BECAUSE GOD GIVES WHAT HE HAS

> *A man lame from birth was being carried, whom they laid daily at the gate of the temple that is called the Beautiful Gate to ask alms of those entering the temple. Seeing Peter and John about to go into the temple, he asked to receive alms. But Peter said, "I have no silver and gold, but what I do have I give to you. In the name of Jesus Christ of Nazareth, rise up and walk!" And he took him by the right hand and raised him up, and immediately his feet and ankles were made strong. And leaping up, he stood and began to walk, and entered the temple with them, walking and leaping and praising God.* (Acts 3:2-3, 6-8)

Here John and Peter demonstrate that because God has given to us from what He has, we can give to others from what we have. God is the One who has given us everlasting life, strength, promise, peace, victory, hope, and much more. Indeed, God *graciously give[s] us all things* (Romans 8:32).

We are not called or expected to give of what we do not have. But we who have received much from God are called and blessed to give of what we have received. So that day, giving of what he had received, *Peter said, "I have no silver and gold, but what I do have I give to you. In the name of Jesus Christ of Nazareth rise up and walk!"* And that is precisely what was needed that day.

What has God given to you that you can give to others in His name? As we do so, God is greatly honored, we are very blessed, and lives are forever changed for their good and for His praise and glory.

For Prayerful Reflection: What great gifts has God given to you from what He has? What are some ways you could give to others today from what God has given to you?

Bible in a Year: *Ezekiel 18-19; James 4*

November 23

I CAN Give TODAY . . .
BECAUSE GOD USES WHAT WE CAN GIVE

One of his disciples, Andrew, Simon Peter's brother, said to [Jesus], "There is a boy here who has five barley loaves and two fish, but what are they for so many?" Jesus said, "Have the people sit down."
(John 6:8-10)

Though Jesus knew He was going to care for that hungry crowd, He tested Philip to see if he could envision in faith what God would do. But Philip focused on what they did not have. Andrew, however, demonstrated a mustard seed of faith and focused on what they did have. So he brought a boy to Jesus, who gladly gave his lunch. And oh, what our Lord did with it!

Can you imagine the laughter spilling across that meadow as Jesus turned that boy's gift into baskets and baskets and baskets of food? This is the thing about God: He can do far more than we imagine with whatever we can give Him. Our part is to give what we can and trust God for the outcome. We could give money, time, an ability, or a lunch. It might seem small to us, but watch what God can do.

I learned this lesson in the summer of 1975. I was painting homes with a friend in a small town in Pennsylvania and living in a downtown hotel room. Looking for Christian fellowship on our first Sunday there, I attended worship at a small church nearby where I immediately noticed a piano but no musician, so we sang without accompaniment. Though self-conscious about my piano playing, I heard God asking me throughout that service to offer Him what I had. So I did. For the rest of that summer, I played for worship, and I learned an important life lesson. When I give God whatever I can, He uses it for His glory.

For Prayerful Reflection: When have you seen God do something great with a gift that seemed so little? What "little boy's lunch" can you give to Jesus today?

Bible in a Year: *Ezekiel 20-21; James 5*

November 24

I CAN Give TODAY...
BECAUSE GOD LOVES JOYFUL GIVING

The point is this: whoever sows sparingly will also reap sparingly, and whoever sows bountifully will also reap bountifully. Each one must give as he has decided in his heart, not reluctantly or under compulsion, for God loves a cheerful giver. (2 Corinthians 9:6-7)

Do we think God gives to us grudgingly, not wanting to but doing it anyway? If we think that, we do not yet grasp God's heart of love. Love cannot be given grudgingly, but only willingly and gladly. And as giving reflects and expresses love, it too must be given voluntarily; it must spring from an attitude of willingness and joy.

The main idea of these verses from Paul in 2 Corinthians 9 is that since giving comes from the heart, God looks not only at the gift but also at the heart of the giver. God loves joyful giving, because this reflects a heart of love, gratitude, and joy from His presence in our lives. Though Paul addresses financial giving here, voluntary, cheerful giving goes far beyond our financial giving. It also applies to giving of our time and of ourselves in service to others.

Do you sometimes find yourself complaining about things you do for other people? You do it, but grudgingly. Do you sometimes give money or material things, or do you give of your time in service but inwardly resent it or complain about it? If so, it is time for a heart check. After all, don't we want our giving to please God? God's Word reveals that before Him gift-giving is a matter of the heart, and He especially loves gifts that are not given reluctantly or out of compulsion, but are given voluntarily and cheerfully, reflecting the heart of one who has been made glad by God.

For Prayerful Reflection: On a scale of reluctance to cheerfulness, where has your heart been in giving? What will it look like for you to joyfully give today?

Bible in a Year: *Ezekiel 22-23; 1 Peter 1*

November 25

I CAN Give TODAY...
BECAUSE GOD REWARDS THE
GIVING OF OUR BEST

"Give, and it will be given to you. Good measure, pressed down, shaken together, running over, will be put into your lap. For with the measure you use it will be measured back to you." (Luke 6:38)

How would you live today if you knew there would be a direct correlation between your generosity and the degree of blessing you will receive from God? Our Lord taught that there is such a connection, for He promises to bless those who give to Him their best, *for with the measure [we] use it will be measured back*. As this truth seeps in, are you like me, convicted of having sometimes given only meager leftovers? And are you motivated to give to God your absolute best today?

Paul Harvey told of a woman and her frozen Thanksgiving turkey. The Butterball turkey company set up a telephone hotline to answer consumer questions about preparing holiday turkeys. This woman called to ask about cooking a turkey that had been in the bottom of her freezer for twenty-three years. The Butterball representative told her the turkey would probably be safe to eat if the freezer had been kept below zero the entire twenty-three years. But the representative warned her that even if the turkey was safe to eat, the flavor would likely have deteriorated, so she would not recommend eating it. The caller replied, "That's what I thought. We will give the turkey to our church."[47]

Our Lord reminds us that He rewards those who give their best, not the leftovers. Being reminded of His many blessings, aren't we moved to give God our best?

For Prayerful Reflection: How have you experienced that *with the measure you use it will be measured back to you*? What might it look like for you to give your best today?

Bible in a Year: *Ezekiel 24-26; 1 Peter 2*

---
[47] Paul Harvey daily radio broadcast (11-22-95).

November 26

I CAN Give TODAY . . .
BECAUSE GOD HOLDS ME RESPONSIBLE

"Will man rob God? Yet you are robbing me. But you say, 'How have we robbed you?' In your tithes and contributions. Bring the full tithe into the storehouse, that there may be food in my house. And thereby put me to the test, says the Lord of hosts, if I will not open the windows of heaven for you and pour down for you a blessing until there is no more need." (Malachi 3:8, 10)

My parents taught me about biblical stewardship – that all l I have is God's, entrusted to me to use for Him. They also taught the principle of tithing – returning the first 10 percent as first fruits, which continually reminds me that I am His. I recall earning a dime as a child and then laying aside a penny as my tithe. This might seem easy to do when dealing with dimes and pennies.

But what about when amounts are much larger? Do we still sacrificially give, mindful that we are stewards entrusted with what is His? Through Malachi, God confronted His people with their failure to tithe, for by this neglect they were effectually robbing God.

Randy Alcorn imagined this scenario: If we had an important package to send to someone in need, we would take it to an overnight delivery service. He asked, "What would you think if, instead of delivering the package, the driver took it home? When confronted, he says, 'If you didn't want me to keep it, why'd you give it to me?' You would say, 'That package isn't yours. Your job is to deliver it to the one who needs it.' Because God puts money in our hands, it doesn't mean that He intends for us to keep it."[48] As God's stewards today, we are responsible to give what is His on His behalf.

For Prayerful Reflection: What does it mean to be a steward of what is God's? What could it look like for you to give on God's behalf today?

Bible in a Year: *Ezekiel 27-29; 1 Peter 3*

---
48   Randy Alcorn, *Letting Go of What Isn't Mine* (Focus on the Family, December 2006), 13.

November 27

I CAN Give TODAY...
BECAUSE GOD HAS A GIVING NATURE

If God is for us, who can be against us? He who did not spare his own Son but gave him up for us all, how will he not also with him graciously give us all things? (Romans 8:31-32)

God's nature is to give. Scripture reminds us of this, as God gave daily manna, miraculous provision, and even His Son for us. In light of this, the apostle Paul asks, *How will he not also with him graciously give us all things?* Our God keeps on giving.

Annie Johnson Flint powerfully stated this in her hymn "He Giveth More Grace," with lyrics that are based on 2 Corinthians 12:9: *"My grace is sufficient for you, for my power is made perfect in weakness."* The song speaks of God's love having no limits and His grace having no measure, which causes Him to give over and over again.

Because God has such a giving nature and because He made us in His own image, we will increasingly develop His giving nature as we follow the Lord Jesus Christ. We will be giving not because of the attention we may gain, but because this is now our nature too.

Charles Spurgeon urged, "Give . . . as a matter of course, that you no more take note that you have helped the poor than that you have eaten your regular meals. Do your alms without whispering to yourself, 'How generous I am!' Do not thus attempt to reward yourself. Leave the matter with God, who never fails to see, to record, and to reward. . . . How can I indulge myself today with this delightful luxury?"[49]

For Prayerful Reflection: How have you experienced and been blessed by God's giving nature? How is God's giving nature evident in you?
Bible in a Year: *Ezekiel 30-32; 1 Peter 4*

---

[49] C. H. Spurgeon, "C. H. Spurgeon in Faith's Checkbook," *Christianity Today*, Vol. 32, No. 5.

November 28

I CAN Give TODAY . . .
BECAUSE GOD IS GLORIFIED IN GRATEFUL GIVING

It is all for your sake, so that as grace extends to more and more people it may increase thanksgiving, to the glory of God. (2 Corinthians 4:15)

[Titus] has been appointed by the churches to travel with us as we carry out this act of grace that is being ministered by us, for the glory of the Lord himself. (2 Corinthians 8:19)

I heard what seemed to be the voice of a great multitude, like the roar of many waters and like the sound of mighty peals of thunder, crying out, "Hallelujah! For the Lord our God the Almighty reigns. Let us rejoice and exult and give him the glory." (Revelation 19:6-7)

As Paul encouraged Christians in Corinth about offerings being collected among the churches for God's work in the church of Jerusalem, he said *it may increase thanksgiving, to the glory of God,* and this act of grace was being ministered *for the glory of the Lord himself.* Isn't it amazing to think that by our grateful giving we are glorifying God?

Glorifying God is our joyful purpose now, and it is excellent preparation for heaven when we will *rejoice and exult and give him the glory* with the saints of all the ages. What a day that will be. But until then, one way we are blessed to accomplish this purpose of glorifying God is through giving of our resources and ourselves for the work and glory of God.

I keep thinking of the dear children I saw fervently praying in Myanmar, asking God to provide a permanent home, so they would not continue to face repeated eviction. I also think of those who gave toward this need, thereby glorifying God, and of the children's joyful thanksgiving that was increased. Because God is glorified in grateful giving, we are blessed to give gratefully.

For Prayerful Reflection: When have you seen God glorified through grateful giving? How could you glorify Him through grateful giving today?

Bible in a Year: *Ezekiel 33-34; 1 Peter 5*

November 29

I CAN Give TODAY...
BECAUSE GOD IS SO GENEROUS TO ME

In him we have redemption through his blood, the forgiveness of our trespasses, according to the riches of his grace, which he lavished upon us, in all wisdom and insight making known to us the mystery of his will, according to his purpose, which he set forth in Christ as a plan for the fullness of time, to unite all things in him, things in heaven and things on earth. In him we have obtained an inheritance. (Ephesians 1:7-11)

If anyone has the world's goods and sees his brother in need, yet closes his heart against him, how does God's love abide in him? Little children, let us not love in word or talk but in deed and in truth. (1 John 3:17-18)

Consider how generous God has been to you. Hasn't He given you life? Hasn't He forgiven all of your sin through the supreme sacrifice of Jesus Christ? Hasn't He lavished grace on you so that you have grasped the wisdom of God and believed in the salvation of God? Hasn't He made you His own child and bestowed on you an eternal and glorious inheritance? Hasn't God blessed you in many ways in this life and given you glorious hope for the life to come? Hasn't God been exceedingly generous to you? If your answer is yes, then you will be drawn to excel in generosity.

In fact, if generosity is lacking in us, as John asked in his letter, *how does God's love abide in [us]?* John's point is that it is not possible to know Jesus and fully experience His amazing grace and generosity without becoming profoundly generous in response. So, to respond on this theme of giving, each of us should consider how generous God has been to us and to prayerfully respond in kind.

For Prayerful Reflection: How has God been generous to you? How is this realization evident in your generosity?

Bible in a Year: *Ezekiel 35-36; 2 Peter 1*

November 30

I CAN Give TODAY . . .
BECAUSE GOD GAVE HIMSELF FOR ME

We want you to know, brothers, about the grace of God that has been given among the churches of Macedonia, for in a severe test of affliction, their abundance of joy and their extreme poverty have overflowed in a wealth of generosity on their part. For they gave according to their means, as I can testify, and beyond their means, of their own accord, begging us earnestly for the favor of taking part in the relief of the saints—and this, not as we expected, but they gave themselves first to the Lord and then by the will of God to us. (2 Corinthians 8:1-5)

The churches of Macedonia were so impacted by the grace and love of Jesus Christ who gave of Himself for them, that even in the face of severe affliction because of their faith in the Lord, they *overflowed in a wealth of generosity on their part*. Being aware of their extreme poverty and the trials they endured, Paul was surprised when they came *begging earnestly for the favor of taking part in the relief of the saints*. Clearly their giving was not from obligation but was entirely from willingness and joy.

Paul explained how such giving was made possible for them and for us. It was because *they gave themselves first to the Lord and then by the will of God to us*. When we devote ourselves to the One who gave Himself for us, we will see no difficulty in generous giving, but we will seek such opportunities like the Macedonians, for we know that our Lord always takes care of us. Since the Macedonian Christians could respond despite their trials and poverty, we can too, if we have first devoted ourselves to the Lord.

For Prayerful Reflection: How has knowing that God gave Himself for you affected your giving? Why does exemplary giving to and for God necessitate first giving yourself to Him?

Bible in a Year: *Ezekiel 37-39; 2 Peter 2*

12 Themes on Following Jesus

DECEMBER

Because God . . .
I Can *Hope* Today

December 1

I CAN Hope TODAY...
BECAUSE GOD OFFERS HOPE IN HIM

"And now, O Lord, for what do I wait? My hope is in you." (Psalm 39:7)

Why are you cast down, O my soul, and why are you in turmoil within me? Hope in God; for I shall again praise him, my salvation. (Psalm 42:5)

For you, O Lord, are my hope, my trust, O Lord, from my youth. (Psalm 71:5)

O Israel, hope in the Lord from this time forth and forevermore. (Psalm 131:3)

In a world that is suffering from the curses of uncertainty, fear, and doubt, hope is desperately needed! But what is hope exactly, and where can it be found?

When you were young and desperately wanted something to happen, did you ever cross your fingers, throw a coin in a well, or pretend in another superstitious way that wishing hard enough might help make it happen? This sort of hope has no certainty in it, for it is merely a desire for a certain outcome.

But God offers hope in Himself. And when the Bible tells us to *hope in God*, it has nothing at all to do with wishful thinking. Biblical hope is about certainty because of God whom we trust. The Hebrew and Greek words that are translated into the English word *hope* express confident expectation. When we see the word *hope* in the Bible, we know it refers to something we greatly need and that God is freely offering to us. It refers to confident expectation. Would you like some of that as you live today and look toward the future?

Biblical hope is knowing we can let go of our uncertainties, fears, and doubts because God is faithful and His promises are true. And as the psalmists testified, in faith we can say to the Lord, *"My hope is in you."*

For Prayerful Reflection: In what areas of your life do you need and desire biblical hope today? What will it mean for you to look to the Lord and receive from Him confident expectation?

Bible in a Year: *Ezekiel 40-41; 2 Peter 3*

December 2

I CAN Hope TODAY...
BECAUSE GOD PROMISES HOPE

Rejoice greatly, O daughter of Zion! Shout aloud, O daughter of Jerusalem! Behold, your king is coming to you; righteous and having salvation is he, humble and mounted on a donkey, on a colt, the foal of a donkey. Return to your stronghold, O prisoners of hope; today I declare that I will restore to you double. On that day the Lord their God will save them, as the flock of his people; for like the jewels of a crown they shall shine on his land. For how great is his goodness, and how great his beauty! (Zechariah 9:9, 12, 16-17)

Have you ever been like the people whom Zechariah addressed? They were discouraged and felt hopeless about their circumstances. Twenty years earlier they had been hopeful when, by the proclamation of Cyrus, they returned from captivity to rebuild Jerusalem, which had been destroyed. But life for them was hard. Facing strong opposition, progress on rebuilding the temple had stalled. Their taxes were high, and their situation was dismal. They had lost hope. But God knew; He cared, and He spoke.

It has been said that humans can live forty days without food, four days without water, and four minutes without air – but we cannot live four seconds without hope. There is some truth to that. We need hope more than we know. And the only true source is God, for God is much greater than our circumstances; He promises hope to those who will trust Him.

To people lacking hope, Zechariah pointed toward a wonderful promise of God: the coming Messiah. Our hope or confident expectation in what God will do is also centered on the long-awaited Christ whose first advent we now celebrate and whose second advent we now anticipate. We can hope today because God has promised it, and Messiah Jesus has delivered it.

For Prayerful Reflection: When have you lacked hope until you heard and believed God's promise? How are you finding hope today in the good news of Christ's advent?

Bible in a Year: *Ezekiel 42-44; 1 John 1*

December 3

I CAN Hope TODAY...
BECAUSE GOD IS MY VERY PRESENT HELP

God is our refuge and strength, a very present help in trouble. Therefore we will not fear though the earth gives way, though the mountains be moved into the heart of the sea. The nations rage, the kingdoms totter; he utters his voice, the earth melts. The Lord of hosts is with us; the God of Jacob is our fortress. "Be still, and know that I am God. I will be exalted among the nations, I will be exalted in the earth!" The Lord of hosts is with us; the God of Jacob is our fortress. (Psalm 46:1-2, 6-7, 10-11)

This psalm has meant much to me through the years, especially in times of uproar and distress internationally, nationally, in political or cultural turmoil, in our Lord's church, and in my own life and circumstances. We have all known trials, because this world, just like the psalmist's world, always seems to be facing some level of chaos. We have lately faced a worldwide pandemic, financial uncertainties, racial injustice, political turmoil, wars, violence, horrific crimes, raging wildfires, earthquakes, hurricanes, and floods. And the list goes on.

Does it sometime seem, as it did to the psalmist, that this world is giving way and the mountains are falling into the sea? When it feels that way, and we are intentional enough to seek the Lord and listen, we can hear God calling to us: *"Be still, and know that I am God."*

When surrounded by an uproar, God calls us to stillness. How is this possible? How can I have hope, no matter what the turmoil is? Because I can know God is with me now. He is our *very present help in trouble.* God is *our fortress.* He is advent's hope and our hope today.

For Prayerful Reflection: When and how has God been *a very present help in trouble* for you? How can you fully live and demonstrate in this Advent season the hope of God, your very present help?

Bible in a Year: *Ezekiel 45-46; 1 John 2*

December 4

I CAN Hope TODAY . . .
BECAUSE GOD INVITES ME TO THE MOUNTAINTOP

It shall come to pass in the latter days that the mountain of the house of the Lord shall be established as the highest of the mountains, . . . and all the nations shall flow to it, and many peoples shall come, and say: "Come, let us go up to the mountain of the Lord, to the house of the God of Jacob, that he may teach us his ways and that we may walk in his paths." . . . He shall judge between the nations, and shall decide disputes for many peoples; and they shall beat their swords into plowshares, and their spears into pruning hooks; nation shall not lift up sword against nation, neither shall they learn war anymore. O house of Jacob, come, let us walk in the light of the Lord. (Isaiah 2:2-5)

The tallest mountain I ever climbed is Mount Fuji in Japan, measuring 12,388 feet. On that clear day, I could see far from the summit. It was beautiful. As I climbed, I passed many Shinto and Buddhist pilgrims who were also climbing the mountain, but they believed that doing so would cleanse them of their sins and impurities. Though they are mistaken in that notion, I was reminded that God is calling us to the mountaintop with Him, where there is real hope.

The vision given to Isaiah is of God's house on the highest mountain in the world that draws all nations to it. As rivers flow to the sea, nations flow to be with God and learn from Him. When we have heard God's invitation to us, we can respond with hope. Do you hear Him now? *"Come, let us go up to the mountain of the Lord."* How very blessed we are to be on this mountain today.

For Prayerful Reflection: How amazed are you that God beckons you to come up and be near Him? How determined have you been to say yes to His invitation each day? How does this affect your hope?

Bible in a Year: *Ezekiel 47-48; 1 John 3*

December 5

I CAN Hope TODAY...
BECAUSE GOD SEES AND ACTS

And he said, "I am the God of your father, the God of Abraham, the God of Isaac, and the God of Jacob." And Moses hid his face, for he was afraid to look at God. Then the Lord said, "I have surely seen the affliction of my people who are in Egypt and have heard their cry because of their taskmasters. I know their sufferings, and I have come down to deliver them out of the hand of the Egyptians and to bring them up out of that land to a good and broad land, a land flowing with milk and honey.... And now, behold, the cry of the people of Israel has come to me, and I have also seen the oppression with which the Egyptians oppress them. Come, I will send you to Pharaoh that you may bring my people, the children of Israel, out of Egypt." (Exodus 3:6-10)

Advent is about God seeing, hearing, and acting in mercy and power for the people He loves. What God did in the days of Moses, He did even more wonderfully in the days of Messiah Jesus' first advent, in His life, and in His triumphal victory for us over sin and death.

Some presumed that God neither saw nor cared about His suffering people. But God informed Moses that He did in fact see them. God had heard their cries and now acted for their deliverance. Biblical hope is rooted in believing that God sees, and that nothing escapes His notice. The heart of advent is knowing that God in fact sees where this world has gone wrong, and in grace He acts to make it right. Though in our suffering we might wrongly conclude that God is far off or unconcerned, in fact, God sees us, upholds His covenant, and lovingly acts. This is the message of advent and the reason for our hope.

For Prayerful Reflection: When and how have you become aware that God really sees, hears, and acts to aid you? How is this realization affecting your hope for today and for the future?

Bible in a Year: *Daniel 1-2; 1 John 4*

December 6

I CAN Hope TODAY . . .
BECAUSE GOD BRINGS HOPE TO HOPELESSNESS

Martha said to Jesus, "Lord, if you had been here, my brother would not have died. But even now I know that whatever you ask from God, God will give you." Jesus said to her, "Your brother will rise again." Martha said to him, "I know that he will rise again in the resurrection on the last day." Jesus said to her, "I am the resurrection and the life. Whoever believes in me, though he die, yet shall he live, and everyone who lives and believes in me shall never die." (John 11:21-26)

Three times I pleaded with the Lord about this. . . . But he said to me, "My grace is sufficient for you, for my power is made perfect in weakness." (2 Corinthians 12:8-9)

I heard again from my dear friend for whom I have been praying, who shepherds some of God's churches in Myanmar. He updated me on the hard struggles in that land with a third major wave of COVID-19 causing many deaths, including that of a number of pastors. There is much grief and suffering there with added uncertainties due to economic devastation, political oppression, and violence. In the face of so much hopelessness, those who know and trust in Christ are holding firmly to Him and are shining for God in the darkness.

Jesus Christ reminds us that He comes today bringing hope to hopelessness. He did this on that day when Mary and Martha were mourning the death of their brother Lazarus. When Paul faced a hard, personal trial which he called his *thorn in the flesh*, God brought grace and power to his weakness.

We can hope today, not because life is easy, but because God is here, bringing real hope to people and situations that would be hopeless without Him.

For Prayerful Reflection: What seemingly hopeless situations have you known where God brought hope? When facing trials, how is your faith affected by believing in His promises and His presence with you?

Bible in a Year: *Daniel 3-4; 1 John 5*

December 7

I CAN Hope TODAY . . .
BECAUSE GOD MAKES A
STRAIGHT PATH FOR ME

A voice cries: "In the wilderness prepare the way of the Lord; make straight in the desert a highway for our God. Every valley shall be lifted up, and every mountain and hill be made low; the uneven ground shall become level, and the rough places a plain. And the glory of the Lord shall be revealed, and all flesh shall see it together, for the mouth of the Lord has spoken." (Isaiah 40:3-5)

Perhaps you have traveled along circuitous roads, twisting and turning around mountains, rivers, valleys, and obstacles of many kinds. Sometimes such journeys seem thrilling, and at other times dangerous and scary. Life is like that. Spiritually we can seem to weave and wander, sometimes unsure of our destination or even if we are on the right road.

Knowing our dilemma, God makes a straight road to lead us to blessing, peace, and everlasting life. This was His promise through Isaiah, which was fulfilled when John the Baptist pointed to Jesus and essentially said, "Here is hope. Now you can walk on the straight path, for Jesus is coming, and here He is."

In an advent devotion titled "On Building a Highway," John Goldingay described how the Israeli National Roads Authority built a network of highways through the country, including an urban artery with tunnels and bridges, to take people straight into the center of Jerusalem.[50] The construction involved disturbing some ancient Roman graves, which sparked protests. But people wanted to get into Jerusalem fast on a highway that overcame all obstacles.

We also want a straight path in life, straight to the destination of God's glory and will for us. God comes today with hope, for He has made the way straight through faith in Jesus Christ.

For Prayerful Reflection: What are some ways your life has straightened out through faith in Jesus Christ? What hope have you gained for today and tomorrow by walking on the path of faith in Jesus?

Bible in a Year: *Daniel 5-7; 2 John*

---
[50] John Goldingay, "On Building a Highway," *ChristianityToday.com*, (November 2020).

December 8

I CAN Hope TODAY . . .
BECAUSE GOD SHINES A GREAT LIGHT

The people who walked in darkness have seen a great light; those who dwelt in a land of deep darkness, on them has light shone. (Isaiah 9:2)

In him was life, and the life was the light of men. The light shines in the darkness, and the darkness has not overcome it. The true light, which gives light to everyone, was coming into the world. (John 1:4-5, 9)

Haven't we all experienced darkness when we could not even see a hand in front of our eyes? I recall such a time when I was assigned with infantry marines, and we were doing night ops, stealthily finding our way in the darkness. Because there was no light from the moon or stars that night, the danger of falling was real, and in fact at one point I did fall. When we face darkness and are afraid, we long for and need hope that a light will shine. Spiritually speaking, we need the same light.

Notice that the Bible says those *who walked in darkness have seen a great light,* but not a light we can turn on of our own volition. Rather, God shines it upon us. In mercy God breaks into the darkness of sin with the Light of the World, who brings hope. The apostle John tells us that God did this in the incarnation of Jesus Christ, for *in him was life, and the life was the light of men.* The light of Christ is shining today into the darkness of this world.

In this season of Advent, God reminds us that He sent His Light into the darkness of the world to give salvation to all who will believe in Him. He is our source of hope today.

For Prayerful Reflection: When have you felt lost in the dark but called on the Lord who turned on the light for you? What areas of darkness in the world or in your own life do you need Christ's light and hope?

Bible in a Year: *Daniel 8-10; 3 John*

December 9

I CAN Hope TODAY . . .
BECAUSE GOD CHANGES *SHALL* TO *IS*

"Therefore the Lord himself will give you a sign. Behold, the virgin shall conceive and bear a son, and shall call his name Immanuel." (Isaiah 7:14)

"For unto you is born this day in the city of David a Savior, who is Christ the Lord." (Luke 2:11)

A message of advent and Christmas is that God keeps all of His promises, including His most remarkable promise that His own Son would come to be our Savior, *Immanuel* – "God with us." This promise of His first advent was repeatedly expressed in Old Testament Scriptures, including the verse quoted above. About seven centuries before Messiah's birth, God promised through Isaiah that the Lord *will* and *shall* do this. Isaiah declared, *"The Lord himself will give you a sign. Behold, the virgin shall conceive and bear a son, and shall call his name Immanuel"* (emphasis added).

Like every promise, this promise of God was at first future-focused, for this was something God's people could hope for and believe with confident expectation that because God promised this, it would surely come to be. Then, in the fullness of time, it did come to be, and our Lord changed the promise of *shall* and *will* to the fulfillment of *is*: *"For unto you is born this day in the city of David a Savior, who is Christ the Lord"* (emphasis added).

That is the thing about God's promises. Whenever we hear a promise of God, we can know with confident expectation that in His time, God will change *shall* or *will* to *is*, for God's every promise is wholly guaranteed. On the night of Jesus' birth, it was so. And on the day or night of Jesus' return, it will be so. And today it is so, for God is changing *shall* and *will* to *is*. God *is* with us.

For Prayerful Reflection: What are some fulfilled promises of God in which you have seen Him change *shall* to *is*? What are some effects of your hope in God's promise-keeping in your life today?

Bible in a Year: *Daniel 11-12; Jude*

December 10

I CAN Hope TODAY . . .
BECAUSE GOD ENTERS MY WARFARE

Herod, when he saw that he had been tricked by the wise men, became furious, and he sent and killed all the male children in Bethlehem and in all that region who were two years old or under, according to the time that that he had ascertained from the wise men. (Matthew 2:16)

For we do not wrestle against flesh and blood, but against the rulers, against the authorities, against the cosmic powers over this present darkness, against the spiritual forces of evil in the heavenly places. (Ephesians 6:12)

If life sometimes feels like a battle, it is because it is a battle. Ever since sin first entered this world, humanity has been embroiled in conflict. Our lives reflect this in various ways. Having served in the military, I am familiar with training for war and being in war. Having served as a shepherd of God's flock, I am also familiar with conflict in the church. And having been a husband, father, and pastoral counselor for many families in crisis, I am also familiar with marriage and family conflict and the hopelessness that can often arise. The reality of our warfare has been evident since the dawn of human history, for the first man born on earth killed his own brother.

The wonderful story of Christ's advent proclaims hope to people embroiled in various forms of warfare, for we see God entering the conflict. We see the darkness of warfare in Herod's evil actions, as his hateful rage brought the horror of death squads to Bethlehem, killing sweet baby boys. God's Son entered our conflicted world.

Warfare still exists all around us in this world. Paul reminds us of *spiritual forces of evil in the heavenly places.* But we have hope today. Our hope is centered in God Himself, who is with us in the battles, granting us confident expectation of what He will do.

For Prayerful Reflection: What warfare have you faced into which God came? What good effect does believing the advent story and hoping in Jesus Christ have in your current conflicts?

Bible in a Year: *Hosea 1-4; Revelation 1*

December 11

I CAN Hope TODAY . . .
BECAUSE GOD CALLED MARY WHO SAID YES

"Greetings, O favored one, the Lord is with you!" And the angel said to her, "Do not be afraid, Mary, for you have found favor with God. And behold, you will conceive in your womb and bear a son, and you shall call his name Jesus. He will be great and will be called the Son of the Most High. And the Lord God will give to him the throne of his father David, and he will reign over the house of Jacob forever, and of his kingdom there will be no end." And Mary said to the angel, "How will this be, since I am a virgin?" And the angel answered her, "The Holy Spirit will come upon you, and the power of the Most High will overshadow you; therefore the child to be born will be called holy—the Son of God." And Mary said, "Behold, I am the servant of the Lord; let it be to me according to your word." (Luke 1:28, 30-35, 38)

Prayerful consideration of the advent of God's Son and our Messiah with all the hope He brings also requires considering Mary, His mother. Through God's angelic messenger Gabriel, Mary was hailed with *"Greetings, O favored one, the Lord is with you!"* and *"you have found favor with God."*

God saw Mary's devotion and her glad willingness to say yes to His amazing plan for her life. Mary responded with faith and hope to this divine encounter and to God's amazing plan, saying, *"Behold, I am the servant of the Lord; let it be to me according to your word."*

In this Advent season, can we follow Mary's example? Can we say yes to God, knowing in faith that His plan for us is good, and that He will surely do what He has said?

For Prayerful Reflection: How has your answer to God's call compared with Mary's answer of yes? How does your hope in God's promises affect your willingness to say yes to Him today?

Bible in a Year: *Hosea 5-8; Revelation 2*

December 12

I CAN Hope TODAY . . .
BECAUSE GOD MADE A WAY FOR ME TO HOPE

Again Isaiah says, "The root of Jesse will come, even he who arises to rule the Gentiles; in him will the Gentiles hope." May the God of hope fill you with all joy and peace in believing, so that by the power of the Holy Spirit you may abound in hope. (Romans 15:12-13)

Here Paul quotes from Isaiah 11:10 that emphasizes the inclusion of Gentiles, for the salvation brought by God's Messiah is intended for all peoples of this world. Everyone who looks to Jesus can find hope, for God sees and cares for us all.

Some years ago, I read of a grieving widow named Stella who was facing deep loneliness in her first Christmas without her husband. On Christmas Eve her doorbell rang, and she was greeted by a messenger holding a box. "What's in the box?" she asked.

The messenger opened the flap, revealing a Labrador retriever puppy. "For you, ma'am."

Puzzled, Stella asked, "But . . . who sent this puppy?"

Turning to leave, the man said, "Your husband. Merry Christmas." She then opened an enclosed letter written by her husband, expressing his love and encouragement. He had purchased the puppy shortly before he died and requested that it be delivered for Christmas. The puppy climbed over Stella and licked away her tears. Hearing "Joy to the World" on her radio and holding this gift from one who loved her, she was filled again with hope and delight.

This Christmas season, please know that you are loved. God has given an amazing gift, so you can know it. *May the God of hope fill you with all joy and peace in believing, so that by the power of the Holy Spirit you may abound in hope.*

For Prayerful Reflection: What gifts has the God of hope given to encourage you? How is God filling you with joy and peace in believing, so that you can abound in hope and bring His hope to others?

Bible in a Year: *Hosea 9-11; Revelation 3*

December 13

I CAN Hope TODAY...
BECAUSE GOD SAYS THE DAYS ARE COMING

"Behold, the days are coming, declares the Lord, when I will fulfill the promise I made to the house of Israel and the house of Judah. In those days and at that time I will cause a righteous Branch to spring up for David, and he shall execute justice and righteousness in the land. In those days Judah will be saved, and Jerusalem will dwell securely. And this is the name by which it will be called: 'The Lord is our righteousness.'" (Jeremiah 33:14-16)

Sometimes when life is hard, promises that a better day is coming might not seem helpful. Many who heard Jeremiah's prophecy felt this way, for the chaos around them was great, and the suffering was profound. Still, God spoke words of hope through His prophet. Jeremiah declared the hopeful news *that the days are coming* when the Messiah King will rule, and then *he shall execute justice and righteousness in the land*. When life is hard for us, hope can be hard too, but God declares that *the days are coming*.

In *Hope and Suffering*, by South African Bishop Desmond Tutu, Bishop Tutu told of hope that was and is available in Christ, even during the horrors of the apartheid regime.[51] His message was that life in South Africa was going to change, for the days were surely coming. He encouraged believers in Christ to hold on to hope. Of course, that time did come when, as promised, the horrors of the apartheid regime ended.

Far more so, do we know and can we hold on in faith and confident expectation to our hope in Jesus Christ, for God promises that *the days are coming*.

For Prayerful Reflection: What promises of God have you struggled to hold on to in faith? How does the sure promise and hope of the days of Christ's coming encourage you today?

Bible in a Year: *Hosea 12-14; Revelation 4*

---

[51] Desmond Tutu, *Hope and Suffering: Sermons and Speeches* (Grand Rapids, MI: Wm. B. Eerdmans Publishing Co., 1984).

December 14

I CAN Hope TODAY...
BECAUSE GOD IS PRESENT IN THE HARDEST TIMES

[Stephen], full of the Holy Spirit, gazed into heaven and saw the glory of God, and Jesus standing at the right hand of God. And he said, "Behold, I see the heavens opened, and the Son of Man standing at the right hand of God." But they cried out with a loud voice and stopped their ears and rushed together at him. And as they were stoning Stephen, he called out, "Lord Jesus, receive my spirit." And falling to his knees he cried out with a loud voice, "Lord, do not hold this sin against them." And when he had said this, he fell asleep. (Acts 7:55-57, 59-60)

As I was named after Stephen, this servant of Jesus and the first Christian martyr, I have always felt some affinity with him. As a young boy, I reflected on Stephen's faithfulness and on the suffering that he endured for his faith in Jesus; I marveled at how God was with him through it all. Stephen's story and my own have taught me that our God is present with us in the hardest times.

From Stephen's example, I have learned these lessons on hope in Jesus Christ: (1) hope allows us to see a glimpse of heaven; (2) hope allows us to forgive, even those who mortally wound us, as Christ forgives us; (3) hope allows us to die in peace, for He is present with us and leads us home; and (4) hope allows us to trust that God will bring good from the struggle. Young Saul, who approved Stephen's suffering and death, later came to faith and proclaimed Jesus.

Because God is with us in our hardest times, we have much cause for hope today.

For Prayerful Reflection: When have you been aware of God's presence in a hard time like Stephen was? How does this assurance of God's presence and hope make a difference for you today?

Bible in a Year: *Joel 1-3; Revelation 5*

December 15

I CAN Hope TODAY . . .
BECAUSE GOD ENABLES PATIENT ENDURANCE

> *I, John, your brother and partner in the tribulation and the kingdom and the patient endurance that are in Jesus, was on the island called Patmos on account of the word of God and the testimony of Jesus. I was in the Spirit on the Lord's day, and I heard behind me a loud voice like a trumpet saying, "Write what you see in a book and send it to the seven churches."* (Revelation 1:9-11)

At the start of John's heavenly vision and God's promise to us, we might miss a certain line – John's brief description of his own life and the lives of recipients of this account. John writes that he is a *brother and partner in the tribulation and the kingdom and the patient endurance that are in Jesus.*

God gave these revelations while John was exiled on the prison island of Patmos. John's written record was circulated among suffering churches that faced trials which were going to worsen in the following years. Christians then lived and now live in two intersecting realities: assurance in the present reign and future return of Jesus Christ, and our present day-to-day experience of waiting and suffering. Hope was and is needed.

John's honest words about the need for patient endurance are woven among visions of God's glory, for our faith in Christ's first coming and our anticipation of His second coming and the glory that will then be revealed enable us to hope and endure today. This concept of patient endurance is often repeated with the language of overcoming in the early chapters of Revelation.

Because God enables our patient endurance, as an old hymn declares, in Him we find "strength for today and bright hope for tomorrow."

For Prayerful Reflection: In what areas of life have you needed patient endurance? How is your hope in Jesus Christ providing the patient endurance you need today?

Bible in a Year: *Amos 1-3; Revelation 6*

December 16

I CAN Hope TODAY . . .
BECAUSE GOD SPEAKS HOPE TO CATASTROPHE

"And there will be signs in sun and moon and stars, and on the earth distress of nations in perplexity because of the roaring of the sea and the waves, people fainting with fear and with foreboding of what is coming on the world. For the powers of the heavens will be shaken. And then they will see the Son of Man coming in a cloud with power and great glory." (Luke 21:25-27)

Catastrophes keep happening. We see them often in the news, and our hearts break. We experience them ourselves or share them with people dear to us. Sometimes the chaos and confusion is so intense and long-lasting that burnout weakens us, and hopelessness makes us ill like a virus of the soul.

In times of crises, we can and will pray and do what we can to show God's love, but we cannot fix everything. In fact, Jesus bluntly warned that catastrophe and crisis will keep coming, but He promises and offers hope. Speaking apocalyptically, Jesus foretold *signs in sun and moon and stars, and on the earth distress of nations in perplexity.* Then He offered us eternal hope and promised that humanity will *see the Son of Man coming in a cloud with power and great glory.*

Here the Lord speaks of His second advent and urges us to believe it in faith, anticipating His promised and glorious return that this might always be our confident expectation. The increasing chaos and catastrophes of this world cannot be stopped by human development or achievement, but only by Jesus Christ Himself. The advent message of hope calls us to see the darkness, naming it for what it is; it calls us to *"straighten up and raise your heads, because your redemption is drawing near"* (Luke 21:28).

For Prayerful Reflection: When have catastrophes and crises weakened you with hopelessness? In this world with so many crises, what is the Lord's invitation to hope saying to you?

Bible in a Year: *Amos 4-6; Revelation 7*

December 17

I CAN Hope TODAY...
BECAUSE GOD PROMISES ETERNAL LIFE

Paul, a servant of God and an apostle of Jesus Christ, for the sake of the faith of God's elect and their knowledge of the truth, which accords with godliness, in hope of eternal life, which God, who never lies, promised before the ages began. (Titus 1:1-2)

Then I heard what seemed to be the voice of a great multitude, ... crying out, "Hallelujah! For the Lord our God the Almighty reigns. Let us rejoice and exult and give him the glory, for the marriage of the Lamb has come, and his Bride has made herself ready." (Revelation 19:6-7)

Writing to Pastor Titus who was then serving the church on the island of Crete, Paul reminded Titus at the beginning of his letter that the mission of the church and of every Christian is rooted in God's promise of eternal life. This is our permanent source of hope, because God who has promised it never lies.

When Helen and I announced our engagement to be married, we set a date and counted down the days with anticipation of what was coming. We had no doubt about it, for we had promised one another. The Bible uses such imagery to portray our relationship with Jesus Christ. We are His bride, looking forward with the Lord to a heavenly wedding and eternity together. What cause for hope! But to have this hope we must be fully committed to Him.

A young marine once came to me as his chaplain to schedule his wedding upon our return from deployment. When I inquired about his fiancée, he said he had two, and was unsure which one he would marry. How foolish. And how foolish it is to go through this life without a firm commitment to Jesus who loves us and promises eternity together with Him.

For Prayerful Reflection: What has God's promise of eternal life meant to you? How firm is your commitment to Jesus today and your own confident expectation of eternity with Him?

Bible in a Year: *Amos 7-9; Revelation 8*

December 18

I CAN Hope TODAY . . .
BECAUSE GOD RAISED JESUS FROM DEATH

"Yet a little while and the world will see me no more, but you will see me. Because I live, you also will live." (John 14:19)

We shall not all sleep, but we shall all be changed, in a moment, in the twinkling of an eye, at the last trumpet. For the trumpet will sound, and the dead will be raised imperishable, and we shall be changed. Therefore, my beloved brothers, be steadfast, immovable, always abounding in the work of the Lord, knowing that in the Lord your labor is not in vain. (1 Corinthians 15:51-52, 58)

Because God has raised Jesus from the grave, we have much cause for hope today. Shortly before His crucifixion, Jesus told His disciples He would rise again and declared, *"Because I live, you also will live."* He speaks these words to us today.

In *Time Magazine*'s column "10 Questions," readers were given an opportunity to submit questions via email to be asked of celebrities and world leaders. In the March 22, 2010, issue, South African Archbishop Desmond Tutu, author of *Made for Goodness,* was featured.[52] One reader asked, "After all you have seen and endured, are you as optimistic as your book says you are?"

Tutu answered, "I am not optimistic. No, I am quite different. I am hopeful. I am a prisoner of hope. In the world you have very bad people – Hitler, Idi Amin – and they look like they are going to win. But *all* of them have bitten the dust. Our hope and confident expectation is centered on the One who conquered death, rose again, and ascended to heaven. Our hope is in the One who defeated that enemy, for we know that because He lives, we shall live also.

Yes, this is our cause for hope today, tomorrow, and forever.

For Prayerful Reflection: What has Jesus' promise meant to you that *"because I live, you also will live"*? How will your hope in the resurrection affect your life and witness today?

Bible in a Year: *Obadiah; Revelation 9*

---

[52] Desmond Tutu, "10 Questions for Desmond Tutu," *Time Magazine* (March 22, 2010), http://content.time.com/ time/subscriber/article/0,33009,1971410,00.html (July 2, 2021).

December 19

I CAN Hope TODAY . . .
BECAUSE GOD COMES TO UNNOTICED PEOPLE

There were shepherds out in the field, keeping watch over their flock by night. And an angel of the Lord appeared to them, and the glory of the Lord shone around them, . . . And the shepherds returned, glorifying and praising God for all they had heard and seen, as it had been told them. (Luke 2:8-9, 20)

Of all the peoples in the world who could have received that first magnificent announcement of Messiah's birth, God chose a group of poor, unnoticed, largely forgotten shepherds. God came so all would see, hear, believe, and follow.

Some might think that their lives matter little to anyone; they even presume that God does not care about someone like them. Perhaps you have personally struggled with such thoughts. But the God of the universe says otherwise. Coming to lowly shepherds to announce the glorious news of Messiah's birth, He also comes to you and me, letting us know we matter to Him.

And when this happens, and we have truly encountered God like those blessed shepherds on that holy night, we too can never be the same again. For we have seen the source of our hope, and we believe in God's Messiah.

For Prayerful Reflection: How is hope affected by knowing that God comes to unnoticed people? How were those shepherds never the same again? How have you been changed similarly?

Bible in a Year: *Jonah 1-4; Revelation 10*

December 20

I CAN Hope TODAY...
BECAUSE GOD'S SON LAY IN A FEEDING TROUGH

And the angel said to [the shepherds], "... behold, I bring you good news of great joy that will be for all the people. For unto you is born this day in the city of David a Savior, who is Christ the Lord. And this will be a sign for you: you will find a baby wrapped in swaddling cloths and lying in a manger." And they went with haste and found Mary and Joseph, and the baby lying in a manger. (Luke 2:10-12, 16)

The location of the birth of God's own Son and our Messiah is remarkable in many ways, and this was wonderfully ordained by God Himself. Being a dad, I remember the excitement with which I approached the birth of our children. Helen and I made careful preparations to ensure we were as prepared as we could be. And when the time came, we were in the best hospital possible, and the nursery was ready at home.

Didn't our eternal Father do the same when the time came for Jesus' birth? He planned it all. As prophesied, God's Son and the offspring of David was born in Bethlehem. The overcrowded inn was no disappointment to God, for He intended a humble birth for His Son. In that stable, baby Jesus, the Son of God and Son of Man, was not surrounded by elegance, but His tiny body was lovingly wrapped by Mary and Joseph in swaddling cloths brought for this purpose. They then gently laid our Lord on a bed of straw in a feeding trough.

From the earliest moments of our Savior's incarnation, He identified with us. He is now and forever our source of hope, for He came, and comes today, into our humanity, frailty, poverty, and humility.

For Prayerful Reflection: What does it mean to you that God's Son who came for you was born in a stable and laid in a feeding trough? How is your hope affected by this powerful expression of humility?

Bible in a Year: *Micah 1-3; Revelation 11*

December 21

I CAN Hope TODAY . . .
BECAUSE GOD IS PLANNING A SURPRISE PARTY

For the Lord himself will descend from heaven with a cry of command, with the voice of an archangel, and with the sound of the trumpet of God. And the dead in Christ will rise first. Then we who are alive, who are left, will be caught up together with them in the clouds to meet the Lord in the air, and so we will always be with the Lord. Therefore encourage one another with these words. (1 Thessalonians 4:16-18)

As Christmas approaches, we may recall parties we have hosted or been invited to; likewise, in remembering our Lord's first coming, we have much to celebrate. In the Gospel accounts of Jesus' birth, there are elements of a party, as we read about the angels singing celebratory birthday praises in their anthem, *"Glory to God in the highest!"* (Luke 2:14).

This makes us ponder the triumphal party that will happen on the day of Christ's second advent. As only our Father in heaven knows when that day will be, this coming event has the characteristics of a surprise party. If you belong to the Lord Jesus by faith, you have an engraved invitation and will be there for sure. I will be there too. Can you imagine our joy on that day?

We are encouraged to be looking toward this future event with enduring faith and confident hope. On the day of Christ's return, His arrival will be magnificent. It will include *the sound of the trumpet of God.* The Thessalonians would have known that this represented the welcoming of a returning victorious leader, in this case the greatest leader of all, for He raises from the dead all who are in Christ Jesus. We can therefore be filled with hope today, for we will soon be together at this most glorious surprise party.

For Prayerful Reflection: What do you have to celebrate this Christmas? How will you do it? How are you encouraged and blessed through your hope in the return of Jesus Christ?

Bible in a Year: *Micah 4-5; Revelation 12*

December 22

I CAN Hope TODAY . . .
BECAUSE GOD INVITES EXPECTANCY

While they were gazing into heaven as he went, behold, two men stood by them in white robes, and said, "Men of Galilee, why do you stand looking into heaven? This Jesus, who was taken up from you into heaven, will come in the same way as you saw him go into heaven." (Acts 1:10-11)

"Behold, I am coming soon, bringing my recompense with me, to repay each one for what he has done. I am the Alpha and the Omega, the first and the last, the beginning and the end." He who testifies to these things says, "Surely I am coming soon." Amen. Come, Lord Jesus! (Revelation 22:12-13, 20)

As biblical hope is confident expectation of what God has promised, He invites us to live today with expectancy of His faithfulness, presence, and answers to our prayers; He wants us to know He is surely coming again. Living with such expectancy flows out of a close, personal relationship with God, which allows us to find His peace in any circumstance, because we know God is here; He is able, and He will do whatever He has promised.

God wants His children to enjoy expectancy regarding His promised return, for we will soon see Him in the fullness of His glory. Such hope means knowing that when He returns, the righteous will be vindicated, evil will be defeated, and all will at last be made right. Because having such confident expectation is transformative in impact, how are we going to live today?

As we follow the Lord Jesus and live in relationship with Him – praying, listening, and sharing life with Him – we will see God in our past, present, and future. Some years ago, I obtained a refrigerator magnet with a succinct reminder that has encouraged me to live expectantly. It says, "Look Back . . . Thank Him. Look Around . . . Serve Him. Look Forward . . . Trust Him. Look Up . . . Expect Him." Amen.

For Prayerful Reflection: Why does God invite us to live with expectancy? What are the benefits of doing so? What would it mean for you to live with hope and expectancy today?

Bible in a Year: *Micah 6-7; Revelation 13*

December 23

I CAN Hope TODAY . . .
BECAUSE GOD REMEMBERS HIS COVENANT

> *Immediately his mouth was opened and his tongue loosed, and he spoke, blessing God. . . . Zechariah was filled with the Holy Spirit and prophesied, saying, "Blessed be the Lord God of Israel, for he has visited and redeemed his people and has raised up a horn of salvation for us in the house of his servant David, as he spoke by the mouth of his holy prophets from of old, that we should be saved from our enemies and from the hand of all who hate us; to show the mercy promised to our fathers and to remember his holy covenant."* (Luke 1:64, 67-72)

Zechariah had been quiet for nine months since the day God sent an angel to him, who said, *"I am Gabriel. I stand in the presence of God, and I was sent to speak to you and to bring you this good news"* (Luke 1:19). Gabriel foretold the birth of a son who would *"make ready for the Lord a people prepared"* (Luke 1:17). This promise was in fulfilment of God's holy covenant, and because Zechariah did not believe it, he was silenced until the day the promise was fulfilled.

On the day of John's birth, nine months' worth of God's stirring in Zechariah's soul came pouring out, as he testified that God had remembered His holy covenant. His prophecy that day (Luke 1:68-69), affirming God's faithfulness, is often called the *Benedictus*. It is one long sentence celebrating God's remembrance of His covenant.

Perhaps, like Zechariah, we have also refused to believe the promises of God. If so, we have also faced some consequences of unbelief. But when God in great mercy opens our eyes and hearts to the wonder of His faithfulness, we too can respond with praise.

For Prayerful Reflection: When have you faced consequences for not believing God's promises? What *Benedictus* of praise can you offer today to celebrate God's faithfulness?

Bible in a Year: *Nahum 1-3; Revelation 14*

December 24

I CAN Hope TODAY...
BECAUSE GOD DISPELS GLOOM

There will be no gloom for her who was in anguish. In the former time he brought into contempt the land of Zebulun and the land of Naphtali, but in the latter time he has made glorious the way of the sea, the land beyond the Jordan, Galilee of the nations. The people who walked in darkness have seen a great light; those who dwelt in a land of deep darkness, on them has light shone. For to us a child is born, to us a son is given; and the government shall be upon his shoulder, and his name shall be called Wonderful Counselor, Mighty God, Everlasting Father, Prince of Peace. (Isaiah 9:1-2, 6)

The arrival of Messiah Jesus dispels our gloom. Isaiah prophesied of this; he foretold the birth of a child whose name would *be called Wonderful Counselor, Mighty God, Everlasting Father, Prince of Peace.* Though Israel was then in deep gloom and anguish, as their captivity was just beginning, God promised the Messiah, who would rule and remove gloom.

Isaiah specifically mentioned the lands of Zebulun and Naphtali, which had been utterly humiliated when annexed by Assyria and reduced to puppet states. But the day was coming, said the Lord, when honor would be restored to that region, as *people who walked in darkness have seen a great light.* This prophecy was fulfilled and quoted in Matthew 4, when Jesus began His ministry in that very region.

The Christmas message is about hope and rebirth, for in Christ, God comes and dispels gloom; He brings hope in its place. By His coming, hope flows like a powerful and beautiful river of life into places of death, failure, and despair, even flowing uphill. Devastation gives way to honor, and death gives way to life, for God, who entered this world, has come into my life, my family, and my neighborhood. We hope today because God is dispelling gloom.

For Prayerful Reflection: When did God enter your life and dispel gloom? How is the message of Christmas like a light removing gloom for you – in this past year, today, and for the year ahead?

Bible in a Year: *Habakkuk 1-3; Revelation 15*

December 25

I CAN Hope TODAY . . .
BECAUSE GOD INCARNATE WAS BORN

While they were there, the time came for her to give birth. And she gave birth to her firstborn son and wrapped him in swaddling cloths and laid him in a manger. (Luke 2:6-7)

And the Word became flesh and dwelt among us, and we have seen his glory, glory as of the only Son from the Father, full of grace and truth. (John 1:14)

The apostle John powerfully declared that on the day of Jesus' birth *the Word became flesh and dwelt among us.* God incarnate was born. The Creator of everything entered His own creation and arrived in our dusty, broken, and harsh world. Luke tells us Jesus' birth interrupted a Roman census ordered by the emperor Caesar Augustus, and Matthew describes the dark hatred in that region's King Herod who would soon be targeting and killing baby boys.

Into this broken world, God came. This small and helpless baby fell into the arms of His mother, as we all do. This is the incredible news of Christmas. God came to where we are, so that by His grace He might bring us to where He is. Divinity took on flesh. If on this Christmas Day we genuinely believe this, we will surely want to welcome, love, and serve Him today and every day to come.

But sadly, too many go through the motions of Christmas without believing or being changed by the truth of it. What I witnessed in Japan several years ago I have also observed throughout the United States: beautiful Christmas decorations are in abundance, and the message is even heard in the public square through Christmas carols that proclaim the truth of it. But multitudes move about neither seeing nor hearing.

If today we are blessed to see and hear the wonder of Christmas, then let us be changed by it, for God incarnate is born.

For Prayerful Reflection: What does the incarnation of God mean to you today? How does the message of Christmas influence and strengthen your hope?

Bible in a Year: *Zephaniah 1-3; Revelation 16*

December 26

I CAN Hope TODAY . . .
BECAUSE GOD FILLS MY LONGING WITH JOY

> *There was a man in Jerusalem, whose name was Simeon, and this man was righteous and devout, waiting for the consolation of Israel, and the Holy Spirit was upon him. And it had been revealed to him by the Holy Spirit that he would not see death before he had seen the Lord's Christ. And he came in the Spirit into the temple, and when the parents brought in the child Jesus, to do for him according to the custom of the Law, he took him up in his arms and blessed God and said, "Lord, now you are letting your servant depart in peace, according to your word; for my eyes have seen your salvation that you have prepared in the presence of all peoples, a light for revelation to the Gentiles, and for glory to your people Israel."* (Luke 2:25-32)

What have been the deepest longings of your heart? How deeply have you hoped for them to be fulfilled? Simeon's hope was that before breathing his last, he might behold God's Messiah. Knowing Simeon's faith and longing, God the Holy Spirit assured Simeon that He would fulfill this longing and answer his prayer. So it happened that memorable day in the sunset of Simeon's life that God fulfilled His promise, and Mary and Joseph gently placed baby Jesus, the Messiah, into Simeon's arms. What joy was Simeon's that day! Subsequent verses describe the same thing happening to a woman of faith named Anna.

Their stories remind us that God keeps filling our longings with unimaginable joy and pointing us forward to when our hopes and dreams will be fully realized in God Himself. Today we can bring our longings to God and trust Him as Simeon and Anna did, for God fills our longings with joy.

For Prayerful Reflection: What deep longings of your heart has God already fulfilled? How does the example of Simeon encourage you with hope for what God will do for you?

Bible in a Year: *Haggai 1-2; Revelation 17*

December 27

I CAN Hope TODAY . . .
BECAUSE GOD PROMISES ANOTHER CHRISTMAS

For the Lord himself will descend from heaven with a cry of command, with the voice of an archangel, and with the sound of the trumpet of God. And the dead in Christ will rise first. (1 Thessalonians 4:16)

Behold, he is coming with the clouds, and every eye will see him. (Revelation 1:7)

For children of all ages, Christmas can be the most anticipated day of the year. It was certainly like that for me as a child. There is rehearsing and celebrating the Christmas story, as we enjoy reminders of it in Christmas pageants, Christmas cards, and the Christmas tree. There are Christmas decorations, Christmas carols, Christmas cookies and other food – and of course, giving and receiving Christmas presents. Then came Christmas Day, and I hate to say it, but when it was all over, sometimes I felt a little let down. Many people feel this way when the celebration of Christmas is not all they had hoped for.

We can remember that God has promised that another Christmas is coming – not like the imperfect day just completed, but a perfect one that is coming soon. God has promised that Jesus Christ is coming again, and it will be a day like no other. If you have imagined the wonder of that first Christmas when the angel announced Messiah's glorious birth to the shepherds, and a choir of angels sang, *"Glory to God in the highest,"* imagine now His second advent. Our Lord will then *descend from heaven with a cry of command, with the voice of an archangel, and with the sound of the trumpet of God.*

Another Christmas is coming. What a glorious reason for hope today!

For Prayerful Reflection: How has your hope in God helped in dealing with Christmas disappointments? How can confident expectation of the Lord's second coming be helpful to you today?

Bible in a Year: *Zechariah 1-4; Revelation 18*

December 28

I CAN Hope TODAY . . .
BECAUSE GOD MAKES ME BE RESOLUTE

Wait for the revealing of our Lord Jesus Christ, who will sustain you to the end, guiltless in the day of our Lord Jesus Christ. God is faithful, by whom you were called into the fellowship of his Son, Jesus Christ our Lord. (1 Corinthians 1:7-9)

Therefore, preparing your minds for action, and being sober-minded, set your hope fully on the grace that will be brought to you at the revelation of Jesus Christ. (1 Peter 1:13)

When a year draws to an end, and a new year quickly approaches, it is common to ponder anew where we have been and where we are going. Resolutions of targets to aim for and intended goals to achieve may then develop. This sort of process has been helpful in my life; I have often prayerfully discerned goals and assignments from God, which included listening and writing this yearlong devotional book.

But far more than being resolute about specific things to do, God calls us to be resolute about the priority of our relationship with Him and all that it entails. To be resolute is to be purposeful, determined, and unwavering.

Because we have all made resolutions and failed to follow them through, we might erroneously conclude that we are incapable of faithfulness in resolutions, even those we long to keep. But the good news today and our reason for hope is that God has promised to help us. As Paul said, *Our Lord Jesus Christ . . . will sustain you to the end.*

With confidence in God's help and in His soon coming, Peter also encourages us to be resolute in our minds and actions by setting our hope on the grace that Jesus Christ gives. Because God makes us resolute, we can confidently hope, for God helps us to be faithful.

For Prayerful Reflection: What resolutions can you make on the priority of your relationship with Him? How has your hope been affected by God's promise to help you be resolute in purpose and faithfulness?

Bible in a Year: *Zechariah 5-8; Revelation 19*

December 29

I CAN Hope TODAY . . .
BECAUSE GOD IS PATIENT WITH ME

But do not overlook this one fact, beloved, that with the Lord one day is as a thousand years, and a thousand years as one day. The Lord is not slow to fulfill his promise as some count slowness, but is patient toward you, not wishing that any should perish, but that all should reach repentance. (2 Peter 3:8-9)

What is taking so long? Why haven't my prayers been fully answered already? Why does it feel like this world is crumbling and I am failing? As followers of Jesus, perhaps we relate to the Little Leaguer whose grandpa had arrived late for the game and yelled to his grandson who was in the dugout, "How's the game going?"

The boy yelled back, "We're behind ten to zero!"

The grandpa yelled, "Ooh, that's not good!"

The boy replied, "It's okay, Grandpa; we haven't been up to bat yet!"

As Christians, we can sometimes feel discouraged, as if we are losing "ten to zero." But God reminds us not to give up. In faith, we can confidently hope, for we will triumph. Because God is with us, victory is certain. In times when our circumstances seem hard, and our wait for relief seems long, we who belong to Christ can have His patience to hope because of God's patience with us. Like the recipients of Peter's letter, we need this reminder today – to hold on to our hope in the Lord. God's patience invites others to come to Him and reminds us that He is not finished with any of us yet.

Because God is patient, we who follow Jesus can be patient too. We who are people of hope know that the end of the story has not yet come, but it is coming. And it is good.

For Prayerful Reflection: How has God been patient with you? How does this encourage you to hope? In what areas of personal discouragement will you determine to patiently hope?

Bible in a Year: *Zechariah 9-12; Revelation 20*

December 30

I CAN Hope TODAY . . .
BECAUSE GOD SATISFIES FULLY

After Jesus was born in Bethlehem of Judea in the days of Herod the king, behold, wise men from the east came to Jerusalem, saying, "Where is he who has been born king of the Jews? For we saw his star when it rose and have come to worship him." When they saw the star, they rejoiced exceedingly with great joy. And going into the house, they saw the child with Mary his mother, and they fell down and worshiped him. Then, opening their treasures, they offered him gifts, gold and frankincense and myrrh. (Matthew 2:1-2, 10-11)

"Blessed are those who hunger and thirst for righteousness, for they shall be satisfied." (Matthew 5:6)

God draws people to Himself in remarkable ways, and satisfies all who come with believing hope. This is evident in the biblical account of the magi who journeyed many hundreds of miles seeking Him. They had little clue as to where they were going or what they would find, but God was drawing them by the hunger of their hearts and the supernatural sign of a guiding star. They came and were fully satisfied.

Most Bible scholars suggest the magi came from Persia, because six centuries earlier many Jews were exiled from Jerusalem to Babylon, which was later conquered by the Persian empire. These magi likely had some awareness of Jewish Scriptures. They were being drawn by God with a longing to worship the promised King.

God still draws people like us who are filled with a hopeful longing for God. There are inspiring examples of this happening today across the Muslim world, which are shared in some personal testimonies on prayercast.com. How sweet to hear of God blessing people being drawn to Him with hope. Jesus' promise remains that all who hunger and thirst after righteousness will be fully satisfied in Him.

For Prayerful Reflection: In what ways have you, like the magi, found satisfaction in coming to Jesus? How is your hunger and thirst for righteousness affecting your hope for what God is going to do?

Bible in a Year: Zechariah 13-14; Revelation 21

December 31

I CAN Hope TODAY . . .
BECAUSE GOD MAKES ALL THINGS NEW

If anyone is in Christ, he is a new creation. The old has passed away; behold, the new has come. All this is from God, who through Christ reconciled us to himself and gave us the ministry of reconciliation. (2 Corinthians 5:17-18)

And he who was seated on the throne said, "Behold, I am making all things new." Also he said, "Write this down, for these words are trustworthy and true." (Revelation 21:5)

Looking back on what the past year held for you, are you feeling encouraged or discouraged, pleased or displeased, filled with faith or doubt, gratitude or grumbling? Now on the cusp of a new year, are you filled today with worry or trust, foreboding or confident hope in the good that God is surely going to do?

Though none of us can know with certainty what the new year will bring, in Christ we can have confident hope for the future, because we know the faithfulness of God who has always been and will always be with us. The Bible reminds us that God is present through every transition, and by His grace He makes all things new. Paul reminds us that we who are in Christ are already *a new creation*, and we have been entrusted by God with *the ministry of reconciliation*, which includes leading others to the Lord to be made new by Him.

We can hold firmly to God's promise today in hope of a coming day when all wrongs will be righted, and God's new and perfect order will replace the old. Like the past year, the Bible begins with God's beginning and concludes with God's new beginning. As God makes all things new, whether we're looking back or looking forward, we can fix our hope firmly in the Lord Jesus Christ.

For Prayerful Reflection: In this past year, how have you seen God's faithfulness as He fulfilled your hopes? Looking ahead now, what confident hope do you hold on to through faith in Jesus Christ?

Bible in a Year: *Malachi 1-4; Revelation 22*

About the Author

Dr. Stephen Gammon is a third-generation minister who has walked with God since early childhood, enjoying a lifetime of treasured quiet times with Jesus. A pastor for forty years, wherever and whenever God has led him, he has served as pastor in three local churches, as a denominational leader, and as an Active Duty and Navy Reserve Chaplain. Steve and his wife Helen are both cancer survivors and reside in Northfield, Minnesota. They are blessed with three adult children and four grandsons.

Connect with the Author
www.walkingwithgodforlife.com

Walking with God, by Stephen A. Gammon

Are you longing to walk closer to God, or wondering if it's even really possible? Would you and your sphere of influence benefit from being mentored for a lifetime of walking with God? Or, are you a minister leading people of various ages and in various seasons of life, but finding it difficult to relate to them?

God teaches priceless lessons through life, including some we may resist learning. Dr. Stephen Gammon shares timeless biblical wisdom and treasured personal insights learned through 14 successive chapters of life in *Walking With God: 101 Lessons for Life and Ministry*.

Available where books are sold.

Walking with God through Deep Valleys,
by Stephen A. Gammon

All of life is not lived on mountaintops. We will experience some deep valleys of pain, disappointment, uncertainty, sickness, grief, and even *the valley of the shadow of death*. Sometimes multitudes enter long and deep valleys together, as in prolonged seasons of war, or the COVID-19 pandemic that brought many to hardship, uncertainty, and fear. Yet, it often feels like we are walking through a deep valley alone. It doesn't have to be that way – Scripture makes it clear that if we have even a little faith, the Lord walks with us and guides us. If we keep our eyes on Him, our deepest valleys will strengthen and enrich our walk with God.

Stephen Gammon faithfully served God for 40 years as a pastor and military chaplain. Then, in October 2018, he was diagnosed with cancer (Multiple Myeloma); he and his wife Helen entered this deep valley, walking with God by faith. With personal vulnerability and spiritual insight, he posted regular medical updates on the CaringBridge website, sharing many priceless lessons learned while walking with God through their valley. Tens of thousands of online visits and innumerable personal responses and reflections from readers attest to the power of these truths. Now edited and published in this book, these lessons will point you towards genuine contentment and peace as you walk through your own deep valleys.

Available where books are sold.

Printed in Great Britain
by Amazon